Isabel McClintock Garland: A Daughter of the Middle Border.

Zulime Taft: "The New Daughter."

A DAUGHTER OF THE MIDDLE BORDER

HAMLIN GARLAND

DOVER PUBLICATIONS, INC.
Mineola, New York

Published in Canada by General Publishing Company, Ltd., 30
Lesmill Road, Don Mills, Toronto, Ontario.
Published in the United Kingdom by Constable and Company,
Ltd., 3 The Lanchesters, 162–164 Fulham Palace Road, London W6
9ER.

Bibliographical Note

This Dover edition, first published in 1998, is an unabridged
republication of the work first published by The Macmillan
Company, New York, in 1921.

Library of Congress Cataloging-in-Publication Data

Garland, Hamlin, 1860–1940.
    A daughter of the middle border / Hamlin Garland.
        p.   cm.
    Originally published: New York : Macmillan, 1921.
    ISBN 0-486-40217-7 (pbk.)
    1. Garland, Hamlin, 1860–1940—Biography.   2. Authors,
American—19th century—Biography.   3. Authors, American—
20th century—Biography.   I. Title.
PS1733.A42   1998
813'.52—dc21   98-14814
    [B]   CIP

Manufactured in the United States of America
Dover Publications, Inc., 31 East 2nd Street, Mineola, N.Y. 11501

To my wife Zulime Taft, who for more than twenty years has shared my toil and borne with my shortcomings, I dedicate this story of a household on the vanishing Middle Border, with an ever-deepening sense of her fortitude and serenity.

Acknowledgments are made to Florence Huber Schott, Edward Foley and Arthur Dudley for the use of the photographs which illustrate this volume.

FOREWORD

—I—

To My New Readers

IN the summer of 1893, after nine years of hard but
happy literary life in Boston and New York, I decided
to surrender my residence in the East and reëstablish my
home in the West, a decision which seemed to be—as it was
—a most important event in my career.

This change of headquarters was due not to a diminish-
ing love for New England, but to a deepening desire to be
near my aging parents, whom I had persuaded, after much
argument, to join in the purchase of a family homestead,
in West Salem, Wisconsin, the little village from which we
had all adventured some thirty years before.

My father, a typical pioneer, who had grown gray in
opening new farms, one after another on the wind-swept
prairies of Iowa and Dakota, was not entirely content with
my plan but my mother, enfeebled by the hardships of a
farmer's life, and grateful for my care, was glad of the
arrangement I had brought about. In truth, she realized
that her days of pioneering were over and the thought of
ending her days among her friends and relatives was a comfort to her. That I had rescued her from a premature grave
on the barren Dakota plain was certain, and the hope of
being able to provide for her comfort was the strongest
element in my plan.

After ten years of separation we were agreed upon a

project which would enable us as a family to spend our summers together; for my brother, Franklin, an actor in New York City, had promised to take his vacation in the home which we had purchased.

As this homestead (which was only eight hours by rail from Chicago) is to be one of the chief characters in this story, I shall begin by describing it minutely. It was not the building in which my life began—I should like to say it was, but it was not. My birthplace was a cabin—part logs and part lumber—on the opposite side of the town. Originally a squatter's cabin, it was now empty and forlorn, a dreary monument of the pioneer days, which I did not take the trouble to enter. The house which I had selected for the final Garland homestead, was entirely without any direct associations with my family. It was only an old frame cottage, such as a rural carpenter might build when left to his own devices, rude, angular, ugly of line and drab in coloring, but it stood in the midst of a four-acre field, just on the edge of the farmland. Sheltered by noble elms and stately maples, its windows fronted on a low range of wooded hills, whose skyline (deeply woven into my childish memories) had for me the charm of things remembered, and for my mother a placid beauty which (after her long stay on the treeless levels of Dakota) was almost miraculous in effect. Entirely without architectural dignity, our new home was spacious and suggested the comfort of the region round about.

My father, a man of sixty-five, though still actively concerned with a wide wheat farm in South Dakota, had agreed to aid me in maintaining this common dwelling place in Wisconsin provided he could return to Dakota during seeding and again at harvest. He was an eagle-eyed, tireless man of sixty-five years of age, New England by origin, tall, alert, quick-spoken and resolute, the kind of natural pioneer who prides himself on never taking the back trail. In truth he had yielded most reluctantly to my plan, influenced almost wholly by the failing health of my mother, to whom the work of a farm household had become an intolerable burden. As I had gained possession of the premises early in November we were able to eat our Thanksgiving Dinner in our new home, happy in the companionship of old friends and neighbors. My mother and my Aunt Susan were entirely content. The Garlands seemed anchored at last.

—II—

To the Readers of
"A Son of the Middle Border"

IN taking up and carrying forward the theme of "A Son of the Middle Border" I am fully aware of my task's increasing difficulties, realizing that I must count on the clear understanding and continuing good will of my readers.

First of all, you must grant that the glamor of childhood, the glories of the Civil War, the period of prairie conquest which were the chief claims to interest in the first volume of my chronicle can not be restated in these pages. The action of this book moves forward into the light of manhood, into the region of middle age. Furthermore, its theme is more personal. Its scenes are less epic. It is a study of individuals and their relationships rather than of settlements and migrations. In short, "A Daughter of the Middle Border" is the complement of "A Son of the Middle Border," a continuation, not a repetition, in which I attempt to answer the many questions which readers of the first volume have persistently put to me.

Foreword

"Did your mother get her new daughter?" "How long did she live to enjoy the peace of her Homestead?" "What became of David and Burton?" "Did your father live to see his grandchildren?" These and many other queries, literary as well as personal, are—I trust—satisfactorily answered in this book. Like the sequel to a novel, it attempts to account for its leading characters and to satisfy the persistent interest which my correspondents have so cordially expressed.

It remains to say that the tale is as true as my memory will permit—it is constructed only by leaving things out. If it reads, as some say, like fiction, that result is due not to invention but to the actual lives of the characters involved. Finally this closes my story of the Garlands and McClintocks and the part they took in a marvelous era in American settlement.

CONTENTS

BOOK I

Contents

ILLUSTRATIONS

A Daughter of the Middle Border

BOOK I

CHAPTER ONE

My First Winter in Chicago

"WELL, Mother," I said as I took my seat at the break-fast table the second day after our Thanksgiving dinner, "I must return to Chicago. I have some lectures to deliver and besides I must get back to my writing."

She made no objection to my announcement but her eyes lost something of their happy light. "When will you come again?" she asked after a pause.

"Almost any minute," I replied assuringly. "You must remember that I'm only a few hours away now. I can visit you often. I shall certainly come up for Christmas. If you need me at any time send me word in the afternoon and I'll be with you at breakfast."

That night at six o'clock I was in my city home, a lodging quite as humble in character as my fortunes.

In a large chamber on the north side of a house on Elm Street and only three doors from Lake Michigan, I had assembled my meager library and a few pitiful mementoes of my life in Boston. My desk stood near a narrow side window and as I mused I could look out upon the shore-less expanse of blue-green water fading mistily into the north-east sky, and, at night, when the wind was in the

East the crushing thunder of the breakers along the concrete wall formed a noble accompaniment to my writing, filling me with vaguely ambitious literary plans. Exalted by the sound of this mighty orchestra I felt entirely content with the present and serenely confident of the future.

"This is where I belong," I said. "Here in the great Midland metropolis with this room for my pivot, I shall continue my study of the plains and the mountains."

I had burned no bridges between me and the Island of Manhattan, however! Realizing all too well that I must still look to the East for most of my income, I carefully retained my connections with *Harper's,* the *Century* and other periodicals. Chicago, rich and powerful as it had become, could not establish—or had not established—a paying magazine, and its publishing firms were mostly experimental and not very successful; although the Columbian Exposition which was just closing, had left upon the city's clubs and societies (and especially on its young men) an esthetic stimulation which bade fair to carry on to other and more enduring enterprises.

Nevertheless in the belief that it was to become the second great literary center of America I was resolved to throw myself into the task of hurrying it forward on the road to new and more resplendent achievement.

My first formal introduction to the literary and artistic circle in which I was destined to work and war for many years, took place through the medium of an address on *Impressionism in Art* which I delivered in the library of Franklin Head, a banker whose home had become one of the best-known intellectual meeting places on the North Side. This lecture, considered very radical at the time, was the direct outcome of several years of study and battle in Boston in support of the open-air school of painting, a school which was astonishing the West with its defiant play of reds and yellows, and the flame of its purple shadows. As a missionary in the interest of the New Art, I rejoiced in this opportunity to advance its inspiring heresies.

While uttering my shocking doctrines (entrenched behind a broad, book-laden desk), my eyes were attracted to the face of a slender black-bearded young man whose shining eyes and occasional smiling nod indicated a joyous agreement with the main points of my harangue. I had never seen him before, but I at once recognized in him a fellow conspirator against "The Old Hat" forces of conservatism in painting.

At the close of my lecture he drew near and putting out his hand, said, "My name is Taft—Lorado Taft. I am a sculptor, but now and again I talk on painting. Impressionism is all very new here in the West, but like yourself I am an advocate of it, I am doing my best to popularize a knowledge of it, and I hope you will call upon me at my studio some afternoon—any afternoon and discuss these isms with me."

Young Lorado Taft interested me, and I instantly accepted his invitation to call, and in this way (notwithstanding a wide difference in training and temperament), a friendship was established which has never been strained even in the fiercest of our esthetic controversies. Many others of the men and women I met that night became my co-workers in the building of the "greater Chicago," which was even then coming into being—the menace of the hyphenate American had no place in our thoughts.

In less than a month I fell into a routine as regular, as peaceful, as that in which I had moved in Boston. Each morning in my quiet sunny room I wrote, with complete absorption, from seven o'clock until noon, confidently composing poems, stories, essays, and dramas. I worked like a painter with several themes in hand passing from one to the other as I felt inclined. After luncheon I walked down town seeking exercise and recreation. It soon became my habit to spend an hour or two in Taft's studio (I fear to his serious detriment), and in this way I soon came to know most of the "Bunnies" of "the Rabbit-Warren" as Henry B. Fuller characterized this studio building —and it well deserved the name! Art was young and timid in Cook County.

Among the women of this group Bessie Potter, who did lovely statuettes of girls and children, was a notable figure. Edward Kemeys, Oliver Dennett Grover, Charles Francis Browne, and Hermon MacNeill, all young artists of high endowment, and marked personal charm became my valued associates and friends. We were all equally poor and equally confident of the future. Our doubts were few and transitory as cloud shadows, our hopes had the wings of eagles.

As Chicago possessed few clubs of any kind and had no common place of meeting for those who cultivated the fine arts, Taft's studio became, naturally, our center of esthetic exchange. Painting and sculpture were not greatly encouraged anywhere in the West, but Lorado and his brave colleagues, hardy frontiersmen of art, laughed in the face of all discouragement.

A group of us often lunched in what Taft called "the Beanery"—a noisy, sloppy little restaurant on Van Buren Street, where our lofty discussions of Grecian sculpture were punctuated by the crash of waiter-proof crockery, or smothered with the howl of slid chairs. However, no one greatly minded these barbarities. They were all a part of the game. If any of us felt particularly flush we dined, at sixty cents each, in the basement of a big department store a few doors further west; and when now and then some good "lay brother" like Melville Stone, or Franklin Head, invited us to a "royal gorge" at Kinsley's or to a princely luncheon in the tower room of the Union League, we went like minstrels to the baron's hall. None of us possessed evening suits and some of us went so far as to denounce swallowtail coats as "undemocratic." I was one of these.

This "artistic gang" also contained several writers who kept a little apart from the journalistic circle of which Eugene Field and Opie Read were the leaders, and though I passed freely from one of these groups to the other I acknowledged myself more at ease with Henry Fuller and Taft and Browne, and a little later I united with them in organizing a society to fill our need of a common meeting place. This association we called *The Little Room,* a name suggested by Madelaine Yale Wynne's story of an intermittently vanishing chamber in an old New England homestead.

For a year or two we met in Bessie Potter's studio, and on the theory that our club, visible and hospitable on Friday afternoon, was non-existent during all the other days of the week, we called it "the Little Room." Later still we shifted to Ralph Clarkson's studio in the Fine Arts Building—where it still flourishes.

The fact is, I was a poor club man. I did not smoke, and never used rum except as a hair tonic—and beer and tobacco were rather distasteful to me. I do not boast of this singularity, I merely state it. No doubt I was considered a dull and profitless companion even in "the Little Room," but in most of my sobrieties Taft and Browne upheld me, though they both possessed the redeeming virtue of being amusing, which I, most certainly, never achieved.

Taft was especially witty in his sly, sidewise comment, and often when several of us were in hot debate, his sententious or humorous retorts cut or stung in defence of some esthetic principle much more effectively than most of my harangues. Sculpture, with him, was a religious faith, and he defended it manfully and practiced it with skill and an industry which was astounding.

Though a noble figure and universally admired, he had, like myself, two very serious defects, he was addicted to frock coats and the habit of lecturing! Although he did not go so far as to wear a plaid Windsor tie with his "Prince Albert" coat (as I have been accused of doing), he displayed something of the professor's zeal in his platform addresses. I would demur against the plaid Windsor tie indictment if I dared to do so, but a certain snapshot portrait taken by a South-side photographer of that day (and still extant) forces me to painful confession—I had such a tie, and I wore it with a frock coat. My social status is thus clearly defined.

Taft's studio, which was on the top floor of the Athenæum Building on Van Buren Street, had a section which he called "the morgue," for the reason that it was littered with piaster duplicates of busts, arms, and hands. This room, fitted up with shelf-like bunks, was filled nearly every night with penniless young sculptors who camped in primitive simplicity amid the grewsome discarded portraits of Cook County's most illustrious citizens. Several of these roomers have since become artists of wide renown, and I refrain from disclosing their names. No doubt they will smile as they recall those nights amid their landlord's cast-off handiwork.

Taft was an "easy mark" in those times, a shining hope to all the indigent models, discouraged painters and other esthetic derelicts of the Columbian Exposition. No artist suppliant ever knocked at his door without getting a dollar, and some of them got twenty. For several years Clarkson and I had him on our minds because of this gentle and yielding disposition until at last we discovered that in one way or another, in spite of a reckless prodigality, he pros-

pered. The bread which he cheerfully cast upon these
unknown waters, almost always returned (sometimes from
another direction) in loaves at least as large as biscuits.
His fame steadily increased with his charity. I did not
understand the principle of his manner of life then, and I
do not now. By all the laws of my experience he should
at this moment be in the poorhouse, but he isn't—he is
rich and honored and loved.

In sculpture he was, at this time a conservative, a wor-
shiper of the Greek, and it would seem that I became his
counter-irritant, for my demand for "A native art" kept
him wholesomely stirred up. One by one as the years
passed he yielded esthetic positions which at first he most
stoutly held. He conceded that the Modern could not be
entirely expressed by the Ancient, that America might
sometime grow to the dignity of having an art of its own,
and that in sculpture (as in painting and architecture)
new problems might arise. Even in his own work (although he professed but one ideal, the Athenian) he came
at last to include the plastic value of the red man, and to
find in the expression of the Sioux or Omaha a certain
sorrowful dignity which fell parallel with his own grave
temperament, for, despite his smiling face, his best work
remained somber, almost tragic in spirit.

Henry B. Fuller, who in *The Chevalier of Pensieri-Vani*
had shown himself to be the finest literary craftsman in
the West, became (a little later) a leader in our group
and a keen delight to us all. He was at this time a small,
brown-bearded man of thirty-five, whose quick humor, keen
insight and unfailing interest in all things literary made
him a caustic corrective of the bombast to which our local
reviewers were sadly liable. Although a merciless critic
of Chicago, he was a native of the city, and his comment
on its life had to be confronted with such equanimity as
our self-elected social hierarchy could assume.

Elusive if not austere with strangers, Henry's laugh (a musical "ha ha") was often heard among his friends. His face could be impassive not to say repellent when approached by those in whom he took no interest, and there were large numbers of his fellow citizens for whom the author of *Pensieri-Vani* had only contempt. Strange to say, he became my most intimate friend and confidant— antithetic pair!

Eugene Field, his direct opposite, and the most distinguished member of "the journalistic gang," took very little interest in the doings of "the Bunnies" and few of them knew him, but I often visited him in his home on the North Side, and greatly enjoyed his solemn-faced humor. He was a singular character, as improvident as Lorado but in a far different way.

I recall meeting him one day on the street wearing, as usual, a long, gray plaid ulster with enormous pockets at the sides. Confronting me with coldly solemn visage, he thrust his right hand into his pocket and lifted a heavy brass candlestick to the light. "Look," he said. I looked. Dropping this he dipped his left hand into the opposite pocket and displayed another similar piece, then with a faint smile lifting the corners of his wide, thin-lipped mouth, he gravely boomed, "Brother Garland—you see before you—a man—who lately—had ten dollars."

Thereupon he went his way, leaving me to wonder whether his wife would be equally amused with his latest purchase.

His library was filled with all kinds of curious objects— worthless junk they seemed to me—clocks, snuffers, butterflies, and the like but he also possessed many autographed books and photographs whose value I granted. His cottage which was not large, swarmed with growing boys and noisy dogs; and Mrs. Field, a sweet and patient soul, seemed sadly out of key with her husband's habit of buying collections of rare moths, door-knockers, and candle molds with money which should have gone to buy chairs and carpets or trousers for the boys.

Eugene was one of the first "Colyumists" in the country, and to fill his "Sharps and Flats" levied pitilessly upon his friends. From time to time we all figured as subjects for his humorous paragraphs; but each new victim understood and smiled. For example, in his column I read one morning these words: "La Crosse, a small city in Wisconsin, famous for the fact that all its trains back into town, and as the home of Hamlin Garland."

He was one of the most popular of Western writers, and his home of a Sunday was usually crowded with visitors, many of whom were actors. I recall meeting Francis Wilson there—also E. S. Willard and Bram Stoker—but I do not remember to have seen Fuller there, although, later, Roswell, Eugene's brother, became Fuller's intimate friend.

George Ade, a thin, pale, bright-eyed young Hoosier, was a frequent visitor at Field's. George had just begun to make a place for himself as the author of a column in the *News* called "Stories of the Street and of the Town"; and John T. McCutcheon, another Hoosier of the same lean type was his illustrator. I believed in them both and took a kind of elder brother interest in their work.

In the companionship of men like Field and Browne and Taft, I was happy. My writing went well, and if I regretted Boston, I had the pleasant sense of being so near West Salem that I could go to bed in a train at ten at night, and breakfast with my mother in the morning, and just to prove that this was true I ran up to the Homestead at Christmas time and delivered my presents in person—keenly enjoying the smile of delight with which my mother received them.

West Salem was like a scene on the stage that day—a setting for a rural mid-winter drama. The men in their gayly-colored Mackinac jackets, the sleighbells jingling pleasantly along the lanes, the cottage roofs laden with snow, and the sidewalks, walled with drifts, were almost arctic in their suggestion, and yet, my parents in the shelter of the friendly hills, were at peace. The cold was not being driven against them by the wind of the plain, and a plentiful supply of food and fuel made their fireside comfortable and secure.

During this vacation I seized the opportunity to go a little farther and spend a few days in the Pineries which I had never seen. Out of this experience I gained some beautiful pictures of the snowy forest, and a suggestion for a story or two. A few days later, on a commission from *McClure's,* I was in Pittsburg writing an article on "Homestead and Its Perilous Trades," and the clouds of smoke, the flaming chimneys, the clang of steel, the roar of blast-furnaces and the thunder of monstrous steel rollers made Wisconsin lumber camps idyllic. The serene white peace of West Salem set Pittsburg apart as a sulphurous hell and my description of it became a passionate indictment of an industrial system which could so work and so house its men. The grimy hovels in which the toilers lived made my own homestead a poem. More than ever convinced that our social order was unjust and impermanent, I sent in my "story," in some doubt about its being accepted. It was printed with illustrations by Orson Lowell and was widely quoted at the time.

Soon after this I made a trip to Memphis, thus gaining my first impression of the South. Like most northern visitors, I was immediately and intensely absorbed in the negroes. Their singing entranced me, and my hosts, Mr. and Mrs. Judah, hired a trio of black minstrels to come in and perform for me. Their songs so moved me, and I became so interested in one old negro's curious chants that

My First Winter in Chicago

I fairly wore them out with demands for their most characteristic spirituals. Some of the hymns were of such sacred character that one of the men would not sing them. "I ain't got no right to sing dem songs," he said.

In Atlanta I met Joel Chandler Harris, who had done so much to portray the negro's inner kindliness, as well as his singularly poetic outlook. Harris was one of the editors of the *Atlanta Constitution*, and there I found him in a bare, prosaic office, a short, shy, red-haired man whom I liked at once. Two nights later I was dining with James A. Herne and William Dean Howells in New York City, and the day following I read some of my verses for the Nineteenth Century Club. At the end of March I was again at my desk in Chicago.

These sudden changes of scene, these dramatic meetings, so typical of my life for many years, took away all sense of drudgery, all routine weariness. Seldom remaining in any one place long enough to become bored I had little chance to bore others. Literary clubs welcomed my readings and lectures; and, being vigorous and of good digestion, I accepted travel as a diversion as well as a business. As a student of American life, I was resolved to know every phase of it.

Among my pleasant jobs I recall the putting into shape of a "Real Conversation" with James Whitcomb Riley, the material for which had been gained in a visit to Greenfield, Riley's native town, during August of the previous year.

My first meeting with Riley had been in Boston at a time when I was a penniless student and he the shining, highly-paid lecturer; and I still suffered a feeling of wonder that a poet—any poet—could demand such pay. I did not resent it—I only marveled at it—for in our conversation he had made his philosophy plain.

"Tell of the things just like they was, they don't need

no excuse," one of his characters said. "Don't tech 'em up as the poets does till they're all too fine fer use," and in his talk with me Riley quaintly added, "Nature is good enough for God, it's good enough for me."

In this article which I wrote for *McClure's,* I made comment on the essential mystery of the poet's art, a conjury which is able to transmute a perfectly commonplace landscape into something fine and mellow and sweet; for the region in which Riley spent his youth, and from which he derived most of his later material, was to me a depressing land, a country without a hill, a river or a lake; a commonplace country, flat, unkempt and without a line of beauty, and yet from these rude fields and simple gardens the singer had drawn the sweetest honey of song, song with a tang in it, like the odor of ripe buckwheat and the taste of frost-bit persimmons. It reinforced my resolution that the mid-land was about to blossom into art.

In travel and in work such as this and in pleasant intercourse with the painters, sculptors, and writers of Chicago my first winter in the desolate, drab, and tumultuous city passed swiftly and on the whole profitably, I no longer looked backward to Boston, but as the first warm spring-winds began to blow, my thoughts turned towards my newly-acquired homestead and the old mother who was awaiting me there.

Eager to start certain improvements which should tend to make the house more nearly the kind of dwelling place I had promised myself it should become, hungry for the soil, rejoicing in the thought of once more planting and building, I took the train for the North with all my summer ward-robe and most of my manuscripts, with no intention of reëntering the city till October at the earliest.

CHAPTER TWO

I Return to the Saddle

TO pass from the crowds, the smoke and the iron clangor of Chicago into the clear April air of West Salem was a celestial change for me. For many years the clock of my seasons had been stilled. The coming of the birds, the budding of the leaves, the serial blossoming of spring had not touched me, and as I walked up the street that exquisite morning, a reminiscent ecstasy filled my heart. The laughter of the robins, the shrill ki-ki-ki of the golden-wing woodpeckers, and the wistful whistle of the lark, brought back my youth, my happiest youth, and when my mother met me at the door it seemed that all my cares and all my years of city life had fallen from me.

"Well, here I am!" I called, "ready for the spring's work."

With a silent laugh, as preface, she replied, "You'll get a-plenty. Your father is all packed, impatient to leave for Ordway."

The old soldier, who came in from the barn a few moments later, confirmed this. "I'm no truck farmer," he explained with humorous contempt. "I turn this onion patch over to you. It's no place for me. In two days I'll be broad-casting wheat on a thousand-acre farm. That's my size"—a fact which I admitted.

As we sat at breakfast he went on to say that he found Wisconsin woefully unprogressive. "These fellows back here are all stuck in the mud. They've got to wake up to

13

the reform movements. I'll be glad to get back to Dakota where people are alive."

With the spirit of the seed-sower swelling within him he took the noon train, handing over to me the management of the Homestead.

An hour later mother and I went out to inspect the garden and to plan the seeding. The pie-plant leaves were unfolding and slender asparagus spears were pointing from the mold. The smell of burning leaves brought back to us both, with magic power, memories of the other springs and other plantings on the plain. It was glorious, it was medicinal!

"This is the life!" I exultantly proclaimed. "Work is just what I need. I shall set to it at once. Aren't you glad you are here in this lovely valley and not out on the bleak Dakota plain?"

Mother's face sobered. "Yes, I like it here—it seems more like home than any other place—and yet I miss the prairie and my Ordway friends."

As I went about the village I came to a partial understanding of her feeling. The small dark shops, the uneven sidewalks, the ricketty wooden awnings were closely in character with the easy-going citizens who moved leisurely and contentedly about their small affairs. It came to me (with a sense of amusement) that these coatless shopkeepers who dealt out sugar and kerosene while wearing their derby hats on the backs of their heads, were not only my neighbors, but members of the Board of Education. Though still primitive to my city eyes, they no longer appeared remote. Something in their names and voices touched me nearly. They were American. Their militant social democracy was at once comical and corrective.

O, the peace, the sweetness of those days! To be awakened by the valiant challenge of early-rising roosters; to

I Return to the Saddle

hear the chuckle of dawn-light worm-hunting robins brought a return of boy-hood's exultation. Not only did my muscles harden to the spade and the hoe, my soul rejoiced in a new and delightful sense of establishment. I had returned to citizenship. I was a proprietor. The clock of the seasons had resumed its beat.

Hiring a gardener, I bought a hand-book on Horticulture and announced my intent to make those four fat acres feed my little flock. I was now a land enthusiast. My feet laid hold upon the earth. I almost took root!

With what secret satisfaction I planned to widen the front porch and build a two-story bay-window on the north end of the sitting room—an enterprise of such audacity that I kept it strictly to myself! It meant the extravagant outlay of nearly two hundred dollars—but above and beyond that, it involved cutting a hole in the wall and cluttering up the yard; therefore I thought it best to keep my plot hidden from my mother till mid-summer gave more leisure to us all.

My notebook of that spring is crowded with descriptions, almost lyrical, of the glory of sunsets and the beauty of bird-song and budding trees—even the loud-voiced, cheerful democracy of the village was grateful to me.

"Yesterday I was deep in the tumult of Chicago," runs the entry, "to-day, I am hoeing in my sun-lit garden, hearing the mourning-dove coo and the cat-birds cry. Last night as the sun went down the hill-tops to the west became vividly purple with a subtle illusive deep-crimson glow beneath, while the sky above their tops, a saffron dome rose almost to the zenith. These mystical things are here joined: The trill of black-birds near at hand, the cackle of barn-yard fowls, the sound of hammers, a plowman talking to his team, the pungent smoke of burning leaves, the cool, sweet, spring wind and the glowing downpouring sunshine—all marvelous and satisfying to me and mine. *This is home!*"

On the twelfth of April, however, a most dramatic reversal to winter took place. "The day remained beautifully springlike till about two o'clock when a gray haze came rushing downward from the north-west. Big black clouds developed with portentous rapidity. Thunder arose, and an icy wind, furious and swift as a tornado roared among the trees. The rain, chilled almost into hail, drummed on the shingles. The birds fell silent, the hens scurried to shelter. In ten minutes the cutting blast died out. A dead calm succeeded. Then out burst the sun, flooding the land with laughter! The black-birds resumed their piping, the fowls ventured forth, and the whole valley again lay beaming and blossoming under a perfect sky."

The following night I was in the city watching a noble performance of "Tristan and Isolde!"

I took enormous satisfaction in the fact that I could plant peas in my garden till noon and hear a concert in Chicago on the same day. The arrangement seemed ideal.

On May 9th I was again at home, "the first whippoor-will sang to-night—trees are in full leaf," I note.

In a big square room in the eastern end of the house, I set up a handmade walnut desk which I had found in LaCrosse, and on this I began to write in the inspiration of morning sun-shine and bird-song. For four hours I bent above my pen, and each afternoon I sturdily flourished spade and hoe, while mother hobbled about with cane in hand to see that I did it right. "You need watching," she laughingly said.

With a cook and a housemaid, a man to work the garden, and a horse to plow out my corn and potatoes, I began to wear the composed dignity of an earl. I pruned trees, shifted flower beds and established berry patches with the large-handed authority of a southern planter. It was comical, it was delightful!

To eat home-cooked meals after years of dreadful restaurants gave me especial satisfaction, but alas! there was a flaw in my lute. We had to eat in our living room; and when I said "Mother, one of these days I'm going to move the kitchen to the south and build a real sure-enough dining room in between," she turned upon me with startled gaze.

"You'd better think a long time about that," she warningly replied. "We're perfectly comfortable the way we are."

"Comfortable? Yes, but we must begin to think of being luxurious. There's nothing too good for you, mother."

Early in July my brother Franklin joined me in the garden work, and then my mother's cup of contentment fairly overflowed its brim. So far as we knew she had no care, no regret. Day by day she sat in an easy chair under the trees, watching us as we played ball on the lawn, or cut weeds in the garden; and each time we looked at her, we both acknowledged a profound sense of satisfaction, of relief. Never again would she burn in the suns of the arid plains, or cower before the winds of a desolate winter. She was secure. "You need never work again," I assured her. "You can get up when you please and go to bed when you please. Your only job is to sit in the shade and boss the rest of us," and to this she answered only with a silent, characteristic chuckle of delight.

"The Junior," as I called my brother, enjoyed the homestead quite as much as I. Together we painted the porch, picked berries, hoed potatoes, and trimmed trees. Everything we did, everything we saw, recovered for us some part of our distant boyhood. The noble lines of the hills to the west, the weeds of the road-side, the dusty weather-beaten, covered-bridges, the workmen in the fields, the voices of our neighbors, the gossip of the village—all these sights and sounds awakened deep-laid, associated tender memories. The cadence of every song, the quality of every resounding jest made us at home, once and for all. Our twenty-five-year stay on the level lands of Iowa and Dakota seemed only an unsuccessful family exploration—our life in the city merely a business, winter adventure.

To visit among the farmers—to help at haying or harvesting, brought back minute touches of the olden, wondrous prairie world. We went swimming in the river just as we used to do when lads, rejoicing in the caress of the wind, the sting of the cool water, and on such expeditions we often thought of Burton and others of our play-mates far-away, and of Uncle David, in his California exile. "I wish he, too, could enjoy this sweet and tranquil world," I said, and in this desire my brother joined.

We wore the rudest and simplest clothing, and hoed (when we hoed) with furious strokes; but as the sun grew hot we usually fled to the shade of the great maples which filled the back yard, and there, at ease, recounted the fierce toil of the Iowa harvest fields, recalling the names of the men who shared it with us,—and so, while all around us green things valorously expanded, and ripening apples turned to scarlet and gold in their coverts of green, we burrowed deep in the soil like the badger which is the symbol of our native state.

After so many years of bleak and treeless farm-lands, it seemed that our mother could not get enough of the luxuriant foliage, the bloom and the odorous sweetness of this lovely valley. Hour by hour, day by day, she sat on the porch, or out under the trees, watching the cloud shadows slide across the hills, hearing the whistle of the orioles and the love songs of the cat-bird, happy in the realization that

I Return to the Saddle

both her sons were, at last, within the sound of her voice. She had but one unsatisfied desire (a desire which she shyly reiterated), and that was her longing for a daughter, but neither Frank nor I, at the moment, had any well-defined hope of being able to fulfill that demand.

My life had not been one to bring about intimate relationships with women. I had been too poor and too busy in Boston to form any connections other than just good friendships, and even now, my means would not permit a definite thought of marriage. "Where can I keep a wife? My two little rooms in Chicago are all the urban home I can afford, and to bring a daughter of the city to live in West Salem would be dangerous." Nevertheless, I promised mother that on my return to Chicago, I would look around and see what I could find.

For three months—that is to say during May, June and July, I remained concerned with potato bugs, currant worms, purslane and other important garden concerns, but in August I started on a tour which had far-reaching effects. Though still at work upon *Rose of Dutcher's Coolly*, I was beginning to meditate on themes connected with Colorado, and as the heat of July intensified in the low country, I fell to dreaming of the swift mountain streams whose bright waters I had seen·in a previous trip, and so despite all my protestations, I found myself in Colorado Springs one August day, a guest of Louis Ehrich, a New Yorker and fellow reformer, in exile for his health. It was at his table that I met Professor Fernow, chief of the National Bureau of Forestry, who was in the west on a tour of the Federal Forests, and full of enthusiasm for his science.

His talk interested me enormously. I forecast, dimly, something of the elemental change which scientific control was about to bring into the mountain west, and when (sensing my genuine interest) he said "Why not accompany me on my round?" I accepted instantly, and my good friends, the Ehrichs out-fitted me for the enterprise.

We left next day for Glenwood Springs, at which point Fernow hired horses and a guide who knew the streams and camps of the White River Plateau, and early on the second morning we set out on a trail which, in a literary sense, carried me a long way and into a new world. From the plain I ascended to the peaks. From the barbed-wire lanes of Iowa and Kansas I entered the thread-like paths of the cliffs, and (most important of all) I returned to the saddle. I became once more the horseman in a region of horsemen.

For the first time in nearly twenty years I swung to the saddle, and by that act recovered a power and a joy which only verse could express. I found myself among men of such endurance and hardihood that I was ashamed to complain of my aching bones and overstrained muscles— men to whom dark nights, precipitous trails, noxious insects, mud and storms were all "a part of the game."

In those few days I absorbed the essential outlines of a new world. My note-book of the time is proof of it—and "The Prairie in the Sky," which was the title of the article I wrote for *Harper's Weekly*, is further evidence of it. How beautiful it all was! As I look back upon it I see green parks lit with larkspur and painter's brush. I taste the marvelous freshness of the air. The ptarmigan scuttles away among the rocks, the marmot whistles, the conies utter their slender wistful cries.

That trail led me back to the hunter's cabin, to the miner's shack on whose rough-hewn walls the fire-light flickered in a kind of silent music. It set me once again in the atmosphere of daring and filled me with the spirit of pioneer adventure.

I Return to the Saddle

In a physical sense I ended my exploration ten days later, but in imagination I continued to ride "The High Country." I had entered a fresh scene—discovered a new enthusiasm.

By this I do not mean to imply that I at once set about the composition of a Wild West novel, but for those who may be interested in the literary side of this chronicle, I will admit that this splendid trip into high Colorado, marks the beginning of my career as a fictionist of the Mountain West.

Thereafter neither the coulee country nor the prairie served exclusively as material for my books. From the plains, which were becoming each year more crowded, more prosaic, I fled in imagination as in fact to the looming silver-and-purple summits of the Continental Divide, while in my mind an ambition to embody, as no one at that time had done, the spirit and the purpose of the Rocky Mountain trailer was vaguely forming in my mind. To my home in Wisconsin I carried back a fragment of rock, whose gray mass, beautifully touched with gold and amber and orange-colored lichens formed a part of the narrow causeway which divides the White River from the Bear. It was a talisman of the land whose rushing waters, majestic forests and exquisite Alpine meadows I desired to hold in memory, and with this stone on my desk I wrote. It aided me in recalling the scenes and the characters I had so keenly admired.

*   *   *   *   *   *

In calling upon Lorado one afternoon soon after my return to Chicago I was surprised and a little disconcerted to find two strange young ladies making themselves very much at home in his studio. In greeting me he remarked in a mood of sly mischief, "You will not approve of these girls—they are on their way to Paris to study sculpture, but

I want you to know them. They are Janet Scudder and my sister Zulime."

Up to this time, notwithstanding our growing friendship, I was not aware that he had a sister, but I greeted Miss Taft with something like fraternal interest. She was a handsome rather pale girl with fine, serious gray-blue eyes, and a composed and graceful manner. Her profile was particularly good and as she was not greatly interested in looking at me I had an excellent chance to study her.

Lorado explained "My sister has been in Kansas visiting mother and father and is now on her way to New York to take a steamer for France. . . . She intends to remain abroad for two years." he added.

Knowing that I was at that moment in the midst of writing a series of essays on *The National Spirit in American Art,* he expected this to draw my fire—and it did. "Why go abroad," I demanded bluntly. "Why not stay right here and study modeling with your brother? Paris is no place for an American artist."

With an amused glance at her friend, Miss Scudder, Miss Taft replied in a tone of tolerant contempt for my ignorance, "One doesn't get very far in art without Paris."

Somewhat nettled by her calm inflection and her supercilious glance I hotly retorted, "Nonsense! You can acquire all the technic you require, right here in Chicago. If you are in earnest, and are really in search of instruction you can certainly get it in Boston or New York. Stay in your own country whatever you do. This sending students at their most impressionable age to the Old World to absorb Old World conventions and prejudices is all wrong. It makes of them something which is neither American nor European. Suppose France did that? No nation has an art worth speaking of unless it has a national spirit."

Of course this is only a brief report of my harangue

which might just as well have remained unspoken, so far as Miss Taft was concerned, and when her brother came to her aid I retired worsted. The two pilgrims went their way leaving me to hammer Lorado at my leisure.

I wish I could truthfully say that this brief meeting with Zulime Taft filled me with a deep desire to see her again but I cannot do so. On the contrary, my recollection is that I considered her a coldly-haughty young person running away from her native land, not to study art but to have a pleasant time in Paris—while she (no doubt) regarded me as a rude, forth-putting anarch—which I was. At this point our acquaintance and our controversy rested.

As the months and years passed I heard of her only through some incidental remark of her brother. Having no slightest premonition of the part she was to play in my after life, I made no inquiries concerning her. She, however, followed me—as I afterward learned, by means of my essays and stories in the magazines but remained quite uninterested (so far as I know) in the personality of their author.

CHAPTER THREE

In the Footsteps of General Grant

AMONG the new esthetic and literary enterprises which the Exposition had brought to Chicago was the high-spirited publishing firm of Stone and Kimball, which started out valiantly in the spring of '94. The head of the house, a youth just out of Harvard, was Herbert Stone, son of my friend Melville Stone, manager of the Associated Press. Kimball was Herbert's classmate.

Almost before he had opened his office, Herbert came to me to get a manuscript. "Eugene Field has given us one," he urged, "and we want one from you. We are starting a real publishing house in Chicago and we need your support."

There was no resisting such an appeal. Having cast in my lot with Chicago, it was inevitable that I should ally myself with its newest literary enterprise, a business which expressed something of my faith in the west. Not only did I turn over to Stone the rights to *Main Traveled Roads,* together with a volume of verse—I promised him a book of essays—and a novel.

These aspiring young collegians were joined in '95 by another Harvard man, a tall, dark, smooth-faced youth named Harrison Rhodes, and when, of an afternoon these three missionaries of culture each in a long frock coat, tightly buttoned, with cane, gloves and shining silk hats, paced side by side down the Lake Shore Drive they had the effect of an esthetic invasion, but their crowning audacity

24

was a printed circular which announced that tea would be served in their office in the Caxton Building on Saturday afternoons! Finally as if to convince the city of their utter madness, this intrepid trio adventured the founding of a literary magazine to be called *The Chap Book!* Culture on the Middle Border had at last begun to hum!

Despite the smiles of elderly scoffers, the larger number of my esthetic associates felt deeply grateful to these devoted literary pioneers, whose taste, enterprise and humor were all sorely needed "in our midst." If not precisely cosmopolitan they were at least in touch with London.

Early in '94 they brought out a lovely edition of *Main Traveled Roads* and a new book called *Prairie Songs.* Neither of these volumes sold—the firm had no special facilities for selling books, but their print and binding delighted me, and in the autumn of the same year I gladly let them publish a collection of essays called *Crumbling Idols,* a small screed which aroused an astonishing tumult of comment, mostly antagonistic. Walter Page, editor of the *Forum,* in which one of the key-note chapters appeared, told me that over a thousand editorials were written upon my main thesis.

In truth the attention which this iconoclastic declaration of faith received at the hands of critics was out of all proportion to its size. Its explosive power was amazing. As I read it over now, with the clamor of "Cubism," "Imagism" and "Futurism" in my ears, it seems a harmless and on the whole rather reasonable plea for National Spirit and the freedom of youth, but in those days all of my books had mysterious power for arousing opposition, and most reviews of my work were so savage that I made a point of not reading them for the reason that they either embittered me, or were so lacking in discrimination as to have no value. In spite of all appearances to the contrary, I hated contention, therefore I left consideration of these assaults entirely to my publishers. (I learned afterwards that Miss Taft was greatly interested in *Crumbling Idols*. Perhaps she assumed that I was writing at her.)

Meanwhile in *Rose of Dutcher's Coolly*, the manuscript of which I had carried about with me on many of my lecturing trips, I was attempting to embody something of Chicago life, a task which I found rather difficult. After nine years of life in Boston, the city by the lake seemed depressingly drab and bleak, and my only hope lay in representing it not as I saw it, but as it appeared to my Wisconsin heroine who came to it from Madison and who perceived in it the mystery and the beauty which I had lost. To Rose, fresh from the farm, it was a great capital, and the lake a majestic sea. As in *A Spoil of Office*, I had tried to maintain the point of view of a countryman, so now I attempted to embody in *Rose of Dutcher's Coolly*, a picture of Chicago as an ambitious young girl from the Wisconsin farm would see it.

In my story Rose Dutcher made her way from Bluff Siding to the State University, and from Madison to a fellowship in the artistic and literary Chicago, of which I was a part. Her progress was intended to be typical. I said, "I will depict the life of a girl who has ambitious desires, and works toward her goal as blindly and as determinedly as a boy." It was a new thesis so far as Western girls were concerned, and I worked long and carefully on the problem, carrying the manuscript back and forth with me for two years.

As spring came on, I again put "Rose" in my trunk and hastened back to West Salem in order to build the two-story bay-window which I had minutely planned, which was, indeed, almost as important as my story and much more exciting. To begin the foundation of that extension was like setting in motion the siege of a city! It was extravagant—reckless—nevertheless assisted by a neighbor who was clever at any kind of building, I set to work in boyish, illogical enthusiasm.

Mother watched us tear out and rebuild with uneasy glance but when the windows were in and a new carpet with an entire "parlor suite" to match, arrived from the city, her alarm became vocal. "You mustn't spend your money for things like these. We can't afford such luxuries."

"Don't you worry about my money," I replied, "There's more where I found this. There's nothing too good for you, mother."

How sweet and sane and peaceful and afar off those blessed days seem to me as I muse over this page. At the village shops sirloin steak was ten cents a pound, chickens fifty cents a pair and as for eggs—I couldn't give ours away, at least in the early summer,—and all about us were gardens laden with fruit and vegetables, more than we could eat or sell or feed to the pigs. Wars were all in the past and life a simple matter of working out one's own individual problems. Never again shall I feel that confidence in the future, that joy in the present. I had no doubts—none that I can recall.

My brother came again in June and joyfully aided me in my esthetic pioneering. We amazed the town by seeding down a potato patch and laying out a tennis court thereon, the first play-ground of its kind in Hamilton township, and often as we played of an afternoon, farmers on their way to market with loads of grain or hogs, paused to watch our game and make audible comment on our folly. We also bought a lawn-mower, the second in the town, and shaved our front yard. We took down the old picket fence in front of the house and we planted trees and flowers, until at last some of the elderly folk disgustedly exclaimed, "What won't them Garland boys do next!"

Without doubt we "started something" in the sleepy village. Others following our example went so far as to take down their own fences and to buy lawn-mowers. That we were planning waterworks and a bath-room remained a secret—this was too revolutionary to be spoken of for the present. We were forced to make progress slowly.

Rose of Dutcher's Coolly, published during this year, was attacked quite as savagely as *Main Traveled Roads* had been, and this criticism saddened and depressed me. With a foolish notion that the Middle West should take a moderate degree of pride in me, I resented this condemnation. "Am I not making in my small way the same sort of historical record of the west that Whittier and Holmes secured for New England?" I asked my friends. "Am I not worthy of an occasional friendly word, a message of encouragement?"

Of course I should have risen superior to these local misjudgments, and in fact I did keep to my work although only a faint voice here and there was raised in my defence. Even after *Rose* had been introduced to London by William Stead, and Henry James and Israel Zangwill and James Barrie had all written in praise of her, the editors of the western papers still maintained a consistently militant attitude. Perhaps I should have taken comfort from the fact that they considered me worth assaulting, but that kind of comfort is rather bleak at its best, especially when the sales of your book are so small as to be confirmatory of the critic.

Without doubt this persistent antagonism, this almost universal depreciation of my stories of the plains had something to do with intensifying the joy with which I returned to the mountain world and its heroic types, at any rate I spent July and August of that year in Colorado and New Mexico, making many observations, which turned out to have incalculable value to me in later days. From a round-up in the Current Creek country I sauntered down through Salida, Ouray, Telluride, Durango and the Ute Reservation, a circuit which filled my mind with noble suggestions for stories and poems, a tour which profoundly influenced my life as well as my writing.

The little morocco-covered notebook in which I set down some of my impressions is before me as I write. It still vibrates with the ecstasy of that enthusiasm. Sentences like these are frequent. "From the dry hot plains, across the blazing purple of the mesa's edge, I look away to where the white clouds soar in majesty above the serrate crest of Uncomphagre. Oh, the splendor and mystery of those cloud-hid regions! . . . A coyote, brown and dry and hot as any tuft of desert grass drifts by. . . . Into the coolness and sweetness and cloud-glory of this marvelous land. . . . Gorgeous shadows are in motion on White House Peak. . . . Along the trail as though walking a taut wire, a caravan of burros streams, driven by a wide-hatted graceful horseman. . . . Twelve thousand feet! I am brother to the eagles now! The matchless streams, the vivid orange-colored meadows. The deep surf-like roar of the firs, the wailing sigh of the wind in the grass—a passionate longing wind." Such are my jottings.

In these pages I can now detect the beginnings of a dozen of my stories, a score of my poems. No other of my trips was ever so inspirational.

Not content with the wonders of Colorado I drifted down to Santa Fé and Isleta, with Charles Francis Browne and Hermon MacNeill, and got finally to Holbrook, where we outfitted and rode away across the desert, bound for the

Snake Dance at Walpi. It would seem that we had decided to share all there was of romance in the South West. They were as insatiate as I.

For a week we lived on the mesa at Walpi in the house of Heli. Aided by Dr. Fewkes of Washington, we saw most of the phases of the snake ceremonies. The doctor and his own men were camped at the foot of the mesa, making a special study of the Hopi and their history. Remote, incredibly remote it all seemed even at that time, and some of that charm I put into an account of it which *Harper's* published—one of the earliest popular accounts of the Snake Dance.

One night as I was standing on the edge of the cliff looking out over the sand to the west, I saw a train of pack horses moving toward Walpi like a jointed, canvas-colored worm. It was the outfit of another party of "tourists" coming to the dance, and half an hour later a tall, lean, brown and smiling man of middle life rode up the eastern trail at the head of his train.

Greeting me pleasantly he asked, "Has the ceremony begun?"

"The snakes are in process of being gathered," I replied, "but you are in time for the most interesting part of the festival."

In response to a question he explained, "I've been studying the Cliff-Dwellings of the Mesa Verde. My name is Pruden. I am from New York."

It was evident that "The Doctor" (as his guides called him) was not only a man of wide experience on the trail, but a scientist as well, and I found him most congenial.

We spent the evening together, and together we witnessed the mysterious snake dance which the natives of Walpi give every other year—a ceremony so incredibly primitive that it carried me back into the stone age, and

three days later (leaving Browne and MacNeill to paint
and sculpture the Hopi) we went to Zuni and Acoma and
at last to the Grand Cañon of the Colorado, a trip which
laid upon my mind a thousand glorious impressions of
the desert and its life. It was so beautiful, so marvelous
that sand and flies and hunger and thirst were forgotten.

Aside from its esthetic delight, this summer turned out
to be the most profitable season of my whole career. It
marks a complete 'bout face in my march. Coming just
after *Rose of Dutcher's Coolly,* it dates the close of my
prairie tales and the beginning of a long series of mountain
stories. Cripple Creek and the Current Creek country
suggested *The Eagle's Heart, Witches' Gold, Money Magic,*
and a dozen shorter romances. In truth every page of my
work thereafter was colored by the experiences of this
glorious savage splendid summer.

The reasons are easy to define. All my emotional relationships with the "High Country" were pleasant, my sense
of responsibility was less keen, hence the notes of resentment, of opposition to unjust social conditions which had
made my other books an offense to my readers were almost
entirely absent in my studies of the mountaineers. My pity
was less challenged in their case. Lonely as their lives
were, it was not a sordid loneliness. The cattle rancher was
at least not a drudge. Careless, slovenly and wasteful as
I knew him to be, he was not mean. He had something of
the Centaur in his bearing. Marvelous horsemanship dignified his lean figure and lent a notable grace to his gestures. His speech was picturesque and his observations
covered a wide area. Self-reliant, fearless, instant of action in emergency, his character appealed to me with ever-
increasing power.

I will not say that I consciously and deliberately cut myself off from my prairie material, the desertion came about

naturally. Swiftly, inevitably, the unplowed valleys, the waterless foothills and the high peaks, inspired me, filled me with desire to embody them in some form of prose, of verse.

Laden with a myriad impressions of Indians, mountaineers and miners, I returned to my home as a bee to its hive, and there, during October, in my quiet chamber worked fast and fervently to transform my rough notes into fiction. Making no attempt to depict the West as some one else had seen it, or might thereafter see it, I wrote of it precisely as it appeared to me, verifying every experience, for, although I had not lingered long in any one place—a few weeks at most—I had observed closely and my impressions were clearly and deeply graved.

In fear of losing that freshness of delight, that emotion which gave me inspiration, I had made copious notes while in the field and although I seldom referred to them after I reached my desk, the very act of putting them down had helped to organize and fix them in my mind.

All of September and October was spent at the Homestead. Each morning I worked at my writing, and in the afternoon I drove my mother about the country or wrought some improvement to the place.

In the midst of these new literary enthusiasms I received a message which had a most disturbing effect on my plans. It was a letter from Sam McClure whose new little magazine was beginning to show astonishing vitality. "I want you to write for me a life of Ulysses Grant. I want it to follow Ida Tarbell's *Lincoln* which is now nearing an end. Come to New York and talk it over."

This request arrested me in my fictional progress. I was tempted to accept this commission, not merely because of the editor's generous terms of payment but for the deeper reason that *Grant* was a word of epic significance in my mind. From the time when I was three years of age, this great name had rung in my ears like the sound of a mellow bell. I knew I could write Grant's story—but—I hesitated.

"It is a mighty theme," I replied, "and yet I am not sure that I ought to give so much of my time at this, the most creative period of my life. It may change the whole current of my imagination."

My father, whose attitude toward the great Commander held much of hero-worship and who had influenced my childish thinking, influenced me now, but aside from his instruction I had come to consider Grant's career more marvelous than that of any other American both by reason of its wide arc of experience and its violent dramatic contrasts. It lent itself to epic treatment. With a feeling that if I could put this deeply significant and distinctively American story into a readable volume, I should be adding something to American literature as well as to my own life, I consented. Dropping my fictional plans for the time I became the historian.

In order to make the biography a study from first-hand material I planned a series of inspirational trips which filled in a large part of '96. Beginning at Georgetown, Ohio, where I found several of Grant's boyhood playmates, I visited Ripley, where he went to school, and then at the Academy at West Point I spent several days examining the records. In addition, I went to each of the barracks at which young Grant had been stationed. Sacketts Harbor, Detroit and St. Louis yielded their traditions. A month in Mexico enabled me to trace out on foot not only the battle grounds of Monterey, but that of Vera Cruz, Puebla and Molina del Rey. No spot on which Grant had lived long enough to leave a definite impression was neglected.

In this work I had the support of William Dean Howells who insisted on my doing the book bravely.

In pursuit of material concerning Grant's later life I interviewed scores of his old neighbors in Springfield and Galena, and in pursuit of his classmates, men like Buckner and Longstreet and Wright and Franklin, I took long journeys. In short I spared no pains to give my material a first-hand quality, and in doing this I traveled nearly thirty thousand miles, making many interesting acquaintances, in more than half the states of the Union.

During all these activities, however, the old Wisconsin farmhouse remained my pivot. In my intervals of rest I returned to my study and made notes of the vividly contrasting scenes through which I had passed. Orizaba and Jalapa, Perote with its snowy mountains rising above hot, cactus-covered plains, and Mexico City became almost dream-like by contrast with the placid beauty of Neshonoc. Some of my experiences, like "the Passion Play at Coyocan," for example, took on a medieval quality, so incredibly remote was its scene,—and yet, despite all this travel, notwithstanding my study of cities and soldiers and battle maps, I could not forget to lay out my garden. I kept my mother supplied with all the necessaries and a few of the luxuries of life.

In my note book of that time I find these lines: "I have a feeling of swift change in art and literature here in America. This latest trip to New York has shocked and saddened me. To watch the struggle, to feel the bitterness and intolerance of the various groups—to find one clique of artists set against another, to know that most of those who come here will fail and die—is appalling. The City is filled with strugglers, students of art, ambitious poets, journalists, novelists, writers of all kinds—I meet them at the clubs—some of them will be the large figures of 1900, most of them will have fallen under the wheel—This bitter war of Realists and Romanticists will be the jest of those who come after us, and they in their turn will be full of battle ardor with other cries and other banners. How is it possible to make much account of the cries and banners of to-day when I know they will be forgotten of all but the students of literary history?"

My contract with *McClure's* called for an advance of fifty dollars a week (more money than I had ever hoped to earn) and with this in prospect I purchased a new set of dinner china and a piano, which filled my mother's heart with delight. As I thought of her living long weeks in the old homestead with only my invalid aunt for company my conscience troubled me, and as it was necessary for me to go to Washington to complete my history, I attempted to mitigate her loneliness by buying a talking machine, through which I was able send her messages and songs. She considered these wax cylinders a poor substitute for my actual voice, but she got some entertainment from them by setting the machine going for the amazement of her callers.

November saw me settled in Washington, hard at work on my history, but all the time my mind was working, almost unconsciously, on my new fictional problems, "After all, I am a novelist," I wrote to Fuller, and I found time even in the midst of my historical study to compose an occasional short story of Colorado or Mexico.

Magazine editors were entirely hospitable to me now, for my tales of the Indian and the miner had created a friendlier spirit among their readers. My later themes were, happily, quite outside the controversial belt. Concerned less with the hopeless drudgery, and more with the epic side of western life, I found myself almost popular. My critics, once off their guard, were able to praise, cautiously it is true, but to praise. Some of them assured me with paternal gravity that I might, by following their suggestions become a happy and moderately successful writer, and this prosperity, you may be sure, was reflected to some degree in the dining room of the old Homestead.

My father, though glad of the shelter of the Wisconsin hills in winter, was too vigorous,—far too vigorous—to be confined to the limits of a four-acre garden patch, and when I urged him to join me in buying one of the fine level farms in our valley he agreed, but added "I must sell my Dakota land first."

With this I was forced to be content. Though sixty years old he still steered the six-horse header in harvest time, tireless and unsubdued. Times were improving slowly, very slowly in Dakota but opportunities for selling his land were still remote. He was not willing to make the necessary sacrifices. "I will not give it away," he grimly declared.

My return to the Homestead during the winter holidays brought many unforgettable experiences. Memories of those winter mornings come back to me—sunrises with steel-blue shadows lying along the drifts, whilst every weed, every shrub, feathered with frost, is lit with subtlest fire and the hills rise out of the mist, domes of brilliant-blue and burning silver. Splashes of red-gold fill all the fields, and small birds, flying amid the rimy foliage, shake sparkles of fire from their careless wings.

It was the antithesis of Indian summer, and yet it had something of the same dream-like quality. Its beauty was more poignant. The rounded tops of the red-oaks seemed to float in the sparkling air in which millions of sun-lit frost flakes glittered. All forms and lines were softened by this falling veil, and the world so adorned, so transfigured, filled the heart with a keen regret, a sense of pity that such a world should pass.

At such times I was glad of my new home, and my mother found in me only the confident and hopeful son. My doubts of the future, my discouragements of the present I carefully concealed.

CHAPTER FOUR

Red Men and Buffalo

ALTHOUGH my *Ulysses Grant, His Life and Character* absorbed most of my time and the larger part of my energy during two years, I continued to dream (in my hours of leisure), of the "High Country" whose splendors of cloud and peak, combined with the broad-cast doings of the cattleman and miner, had aroused my enthusiasm. The heroic types, both white and red, which the trail has fashioned to its needs continued to allure me, and when in June, '97, my brother, on his vacation, met me again at West Salem, I outlined a tour which should begin with a study of the Sioux at Standing Rock and end with Seattle and the Pacific Ocean. "I must know the North-west," I said to him.

In order to report properly to any army post, I had in my pocket a letter from General Miles which commended me to all agents and officers, and with this as passport I was in the middle of getting my equipment in order when Ernest Thompson Seton and his wife surprised me by dropping off the train one morning late in the month. They too, were on their way to the Rockies, and in radiant holiday humor.

My ·first meeting with Seton had been in New York at a luncheon given for James Barrie only a few months before, but we had formed one of those instantaneous friendships which spring from the possession of many identical interests. His skill as an illustrator and his knowledge of wild

38

animals had gained my admiration but I now learned that he knew certain phases of the West better than I, for though of English birth he had lived in Manitoba for several years. We were of the same age also, and this was another bond of sympathy.

He asked me to accompany him on his tour of the Yellowstone but as I had already arranged for a study of the Sioux, and as his own plans were equally definite, we reluctantly gave up all idea of camping together, but agreed to meet in New York City in October to compare notes.

The following week, on the first day of July, my brother and I were in Bismark, North Dakota, on our way to the Standing Rock Reservation to witness the "White Men's Big Sunday," as the red people were accustomed to call the Fourth of July.

It chanced to be a cool, sweet, jocund morning, and as we drove away, in an open buggy, over the treeless prairie swells toward the agency some sixty miles to the south, I experienced a sense of elation, a joy of life, a thrill of expectancy, which promised well for fiction. I knew the signs.

There was little settlement of any kind for twenty miles, but after we crossed the Cannonball River we entered upon the unviolated, primeval sod of the red hunter. Conical lodges were grouped along the streams. Horsemen with floating feathers and beaded buck-skin shirts over-took us riding like scouts, and when on the second morning we topped the final hill and saw the agency out-spread below us on the river bank, with hundreds of canvas tepees set in a wide circle behind it, our satisfaction was complete. Thousands of Sioux, men, women, and children could be seen moving about the teepees, while platoons of mounted warriors swept like scouting war parties across the plain. I congratulated myself on having reached this famous agency

39

while yet its festival held something tribal and primitive.

After reporting to the Commander at Fort Yates, and calling upon the Agent in his office, we took lodgings at a little half-breed boarding house near the store, and ate our dinner at a table where full-bloods, half-bloods and squaw men were the other guests.

Every waking hour thereafter we spent in observation of the people. With an interpreter to aid me I conversed with the head men and inquired into their history. The sign-talkers, sitting in the shade of a lodge or wagon-top, depicting with silent grace the stirring tales of their youth, were absorbingly interesting. I spent hours watching the play of their expressive hands.

The nonchalant cow-boys riding about the camp, the somber squaw-men (attended by their blanketed wives and groups of wistful half-breed children), and the ragged old medicine men all in their several ways made up a marvelous scene, rich with survivals of pioneer life.

The Gall and the Sitting Bull were both dead, but Rain-in-the-Face (made famous by Longfellow) was alive, very much alive, though a cripple. We met him several times riding at ease (his crutch tied to his saddle), a genial, handsome, dark-complexioned man of middle age, with whom it was hard to associate the acts of ferocity with which he was charged.

My letter of introduction from General Miles not only made me welcome at the Fort, it authorized me to examine the early records of the Agency, and these I carefully read in search of material concerning the Sitting Bull.

In those dingy, brief, bald lines of record, I discovered official evidence of this chief's supremacy long before the Custer battle. As early as 1870 he was set down as one of the "irreconcilables," and in 1874 the Sioux most dreaded by the whites was "Sitting Bull's Band." To Sitting Bull all couriers were sent, and the brief official accounts of their meetings with him were highly dramatic and sometimes humorous.

He was a red man, and proud of it. He believed in remaining as he was created. "The great spirit made me red, and red I am satisfied to remain," he declared. "All my people ask is to be let alone, to hunt the buffalo, and to live the life of our fathers"— and in this he had the sympathy of many white men even of his day.

(In the final count this chieftain, for the reason that he kept the red man's point of view, will outlive the opportunists who truckled to the white man's power. He will stand as a typical Sioux.)

Our days at the Agency passed so swiftly, so pleasantly that we would have lingered on indefinitely had not the report of an "outbreak" among the northern Cheyennes aroused a more intense interest. In the hope of seeing something of this uprising I insisted on hurriedly returning to Bismark, where we took the earliest possible train for Custer City, Montana.

At that strange little cow-town my brother hired a man to drive us to Fort Custer, some forty or fifty miles to the south, a ride which carried us deep into a wild and beautiful land, a country almost untouched of man, and when, toward sun-set, we came in sight of the high bluff which stands at the confluence of the Big Horn and the Little Big Horn rivers, the fort, the ferry, the stream were a picture by Catlin or a glorious illustration in a romance of the Border. It was easy to imagine ourselves back in the stirring days of Sitting Bull and Roman Nose.

The commander of the Garrison, Colonel Anderson, a fine soldierly figure, welcomed us courteously and turned us over to Lieutenant Aherne, a hospitable young Irishman who invited us to spend the night in his quarters. It happened most opportunely that he was serving as Inspector of the meat issue at the Crow Agency, and on the following day we accompanied him on his detail, a deeply instructive experience, for, at night we attended a ceremonial social dance given by the Crows in honor of Chief Two Moon, a visiting Cheyenne.

Two Moon, a handsome broad-shouldered man of fifty, met us at the door of the Dance Lodge, welcomed us with courtly grace, and gave us seats beside him on the honor side of the circle. It appeared that he was master of ceremonies, and under his direction the dancing proceeded with such dramatic grace and skill that we needed very little help to understand its action.

In groups of eight, in perfect order, the young men rose from their seats, advanced to the center of the circle, and there reënacted by means of signs, attitudes and groupings, various notable personal or tribal achievements of the past. With stealthy, silent stride this one delineated the exploit of some ancestral chief, who had darted forth alone on a solitary scouting expedition. Others depicted the enemy, representing his detection and his capture. A third band arose, and trailing the hero spy, swiftly, silently, discovered the captors, attacked and defeated them and with triumphant shouts released the captive and brought him to camp —all in perfect unison with the singers at the drum whose varying rhythm set the pace for each especial episode, almost as precisely as a Chinese orchestra augments or diminishes the action on the stage.

To me this was a thrilling glimpse into prehistoric America, for these young men, stripped of their tainted white-man rags, were wholly admirable, painted lithe-limbed warriors, rejoicing once again in the light of their ancestral moons. On every face was a look like that of a captive leopard, dreaming of far-seen, familiar sands. The present was forgot, the past was momentarily restored.

Red Men and Buffalo

At midnight we went away but the strangely-moving beat of that barbaric drum was still throbbing in my ears as I fell asleep.

*   *   *   *   *   *

Early the following morning, eager to reach the scene of the Cheyenne outbreak we hired saddle horses and rode away directly across the Custer battle field on our way toward Lame Deer, where we were told the troops were still in camp to protect the agency.

What a ride that was! Our trail led us beyond the plow and the wagon wheel, far into the midst of hills where herds of cattle were feeding as the bison had fed for countless ages. Every valley had its story, for here the last battles of the Cheyennes had taken place. I had overtaken the passing world of the red nomad.

We stopped that night at a ranch about half way across the range, and in its cabin I listened while the cattlemen expressed their hatred of the Cheyenne. The violence of their antagonism, their shameless greed for the red man's land revealed to me once and for all the fomenting spirit of each of the Indian Wars which had accompanied the exterminating, century-long march of our invading race. In a single sentence these men expressed the ruthless creed of the land-seeker. "We intend to wipe these red sons-of-dogs from the face of the earth." Here was displayed shamelessly the seamy side of western settlement.

At about ten o'clock next morning we topped the scantily-timbered ridge which walls in the Lame Deer Agency, and looked down upon the tents of the troops. A company of cavalry drilling on the open field to the north gave evidence of active service, and as I studied the mingled huts and tepees of the village, I realized that I had arrived in time to witness some part of the latest staging of the red man's final stand.

A Daughter of the Middle Border

Reporting at once to the agent, Major George Stouch, I found him to be a veteran officer of the regular army "On Special Duty," a middle-aged, pleasant-faced man of unassuming dignity whose crooked wrist (caused by a bullet in the Civil War) gave him a touch of awkwardness; but his eyes were keen, and his voice clear and decisive.

"The plans of the cattlemen have been momentarily checked," he said, "but they are still bitter, and a single pistol-shot may bring renewed trouble. The Cheyennes, as you know, are warriors."

He introduced me to Captain Cooper, in command of the troopers, and to Captain Reed, Commander of the Infantry, who invited us to join his mess, an invitation which we gladly accepted.

Cooper was a soldier of wide experience, a veteran of the Civil War, and an Indian fighter of distinction. But his Lieutenant, a handsome young West Pointer named Livermore, interested me still more keenly, for he was a student of the sign language and had been at one time in command of an experimental troop of red "rookies." Like Major Stouch he was a broad-minded friend of all primitive peoples, and his experiences and stories were of the greatest value to me.

With the aid of Major Stouch I won the confidence of White Bull, Two Moon, Porcupine, American Horse and other of the principal Cheyennes, and one of the Agency policemen, a fine fellow called Wolf Voice, became my interpreter. Though half-Cheyenne and half-Assiniboin, he spoke English well, and manifested a marked sense of humor. He had served one summer as guide to Frederick Remington, and had some capital stories concerning him. "Remington fat man—too heavy on pony. Him 'fraid Injuns sure catch him," he said with a chuckle. "Him all-time carry box—take pictures. Him no warrior."

44

Red Men and Buffalo

For two weeks I absorbed "material" at every pore, careless of other duties, thinking only of this world, avid for the truth, yet selecting my facts as every artist must, until, at last, measurably content I announced my intention to return to the railway. "We have tickets to Seattle," I said to Stouch, "and we must make use of them."

"I'm sorry to have you go," he replied, "but if you must go I'll send Wolf Voice with you as far as Custer."

We had no real need of a guide but I was glad to have Wolf Voice riding with me, for I had grown to like him and welcomed any opportunity for conversing with him. He was one of the few full-bloods who could speak English well enough to enjoy a joke.

As we were passing his little cabin, just at the edge of the Agency, he said, "Wait, I get you somesing."

In a few moments he returned, carrying a long eagle feather in his hand. This he handed to me, saying, "My little boy—him dead. Him carry in dance dis fedder. You my friend. You take him."

Major Stouch had told me of this boy, a handsome little fellow of only five years of age, who used to join most soberly and cunningly with the men in their ceremonial dances; and so when Wolf Voice said, "I give you dis fedder—you my friend. You Indian's friend," I was deeply moved.

"Wolf Voice, I shall keep this as a sign, a sign that we are friends."

He pointed toward a woman crouching over a fire in the corral, "You see him—my wife? Him cry—all time cry since him son die. Him no sleep in house. Sleep all time in tepee. Me no sleep in house. Spirit come, cry, *woo-oo-oo* in chimney. My boy spirit come,—cry—me 'fraid! My heart very sore."

The bronze face of the big man was quivering with emotion as he spoke, and not knowing what to say to comfort him I pretended to haste. "Let us go. You can tell me about it while we ride.

As we set forth he recovered his smile, for he was naturally of a cheerful disposition, and in our long, leisurely journey I obtained many curious glimpses into his psychology— the psychology of the red man. He led us to certain shrines or "medicine" rocks and his remarks concerning the offer- ings of cartridges, calico, tobacco and food which we found deposited beside a twisted piece of lava on the side of a low hill were most revealing.

"Wolf Voice, do you believe the dead come back to get these presents," I asked.

"No," he soberly replied. "Spirit no eat tobacco, spirit eat spirit of tobacco."

His reply was essentially Oriental in its philosophy. It was the *essence* of the offering, the *invisible* part which was taken by the invisible dead.

Many other of his remarks were almost equally revela- tory. "White soldier heap fool," he said. "Stand up in rows to be shot at. Injun fight running—in bush—behind trees."

We stopped again at The Half-Way Ranch, and the manner in which the cattlemen treated Wolf Voice angered me. He was much more admirable than they, and yet they would not allow him to sleep in the house.

He rode all the way back to Fort Custer with us and when we parted I said, "Wolf Voice, I hope we meet again," and I meant it. His spirit is in all that I have since written of the red men. He, Two Moon, American Horse, and Por- cupine were of incalculable value to me in composing *The Captain of the Gray Horse Troop,* which was based upon this little war.

From Billings we went almost directly to the Flat Head

Red Men and Buffalo

Reservation. We had heard that a herd of buffalo was to be seen in its native pastures just west of Flat Head Lake and as I put more value on seeing that herd than upon any other "sight" in the state of Montana, we made it our next objective.

Outfitting at Jocko we rode across the divide to the St. Ignacio Mission. Less wild than the Cheyenne reservation the Flat Head country was much more beautiful, and we were entirely happy in our camp beside the rushing stream which came down from the Jocko Lakes.

"Yes, there is such a herd," the trader said. "It is owned by Michel Pablo and consists of about two hundred, old and young. They can be reached by riding straight north for some twenty miles and then turning to the west. You will have to hunt them, however; they are not in a corral. They are feeding just as they used to do. They come and go as they happen to feel the need of food or water."

With these stimulating directions we set forth one morning to "hunt a herd of buffalo," excited as a couple of boys, eager as hunters yet with only the desire to see the wild kine.

After we left the road and turned westward our way led athwart low hills and snake-like ravines and along deep-worn cattle paths leading to water holes. All was magnificently primeval. No mark of plow or spade, no planted stake or post assailed our eyes. We were deep in the land of the bison at last.

Finally, as we topped a long, low swell, my brother shouted, "Buffalo!" and looking where he pointed, I detected through the heated haze of the midday plain, certain vague, unfamiliar forms which hinted at the prehistoric past. They were not cows or horses, that was evident. Here and there purple-black bodies loomed, while close beside them other smaller objects gave off a singular and striking contrast. There was no mistaking the character of these animals. They were bison.

To ride down upon them thus, in the silence and heat of that uninhabited valley, was to realize in every detail, a phase of the old-time life of the plains. We moved in silence. The grass-hoppers springing with clapping buzz before our horses' feet gave out the only sound. No other living thing uttered voice. Nothing moved save our ponies and those distant monstrous kine whose presence filled us with the same emotion which had burned in the hearts of our pioneer ancestors.

As we drew nearer, clouds of dust arose like lazy smoke from smoldering fires, curtains which concealed some mighty bull tossing the powdery earth with giant hoof. The cows seeing our approach, began to shift and change. The bulls did not hurry, on the contrary, they fell to the rear and grimly halted our advance. Towers of alkali dust, hot and white, lingering smoke-like in the air shielded us like a screen, and so—slowly riding—we drew near enough to perceive the calves and hear the mutter of the cows as they reënacted for us the life of the vanished millions of their kind.

Here lay a calf beside its dam. Yonder a solitary ancient and shaggy bull stood apart, sullen and brooding. Nearer a colossal chieftain, glossy, black, and weighing two thousand pounds moved from group to group, restless and combative, wrinkling his ridiculously small nose, and uttering a deep, menacing, muttering roar. His rivals, though they slunk away, gave utterance to similar sinister snarls, as if voicing bitter resentment. They did not bellow, they *growled*, low down in their cavernous throats, like angry lions. Nothing that I had ever heard or read of buffaloes had given me the quality of this majestic clamor.

Occasionally one of them, tortured by flies, dropped to

earth, and rolled and tore the sod, till a dome of dust arose and hid him. Out of this gray curtain he suddenly reappeared, dark and savage, like a dun rock emerging from mist. One furious giant, moving with curling upraised tail, challenged to universal combat, whilst all his rivals gave way, reluctant, resentful, yet afraid. The rumps of some of the veterans were as bare of hair as the loins of lions, but their enormous shoulders bulked into deformity by reason of a dense mane. They moved like elephants— clumsy, enormous, distorted, yet with astonishing celerity.

It was worth a long journey to stand thus and watch that small band of bison, representatives of a race whose myriads once covered all America, for though less than two hundred in number, they were feeding and warring precisely as their ancestors had fed and warred for a million years. Small wonder that the red men believe the white invader must have used some evil medicine, some magic power in sweeping these majestic creatures from the earth. Once they covered the hills like a robe of brown, now only a few small bands are left to perpetuate the habits and the customs of the past.

As we watched, they fed, fought, rose up and lay down in calm disdain of our presence. It was as if, unobserved, and yet close beside them, we were studying the denizens of a small corner of aboriginal America, America in pre-Columbian times. Reluctantly, slowly we turned and rode away, back to our tent, back to the railway and the present day.

*   *   *   *   *   *

On our return to Missoula we found the town aflame with a report that a steamer had just landed at Seattle, bringing from Alaska nearly three million dollars in gold-dust, and that the miners who owned the treasure had said, "We dug it from the valley of the Yukon, at a point called the

Klondike. A thousand miles from anywhere. The Yukon is four thousand miles long, and flows north, so that the lower half freezes solid early in the fall, and to cross overland from Skagway—the way we came out—means weeks of travel. It is the greatest gold camp in the world but no one can go in now. Everybody must wait till next June."

It was well that this warning was plainly uttered, for the adventurous spirits of Montana instantly took fire. Nothing else was talked of by the men on the street and in the trains. Even my brother said, "I wish I could go."

"But you can't," I argued. "It is time you started for New York. Herne will drop you if you don't turn up for rehearsal in September."

Reluctantly agreeing to this, he turned his face toward the East whilst I kept on toward Seattle, to visit my classmate Burton Babcock, who was living in a village on Puget Sound.

The coast towns were humming with mining news and mining plans. The word "Klondike" blazed out on banners, on shop windows and on brick walls. Alert and thrifty merchants at once began to advertise Klondike shoes, Klondike coats, Klondike camp goods. Hundreds of Klondike exploring companies were being organized. In imagination each shop-keeper saw the gold seekers of the world in line of march, their faces set toward Seattle and the Sound. Every sign indicated a boom.

This swift leaping to grasp an opportunity was characteristically American, and I would have gladly taken part in the play, but alas! my Grant history was still unfinished, and I had already overstayed my vacation limit. I should have returned at once, but my friend Babcock was expecting me to visit him, and this I did.

Anacortes (once a port of vast pretentions), was, at this time, a boom-town in decay, and Burton whom I had

not seen for ten years, seemed equally forlorn. After
trying his hand at several professions, he had finally drifted
to this place, and was living alone in a rude cabin, camping
like a woodsman. Being without special training in any
trade, he had fallen into competition with the lowest kind
of unskilled labor.

Like my Uncle David, another unsuccessful explorer, he
had grown old before his time, and for a few minutes I
could detect in him nothing of the lithe youth I had known
at school on the Iowa prairie twenty years before. Shaggy
of beard, wrinkled and bent he seemed already an old
man.

By severest toil in the mills and in the forest he had
become the owner of two small houses on a ragged street—
these and a timber claim on the Skagit River formed his
entire fortune.

Though careless of dress and hard of hand, his speech
remained that of the thinker, and much of his reading was
still along high, philosophical lines. He had been a singular
youth, and he had developed into a still more singular man.
With an instinctive love of the forest, he had become a
daring and experienced mountaineer. As he described to
me his solitary trips over the high Cascades I was reminded
of John Muir, for he, too, often spent weeks in the high
peaks above his claim with only such outfit as he could
carry on his back.

"What do you do it for?" I asked. "Are you gold-
hunting?"

With a soft chuckle he answered, "Oh, no; I do it just
for the fun of it. I love to move around up there, alone,
above timber line. It's beautiful up there."

Naturally, I recalled the scenes of our boyhood. I spoke
of the Burr Oak Lyceums, of our life at the Osage Seminary,
and of the boys and girls we had loved, but he was not

disposed, at the moment, to dwell on them or on the past. His heart (I soon discovered) was aflame with desire to join the rush of gold-seekers. "I wish you would grub-stake me," he timidly suggested. "I'd like to try my hand at digging gold in the Klondike."

"It's too late in the season," I replied. "Wait till spring. Wait till I finish my history of Grant and I'll go in with you."

With this arrangement (which on my part was more than half a jest) I left him and started homeward by way of Lake MacDonald, the Blackfoot Reservation and Fort Benton, my mind teeming with subjects for poems, short stories and novels. My vacation was over. Aspiring vaguely to qualify as the fictionist of this region, I was eager to be at work. Here was my next and larger field. As my neighbors in Iowa and Dakota were moving on into these more splendid spaces, so now I resolved to follow them and be their chronicler.

This trip completed my conversion. I resolved to pre-empt a place in the history of the great Northwest which was at once a wilderness and a cosmopolis, for in it I found men and women from many lands, drawn to the mountains in search of health, or recreation, or gold. I perceived that almost any character I could imagine could be verified in this amazing mixture. I began to sketch novels which would have been false in Wisconsin or Iowa. With a sense of elation, of freedom, I decided to swing out into the wider air of Colorado and Montana.

CHAPTER FIVE

The Telegraph Trail

THE writing of the last half of my Grant biography demanded a careful study of war records, therefore in the autumn of '97 I took lodgings in Washington, and settled to the task of reading my way through the intricacies of the Grant Administrations. Until this work was completed I could not make another trip to the Northwest.

The new Congressional Library now became my grandiose work-shop. All through the winter from nine till twelve in the morning and from two till six in the afternoon, I sat at a big table in a special room, turning the pages of musty books and yellowed newspapers, or dictating to a stenographer the story of the Reconstruction Period as it unfolded under my eyes. I was for the time entirely the historian, with little time to dream of the fictive material with which my memory was filled.

I find this significant note in my diary. "My Grant life is now so nearly complete that I feel free to begin a work which I have long meditated. I began to dictate, to-day, the story of my life as boy and man in the West. In view of my approaching perilous trip into the North I want to leave a fairly accurate chronicle of what I saw and what I did on the Middle Border. The truth is, with all my trailing about in the Rocky Mountains I have never been in a satisfying wilderness. It is impossible, even in Wyoming, to get fifty miles from settlement. I long to undertake a journey which demands hardihood, and so, after careful in-

53

vestigation, I have decided to go into the Yukon Valley by
pack train over the British Columbian Mountains, a route
which offers a fine and characteristic New World adventure."

To prepare myself for this expedition I ran up to Ottawa
in February to study maps and to talk with Canadian of-
ficials concerning the various trails which were being surveyed and blazed. "No one knows much about that country," said Dawson with a smile.

I returned to Washington quite determined on going to
Teslin Lake over a path which followed an abandoned telegraph survey from Quesnelle on the Fraser River to the
Stickeen, a distance estimated at about eight hundred miles,
and I quote these lines as indicating my mind at the time:

> The way is long and cold and lone—
>   But I go!
> It leads where pines forever moan
>   Their weight of snow—
>   But I go!
> There are voices in the wind which call
> There are shapes which beckon to the plain·
> I must journey where the peaks are tall,
> And lonely herons clamor in the rain.

One of my most valued friends in Washington at this
time was young Theodore Roosevelt, who had resigned his
position as Police Commissioner in New York City to become Assistant Secretary of the Navy. His life on a Dakota
ranch had not only filled him with a love for western trails
and sympathy with western men, but had created in him a
special interest in western writers. No doubt it was this
regard for the historians of the West which led him to invite
me to his house; for during the winter I occasionally lunched
or dined with him. He also gave me the run of his office,
and there I sometimes saw him in action, steering the department toward efficiency.

The Telegraph Trail

Though nominally Assistant Secretary he was in fact the Head of the Navy, boldly pushing plans to increase its fighting power. This I know, for one day as I sat in his office I heard him giving orders for gun practice and discussing the higher armament of certain ships. I remember his words as he showed me a sheet on which was indicated the relative strength of the world's navies. "We must raise all our guns to a higher power," he said with characteristic emphasis.

John Hay, Senator Lodge, Major Powell and Edward Eggleston were among my most distinguished hosts during this winter and I have many pleasant memories of these highly distinctive personalities. Major Powell appealed to me with especial power by reason of his heroic past. He had been an engineer under Grant at Vicksburg and was very helpful to me in stating the methods of the siege, but his experiences after the war were still more romantic. Though a small man and with but one arm, he had nevertheless led a fleet of canoes through the Grand Cañon of the Colorado—the first successful attempt at navigating that savage and sullen river, and his laconic account of it enormously impressed me. He was, at this time, the well-known head of the Ethnological Bureau, and I frequently saw him at the Cosmos Club, grouped with Langley, Merriam, Howard and other of my scientific friends. He was a somber, silent, and rather unkempt figure, with the look of a dreaming lion on his face. It was hard to relate him with the man who had conquered the Grand Cañon of the Colorado.

His direct antithesis was Edward Eggleston, whose residence was a small brick house just back of the Congressional Library. Eggleston, humorous, ready of speech, was usually surrounded by an attentive circle of delighted listeners and I often drew near to share his monologue. He was a handsome man, tall and shapely with abundant gray hair and a full beard, and was especially learned in American early history. "Edward loves to monologue," his friends smilingly said as if in criticism, but to me his talk was always interesting.

We became friends on the basis of a common love for the Western prairie, which he, as a "circuit rider" in Minnesota had minutely explored. I told him, gladly and in some detail, of my first reading of *The Hoosier School-master*, and in return for my interest he wrote a full page of explanation on the fly leaf of a copy which I still own and value highly, for I regard him now, as I did then, as one of the brave pioneers of distinctive Middle Border fiction.

Roosevelt considered me something of a Populist, (as I was), and I well remember a dinner in Senator Lodge's house where he and Henry Adams heckled me for an hour or more in order to obtain a statement of what I thought "ailed" Kansas, Nebraska and Dakota. They all held the notion that I understood these farmer folk well enough to reflect their secret antagonisms, which I certainly did. I recall getting pretty hot in my plea, but Roosevelt seemed rather proud of me as I warmly defended my former neighbor. "The man on the rented farm who is raising corn at fifteen cents per bushel to pay interest on a mortgage is apt to be bitter," I argued.

However, this evening was an exception. Generally we talked of the West, of cattle ranching, of trailing and of the splendid types of pioneers who were about to vanish from the earth. One night as we sat at dinner in his house, he suddenly leaned back in his chair and said with a smile "I can't tell you how I enjoy having a man at my table who knows the difference between a *parfleshche* and an *apparejo*."

Although I loved the trail I had given up shooting. I no longer carried a gun even in the hills—although, I will admit, I permitted my companions to do so. Roosevelt differed from me in this. He loved "the song of the bullet." "It gives point and significance to the trail," he explained.

The Telegraph Trail

I recall quoting to him one of his own vividly beautiful descriptions of dawn among the hills, a story which led up to the stalking and the death of a noble elk. "It was fine, all fine and true and poetic," I declared, "but I should have listened with gratitude to the voice of the elk and watched him go his appointed way in peace."

"I understand your position perfectly," he replied, "but it is illogical. You must remember every wild animal dies a violent death. Elk and deer and pheasants are periodically destroyed by snows and storms of sleet—and what about the butcher killing lambs and chickens for your table? I notice you accept my roast duck."

He was greatly interested in my proposed trip into the Yukon. "By George, I wish I could go with you," he said, and I had no doubt of his sincerity. Then his tone changed. "We are in for trouble with Spain and I must be on the job."

To this I replied, "If I really knew that war was coming, I'd give up my trip, but I can't believe the Spaniards intend to fight, and this is my last and best chance to see the Northwest."

In my notebook I find this entry: "Jan., 1898. Dined again last night with Theodore Roosevelt, Assistant Secretary of the Navy, a man who is likely to be much in the public eye during his life. A man of great energy, of noble impulses, and of undoubted ability."

I do not put this forward as evidence of singular perception on my part, for I imagine thousands were saying precisely the same thing. I merely include it to prove that I was not entirely lacking in penetration.

Henry B. Fuller, who came along one day in January, proved a joy and comfort to me. His attitude toward Washington amused me. Assuming the air of a Cook tourist, he methodically, and meticulously explored the city, bringing to me each night a detailed report of what he had seen. His concise, humorous and self-derisive comment was litera-

57

ture of a most delightful quality, and I repeatedly urged him to write of the capital as he talked of it to me, but he professed to have lost his desire to write, and though I did not believe this, I hated to hear him say it, for I valued his satiric humor and his wide knowledge of life.

He was amazed when I told him of my plan to start, in April, for the Yukon, and in answer to his question I said, "I need an expedition of heroic sort to complete my education, and to wash the library dust out of my brain."

In response to a cordial note, I called upon John Hay one morning. He received me in a little room off the main hall of his house, whose spaciousness made him seem diminutive. He struck me as a dapper man, noticeably, but not offensively, self-satisfied. His fine black beard was streaked with white, but his complexion was youthfully clear. Though undersized he was compact and sturdy, and his voice was crisp, musical, and decisive.

We talked of Grant, of whom he had many pleasing personal recollections, and when a little later we went for a walk, he grew curiously wistful and spoke of his youth in the West and of the simple life of his early days in Washington with tenderness. It appeared that wealth and honor had not made him happy. Doubtless this was only a mood, for in parting he reassumed his smiling official pose.

A few days later as I entered my Hotel I confronted the tall figure and somber, introspective face of General Longstreet whom I had visited a year before at his home in Gainesville, Georgia. We conversed a few moments, then shook hands and parted, but as he passed into the street I followed him. From the door-step I watched him slowly making his cautious way through throngs of lesser men (who gave no special heed to him), and as I thought of the days when his dread name was second only to Lee's in the fear and admiration of the North, I marveled at the change in twenty years. Now he was a deaf, hesitant old man, sorrowful of aspect, poor, dim-eyed, neglected, and alone.

"Swift are the changes of life, and especially of American life," I made note. "Most people think of Longstreet as a dead man, yet there he walks, the gray ghost of the Confederacy, silent, alone."

As spring came on and the end of my history of Grant drew near, my longing for the open air, the forest and the trail, made proof-reading a punishment. My eyes (weary of newspaper files and manuscripts) filled with mountain pictures. Visioning my plunge into the wilderness with keenest longing, I collected a kit of cooking utensils, a sleeping bag and some pack saddles (which my friend, A. A. Anderson, had invented), together with all information concerning British Columbia and the proper time for hitting The Long Trail.

In showing my maps to Howells in New York, I casually remarked, "I shall go in *here,* and come out *there*—over a thousand miles of Trail," and as he looked at me in wonder, I had a sudden realization of what that remark meant. A vision of myself, a minute, almost indistinguishable insect— creeping hardily through an illimitable forest filled my imagination, and a momentary awe fell upon me.

"How easy it would be to break a leg, or go down with my horse in an icy river!" I thought. Nevertheless, I proceeded with my explanations, gayly assuring Howells that it was only a magnificent outing, quoting to him from certain circulars, passages of tempting descriptions in which "splendid savannahs" and "herds of deer and caribou" were used with fine effect.

In my secret heart I hoped to recapture some part of that Spirit of the Sunset which my father had found and loved in Central Minnesota in Fifty-eight. Deeper still, I had a hope of reënacting, in helpful degree, the epic days of

Forty-nine, when men found their painful way up the Platte Cañon, and over the Continental Divide to Oregon. "It is my last chance to do a bit of real mountaineering, of going to school to the valiant wilderness," I said, "and I can not afford to miss the opportunity of winning a master's degree in hardihood."

That I suffered occasional moments of depression and doubt, the pages of my diary bear witness. At a time when my stories were listed in half the leading magazines, I gravely set down the facts of my situation. "In far away Dakota my father is living alone on a bleak farm, cooking his own food and caring for a dozen head of horses, while my mother, with failing eyes and shortening steps, waits for him and for me in West Salem with only an invalid sister-in-law to keep her company. In a very real sense they are all depending upon me for help and guidance. I am now the head of the house, and yet—here I sit planning a dangerous adventure into Alaska at a time when I should be at home."

My throat ached with pity whenever I received a letter from my mother, for she never failed to express a growing longing for her sons, neither of whom could be with her. To do our chosen work a residence in the city was necessary, and so it came about that all my victories, all my small successes were shadowed by my mother's failing health and loneliness.

* * * * * *

It remains to say that during all this time I had heard very little of Miss Zulime Taft. No letters had passed between us, but I now learned through her brother that she was planning to come home during the summer, a fact which should have given me a thrill, but as more than four years had passed since our meeting in Chicago, I merely wondered whether her stay in Paris had greatly changed her character for the better. "She will probably be more

French than American when she returns," I said to Lorado, when he spoke of her.

"Her letters do not sound that way," he answered. "She seems eager to return, and says that she intends to work with me here in Chicago."

Early in March, I notified Babcock to meet me at Ashcroft in British Columbia on April 15th. "We'll outfit there, and go in by way of Quesnelle," I added, and with a mind filled with visions of splendid streams, grassy valleys and glorious camps among eagle-haunted peaks, I finished the final pages of my proof and started West, boyishly eager to set forth upon the mighty circuit of my projected exploration.

"This is the end of my historical writing," I notified McClure. "I'm going back to my fiction of the Middle Border."

On a radiant April morning I reached the homestead finding mother fairly well, but greatly disturbed over my plan. "I don't like to have you go exploring," she said. "It's dangerous. Why do you do it?"

Her voice, the look of her face, took away the spirit of my adventure. I felt like giving it up, but with all arrangements definitely made I could do nothing but go on. The weather was clear and warm, with an odorous south wind drawing forth the leaves, and as I fell to work, raking up the yard, the smell of unfolding blooms, the call of exultant "high-holders" and the chirp of cheerful robins brought back with a rush, all the sweet, associated memories of other springs and other gardens, making my gold-seeking expedition seem not only chimerical, but traitorous to my duties.

The hens were singing their cheerful, changeless song below the stable wall; calves were bawling from the neighboring farm-yards and on the mellow soil the shining, broadcast seeders were clattering to their work, while over the greening hills a faint mist wavered, delicate as a bride's veil. Was it not a kind of madness to exchange the security, the peace, the comfort of this homestead, for the hardships of a trail whose circuit could not be less than ten thousand miles, a journey which offered possible injury and certain deprivation?

The thought which gave me most uneasiness was not my danger but the knowledge that in leaving my mother to silently brood over the perils which she naturally exaggerated, I was recreant to my pledge. Expression was always elliptical with her, and I shall never know how keenly she suffered during those days of preparation. Instead of acquiring a new daughter, she seemed on the point of losing a son.

She grudged every moment of the hours which I spent in my study. There was so little for her to do! She kept her chair during her waking hours either on the porch overlooking the garden or in the kitchen supervising the women at their work. Every slightest event was pitifully important in her life. The passing of the railway trains, the milking of the cow, the watering of the horses, the gathering of the eggs—these were important events in her diary. My incessant journeyings, my distant destinations lay far beyond her utmost imagining. To her my comings and goings were as mysterious, as incalculable as the orbits of the moon, and I think she must have sometimes questioned whether Hamlin Garland, the historian, could possibly be the son for whom she had once knit mittens and repaired kites.

If I had not been under contract, if I had not gone so far in preparation and announcement that to quit would have been disgraceful, I would have given up my trip on her account. "I am ashamed to turn back. I must go on," I said. "I won't be gone long. I'll come out by way of the Stickeen."

When the time came to say good-bye, she broke down

utterly and I went away with a painful constriction in my own throat, a lump which lasted for hours. Not till on the second day as I saw droves of Canadian antelope racing with the train, whilst flights of geese overhead gave certain sign of the wilderness, did I regain my desire to explore the valleys of the North. That lonely old woman on the porch of the Homestead was never absent from my mind.

Promptly on the afternoon of my arrival at Ashcroft on the Canadian Pacific Railway, Burton Babcock, wearing a sombrero and a suit of corduroy, dropped from the east-bound train, a duffel bag in his right hand, and a newly-invented camp-stove in the other. "Well, here I am," he said, with his characteristic chuckle.

Ready for the road, and with no regrets, no hesitancies, no fears, he set to work getting our outfit together leaving me to gather what information I could concerning the route which we had elected to traverse.

It was hard for me to realize that this bent, bearded, grizzled mountaineer was Burt Babcock, the slim companion of my Dry Run Prairie boyhood—it was only in peculiar ways of laughter, and in a certain familiar pucker of wrinkles about his eyes, that I traced the connecting link. I must assume that he found in me something quite as alien—perhaps more so, for my life in Boston and New York had given to me habits of speech and of thought which obscured, no doubt, most of my youthful characteristics.

As I talked with some of the more thoughtful and conscientious citizens of the town, I found them taking a very serious view of the trip we were about to undertake. "It is a mighty long, hard road," they said, "and a lot of men are going to find it a test of endurance. Nobody knows anything about the trail after you leave Quesnelle. You want to go with a good outfit, prepared for two months of hardship."

In view of this warning I was especially slow about buying ponies. "I want the best and gentlest beasts obtainable," I said to Burton. "I am especially desirous of a trustworthy riding horse."

That evening, as I was standing on the hotel porch, my attention was attracted to a man mounted on a spirited gray horse, riding up the street toward the hotel. There was something so noble in the proud arch of this horse's neck, something so powerful in the fling of his hooves that I exclaimed to the landlord, "*There* is the kind of saddle-horse I am looking for! I wonder if by any chance he is for sale?"

The landlord smiled. "He is. I sent word to the owner and he has come on purpose to see you. You can have the animal if you want him bad enough."

The rider drew rein and the landlord introduced me as the man who was in need of a mount. Each moment my desire to own the horse deepened, but I was afraid to show even approval. "How much do you want for him?" I asked indifferently.

"Well, stranger, I must have fifty dollars for this horse. There is a strain of Arabian in him, and he is a trained cow-pony besides."

Fifty dollars for an animal like that! It was like giving him away. I was at once suspicious. "There must be some trick about him. He is locoed or something," I remarked to my partner.

We could find nothing wrong, however, and at last I passed over a fifty dollar bill and led the horse away.

Each moment increased my joy and pride in that dapple-gray gelding. Undoubtedly there was Arabian blood in his veins. He had a thoroughbred look. He listened to every word I spoke to him. He followed me as cheerfully and as readily as a dog. He let me feel his ears (which a locoed horse will not do) and at a touch of my hand made room for me in his stall. In all ways he seemed exactly the horse I had been looking for, and I began to think of my long ride over the mountains with confidence.

To put the final touch to my security, the owner as he was leaving the hotel said to me, with a note of sadness in his voice, "I hate to see that horse take the long trail. Treat him well, partner."

Three days later, mounted on my stately gray "Ladrone," I led my little pack-train out of Ashcroft, bound for Teslin Lake, some twelve hundred miles to the Northwest. It was a lovely spring afternoon, and as I rode I made some rhymes to express my feeling of exultation.

> I mount and mount toward the sky,
> The eagle's heart is mine.
> I ride to put the clouds below
> Where silver lakelets shine.
> The roaring streams wax white with snow,
> The granite peaks draw near,
> The blue sky widens, violets grow,
> The air is frosty clear.
> And so from cliff to cliff I rise,
> The eagle's heart is mine;
> Above me, ever-broadening skies—
> Below, the river's shine.

The next day as we were going down a steep slope, one of the pack horses bolted and ran round Ladrone entangling me in the lead rope. When I came to myself I was under my horse, saddle and all, and Ladrone was looking down at me in wonder. The tremendous strain on the rope had pulled me saddle and all under his belly, and had he been the ordinary cayuse he would have kicked me to shreds. To my astonishment and deep gratitude he remained perfectly quiet while I scrambled out from under his feet and put the saddle in place.

My partner, white with excitement, drew near. "I

thought you were a goner," he said, huskily. "That horse of yours is a wonder."

As I thought of the look in that gray pony's brown eyes whilst I lay, helpless beneath him, my heart warmed with gratitude and affection. "Old boy," I said, as I patted his neck, "I will never leave *you* to starve and freeze in the far north. If you carry me through to Telegraph Creek, I will see that you are comfortable for the remaining years of your life."

I mention this incident for the reason that it had far-reaching consequences—as the reader will discover.

In *The Trail of the Goldseekers,* I have told in detail my story of our expedition. Suffice it to say, at this point, that we were seventy-nine days in the wilderness, that we were eaten by flies and mosquitoes, that we traveled in the rain, camped in the rain, packed our saddles in the rain. We toiled through marshes, slopped across miles of tundra, swam our horses through roaring glacial streams and dug them out of bog-holes. For more than two hundred miles we walked in order to lighten the loads of our weakened animals, and when we reached Glenora we were both past-masters of the art of camping through a wilderness. No one could tell us anything about packing, bushing in a slough or managing a pack-train. We were master-trailers!

Burton, though a year or two older than I, proved an invincible explorer, tireless, uncomplaining and imperturbable. In all our harsh experiences, throughout all our eighty days of struggle with mud, rocks, insects, rain, hunger and cold, he never for one moment lost his courage. Kind to our beasts, defiant of the weather, undismayed by any hardship, he kept the trail. He never once lifted his voice in anger. His endurance of my moods was heroic.

Assuming more than half of the physical labor he loyally said, "You are the boss, the historian of this expedition. You are the proprietor. I am only the hired-man."

The Telegraph Trail

Such service could not be bought. It sprang from a friendship which had begun twenty-eight years before, an attachment deep as our lives which could not be broken.

On the seventy-ninth day, ragged, swarthy, bearded like Forty-niners, with only a handful of flour and a lump of bacon left in our kit we came down to the Third Fork of the Stickeen River, without a flake of gold to show for our "panning" the sands along our way. My diaries state that for more than thirty days of this journey it rained, and as I look back upon our three weeks in the Skeena valley I shiver with a kind of retrospective terror. At one time it looked as though we must leave all our horses in that gloomy forest. Ladrone lost the proud arch of his neck and the light lift of his small feet. He could no longer carry me up the steeps and his ribs showed pitifully.

At Glenora, in beautiful sunny weather, we camped for two weeks in blissful leisure while our horses recovered their strength and courage. We were all hungry for the sun. For hours we lay on the grass soaking our hides full of light and heat, discussing gravely but at our ease, the situation.

Our plan had been to pack through to Teslin Lake, build a raft there and float down the Hotalinqua into the Yukon and so on to Dawson City, but at Glenora I found a letter from my mother waiting for me, a pitiful plea for me to "hurry back," and as we were belated a month or more, and as winter comes early in those latitudes, I decided to turn over the entire outfit to Babcock and start homeward by way of Fort Wrangell.

"I can't afford to spend the winter on the Yukon," I said to Burton. "My mother is not well and is asking for me. I will keep Ladrone—I am going to take him home with me—but the remainder of the outfit is yours. If you decide to go on to Teslin—which I advise against—you will need a thousand pounds of food and this I will purchase for you.—It is hard to quit the trail. I feel as if running a pack-train were the main business of my life and that I am deserting my job in going out, but that is what I must do."

The last Hudson Bay trading steamer was due at about this time and I decided to take passage to Fort Wrangell with Ladrone, who was almost as fat and handsome as ever. Two weeks of delicious grass had done wonders for him. I knew that every horse driven through to Teslin Lake would be turned out to freeze and starve at the end of the trail, and I could not think of abandoning my brave pony to such a fate. He had borne me over mud, rocks and streams. He had starved and shivered for me, and now he was to travel with me back to a more amiable climate at least. "I could never look my readers in the face if I left him up here," I explained to my partners who knew that I intended to make a book of my experiences.

It was a sad moment for my partner as for me when I led my horse down to the steamer. Ladrone seemed to realize that he was leaving his comrades of the trail for he called to them anxiously, again and again. He had led them for the last time. When the cry "HYak KILpy" came next day he would not be there!

Having seen him safely stowed below deck I returned to the trail for a final word with Burton.

There he stood, on the dock, brown with camp-fire smoke, worn and weather beaten, his tireless hands folded behind his back, a remote, dreaming, melancholy look in his fearless eyes. His limp sombrero rested grotesquely awry upon his shaggy head, his trousers bulged awkwardly at the knees —but he was a warrior! Thin and worn and lame he was about to set forth single-handedly on a journey whose circuit would carry him far within the Arctic Circle.

The boat began to move. "Good luck, Old Man," I called.

"Good Luck!" he huskily responded. "My love to the folks."

I never saw him again.

I went to Wrangell, and while camped there waiting for a boat to take me back to the States I heard of a "strike" at Atlin, somewhere back of Skaguay. I decided to join this rush, and so, leaving my horse to pasture in the lush grass of the hill-side, I took steamer for the north. Again I outfitted, this time at Skaguay. I crossed the famous White Pass. I reached Atlin City. I took a claim.

A month later I returned to Wrangell, picked up Ladrone, shipped with him to Seattle and so ceased to be a gold-seeker.

In Seattle my wonder and affection for Ladrone increased. He had never seen a big town before, or heard a street car, or met a switching engine, and yet he followed me through the city like a trustworthy dog, his nose pressed against my shoulder as if he knew I would protect him. At the door of the freight car which I had chartered, he hesitated, but only for an instant. At the word of command he walked the narrow plank into the dark interior and there I left him with food and water, billed for St. Paul where I expected to meet him and transfer him to a car for West Salem. It all seemed very foolish to some people and my only explanation was suggested by a brake-man who said, "He's a runnin' horse, ain't he?"

"Yes, he's valuable. Take good care of him. He is Arabian."

CHAPTER SIX

The Return of the Artist

AFTER an absence of five months I returned to La Crosse just in time to eat Old Settlers Dinner with my mother at the County Fair, quite as I used to do in the "early days" of Iowa. It was the customary annual round-up of the pioneers, a time of haunting, sweetly-sad recollections, and all the speeches were filled with allusions to the days when deer on the hills and grouse in the meadows gave zest to life upon the farms.

How peaceful, how secure, how abundant my native valley appeared to me, after those gloomy toilsome months in the cold, green forests of British Columbia—and how incredible my story must have seemed to my mother as I told her of my journey eastward by boat and train, bringing my saddle horse across four thousand miles of wood and wave, in order that he might spend his final years with me in the oat-filled, sheltered valley of Neshonoc. "His courage and faithfulness made it impossible for me to leave him up there," I explained.

He had arrived on the train which preceded me, and was still in the car. At the urgent request of my Uncle Frank I unloaded him, saddled him, and rode him down to the fair-ground, wearing my travel-scarred sombrero, my faded trailer's suit and my leggings, a mild exhibition of vanity which I trust the reader will overlook, for in doing this I not only gave keen joy to my relatives, but furnished another "Feature" to the show.

The Return of the Artist

My friend, Samuel McKee, the Presbyterian minister in the village, being from Kentucky, came nearer to understanding the value of my horse than any other spectator. "I don't wonder you brought him back," he said, after careful study. "He is a beauty. There's a strain of Arabian in him."

My mother's joy over my safe return was quite as wordless as her sorrow at our parting (in April) had been. To have me close beside her, to lay her hand upon my arm, filled her with inexpressible content. She could not imagine the hundredth part of the hardships I had endured, and I made no special effort to enlighten her—I merely said, "You needn't worry, mother, one such experience is enough. I shall never leave you for so many months again," and I meant it.

With a shy smile and a hesitant voice, she reverted to a subject which was of increasing interest to her. "What about my new daughter? When am I to see her? I hope now you'll begin to think of a wife. First thing you know you'll be too old."

My reply was vaguely jocular. "Be patient a little while longer. I shall seriously set to work and see what I can find for you by way of a daughter-in-law."

"Choose a nice one," she persisted. "One that will like the old house—and me. Don't get one who will be too stylish to live here with us."

In this enterprise I was not as confident as I appeared, for the problem was not simple. "The girl who can consent to be my wife must needs have a generous heart and a broad mind, to understand (and share) the humble conditions of my life, and to tolerate the simple, old-fashioned notions of my people. It will not be easy," I acknowledged. "I can not afford to make a mistake—one that will bring grief and not happiness to the homestead and its mistress."

However, I decided to let that worry stand over. "Sufficient unto the day is the evil thereof," was a saying which my father often repeated—and yet I was nearing the dead line! I was thirty-eight.

That first night of my return to the valley was of such rich and tender beauty that all the suffering, the hardships of my exploration were forgotten. The moon was at its full, and while the crickets and the katydids sang in unison, the hills dreamed in the misty distance like vast, peaceful, patient, crouching animals. The wheat and corn burdened the warm wind with messages of safely-garnered harvests, and my mind, reacting to the serenity, the peace, the opulence of it all, was at rest. The dark swamps of the Bulkley, the poisonous plants of the Skeena, the endless ice-cold marshes of the high country, the stinging insects of the tundra, and the hurtling clouds of the White Pass, all seemed events of another and more austere planet.

On the day following the fair, just as I was stripping my coat and rolling my sleeves to help my father fence in a pasture for Ladrone, a neighbor came along bringing a package from the post office. It was a book, a copy of my *Life of Grant,* the first I had seen; and, as I opened it I laughed, for I bore little resemblance to a cloistered historian at the moment. My face was the color of a worn saddle; my fingers resembled hooks of bronze, and my feet carried huge, hob-nail shoes. "What would Dr. Brander Matthews, Colonel Church and Howells, who had warmly commended the book, think of me at this moment?" I asked myself.

Father was interested, of course, but he was not one to permit a literary interest to interfere with a very important job. "Bring that spade," commanded he, and putting my history on top of a post, I set to work, digging another hole, rejoicing in my strength, for at that time I weighed one hundred and eighty pounds, all bone and muscle. So much the trail had done for me.

The Return of the Artist

I had broadened my palms to the cinch and the axe—
I had laid my breast to the rain."

Nothing physical appalled me, and no labor really wearied
me.

Oh, the wealth of that day's sunlight, the opulence of
those nearby fields—the beauty of those warmly-misted
hills! In the evening, as I mounted Ladrone and rode him
down the lane, I had no desire to share Burton's perilous
journey down the Hotalinqua.

As my mother's excitement over my return passed away,
her condition was disturbing to me. She was walking less
and less and I began at once to consider a course of treatment which might help her. At my aunt's sugestion I
wrote to a physician in Madison whose sanitarium she had
found helpful, and as my brother chanced to be playing in
Milwaukee, I induced mother to go with me to visit him.
She consented quite readily for she was eager to see him
in a real theater and a real play.

We took lodging in one of the leading hotels, which
seemed very splendid to her and that night she saw Franklin on the stage as one of "the three Dromios" in a farce
called "Incog." a piece which made her laugh till she
was almost breathless.

Next day we took her shopping. That is to say she went
along with us a helpless victim, while we purchased for her
a hat and cloak, at an expense which seemed to her almost
criminal. They were in truth very plain garments, and
comparatively inexpensive, but her tender heart overflowed
with pride of her sons and a guilty joy in their extravagance.
Many times afterward I experienced, as I do at this moment, a sharp pang of regret that I did not insist on a better cloak, a more beautiful hat. I only hope she understood!

In this way, or some other way, I bribed her to go with
me to Madison, to the Sanitarium. "You must not run

home," I said to her. "Make a fair trial of the Institution."

To this she uttered no reply and as she did not appear homesick or depressed, I prepared to leave, with a feeling that she was in good hands, and that her health would be greatly benefited by the regimen. "I must go to the city and look up that new daughter," I said to her in excuse for deserting her, and this made her entirely willing to let me go.

Chicago brilliantly illuminated, was filled with the spirit of the Peace Jubilee, as I entered it. State Street, grandly impressive under the sweep of a raw east wind, was gay with banners and sparkling with looping thousands of electric lights, but I hurried at once to my study on Elm Street. In half an hour I was deep in my correspondence. The Telegraph Trail was a million miles away, New York and its publishers claimed my full attention once again.

At two o'clock next day I entered Taft's studio, where I received many cordial congratulations on my return. "I can't understand why you went," Lorado said, and when, at the close of the afternoon, Browne, his brother-in-law, invited me to dinner, saying, "You'll find Miss Zulime Taft there," I accepted. Although in some doubt about Miss Taft's desire to meet me, I was curious to know what four years of Paris had done for her.

Browne explained that she was going to take up some sort of work in Chicago. "She's had enough of the Old World for the present."

As he let us into the hall of his West Side apartment, I caught a momentary glimpse of a young woman seated in the living room, busily sewing. She rose calmly, though a little surprised at our invasion, and with her rising, spools of thread and bits of cloth fell away from her with comic effect, although her expression remained loftily serene.

"Hello, sister Zuhl," called Browne. "Here is an old-time friend of yours."

As she greeted me with entire self-possession I hardly rec-

74

ognized her relationship to the pale, self-possessed art-student, with whom I had held unprofitable argument some four years before. She was much more mature and in better health than when I last saw her. She carried herself with dignity, and her gown, graceful of line and rich in color, fitted her beautifully.

With no allusion to our former differences she was kind enough to say that she had been a delighted reader of my stories in the magazines, and that she approved of America. "I've come back to stay," she said, and we all applauded her statement.

As the evening deepened I perceived that her long stay in England and in France had done a great deal for Zulime Taft. She was not only well informed in art matters, she conversed easily and tactfully, and her accent was refined without being affected. As we settled into our seats around the dinner table, I was glad to find her opposite me.

She had met many interesting and distinguished people, both in London and on the Continent, and she brought to our little circle that night the latest word in French art. Indeed, her comment was so entertaining, and so valuable, that I was quite converted to her brother's judgment concerning her term of exile: "Whether you go on with your sculpture or not," he said, "those four years of Europe have done more for you than a college course."

She represented everything antithetic to the trail and the farm. She knew little of New England and nothing of the Mountain West. In many ways she was entirely alien to my life and yet—or rather because of that—she interested me. Filled with theories concerning art—enthusiasms with which the "American Colony" in Paris was aflame, she stated them clearly, forcibly and with humor. Her temper in argument was admirable and no man had occasion to talk down at her—as Browne, who was a good deal of a conservative, openly acknowledged.

She was all for "technique," it appeared. "What America

needs more than subject is skill, knowledge of how to paint," she declared. "Anything can be made beautiful by the artist's brush."

At the close of a most delightful evening Fuller and I took our departure together, and we were hardly out of the door before he began to express open, almost unrestrained admiration of Zulime Taft. "She's a very remarkable girl," he said. "She will prove a most valuable addition to our circle."

"Yes," I admitted with judicial poise, "she is very intelligent."

"Intelligent!" he indignantly retorted. "She's a beauty. She's a prize. Go in and win."

Although I did not decide at that moment to go in and win, I was profoundly affected by his words. Without knowing anything more about her than these two meetings gave me, I took it for granted—quite without warrant, that Fuller had learned from Lorado that she was not committed to any one. It was fatuous in me but on this assumption I acted.

By reference to letters and other records I find that I dined at the Browne's on the slightest provocation. I suspect I did so without any invitation at all, for while Miss Taft did not betray keen interest in me she did not precisely discourage me. I sought her company as often as possible without calling especial attention to my action, and as she gave no hint of being friendlier with any other man, I went cheerily, blindly along.

One afternoon as I was taking tea at one of the great houses of the Lake Shore Drive, she came into the room with the easy grace of one habituated to meeting people of wealth and distinction. Neither arrogant nor humble, her self-respecting composure fairly sealed her conquest so far as I was concerned.

The group of artists surrounding Taft had formed an

informal Saturday night club, which met in a "Camp Supper," and in these jolly, intimate evenings Miss Taft and her sister, Mrs. Browne, were guiding spirits. Being included in this group I acknowledged these parties to be the most delightful events of my life in Chicago. They appeared a bit of Bohemia, "transmogrified" to suit our conditions, and they made the city seem less like a drab expanse of desolate materialism.

Sometimes a great geologist would help to make the coffee, while an architect carved the turkey; and sometimes banker Hutchinson was permitted to aid in distributing plates and spoons, but always Zulime Taft was one of the hostesses, and no one added more to the distinction and the charm of the company. She was never out of character, never at a loss in an effort to entertain her guests, and yet she did this so effectively that her absence was instantly felt—I, at least, always resented the action of those wealthy guests who occasionally hurried away with her to the Thomas Concert at eight-fifteen. My mood was all the more bitter for the reason that I could not afford to take her there myself. To ask her to sit in the gallery was disgraceful, and seats in the balcony were not only expensive, but almost impossible to get. They were all sold, in advance, for the season. For all these reasons I frequently watched her departure with a sense of defeat.

Israel Zangwill, who came to town at about this time to lecture, was brought to one of our suppers and proved to be of the true artist spirit. During his stay in the city Taft made a quick sketch of him, catching most admirably the characteristics of his homely face! He was a quaint yet powerful personality, witty and wise, and genial, and made friends wherever he went.

Meanwhile, notwithstanding many pleasant meetings with Miss Taft—perhaps because of them—I had my moments of gloomy introspection wherein I cast up accounts in order to determine what I had gained by my six months' vacation in the wilderness. First of all I had become a master trailer—so much was assured, but this acquirement did not promise to be of any practical benefit to me except possibly in the way of a lecture tour. Broadening my hand to the cinch and the axe did not make me any more attractive as a suitor and certainly did not add anything to my capital.

My outing had cost me twice what I had calculated upon, and, thus far, I had only syndicated a few letters and a handful of poems. The book which I had in mind to write was still a mass of notes. My horse, whose transportation and tariff had cost me a thousand dollars, was of little use to me, although I hoped to get back a part of his cost by means of a story. My lecture on "The Joys of the Trail" promised to be moderately successful, and yet with all these things conjoined I did not see myself earning enough to warrant me in asking Zulime Taft or any woman to be the daughter which my mother was so eagerly awaiting.

It was a time of halting, of transition for me. For six years—even while writing my story of Ulysses Grant I had been absorbing the mountain west in the growing desire to put it into fiction, and now with a burden of Klondike material to be disposed of, I was subconsciously at work upon a story of the plains and the Rocky Mountain foothills. In short, as a cattleman would say, I was "milling" in the midst of a wide landscape.

I should have gone on to New York at once, but with the alluring associations of Taft's studio, I lingered on through November and December, excusing myself by saying that I could work out my problem better in my own room on Elm Street than in a hotel in New York, and as a matter of fact I did succeed in writing several chapters of the Colorado novel which I called *The Eagle's Heart*.

At last, late in December, I bundled my manuscripts together and set out for the East. Perhaps this decision was hastened by some editorial suggestion—at any rate I arrived, for I find in my diary the record of a luncheon with Brander Matthews who said he liked my Grant book,—a verdict which heartened me wonderfully. I believed it to be a good book then, as I do now, but it was not selling as well as we had confidently expected it to do and my publishers had lost interest in it.

The reason for the failure of this book was simple. The war with Spain had thrust between the readers of my generation and the Civil War, new commanders, new slogans and new heroes. To this later younger public "General Grant" meant *Frederick* Grant, and all hats were off to Dewey, Wood and Roosevelt. "You are precisely two years late with your story of the Great Commander," I was told, and this I was free to acknowledge.

There is an old proverb which had several times exactly described my situation and which described it then. "It is always darkest just before dawn," proved to be true of this particular period of discouragement, for one day while at The Players, Brett, the head of Macmillans, came up to me and said, "Why don't you let me take over your *Main Traveled Roads, Prairie Folks,* and *Rose of Dutcher's Coolly?* I will do this provided you will write two new books for me, one to be called *Boy Life on the Prairie* and the other a Klondike book based on your experiences in the North."

This offer cleared my sky. It not only gave direction to my pen—it roused my hopes of having a home of my own, for Brett's offer involved the advance of several thousand dollars in royalty. I began to think of marriage in a more definite way. My case was not so hopeless after all. Perhaps Zulime Taft——

Taking a room on Twenty-fifth street I set to work with eager intensity to get these five books in shape for the

Macmillan press, and in two weeks I had carefully revised *Rose* and was hard at work on the record of my story of the Northwest which I called *The Trail of the Gold Seekers*. I was done with "milling." I was headed straight for a home.

In calling upon Howells soon after my arrival I referred to our last meeting wherein I had lightly remarked (putting my finger on the map), "I shall go in here at Quesnelle and come out there, on the Stickeen," and said, "I am now able to report. I did it. In spite of all the chances for failure I carried out my program."

He asked about the dangers I had undergone, and I replied by saying, "A trailer meets his dangers and difficulties one by one. In the mass they are appalling but singly they are surmountable. We took each mile as it came."

"What do you intend to do with your experiences?" he asked.

"I don't know, but I *think* they will take the form of a chronicle, a kind of diary, wherein each chapter will be called a camp. Camp One, Camp Two, and the like."

"That sounds original and promising," he said, and with his encouragement I set to work.

Israel Zangwill was often in the city and we met frequently during January and February. I recall taking him to see Howells whom he greatly admired but had never met. They made a singularly interesting contrast of East and West. Howells was serious, almost sad for some reason, unassuming, self-unconscious and yet masterly in every word. Zangwill on the contrary overflowed with humor, emitting a shower of epigrams concerning America and the things he liked and disliked, and soon had Howells smiling with pleased interest.

As we were leaving the house Zangwill remarked in a musing tone, "What fine humility, or rather modesty. I can't imagine any other man of Howells' eminence taking that tone."

Kipling had just returned to America, and I went at once to call upon him. I had not seen him since the dinner which he gave to Riley and me in the early Nineties, and I was in doubt as to his attitude toward the States. I found him in a very happy mood, surrounded by callers. In the years of his absence the American public had learned to place a very high value on his work and thousands of his readers were eager to do him honor.

"They come in a perfect stream," he said, and there was a note of surprise as well as of pleasure in his voice.

He inquired of Riley and Howells and other of our mutual friends, making it plain that he held us all in his affections. I mention his youth, his happiness, his joy with special emphasis for he was stricken with pneumonia a few days later and came so near death that only the most skillful nursing was able to bring him back to health. For two nights his life was despaired of, and when he recovered consciousness it was only to learn that one of his children had died while he himself was at lowest ebb. It was a most tragic reversal of fortune but it had this compensation, it called forth such a flood of sympathy on the part of his public that the daily press carried hourly bulletins of his conditions. It was as if a great ruler were in danger.

On Saturday the eleventh of February, I attended a meeting (the first meeting) of the National Institute of Arts and Letters. Charles Dudley Warner presided, but Howells was the chief figure. Owen Wister, Robert Underwood Johnson, Augustus Thomas and Bronson Howard took an active part. Warner appointed Thomas and me as a committee to outline a Constitution and By-laws, and I set down in my diary this comment, "Only a few men were out and these few were chilled by a cold room but never-

A Daughter of the Middle Border

theless, this meeting is likely to have far-reaching consequences."

In these months of my stay in New York I had a very busy and profitable time with Howells, Burroughs, Stedman, Matthews, Herne and their like as neighbors but after all, my home was in the West, and many times each day my mind went back to my mother waiting in the snow-covered little village thirteen hundred miles away. As I had established her in Wisconsin to be near me, it seemed a little like desertion to be spending the winter in the East.

My thoughts often returned to the friendly circle in Taft's studio, and late in February I was keenly interested in a letter from Lorado in which he informed me that Wallace Heckman, Attorney for The Art Institute, had offered to give the land to found a summer colony of artists and literary folk on the East bank of Rock River about one hundred miles west of Chicago. "You are to be one of the trustees," Lorado wrote, "and as soon as you get back, Mr. Heckman wants to take us all out to look at the site for the proposed camp."

My return to Chicago on the first day of March landed me in the midst of a bleak period of raw winds, filthy slush and all-pervading grime—but with hopes which my new contract with Macmillans had inspired I defied the weather. I rejoined Lorado's circle at once in the expectation of meeting his sister, and in this I was not disappointed.

Lorado referred at once to Heckman's offer to deed to our group a tract of land. "He wants you to be one of the trustees and has invited us all to go out at once and inspect the site."

Upon learning that Miss Taft was to be one of the members of the colony I accepted the trusteeship very readily. With three thousand dollars advance royalty in sight, I began to imagine myself establishing a little home somewhere in or near Chicago, and the idea of an inexpensive

82

summer camp such as my artist friends had in mind, appealed to me strongly.

Alas for my secret hopes!—Whether on this tour of inspection or a few days later I cannot now be sure, but certainly close upon this date Lorado (moved by some confiding remark concerning my interest in his sister Zulime) explained to me with an air of embarrassment that I must not travel any farther in that direction. "Sister Zuhl came back from Paris not to paint or model but to be married. She is definitely committed to another man." He finally, bluntly said.

This was a bitter defeat. Although one takes such blows better at thirty-nine than at nineteen, one doesn't lightly say "Oh, well—such is life!" I was in truth disheartened. All my domestic plans fell with a crash. My interest in the colony cooled. The camp suppers lost their charm.

It is only fair to me to say that Miss Taft had never indicated in any way that she was mortgaged to another, and no one—so far as I could see, was more in her favor than I, hence I was not entirely to blame in the case. My inferences were logical. So far as her words and actions were concerned I was justified in my hope that she might consent.

However, regarding Lorado's warning as final I turned to another and wholly different investment of the cash with which my new contract had embarrassed me. I decided to go to England.

For several years my friends in London had been suggesting that I visit them and I had a longing to do so. I wanted to see Barrie, Shaw, Hardy, Besant, and other of my kindly correspondents and this seemed my best time to make the journey.

Rose of Dutcher's Coolly had won for me many English friends. Henry James had reviewed it, Barrie had written to me in praise of it and Stead had republished it in a cheap edition which had gained a wide circle of readers. "In going abroad now I shall be going among friends," I said to Fuller who was my confidant, as usual.

Henry James in a long and intimate letter had said, "It is high time for you to visit England. I shall take great pleasure in having you for a week-end here at Old Rye"— and a re-reading of this letter tipped the scale. I took the train for Wisconsin to see my mother and prepare her for my immediate trip to London.

Dear soul! She was doubly deeply disappointed, for I not only failed to bring assurance of a new daughter, I came with an avowal of desertion in my mouth. Pathetically counting on my spending the summer with her, she must now be told that I was about to sail for the Old World!

It was not a happy home-coming. I acknowledged myself to be a base, unfilial, selfish wretch, "and yet—if I am ever to see London now is my time. Each year my mother will be older, feebler. The sooner I make the crossing the safer for us all. Furthermore I am no longer young—and just·now with Barrie, Shaw, Zangwill, Doyle and Henry James, England will be hospitable to me. The London Macmillans are to bring out my books and so——"

Mother consented at last, tearfully, begging me not to stay long and to write often, to which I replied, "You may count on me in July. I shall only be gone three months— four at the outside. I shall send Frank to stay with you— and I shall write every day."

Just before coming to West Salem (with a feeling of guilt in my heart) I had purchased a mechanical piano in the hope that it would cheer her lonely hours, and as this instrument had arrived I unboxed it and set it up in the music room, eager to please the old folks to whom it was an amazing contrivance.

It was on Sunday and Uncle Will came in together with

several of the neighbors, and while I manipulated the stops and worked the pedals, they all sat in silence, marveling at the cunning of the mechanism rather than enjoying "The Ride of the Valkyries." However as I played some simpler things, a song of MacDowells, a study by Grieg, my Uncle's head bowed, and on his face came that somber brooding look which recalled to me the moods of David, his younger brother, whose violin had meant so much to me when as a boy, I lay before the fire and listened with sweet Celtic melancholy to the wailing of its strings.

Something in these northern melodies sank deep into my mother's inherited memories, also, and her eyes were wide and still with inward vision, but my Aunt Susan said, "That's a fine invention, but I'd rather hear you sing," and in this judgment Maria concurred. "It's grand," she admitted, "but 'tain't like the human voice."

In the end I put the machine back in the corner and sang for them, some of the familiar songs. The instrument was surprising and new and wonderful but it did not touch the hearts of my auditors like "Minnie Minturn" and "The Palace of the King."

On the day following I set the date of my departure and at the end of my announcement mother sat in silence, her face clouded with pain, her eyes looking away into space. She had nothing to say in opposition, not a word—she only said, "If you're going I guess the quicker you start the better."

CHAPTER SEVEN

London and Evening Dress

CONFESSION must now be made on a personal matter of capital importance. Up to my thirty-ninth year I had never worn a swallow-tail evening coat, and the question of conforming to a growing sartorial custom was becoming, each day, of more acute concern to my friends as well as to myself.

My first realization of the differences which the lack of evening dress can make in a man's career, came upon me clearly during the social stir of the Columbian Exposition, for throughout my ten years' stay in Boston I had accepted (with serene unconsciousness of the incongruity of my action) the paradoxical theory that a "Prince Albert frock coat" was the proper holiday or ceremonial garment of an American democrat. The claw-hammer suit was to me, as to my fellow artist, "the livery of privilege" worn only by monopolistic brigands and the poor parasites who fawned upon and served them, whereas the double-breasted black coat, royal, as its name denoted, was associated in my mind with judges, professors, senators and doctors of divinity.

It was, moreover, a dignified and logical garment. It clothed with equal charity a man's stomach and his stern. Generous of its skirts, which went far to conceal wrinkled trousers, it could be worn with a light tie at a formal dinner or with a dark tie at a studio tea, and was equally appropriate at a funeral or a wedding. For all these several reasons it remained the uniform of professional men throughout

86

the Middle Border. From my earliest childhood it had been my ideal of manly elegance. Even in New York I had kept pretty close to the social level where it was still accepted.

The World's Fair in '93, however, had not only brought to Chicago many of the discriminating social customs of the East, but also many distinguished guests from the old world to whom dress was a formal, almost sacred routine. To meet these noble aliens, we, the artists and writers of the city, were occasionally invited; and the question "Shall we conform" became ever more pressing in its demand for final settlement. One by one my fellows had deserted from the ranks and were reported as rubbing shoulders with pluto-crats in their great dining-rooms or escorting ladies into gilded reception parlors, wearing garments which had no relationship to learning, or art, or law, as I had been taught to believe. Lorado Taft, Oliver Dennett Grover, and even Henry Fuller had gone over to the shining majority, leaving me almost alone in stubborn support of the cylindrical coat.

To surrender was made very difficult for me by Eugene Field, who had publicly celebrated me as "the sturdy op-ponent of the swallow-tail suit," and yet he himself,— though still outwardly faithful—had been heard to say, "I may be forced to wear the damned thing _yet._"

In all this I felt the wind of social change. That I stood at the parting of the ways was plain to me. To continue on my present line of march would be to have as exemplars Walt Whitman, Joaquin Miller, John Burroughs and other illustrious non-conformists to whom long beards, easy col-lars, and short coats were natural and becoming. To take the other road was to follow Lowell and Stedman and Howells. To shorten my beard—or remove it altogether,— to wear a standing collar, and attached cuffs—to abandon my western wide-rimmed hat—these and many other "re-forms" were involved in my decision. Do you wonder that I hesitated?

That I was being left out of many delightful dinners and receptions had been painfully evident to me for several years, but the consideration which had most weight with me, at this time, was expressed by one of my friends who bluntly declared that all the desirable young women of my acquaintance not only adored men in evening dress but ridiculed those of us who went about at all hours of the day and night in "solemn, shiny, black frocks." I perceived that unless I paid a little more attention to tailors and barbers and haberdashers my chances for bringing a new daughter to my mother were dishearteningly remote. Secretly alarmed and meditating a shameful surrender, I was held in check by the thought of the highly involved system of buttons, ties, gloves, hats, and shoes with which I would be called upon to wrestle.

Zangwill, to whom I confided my perplexity, bluntly advised me to conform. "In truth," said he, "the steel pen suit is the most democratic of garments. It renders the poor author indistinguishable from the millionaire."

As usual I referred the problem to Howells. After explaining that I had in mind a plan to visit England I said, "Every one but John Burroughs says I must get into the swallow-tail coat; and I will confess that even here in New York I am often embarrassed by finding myself the only man in a frock suit at a dinner."

Howells smiled and with delightful humor and that precision of phrase which made him my joy and my despair, answered, "My dear fellow, why don't you make your proposed visit to England, buy your evening suit there and on your return to Chicago plead the inexorability of English social usages?"

He had pointed the way out. "By George, I'll do just that," I declared, vastly elated.

In this account of my hesitations I am *still* the historian. In stating my case I am stating the perplexities of thousands of my fellow citizens of the Middle Border. It has its humorous phases—this reversal of social habit in me, but it also has wide significance. My surrender was coincident with similar changes of thought in millions of other young men throughout the West. It was but another indication that the customs of the Border were fading to a memory, and that Western society, which had long been dominated by the stately figures of the minister and the judge, was on its way to adopt the manners and customs of the openly-derided but secretly admired "four hundred."

Having decided on my sailing date I asked Howells for a few letters of introduction to English authors.

He surprised me by saying, "I have very few acquaintances in England but I will do what I can for you."

At the moment of embarkation I disappointed myself by remaining quite calm. Even when the great ship began to heave and snort and slide away from the wharf I experienced no thrill—it was not till an hour or two later, as I stood on the forward deck, watching the sun go down over the tumbling spread of water, which had something of the majesty I had known in the prairies, that I became exalted. The vast expanse seemed strangely like an appalling desert and lifting my eyes to the cloudy horizon line I could almost imagine myself back on the rocks of Walpi overlooking the Navajo reservation.

In a letter to my mother I gave the story of my trip. "Feeling a bit queer along about nine o'clock I went to my state room.—When I came on deck the next time, my eyes rested upon the green hills of Ireland!—I am certain the ship's restaurant realized the highest possible profit in my case for I remember but two meals, one as we were leaving Sandy Hook, the other as we signaled Queenstown. It may be that I imbibed a bowl of soup in the interim,—I certainly swallowed a great many doses of several kinds of medicine. The ship's doctor declared me to be the worst sailor he had even known in all his thirty years' experience, —so much of distinction I may definitely claim."

In the dark hours of that interminable week, I went over my trail into the Skeena Valley during the previous May, with retrospective delight. In contrast to these endless days of lonely misery in my ship bed those weeks of rain and mud and mosquitoes became a joyous outing. So far from giving any thought to problems of dress or social intercourse I was only interested in reaching land—any land.

"In two minutes after I landed at Liverpool I was perfectly well," I wrote to my mother. "The touch of solid earth under my feet instantly restored my sanity. My desire to live returned. In an hour I was aboard one of the quaint little coaches of the Midland Express and on my way to London.

"Lush meadows, flecked with fat red cattle feeding beside slow streams; broad lawns rising to wooded hills, on which many-towered gray buildings rose; sudden thick-walled towns; factories, winding streams, noble trees, and finally a yellow mist and London!

"I am at a small inn, near the Terminal Hotel. I ate my dinner last night surrounded by English people. With brain still pulsing with the motion of the sea, I went to my bed, rejoicing to feel around me the solid stone walls of this small but ancient hotel."

After a long walk in search of my publishers I was repaid by finding several letters awaiting me, and among them was one from Zangwill, who wrote, "Come at once to my house. I have a message for you."

His address was almost as quaint in my ear as that of Sir Walter Besant, which was Frognals End—or something like it, but I found it at last on the way to 'Ampstead 'Eath. The house was a modest one but his study was made cheery by a real fire of "coals," and many books.

He greeted me heartily and said, "I have an invitation

for you to the Authors' Society Dinner which comes next week. It will be what you would call 'a big round-up' and you can't afford to miss it. You must go at once and order that evening suit."

The idea of the dinner allured me but I shuffled, "Can't I go as I am?"

"Certainly not. It is a full-dress affair."

I argued, "But George Bernard Shaw is reported to be without the dress suit."

"Yes," admitted Zangwill, "Shaw goes everywhere in tweeds, but then he is Shaw, and can afford to do as he pleases. You will not see him at this dinner. He seldom goes to such functions."

With a shudder I plunged. "I'll do it! If I must surrender, let it be on a grand occasion like this. I am in your hands."

Zangwill was highly amused. "We will go at once. That suit must be ready for the dinner which comes on Thursday. There's not a moment to spare. The cow-boy must be tamed."

My hesitation may seem comical to my reader as it did to Zangwill, but I really stood in deep dread of the change. The thought of bulging shirt fronts, standing collars, varnished shoes and white ties appalled me. With especial hatred and timidity I approached the cylindrical hat, which was so wide a departure from my sombrero.—Nevertheless decision had been taken out of my hands! With wry face I followed my guide.

In most unholy glee Zangwill stood looking on whilst I was being measured. "This is the beginning of your moral debacle," said he. "What will they say of you in Wisconsin, when they hear of your appearance at an English dinner wearing 'the livery of the oppressor'?"

I made no reply to these questions, but I felt like the traitor he reported me to be.

However, being in so far I decided to go clean through. I bought a white tie, some high collars, two pairs of gloves and a folding opera hat. I could not bring myself to the point of wearing a high hat in the day time (that was almost too much of a change from my broad brim), although my Prince Albert Frock, which I wore morning, noon, and night, was in conformity with English custom. Even the clerks were so attired.

Meanwhile, Zangwill's study was the only warm place in London—so far as I knew. His glowing fire of hard coal was a powerful lure, and I was often there, reacting to the warmth of his rug like a chilled insect. On his hearth I thawed into something like good humor, and with his knowledge of American steam heat he was fitted to understand my vocal delight.

From my Strand hotel I set out each morning, riding about the city on the tops of 'buses and in this way soon got "the lay of the land." I was able to find Piccadilly Circus, Trafalgar Square, the Houses of Parliament, and a few other landmarks of this character. I spent a week or more, roaming about the old city, searching out, as most Americans do, the literary, the historic. I wanted to see the Tower, "The Cheshire Cheese," and the Law Courts of the Temple. The modern London, which was almost as ugly as Chicago, did not interest me at all.

Between "try-ons" of the new suit I began to meet the men I was most interested in. I lunched with James Barrie and called upon Bret Harte, Sir Walter Besant and Thomas Hardy. Bernard Shaw wrote asking me to Hindhead for a week-end, and Conan Doyle invited me to see a cricket match with him—but all these events were subordinate to the authors' dinner and the accursed suit in which I was about to lose my identity. "My shirt will 'buckle,' my shoes will hurt my feet, my tie will slip up over my collar—I shall take cold in my chest——" (As a hardened diner-out I look back with wonder and a certain incredulity on that uneasy week.)

These were a few of the fears I entertained, but on the fateful night—an hour before the time to start out, I assumed the whole "outfit" and viewed myself as best I could in my half-length mirror and was gratified to note that I resembled almost any other brown-bearded man of forty. I couldn't see my feet and legs in the glass, but my patent leather shoes were illustrious. I began to think I might pull through without accident.

Zangwill with a mischievous grin on his face, met me at the door of the hotel at seven, and conducted me to the reception hall which was already filled with a throng of most distinguished guests running from Sir Walter Besant, the president of the Authors' Society, to Lord Rosebery, who was to be one of the speakers. Zangwill, who seemed to be known of everybody, kept me in hand, introducing me to many of the writers, and kind Sir Walter said, "As an American over-seas member your seat is at the speakers' table"— an honor which I accepted with a swift realization that it was made possible by the new coat and vest I presented to the world.

Zangwill parted with me, smilingly. "I am but one of lower orders," said he, "but I shall have an eye to you during dinner."

My left-hand neighbor at the table was a short, gray, gloomy individual whose name I failed to catch, but the man on my right was Henry Norman, of the *London Chronicle*, and after we had established friendly relations I leaned to him and whispered, "Who is the self-absorbed, gloomy chieftain on my left?"

"That," said he, "is Henry M. Stanley."

"What!" I exclaimed, "not Henry M. Stanley of Africa?"

"Yes, Stanley of Uganda."

It seemed a pity to sit in silence beside this great explorer, who had been one of my boyish heroes, and I decided to break the ice of his reserve in some way. Turning to him suddenly I asked, "Sir Henry, how do you pronounce the name of that poisonous African fly—is it Teetsie or Tettsie?"

He brightened up at once. I was not so great a bore as he feared. After he had given me a great deal of information about this fly, and the sleeping sickness, I asked him what he thought of the future of the continent, to which he responded with growing geniality. We were off!

After a proper interval I volunteered some valuable data concerning the mosquitoes and flies I had encountered on my recent trip into the wilderness of British Columbia. He became interested in me. "Oh! You've been to the Klondike!"

This quite broke down his wall. Thereafter he listened respectfully to all that I could tell him of the black flies, the huge caribou flies, the orange-colored flies, and the mosquitoes who worked in two shifts (the little gray ones in hot sunlight, the big black ones at night), and by the time the speaking began we were on the friendliest terms. "What a bore these orators are!" I said, and in this judgment he instantly agreed.

Sitting there in the faces of hundreds of English authors, I achieved a peaceful satisfaction with my outfit. A sense of being entirely inconspicuous, a realization that I was committed to convention, produced in me an air of perfect ease. By conforming I had become as much a part of the scene as Sir Walter or the waiter who shifted my plates and filled my glass. "Zangwill is right," I said, "the claw-hammer coat is in truth the most democratic of garments."

It pleased me also to dwell upon the fact that the moment of my capitulation had been made glorious by a meeting with Stanley and Hardy and Barrie, and that the dinner which marked this most important change in lifelong habits of dress was appropriately notable. That several hundred of

London and Evening Dress

the best known men and women of England had witnessed my fall softened the shock, and when—on the way out—Zangwill nudged my elbow and said, "Cow-boy, you wore 'em to the manner born," I smiled in lofty disregard of future comment. I faced Chicago and New York with serene and confident composure.

Although I carried this suit with me to Bernard Shaw's (on a week-end visit), I was not called upon to wear it, for he met me in snuff-colored knickerbockers and did not change to any other suit during my stay. Sunday dinner at Conan Doyle's was a midday meal, and Barrie and Hardy and other of my literary friends I met at teas or luncheons. I took my newly-acquired uniform to Paris but as my meetings with my French friends were either teas or lunches, it so happened that—eager as I was to display it I did not put this suit on till after I reached home. My first appearance in it was in the nature of a masquerade, my second was by way of a joke to please my mother.

Knowing that she had never seen a man in evening dress I arrayed myself, one night, as if for a banquet, and suddenly descended upon her with intent to surprise and amuse her. I surprised her but I did not make her laugh in the way I had expected. On the contrary she surveyed me with a look of pride and then quietly remarked, "I like you in it. I wouldn't mind if you dressed that way every day."

This finished my opposition to the swallow-tail coat. If my mother, the daughter of a pioneer, a woman of the farm, accepted it as something appropriate to her son, its ultimate acceptance by all America was inevitable. Thereafter I lay in wait for an opportunity to display myself in all my London finery.

* * * * * *

Two months later as I was mounting the central staircase of the Chicago Art Institute, on my way to the Annual Reception, I met two of my fellow republicans in Prince Albert

Frock suits. At sight of me they started with surprise—surprise and sorrow—exclaiming, "Look at Hamlin Garland!" Assuming an expression of patrician ease, I replied, "Oh, yes, I have conformed. In London one *must* conform, you know.—The English are quite inexorable in all matters of dress, you understand."

Howells, when I saw him next, smilingly listened to my tale and heartily approved of my action, but Burroughs regarded it as a weak surrender. "A silk hat and steel-pen coat on a Whitman Democrat," he said, "seems like a make-believe," which, in a sense, it was.

CHAPTER EIGHT

The Choice of the New Daughter

ALTHOUGH my mother met me each morning with a happy smile, she walked with slower movement, and in studying her closely, after three months' absence, I perceived unwelcome change. She was not as alert mentally or physically as when I went away. A mysterious veil had fallen between her wistful spirit and the outer world. Her vision was dimmer and her spirit at times withdrawn, remote. She laughed in response to my jesting, but there was an absent-minded sweetness in her smile, a tremulous quality in her voice which disturbed me.

Her joy in my return, so accusing in its tenderness, led me to declare that I would never again leave her, not even for a month. "You may count on me hereafter," I said to her. "I'm going to quit traveling and settle down near you."

"I hope you mean it this time," she replied soberly, and her words stung for I recalled the many times I had disappointed her.

With a mass of work and correspondence waiting my hand I went from my breakfast to my study. My forenoons thereafter were spent at my desk, but with the understanding that if she got lonesome, mother was privileged to interrupt, and it often happened that along about eleven I would hear a softly-opened stair-door and then a call,—a timid call as if she feared to disturb me—"Haven't you done enough? Can't you come now?" There was no resisting this appeal. Dropping my pen, I went below and gave the rest of my day to her.

We possessed an ancient low-hung "Surrey," a vehicle admirably fitted for an invalid, and in this conveyance with a stout mare as motive power we often drove away into the country of a pleasant afternoon, sometimes into Gill's Coulee, sometimes to Onalaska.

On these excursions my mother rode in silence, busied with the past. Each hill, each stream had its tender association. Once as we were crossing the Kinney Hill she said, "We used to pick plums along that creek." Or again as we were driving toward Mindora, she said, "When Mc-Eldowney built that house we thought it a palace."

She loved to visit her brother William's farm, and to ride past the old McClintock house in which my father had courted her. Her expression at such times was sweetly sorrowful. The past appeared so happy, so secure, her present so precarious, so full of pain. She sensed the mystery, the tragedy of human life, but was unable to express her conceptions,—and I was of no value as a comforter. I could only jest with a bitter sense of helplessness.

On other days, when she was not well enough to drive, I pushed her about the village in a wheeled chair, which I had bought at the World's Fair. In this way she was able to make return calls upon such of her neighbors as were adjacent to side-walks. She was always in my thought,— only when Franklin took her in charge was it possible for me to concentrate on the story which I had begun before going abroad, and in which I hoped to embody some of the experiences of my trip. *Boy Life on the Prairie* was also still incomplete, and occasionally I put aside *The Hustler,* as I called my fiction, in order to recover and record some farm custom, some pioneer incident which my mother or my brother brought to my mind as we talked of early days in Iowa.

The story (which Gilder afterward called *Her Mountain Lover*) galloped along quite in the spirit of humorous extravaganza with which it had been conceived, and I thoroughly enjoyed doing it for the reason that in it I was able to relive some of the noblest moments of my explorations of Colorado's peaks and streams. It was an expression of my indebtedness to the High Country.

I made the mistake, however, of not using the actual names of localities. Just why I shuffled the names of trails and towns and valleys so recklessly, I cannot now explain, for there was abundant literary precedent for their proper and exact use. Perhaps I resented the prosaic sound of "Sneffles" and "Montrose Junction." Anyhow, whatever my motive, I covered my tracks so well that it was impossible even for a resident to follow me. In *The Eagle's Heart* I was equally elusive, but as only part of that book referred to the High Country the lack of definite nomenclature did not greatly matter.

Personally I like *Her Mountain Lover,* which is still in print, and for the benefit of the possible reader of it, I will explain that the "Wagon Wheel Gap" of the story is Ouray, and that the Grizzly Bear Trail leads off the stage road to Red Mountain.

Our red raspberries were just coming into fruit, and a few strawberries remained on the vines, therefore it happened that during the season we had a short-cake with cream and sugar almost every night for supper,—and such short-cakes!—piping hot, buttered, smothered in berries. I fear they were not very healthful either for my mother or for her sons, but as short-cakes were an immemorial delicacy in our home I could not bring myself to forbid them.

Mother insisted on them all the more firmly when I told her that the English knew nothing of short-cake or our kind of pies, and then, more to amuse her than for any other reason, I told of a visit to my English publisher and of my bragging about her short-cake so shamelessly that he had finally declared: "I am coming to Chicago next year, and I shall journey all the way to West Salem just to test your mother's short-cake."

This made her chuckle. "Let him come," she said confidently. "We'll feed him on it."

Notwithstanding her reaction to my jesting, my anxiety concerning her deepened. The long periods of silence into which she fell alarmed me, and at times, as she sat alone, I detected on her face an expression of pain which was like that of one in despair. When I questioned her, she could not define the cause of her distress, but I feared it came from some weakening of her heart.

She was failing,—that was all too evident to me—failing faster than her years warranted, and then (just as I was becoming a little reassured) she came to me one morning, with both her hands outstretched, as if feeling her way, her face white, her eyes wide and deep and dark with terror. "I can't see! I can't see!" she wailed.

With a sense of impending tragedy I took her in my arms and led her to a chair. "Don't worry, mother!" was all I could say. "It will pass soon. Keep perfectly quiet."

Under the influence of my words she gradually lost her fear, and by the time the doctor arrived she was quite calm and could see—a little—though in a strange way.

In answer to his question she replied with a pitiful little smile, "Yes, I can see you, but only in pieces. I can only see a part of your face,—the rest of you is all black."

This reply seemed to relieve the doctor's mind. His face lighted up. "I understand! Don't worry a mite. You will be all right in a few minutes. It is only a temporary nerve disturbance."

This proved to be true, and as her lips resumed their placid sweetness my courage came back. In a few hours she was able to see quite clearly, or at least as clearly as was normal to her age. Nevertheless I accepted this attack as a distinct and sinister warning. It not only emphasized her dependence upon me, it made me very definitely aware of what would happen to our household if she were to become a helpless invalid. Her need of a larger bed-chamber, with a connecting bathroom was imperative.

"I know you will both suffer from the noise and confusion of the building," I said to my aunt, "but I am going to enlarge mother's room and put in water and plumbing. If she should be sick in that small bedroom it would be horrible."

Up to this time our homestead had remained simply a roomy farmhouse on the edge of a village. I now decided that it should have the conveniences of a suburban cottage, and to this end I made plans for a new dining-room, a new porch, and a bath-room.

Mother was appalled at the audacity of my designs. She wanted the larger chamber, of course, but my scheme for putting in running water appealed to her as something almost criminally extravagant. She was troubled, too, by the thought of the noise, the dirt, the change which were necessary accompaniments of the plan.

I did my best to reassure her. "It won't take long, mother, and as for the expense, you just let *me* walk the floor."

She said no more, realizing, no doubt, that I could not be turned aside from my purpose.

There were no bathrooms in West Salem in 1899—the plumber was still the tinner, and when the news of my ambitious designs got abroad it created almost as much comment as my brother's tennis court had roused some five years earlier. As a force making toward things high-fi-lutin, if not actually un-American, I was again discussed. Some said, "I can't understand how Hamlin makes all his money." Others remarked, "Easy come, easy go!" Something un-

accountable lay in the scheme of my life. It was illogical,
if not actually illegal.

"How can he go skittering about all over the world in
this way?" asked William McEldowney, and Sam McKinley
said to my mother, "I swear, I don't see how you and Dick
ever raised such a boy. He's a 'sport,'—that's what he is,
a freak." To all of which mother answered only with a
silent laugh.

The carpenters came, together with a crew of stone-
masons, and the old kitchen began to move southward,
giving place for the foundations of the new dining-room.
By the end of the week, the lawn was littered with material
and tools, and the frame-work was enclosed.

My mother, in her anxiety to justify the enormous outlay
said, "Well, anyhow, these improvements are not entirely
for me, they will make the house all the nicer for my New
Daughter when she comes."

"That's true," I answered, "I hadn't thought of that."

"It's *time* you thought of it. You're almost forty years
old," she replied with humorous emphasis, then she added,
"I begin to think I never *will* see your wife."

"Just you wait," I jestingly replied. "The case is not so
hopeless as you think—I have just received a letter which
gives me a 'prospect.' "

I said this merely to divert her, but she seized upon my
remark with alarming seriousness. "Read me the letter.
Where does she live?—Tell me all about her."

Being in so far I thought it could do no harm to go a
little farther. I described (still in bantering mood) my first
meeting with Zulime Taft more than five years before. I
pictured her as she looked to me then, and as she afterward appeared when I met her a second time in the home
of her sister in Chicago. "I admit that I was greatly impressed by her," I went on, "but just when I had begun to
hope for a better understanding, her brother Lorado chilled

me with the information that she was about to be claimed by another man. To be honest about it, mother, I am not sure that she is interested in me even now; although one of her friends has just written me to say that Lorado was mistaken, and that Zulime is not engaged to any one. I am going down to visit some friends at the camp to test the truth of this; but don't say a word about it, for my information may be wrong."

My warning went for nothing! My confession was too exciting to be kept a secret, and soon several of mother's most intimate friends had heard of my expedition, and in their minds, as in hers, my early marriage was assured. Did not the proof of it lie in the fact that I was pushing my building with desperate haste? Was this not done in order to make room for my bride?—No other reason was sufficient to account for the astounding improvements which I had planned, and which were going forward with magical rapidity.

Of course no one could convince my mother that her son's "attractions" might not prove sufficiently strong to make his "prospect" a possibility, for to her I was not only a distinguished author, but a "Good provider," something which outweighed literary attainment in a home like ours.

She could not or would not speak of the girl as "Miss Taft," but insisted upon calling her "Zuleema," and her mind was filled with plans for making her at home.

Privately I was more concerned than I cared to show, and I would be giving a false impression if I made light of my feeling at this time. I spoke to mother jestingly in order to prevent her from building her hopes on an unstable foundation.

In the midst of my busiest day I received a letter from my good friends, Wallace and Tillie Heckman, and though I was but a clumsy farmer in all affairs of the heart, I perceived enough of hidden meaning in their invitation to visit

Eagle's Nest, to give me pause even in the welter of my plumbing. I replied at once accepting their hospitality, and on Saturday took the train for Oregon to stay over Sunday at least.

Squire Heckman was good enough to meet me at the train, and as he drove me up the hill to "Ganymede," which was his summer home, he said, "You will breakfast with us, and as it is our custom to dine at the Camp on Sunday we will take you with us and introduce you to the campers, although most of them are known to you."

Mrs. Heckman, who was cordial in her welcome, informed me at breakfast that Miss Taft was the volunteer stewardess of the Camp. "She is expecting us to bring you to dinner to-day."

"As one of the Trustees of the Foundation, a tour of inspection is a duty," I replied.

There was a faint smile on Mrs. Heckman's demure lips, but Wallace, astute lawyer that he was, presented the bland face of a poker player. Without a direct word being spoken I was made to understand that Miss Taft was not indifferent to my coming, and when at half-past eleven we started for Eagle's Nest I had a sense of committing myself to a perilous campaign.

A walk of half a mile through a thick grove of oaks brought us out upon a lovely, grassy knoll, which rose two hundred feet or more above the Rock River, and from which a pleasing view of the valley opened to the north as well as to the south. The camp consisted of a small kitchen cabin, a dining tent, a group of cabins, and one or two rude studios to which the joyous off-hand manners of the Fine Arts Building had been transferred. It was in fact a sylvan settlement of city dwellers—a colony of artists, writers and teachers out for a summer vacation.

In holiday mood Browne, Taft, and Clarkson greeted me warmly, upbraiding me, however, for having so long neg-

Miss Zulime Taft, acting as volunteer housekeeper for the colony, had charge of the long rude table under the tent-fly to which the campers assembled with the appetites of harvest hands and the gayety of uncalculating youth.

lected my official duties as trustee. "We need your counsel."

Mrs. Heckman, laconic, quizzical, walked about "the reservation" with me, and in her smiling eyes I detected a kind of gentle amusement with her unconventional neighbors. She said nothing then (or at any time) which could be interpreted as criticism, but a merry little quirk in the corner of her lip instructed me.

Miss Taft was not visible. "As house-keeper she is busy with preparations for dinner," Mrs. Heckman explained, and so I concealed my disappointment as best I could.

At last at one o'clock, Lorado, as Chief of the tribe, gave the signal for the feast by striking a huge iron bar with a hammer, a sound which brought the campers from every direction, clamoring for food, and when all were seated at the dining table beneath a strip of canvas, some one asked, "Where's Zuhl?"

Browne answered with blunt humor, "Primping! She's gone to smooth her ruffled plumage."

A cry arose, "Here she comes!" and Spencer Fiske the classical scholar of the camp with fervent admiration exclaimed "By Jove—a veritable Diana!"

Browne started the Toreador's song, and all began to beat upon the tables with their spoons in rhythmical clamor. Turning my head I perceived the handsome figure of a girl moving with calm and stately dignity across the little lawn toward the table. She was bareheaded, and wore a short-sleeved, collarless gown of summer design, but she carried herself with a leisurely and careless grace which made evident the fact that she was accustomed to these moments of uproar. As she neared the tent, however, I detected a faint flicker of amusement in the lines about her mouth.

This entrance so dramatic and so lovely was precisely the kind of picture to produce on my mind a deeply influencing impression. I thought her at the moment one of the most gracious and admirable women of my world, a union of European culture and the homely grace of the prairie.

She greeted me with a pleasant word, and took a seat opposite, making no reply to the jocular comment of her boarders. It was evident that she was not only accustomed to demonstrations of this sort, but considered them a necessary part of her stewardship, an office which was entirely without salary—and scantily repaid in honor.

No complaints about the scarcity of butter, or questions concerning the proportions of milk in the cream jug, had power to draw her into defensive explanation. At last her tormentors unable to stampede her by noise, or plague her by petitions, subsided into silence or turned to other matters, and we all settled down to an abundant and very jolly dinner.

It was because the camp loved Zulime Taft that they could carry on in this way. It was all studio *blague,* and she knew it and offered no defense of her economies.

Most of the artists and writers in the camp were already known to me. They were all of small income, some of them were almost as poor as I, and welcomed a method by which they were able to spend a summer comfortably and inexpensively. A common kitchen, and an old white horse and wagon also owned collectively, made it possible to offer board at four dollars per week!

The Heckman home, which the campers called "the Castle," or "The Manor House," a long, two-story building of stone which stood on the southern end of the Bluff, overlooked what had once been Black Hawk's Happy Hunting Ground. It was not in any sense a château, but it pleased Wallace Heckman's artist-tenants to call it so, and by contrast with their cook-house it did, indeed, possess something like grandeur. Furthermore "the Lord of the Manor" added to the majesty of his position by owning and driving a coach (this was before the day of the automobile), and at times those of his tenants most highly in favor, were invited to a seat on this stately vehicle.

"Lady" Heckman possessed a piano, another evidence of wealth, and the pleasantest part of my recollections of this particular visit concerns the evenings I spent with her in singing "Belle Mahone" and "Lily Dale," while Lorado and his sisters sat in the corner and listened—at least I infer that they listened—now that I grow more clear in my mind I recall that Tillie Heckman did not sing, she only played for me; and my conviction is that I sang very well. I may be mistaken in this for (at times) I detected Wallace Heckman addressing a jocose remark to Miss Taft when he should have been giving his undivided attention to my song.

Miss Taft was accused of having a keen relish for the fare at Castle Heckman, and in this relish I shared so frankly that when Tillie invited me to stay on indefinitely, and Wallace suggested that I might make the little pavilion on the lawn serve as my study, I yielded. "Work on the homestead must wait," I wrote to my mother. "Important business here demands my attention."

Zulime Taft appeared pleased when I announced my acceptance of the Heckman hospitality, and Wallace immediately offered me the use of his saddle horses and his carriage, and when he said, "Miss Taft loves to ride," I was convinced not only of his friendly interest but of his hearty coöperation. Furthermore as Mrs. Heckman often kept Miss Taft for supper, I had the pleasant task of walking back to camp with her.

In some way (I never understood precisely how) the campers, one and all, obtained the notion that I was significantly interested in Miss Taft; but, as I was proceeding with extraordinary caution, wearing the bland expression of a Cheyenne chieftain, I could not imagine any one discovering in my action anything more than a frank liking, a natural friendship between the sister of my artist comrade and myself.

It is true I could not entirely conceal the fact that I preferred her company to that of any other of the girls, but there was nothing remarkable in that—nevertheless, the whole camp, as I learned afterward (long afterward), was not only aware of my intentions but, behind my back, almost under my nose, was betting on my chances. Wagers were being offered and taken, day by day, as to whether I would win or lose!

Fortunately, nothing of this disgraceful business reached me. I was serenely unconscious of it all.

Demure as Tillie Heckman looked, slyly humorous as she occasionally showed herself to be, she was a woman of understanding, and from her I derived distinct encouragement. She not only indicated her sympathy; she conveyed to me her belief that I had a fair chance to win. I am not sure, but I think it was from her that I received the final statement that Miss Taft was entirely free. However, this did not clear me from other alarms, for on Friday night the train brought Henry Fuller and several young men visitors who were all quite willing to walk and talk with Miss Taft. It was only during the midweek that I, as the only unmarried man in camp, felt entirely secure.

Henry Fuller stayed on after the others went back to the city, and I would have been deeply disturbed by Zulime's keen interest in him, had I not been fully informed of their relationship, which was entirely that of intellectual camaraderie. Fuller was not merely a resolved bachelor; he was joyously and openly opposed to any form of domesticity. He loved his freedom beyond all else. The Stewardess knew this and revelled in his wit, sharing my delight in his bitter ironies. His verbal inhumanities gave her joy, because she didn't believe in them. They were all "literature" to her.

The Choice of the New Daughter

The weather was glorious September, and as my writing was going forward, my companionship ideal, and my mother's letters most cheerful, I abandoned myself, as I had not done in twenty years, to a complete enjoyment of life. Golden days! Halcyon days! Far and sweet and serene they seem as I look back upon them from the present—days to review with wistful regret that I did not more fully employ them in the way of youth, for alas! my mornings were spent in writing when they should have been given to walking with my sweetheart; yet even as I worked I had a sense of her nearness, and the knowledge that the shimmering summer landscape was waiting for me just outside my door, comforted me. However, I was not wholly neglectful of my opportunities. My afternoons were given over to walking or riding with her, and our evenings were spent in long and quiet excursions on the river or sitting with the artists in the light of a bonfire on the edge of the bluff, talking and singing.

The more I knew of Miss Taft the more her versatility amazed me. She could paint, she could model, she could cook and she could sew. As Stewardess, she took charge of the marketing, and when the kitchen fell into a flutter, her masterly taste and skill brought order—and a delicious dinner—out of chaos. It remains to say that, in addition to all these, her intellectual activities, she held her own in the fierce discussions (concerning Art) which broke out at the table or raged like whirlwinds on the moonlit bluff—discussions which centered around such questions as these: "Can a blue shadow painting ever be restful?" "Is Local Color essential to fiction?" I particularly admired the Stewardess in these moments of controversy, for she never lost her temper or her point of view.

Incredibly sweet and peaceful that week appears as I view it across the gulf which the World War has thrust between that year and this.

We had no fear of hunger in those days, no dread of social unrest, no expectation of any sudden change. All wars were over—in our opinion. The world was at last definitely at peace, and we in America, like the world in general, had nothing to do but to go on getting richer and happier, so happy that we could be just. We were all young—not one of us had gray hair. Life, for each of us as for the Nation, moved futureward on tranquil, shining course, as a river slips southward to the sea, confident, effortless, and serene. Heavenly skies, how happy we were!

That I was aware in some degree of the idyllic, evanescent charm of those days is made certain in a note which I find in my diary, the record of a walk in the woods with Zulime. Her delight in the tender loveliness of leaf and vine, in the dapple of sunlight on the path, I fully shared. Another page tells of a horseback excursion which we made across the river. She rode well, very well, indeed, and her elation, her joy in the motion of the horse, as well as her keen delight in the landscape, added to my own pleasure. We stayed to supper at the Heckmans' that night, and walked back to the camp at nine, loitering through the most magical light of the Harvest Moon.

As she manifested a delightful interest in what I was writing, I fell into the habit of reading to her some pages out of my new manuscript, in order that I might have the value of her comment on it. Of course I expected comment to be favorable, and it was. That this was an unfair advantage to take of a nice girl, I was aware, even then, but as she seemed willing to listen I was in a mood to be encouraged by her smiles and her words of praise.

My growing confidence led to an enlargement of my plans concerning the homestead. "You are right," I wrote to my mother. "A new daughter will make other improvements in the house absolutely necessary. Not merely a new dining-room, but an extra story must be added to the wing—" And in the glow of this design I reluctantly cut short my visit and returned to West Salem, to apprise the carpenters of the radical changes in my design.

Jestingly, and more by way of reconciling my mother to the renewed noise and confusion of the building, I described the walks and rides I had taken with Zulime, warning her at the same time not to enlarge upon these facts. "Miss Taft's interest may be only friendliness," I added.

My words had precisely an opposite effect: thereafter she spoke of my hopes as if they were certainties, and insisted on knowing all about "Zuleema," as she persisted in calling Miss Taft.

"Now, Mother," I again protested, "you must not talk that way to *any* of your callers, for if you do you'll get me into a most embarrassing situation. You'll make it very hard for me to explain in case of failure."

"You mustn't fail," she responded wistfully. "I can't afford to wait much longer."

It was incredible to her that any sane girl would reject such an alliance, but I was very far from her proud confidence.

In this doubt of success, I was entirely honest. I had never presumed on any manly charm, I made no claim to beauty—on the contrary, I had always been keenly aware of my rude frame and clumsy hands. I realized also my lack of nice courtesy and genial humor. Power I had (and relied upon), but of the lover's grace—nothing. That I was a bear was quite as evident to me as to my friends. "If I win this girl it must be on some other score than that of beauty," I admitted.

In the midst of the bustle and cheer of this week another swift and sinister cloud descended upon me. One evening, as mother and I were sitting together, she fell into a terrifying death-like trance from which I could not rouse her, a condition which alarmed me so deeply that I telegraphed to my father in Dakota and to my brother in Chicago, telling them to come at once. It seemed to me that the final moment of our parting was at hand.

All through that night, one of the longest I had ever known (a time of agony and remorse as well as of fear), I blamed myself for bringing on the wild disorder of the building. "If I had not gone away, if I had not enlarged my plan, the house would now be in order," was the thought which tortured me.

The sufferer's speech had failed, and her pitiful attempts to make her wishes known wrung my heart with helpless pity. Her eyes, wide, dark and beautiful, pleaded with me for help, and yet I could only kneel by her side and press her hand and repeat the doctor's words of comfort. "It will pass away, mother, just as your other attacks have done. I am sure of it. Don't try to talk. Don't worry."

As the night deepened, dark and sultry, distant flashes of silent lightning added to the lurid character of my midnight vigil. It seemed that all my plans and all my hopes had gone awry. Helpless, longing for light, I wore out the lagging hours beside my mother's bed, with very little change in her condition to relieve the strain of my anxiety. "Will she ever speak again? Have I heard her voice for the last time?" These questions came again and again to my mind.

Dawn crept into the room at last, and Franklin came on the early train. With his coming, mother regained some part of her lost courage. She grew rapidly stronger before night came again, and was able to falter a few words in greeting and to ask for father.

During the following day she steadily improved, and in the afternoon was able to sit up in her bed. One of the first of her interests was a desire to show my brother a new bonnet which I had recently purchased for her in the city, and at her request I put it into her hands.

Her love and gratitude moved us both to tears. Her action had the intolerable pathos of a child's weakness united with a kind of delirium. To watch her feeble hands exhibiting a head-dress which I feared she would never again wear—displaying it with a pitiful smile of pride and joy— was almost more than I could bear. Her face shone with happiness as she strove to tell my brother of the building I was doing to make her more comfortable. "Zuleema is coming," she said. "My new daughter—is coming."

When Franklin and I were alone for a moment, I said: "She must not die. *I won't let her die.* She must live a little longer to enjoy the new rooms I am building for her."

It would appear that the intensity of my desire, the power of my resolve to bring her back to life, strengthened her, wrought upon her with inexplicable magic, for by the time my father arrived she was able to speak and to sit once more in her wheeled chair. She even joked with me about "Zuleema."

"You'd better hurry," she said, and then the shadow came back upon me with bitter chill. How insecure her hold on life had become!

Haste on the building was now imperative—so much, at least, I could control. With one crew of carpenters, another of painters, and a third of tinners, all working at the same time, I rushed the construction forward. At times my action presented itself to me as a race against death, or at least with death's messenger. What I feared, most of all, was a sudden decline to helpless invalidism on my mother's part, a condition in which a trained nurse would be absolutely necessary. To get the rooms in order while yet our invalid was able to move about the house, was now my all-absorbing interest.

With no time to dream of love, with no thought of

writing, I toiled like a slave, wet with perspiration, dusty and unkempt. With my shirt open at the throat and my sleeves rolled to the elbow, I passed from one phase of the job to another, lending a hand here and a shoulder there. In order that I might hasten the tearing down and clearing away, I plunged into the hardest and dirtiest tasks, but at night, after the men were gone, dark moods of deep depression came over me, moments in which the essential futility of my powers overwhelmed me with something like despair.

"What right have you to ask that bright and happy girl—any girl—to share the uncertainties, the parsimony, the ineludible struggle of your disappointing life?" I demanded of myself, and to this there was but one answer: "I have no right. I have only a need."

Nevertheless, I wrote her each day a short account of my doings, and her friendly replies were a source of encouragement, of comfort. She did not know (I was careful to conceal them) the torturing anxieties through which I was passing, and her pages were, for the most part, a pleasant reflection of the uneventful, care-free routine of the camp. In spite of her caution she conveyed to me, beneath her elliptical phrases, the fact that she missed me and that my return would not be displeasing to her. "When shall we see you?" she asked.

In one of her letters she mentioned—casually—that on Monday she was going to Chicago with her sister, but would return to the camp at the end of the week.

Something in this letter led me to a sudden change of plan. As mother was now quite comfortable again I said to her, "Zuleema has gone to Chicago to do some shopping. I think I'll run down and meet her and ask her to help me select the curtains and wall-paper for your new room. What do you say to that?"

"Go along!" she said instantly, "but I expect you to bring her home with you."

"Oh, I can't do that," I protested. "I haven't any right to do that—yet!"

The mere idea of involving the girl in my household problem seemed exciting enough, and on my way down to the city I became a bit less confident. I decided to approach the matter of my shopping diplomatically. She might be alarmed at my precipitancy.

She was not alarmed—on the contrary her pleased surprise and her keen interest in my mother's new chamber gave me confidence. "I want you to help me buy the furnishings for the new rooms," I said almost at once.

"I shall be glad to help,"she replied in the most natural way.

Evidently, *she* saw nothing especially significant in my request, but to me it was a subtle stratagem. To have her take part in my bargain-hunting was almost as exciting as though we were furnishing OUR home, but I dared not assume that she was thinking along these dangerous lines. That she was genuinely interested in my household problems was evident, but I was not justified in asking anything further. She was distinctly closer to me that day, more tenderly intimate than she had ever been before, and her womanly understanding of my task—the deep sympathy she expressed when I told her of my mother's recent illness— all combined to give me comfort—and hope!

A few days later we rode back to Eagle's Nest Camp together, and all through those three hours on the train a silent, subconscious, wordless adjustment went on between us. That she was secretly debating the question of accepting me was certain, and there was nothing in her manner to dishearten me; on the contrary, she seemed to enjoy playing round the perilous suggestion.

We dined at "the Castle" as usual, and late that night,

as we walked slowly over to the camp through the odorous woods, hearing the whippoorwill's cry and the owlets hoot from their dark coverts, I was made aware that my day's work had drawn her closer into my life. I had made her aware of my need.

The day which followed our return to camp was my thirty-ninth birthday, and I celebrated it by taking a long walk and talk with her. She took some sewing with her, and as we rested under a great oak tree, we spoke of many intimate, personal things, always with the weight of our unsolved problem on our mind.

At last, in approaching my plea for help, I stated the worst of my case. "I am poor and shall always remain poor," I said. "My talent is small and my work has only a very limited appeal. I see no great improvement in my fortunes. I have done an enormous amount of work this year (I've written three volumes), but all of them conjoined will not bring in as much cash as a good stone-mason can earn. But that isn't the worst of it! The hopeless part of it is—I *like* my job. I wouldn't change to a more profitable one if I could. I have only one other way of earning money, and that is by physical labor. If the worst comes to the worst, I can farm or do carpenter work."

Her reply to all this was not entirely disheartening. "To make money is not the most important thing in the world," she said, and then told me of her own childhood in Illinois, of the rigid economies which had always been necessary in the Taft home. "My father's salary as a professor of geology was small, and with six people to feed and clothe, and four children to be educated, my poor little mother had a very busy and anxious time of it. I know by personal experience what it is to lack money for food and clothes. The length of my stay in Paris was dependent on rigid daily economy. I hadn't an extra franc to spare."

The Choice of the New Daughter

This confession of her own lifelong poverty should have turned me aside from my fell purpose, but it did not—it merely encouraged me to go on. In place of saying, "My dear girl, as compensation for all those years of care and humiliating poverty you deserve a spacious home, with servants and a carriage. Realizing that I can offer you only continued poverty and added anxiety, I here and now relinquish my design. I withdraw in favor of a better and richer man"—instead of uttering these noble words, what did I do? I did the exact opposite! I proceeded to press my selfish, remorseless, unwarranted demand!

It is customary for elderly men to refer either flippantly or with gentle humor to their days of courtship, forgetting (or ignoring) the tremulous eagerness, the grave questioning and the tender solemnity of purpose with which they weighed the joys and responsibilities of married life. It is easy to be cynical or evasive or unduly sentimental in writing of our youthful love affairs, when the frosts of sixty years have whitened our heads, after years of toil and care have dimmed our eyes and thinned our blood, but I shall permit neither of these unworthy moods to color my report of this day's emotion. I shall not deny the alternating moments of hope and doubt, of bitterness and content, which made that afternoon both sweet and sad.

The thing I was about to do was tragically destructive—I knew that. To put out a hand, to arrest this happy and tranquil girl, saying, "Come, be my wife. Come, suffer with me, starve with me," was a deed whose consequences scared me while they allured me. I felt the essential injustice of such a marriage, and I foresaw some of its accompanying perplexities, but I did not turn aside as I should have done. With no dependable source of income, with an invalid mother to care for, I asked this artist, so urban, so native to the studio, so closely knit to her joyous companions in the city, to go with me into exile, into a country town, to be the housekeeper of a commonplace cottage filled with aged people! "It is monstrous selfishness; it is wrong," I said, "but I want you."

My philosophy, even at that time, was essentially individualistic. I believed in the largest opportunity to every human soul. Equal rights *meant* Equal rights in my creed. I had no intention of asking Zulime Taft to sink her individuality in mine. I wanted her to remain herself. Marriage, as I contemplated it, was to be not a condition where the woman was a subordinate but an equal partner, and yet how unequal the sacrifice! "I ask you to join your future with mine. It's a frightful risk, but I am selfish enough to wish it."

Under no illusion about my own character, I admitted that there is no special charm in a just man. To have a sense of honor is fine, but to have a joyous and lovely disposition makes a man a great deal easier to live with. I was perfectly well aware that as a husband I would prove neither lovely nor joyous. My temper was not habitually cheerful. Like most writers, I was self-absorbed, filled with a sense of the importance of my literary designs. To be "just" was easy, but to be charming and considerate—these were the points on which I was sure to fail, and I knew it. Did that deter me? Not at all! Bitterly unwilling to surrender Zulime to the richer and kindlier man who was, undoubtedly, waiting at that moment to receive her and cherish her, I pleaded with her to share my poverty and my hope of future fame.

Shaken by my appeal, she asked for time in which to consider this problem. "I ought to talk with Lorado," she said.

The mere fact that she could not decide against me at the moment gave me confidence. "Very well," I said.

The Choice of the New Daughter

"Mother wants me—I shall go home for a week. Let me know when I can come again. I hope it will not be more than a week."

In this arrangement we rested, and as we walked back to camp I cared nothing for the sly words or glances of our fellow artists. I believed I had won my case.

My mother's demand for my presence did not arise—I soon learned—from any return of her malady, but from a desire for news of my courtship. "Where's my new daughter? Why didn't you bring her?" she demanded.

"She couldn't come this time. The question is still unsettled."

"Go right back and settle it," she urged. "Go quick, before some one else gets her. Write to her. Tell her to come right up. Send her a telegram. Seems as though I can't wait another week."

Her urgency made me laugh, even while I perceived the pathos of it. "I can't bring her to you, mother, till she is willing to come as a bride—but she's thinking about it, and I am going back next week to get my answer. Be patient a little while longer. I promise you the whole question will be settled soon, and I *hope* it will be settled our way. Zulime seems to like me."

Dear old mother! Her stammering, tremulous utterance made me smile and it made me weep. She was growing old prematurely, and the need of haste was urgent. "If I can possibly persuade her to come," I added very gravely, "I'll fetch her home to eat Thanksgiving dinner with you."

My tone, rather than my words, silenced her, and gave her a measure of content, although she was childishly impatient of even a day's delay.

All that week I alternately hoped and doubted, assembling all the items on the credit side of my ledger, and at last a letter came in which Zulime indicated that she wished to see me. "I am still undecided," she said, "but you may come." I left at once for the camp, feeling that her confession of indecision was in my favor.

Lorado was not markedly favorable to me as a brother-in-law. He liked me and respected me as a friend, but as a suitor for the hand of his sister—well, that was another and far more serious matter.

The camp "Equipage" met me at the station, and I consented to ride in it as far as the Heckman gate, hoping that Zulime would be there to welcome me. In this I was not disappointed, and something in her face and the firm clasp of her hand reassured me.

For nearly a week, in the midst of the most glorious October landscape, surrounded by the scarlet and gold and crimson branches of the maples and the deep-reds and bronze-greens of the oaks, she and I walked and rode and boated in almost constant companionship. Idyllic days! Days of a quality I had lost all hope of ever again reliving. Days of quiet happiness and almost perfect content, for on an afternoon of dreamlike beauty, in a glade radiant with hazy golden sunshine and odorous with the ripening leaves, she spoke the all-important words which joined her future life with mine.

We were seated at the moment on our favorite bank, under a tall oak tree, gorgeous as a sunset cloud, and as silent. I had been reading to her, and she was busy with some delicate embroidery. The crickets were chirping sleepily in the grass at our feet, and the jays calling harshly seemed warning us of the passing of summer and the coming on of frost.

"Let the wedding day be soon," I pleaded as we rose to return to camp. "I am nearing the dead-line. I am almost forty years old—I can't afford to wait. I want you to come to me now—at once. The old folks are waiting for you. They want you for Thanksgiving Day. Your presence would make them happier than any other good fortune in this world."

She understood my way of putting the argument. She knew that I was veiling my own eagerness under my mother's need, and after a little reflection she said, "I am going out to my father's home in Kansas. You may come for me there on the twenty-third of November. That is— if you still want me at that time."

The end of the camp season was at hand; everybody was packing up, and so my girl and I turned with deep regret from the golden halls of our sylvan meeting-place. "This is my Indian summer," I said to her, "and that you may never have cause to regret the decision which this day has brought to you, is my earnest hope."

More than twenty years have gone over our heads, and as I write these lines our silver wedding is not far off. Our lives have not been all sunshine, but Zulime has met all storms with a brave sweetness, which I cannot over-praise. If she has regrets, she does not permit me to know them. My poverty—which persists—has not embittered her or caused her, so far as I know, a single mood of self-commiseration.

CHAPTER NINE

A Judicial Wedding

ON reaching my Elm Street home the next day, I was surprised and deeply gratified to find on my desk a letter from William Dean Howells, in which he said: "I am at the Palmer House. I hope you will come to see me soon, for I start for Kansas on a lecture trip in a few days."

Although I had long been urging that he should come to Chicago, he had steadfastly declined to accept a lecture engagement west of Ohio, and I could not quite understand what had led him so far afield as Kansas. I hastened to call upon him, and, at the first appropriate pause in the conversation, I spoke to him of my engagement. "Miss Taft loves your books and would keenly appreciate the honor of meeting you."

With instant perception of my wish to have him know my future wife, he replied, "My dear fellow, I am eager to meet *her*. Perhaps my gray hairs will excuse your bringing her to call upon me."

"At your convenience," I replied eagerly. "I want you to know her. She is very much worth while."

"I am sure of that," he smilingly retorted.

He was billed to speak that night, and as he was leaving for Rock Island the following day he arranged that I should bring Zulime to the hotel just before he started for his lecture.

After telling her of his wish to see her, I explained the significance of it. "You must understand that Mr. Howells

A Judicial Wedding

is a kind of literary father confessor to me. He is a man of most delicate courtesy. Once you have seen him, once you have looked into his face, you will love him."

She was as ready as I was to take her, and promptly on the minute we sent up our names and took seats in the Ladies' Parlor. It had been years since I had entered the Palmer House, and as we waited we compared memories of its old-time splendor. "My father still regards it as the grandest hotel in the West, and it is probable that Mr. Howells knew of no other. So far as I know he has never been in Chicago before, unless possibly for a few days during the World's Fair."

Zulime was much excited at the thought of meeting the great novelist, but when he came, she took his hand with graceful composure, expressing just the right mingling of reserve and pleasure. I was proud of her, and the fact that Howells instantly and plainly approved of her, added to my satisfaction.

"I congratulate you both," he said as we were leaving. "You see," he added, addressing himself to Zulime, "your husband-elect is one of my boys. I am particularly concerned with his good fortune. I like his bringing you to see me, and I hope we shall see you both in New York."

In a literary sense this was my paternal blessing, for "Mr. Howells" had been a kind of spiritual progenitor and guide ever since my first meeting with him in '87. His wisdom, his humor, his exquisite art, had been of incalculable assistance to me, as they had been to Clemens, Burroughs, and many others of my fellow-craftsmen, and his commendation of me to my intended wife almost convinced me, for the moment, of my worthiness. How delightful he was! How delicate—how understanding! We both went away, rich in the honor of his approval of our prospective union.

Rich in his friendship, I was but poorly furnished in other

respects. I recall with shame the shopping tour which I made along State Street, searching for an engagement ring, a gauge which Zulime, knowing my poverty, stoutly insisted that she did not need—a statement which I was simple enough to believe until her sister enlightened me. "That's only Zuhl's way. Of course she wants a ring—every girl does. Don't fail to get her one—a nice one!"

I found one at last that Zulime thought I could afford. It was a small gold band with five opals, surrounded by several very minute diamonds, all of which could be had for the sum of thirty-eight dollars. As I bought this ring Zulime's girlish delight in it touched as well as instructed me. Each time she held her finger up for me to see (she had a beautiful hand) I regretted that I had not purchased a better ring. Why did I take a ring at thirty-eight dollars! Why not fifty dollars? But what could be expected of a man who never before had spent so much as one dollar on a piece of jewelry, a man whose chief way of earning money was to save it? Whenever I look at that poor little jewel now I experience a curious mingling of shame and regret. I had so little money at that time, and the future was so uncertain!

Zulime was living with her sister, and there I spent most of my evenings and some of my afternoons during the following week, scarcely able to realize my change of fortune except when alone with her, discussing our future. She agreed at last to a date for the wedding which would enable us to spend Thanksgiving at West Salem, and then for some reason, not clear to me now, I suddenly took the train for Gallup, New Mexico, with the Navajo Indian Agency for final destination.

Just why I should have chosen to visit Ganado at this precise time is inexplicable, but there is no mystery in my leaving Chicago. My future sister-in-law bluntly informed me that my absence from the city would greatly facilitate the necessary dressmaking. Although an obtuse person in some ways, I know when I am bumped. Three days after Fuller's luncheon to Howells, I reached the town of Gallup, which is the point of departure for the Navajo Agency, some twenty-five or thirty miles north of the Santa Fé railway.

For nearly ten years I had been going to the Rocky Mountains at least once during the summer season, and it is probable that I felt the need of something to offset the impressions of my tour in England and France—to lose touch with my material even for twelve months was to be cheated—then, too, I hoped in this way to shorten the weeks of waiting. Anyhow, here I was in Gallup, a drab little town which would have been a horror to my bride-elect.

One of the reasons for my being in New Mexico I am sure about. With the prospect of having some sort of an apartment in the city and a cabin at the camp, I was in the market for Navajo rugs, and silver, and Hopi pottery. It was in pursuit of these (and of literary material) that I mounted the stage the next morning and set off up the sun-lit valley to the north.

In leaving Gallup behind, my spirits rose. I wished that Zulime might have shared this strange landscape with me. On the right a distant, dimly-blue wall of mountains ran, while to the west rolled high, treeless hills, against which an occasional native hut showed like a wolf's den, half-hid among dwarf piñon trees and surrounded by naked children and savage dogs.

At intervals we came upon solitary shepherds tending their piebald flocks, as David and Abner guarded their father's sheep in Judea. That these patient shepherds, watching their lean herds, these Deborahs weaving their bright blankets beneath gnarled branches of sparse cedar trees, should be living less than forty-eight hours from Chicago, was incredible, and yet here they were! Their life and landscape, though of a texture with that of Arabia, were as real as Illinois, and every mile carried me deeper into the silence and serenity of their tribal home.

Brown boys, belted with silver and wearing shirts of gay calico, met us, riding their wiry little ponies with easy grace. Children, naked, shy as foxes, arrested their play beside dry clumps of sage-brush and stared in solemn row, whilst their wrinkled, leathery grand-sires hobbled out, cupping their thin brown hands in prayer for tobacco.

There was something Oriental, fictive in it all, and when at the end of the day I found myself a guest in a pleasant cottage at the Agency, I was fully awake to the contrasts of my "material." My ears, as well as my eyes, were open to the drama of this land whose prehistoric customs were about to pass. For the moment I was inclined to rest there and study my surroundings, but as the real objective of my journey was Ganado, about thirty miles to the west of the Fort, I decided to go on.

Ganado was the home of a famous Indian trader named Hubbell, whose store was known to me as a center of Navajo life. Toward this point I set forth a few days later, attended by a young Navajo whose *hogan* was in that direction, and who had promised to put me on my trail.

He was a fine, athletic youth of pleasant countenance, mounted upon a spotted pony and wearing a shirt of purple calico. With a belt of silver disks around his waist and a fillet of green cloth binding his glossy black hair, he was distinctly and delightfully colorful.

Our way rose at once to the level of a majestic plateau, sparsely set with pines and cedars, a barren land from which the grass and shrubs had long since been cropped by swarms of sheep and goats. Nevertheless, it was lovely to the eye, and as we rode forward we came upon a party of Navajo girls gathering piñon nuts, laughing and singing in happy abandon, untroubled by the white man's world. They greeted my guide with jests, but became very grave as he pointed out a fresh bear-track in the dust of the trail.

"Heap bears," he said to me. "Injun no kill bears. Bears big medicine," and as we rode away he laughed back at the panic-stricken girls, who were hurriedly collecting their nuts in order to flee the spot.

At last my guide halted. "I go here," he signed with graceful hand. "You keep trail; bimeby you come deep valley—stream. On left white man's house. You stop there." All of which was as plain as if in spoken words.

As I rode on alone, the peace, the poetry, the suggestive charm of that silent, lonely, radiant land took hold upon me with compelling power. Here in the midst of busy, commonplace America it lay, a section of the Polished Stone Age, retaining the most distinctive customs, songs and dances of the past. Here was a people going about its immemorial pursuits, undisturbed by the railway and the telephone. Its shepherds, like the Hittites, who wandered down from the hills upon the city of Babylon two thousand years before the Christian Era, were patriarchal and pastoral. They asked but a tent, a piece of goat's flesh, and a cool spring.

Late in the afternoon (I loitered luxuriously) I came to the summit of a long ridge which overlooked a broad, curving valley, at the far-away western rim of which a slender line of water gleamed. How beautiful it all was, but how empty! No furrow, no hut, no hint of human habitation appeared, a land which must ever be lonely, for it is without rains, and barren of streams for irrigation.

An hour later I rode up to the door of a long, low, mud-walled building, and was met by the trader, a bush-bearded, middle-aged man with piercing gray eyes and sturdy, upright figure. This was Lorenzo Hubbell, one of the best-known citizens of New Mexico, living here alone, a day's ride from a white settler.

Though hairy and spectacled he was a comparatively young man, but his mixed blood had already given him a singular power over his dark-skinned neighbors of the territory.

His wife and children were spending the summer in Alberquerque, and in the intimacy of our long days together I spoke of my approaching marriage. "I want to buy some native blankets and some Navajo silver for our new home."

His interest was quick. "Let me send your wife a wedding present. How would she like some Hopi jars?"

The off-hand way in which he used the words, "your wife," startled me—reminded me that in less than two weeks I was due at Professor Taft's home to claim my bride. I accepted his offer of the vases and began to collect silver and turquoise ornaments, in order that I might carry back to Zulime some part of the poetry of this land and its people.

"The more I think about it," I wrote to her, "the more I want you to share my knowledge of 'the High Country.' Why not put our wedding a week earlier and let me take you into the mountains? If you will advance the date to the eighteenth of November, we can have an eight-day trip in Colorado and still reach mother and the Homestead in time for Thanksgiving. I want to show you my best beloved valleys and peaks."

Though addressing the letter to her Chicago home, I knew that she was about to leave for Kansas; therefore I added a postscript: "I am planning to meet you in your father's

A Judicial Wedding

house about the eighteenth of the month, and I hope you will approve my scheme."

In the glow of my plan for a splendid Colorado wedding journey, I lost interest in Ganado and its Indians. Making arrangements for the shipment of my treasures, I saddled my horse one morning, waved Hubbell a joyous farewell, and started back toward the Agency in the hope of finding there a letter from my girl.

In this I was not disappointed. She wrote: "I shall leave for Kansas on the Burlington, Sunday night. You can write me at Hanover." It was plain she had not received my latest word.

I began to figure. "If I leave here to-morrow forenoon, and catch the express at Gallup to-morrow night, I can make the close connection at Topeka, and arrive in St. Joseph just half an hour before Zulime's train comes in on Monday morning. I shall surprise her—and delight myself —by having breakfast with her!"

However, I could not get away till morning, and with an evening to wear away I accepted the Agent's invitation to witness a native dance which had been announced to him by one of the young Navajo policemen. I had never seen a Navajo dance, and gladly accepted the opportunity to do so.

It was a clear, crisp November evening as we started out, the clerk, his sister, one of the teachers and myself riding in a two-seated open wagon, drawn by a pair of spirited horses. The native village was some ten miles to the north, and all the way up hill, so that before we came in sight of it darkness had fallen, and in the light of a bonfire the dancers were assembling.

Of the village, if there was a village, I could see little, but a tall old man (the town crier) was chanting an invitation or command of some sort, and dark forms were moving to and fro among the shadows of the piñon trees. How remote it all was from the white man's world, how self-sufficing and peaceful—how idyllic!

The master of ceremonies met us and gave us seats, and for three hours we sat in the glow of the fire, watching the youthful, tireless dancers circle and leap in monotonous yet graceful evolutions. Here was love and courtship, and jealousy and faithful friendship, just as among the white dancers of Neshonoc. Roguish black eyes gleamed in the light of the fire, small feet beat the earth in joyous rhythm, and the calm faces of the old men lent dignity and a kind of religious significance to the scene. They were dreaming of the past, when no white man had entered their world.

The young people were almost equally indifferent to us, and as the night deepened we who were white merged more and more indistinguishably with the crowd of dusky on-lookers. It was easy to imagine ourselves back in the sixteenth century, looking upon this scene from the wondering viewpoint of the Spanish explorers. Whence came these people, these dances, these ceremonials?

At last the time came for us to set forth upon our long ride back to the Agency, and so, silently, we rose and slipped away into the darkness, leaving the dancers to end their immemorial festival without the aliens' presence. They had no need of us, no care for us. At a little distance I turned and looked back. The songs, interrupted by shrill, wolfish howlings and owl-like hootings, rang through the night with singular savage charm, a chant out of the past, a chorus which was carrying forward into an individualistic white man's world the voices of the indeterminate tribal past.

The sky was moonless, the air frosty, and after we had entered the narrow cañon, which was several miles long and very steep, the clerk, who was not very skilled with horses, turned the reins over to me, and for an hour or more I drove with one foot on the brake, trusting mainly to the horses to find their way. It was bitter cold in the cañon, and my cramped right leg became lame—so lame that I could hardly get out of the wagon after we reached the Agency. Excruciating pain developed in the sciatic nerve, and though I passed a sleepless night I was determined to leave next morning. "I shall go if I have to be carried to my horse," I said grimly to the clerk, who begged me to stay in bed.

Fortunately, the trader was going to the railway and kindly offered to take me with him; and so, laden with Navajo silver (bracelets, buckles and rings), I started out, so lame that I dragged one leg with a groan, hoping that with the warmth of the sun my pain would pass away.

Reaching Gallup at noon, I spent the afternoon sitting in the sun, waiting for the train. At six o'clock it came, and soon I was washed and shaved and eating dinner on the dining-car of the Continental Limited.

All that night and all the next day and far into the second night I rode, my fear of missing connection at Topeka uniting with my rheumatism to make the hours seem of interminable length. It semed at times a long, long "shot" —but I made it! I reached the station at Topeka just in time to catch the connecting train, and I was on the plat-form at St. Joseph at sun-rise a full half-hour before the Burlington coaches from Chicago were due.

As I walked up and down, I smiled with anticipation of the surprise I had in store. "If she keeps her schedule I shall see her step from the Pullman car without the slightest suspicion that I am within six hundred miles of her," I thought, doing my best to walk the kink out of my leg, which was still painful. "She is coming! My wife is coming!" I repeated, incredulous of the fact.

At eight o'clock the engine came nosing in, and while

watching the line of passengers descend, I lost hope. It
was too much to expect!

She was there! I saw her as she stepped down from
the rear Pullman, and just as she was about to take her
valise from the porter, I touched her on the shoulder and
said, "I'll take charge of that."

She started and turned with a look of alarm, a look which
changed to amazement, to delight. "Oh!" she gasped.
"Where did *you* come from?"

"From the Navajo reservation," I replied calmly.

"But how did you *get here?*"

"By train, like yourself."

"But when—how long ago?"

"About thirty minutes," I laughed. "I'm a wizard at
making close connections." Then, seeing that she must
know all about it at once, I added, "Come into the station
restaurant, and while we are eating breakfast I will tell
you where I have been and what brought me back so soon."

While waiting for our coffee I took from my valise a
bracelet of silver, a broad band shaped and ornamented
by some Navajo silversmith. "Hold out your arm," I commanded. She obeyed, and I clasped the barbaric gyve about
her wrist. "That is a sign of your slavery," I said gravely.

Smilingly, meditatively, she fingered it, realizing dimly
the grim truth which ran beneath my jesting. She was
about to take on a relationship which must inevitably bring
work and worry as well as joy.

(That silver band has never left her wrist for a moment.
For twenty-two years she has worn it, keeping it bright
with service for me, for her children and for her friends.
There is something symbolic in the fact that it has never
lost its clear luster and that it has never tarnished the arm
it adorns.)

Her joy in this present, her astonishment at my un-

expected appearance on the railway platform, amused and
delighted me. I could scarcely convince her that at six
o'clock on Saturday night I was in a New Mexico town,
waiting for the eastern express. It was all a piece of miraculous adventure on my part, but her evident pleasure in
its successful working out made me rich—and very humble.
"What did you do it for?" she asked; then, with a look of
dismay, she added, "What am I going to do with you in
Hanover?"

"I think I can find something to do," I answered, and
entered upon a detailed statement of my plan. "I want
you to see the mountains. We'll set our wedding day for
the eighteenth—that will give us a week in Colorado, and
enable us to eat Thanksgiving dinner with the old folks at
the homestead. You say you have never seen a real mountain—well, here's your chance! Say the word, and I'll take
you into the heart of the San Juan Range. I'll show you
the splendors of Ouray and the Uncompagre."

Holding the floor, in order that she might not have a
chance to protest, I spread an alluring panorama of peaks
and valleys before her eyes, with an eloquence which I
intended should overcome every objection. That she was
giving way to my appeal was evident. Her negatives, when
they came, were rather feeble. "I can't do it. It would
be lovely, but—oh, it is impossible!"

"It is done—it is arranged!" I replied. "I have already
sent for the railway tickets. They will be at your home
to-morrow night. All is settled. We are to be married on
the eighteenth, and——"

"But our cards are all in Chicago and printed for the
twenty-third!"

"What of that? Get some more—or, better still, forget
'em! We don't need cards."

"But—my sewing?"

"Never mind your sewing. Would you let a gown come between you and a chance to see the Needle Peaks? I am determined that you shall see Ouray, Red Mountain, and the San Juan Divide."

At last she said, "I'll think about it."

She was obliged to think about it. All the forenoon, as the train ambled over the plain toward the village in which Professor Taft had established his bank, I kept it in her mind. "It may be a long time before we have another chance to visit Colorado. It will be glorious winter up there. Think of Marshall Pass, think of Uncompagre, think of the Toltec Gorge!" My enthusiasm mounted. "Ouray will be like a town in the Andes. We must plan to stay there at least two days."

She fell into silence, a dazed yet smiling silence, but when at last I said, "Every hour in the low country is a loss— let's be married to-morrow," she shook her head. I had gone too far.

She confessed that a stay in Hanover was in the nature of a punishment. "I never liked it here, and neither did my little mother," she said, and then she described her mother's life in Hanover. "I was called home to nurse her in the last days of her illness," she explained. "Poor little mamma! She came out here unwillingly in the first place, and I always resented her living so far away from the city. After her death I seldom came here. Father does not care. He is so absorbed in his business and in his books that it doesn't matter where he lives."

Professor Taft and his son, Florizel, were both at the train to meet Zulime, and both were properly amazed when I appeared. As a totally unexpected guest I was a calamity —but they greeted me cordially. What Zulime said in explanation of my presence I do not know, but the family accepted me as an inevitable complication.

A Judicial Wedding

My lameness, which dated from that ride down the Navajo cañon, persisted, which was another worriment; for Zulime was too busy with sewing-women to give much time to me and walking was very painful, hence I spent most of my day down at the bank, talking with my prospective father-in-law, who interested me much more than the sordid little village and its empty landscape. He was a sturdy, slow-moving man with long, gray beard, a powerful and strongly individual thinker, almost as alien to his surroundings as a Hindoo Yoghi would have been. With the bland air of a kindly teacher he met his customers in the outer office and genially discoursed to them of whatever happened to be in his own mind—what they were thinking about was of small account to him.

As a deeply-studied philosopher of the old-fashioned sort, his words, even when addresesd to a German farmer, were deliberately chosen, and his sentences stately, sonorous and precise. Regarding me as a man of books, he permitted himself to roam widely over the fields of medieval history, and to wander amid the gardens of ancient faiths and dimly remembered thrones.

Although enormously learned, his knowledge was expressed in terms of the past. His quotations, I soon discovered, were almost entirely confined to books whose covers were of a faded brown. His scientists, his historians were all of the Victorian age or antecedent thereto. Breasted and Ferrero did not concern him. His biologists were of the time of Darwin, his poets of an age still earlier, and yet, in spite of his musty citations, he was a master mind. He knew what he knew (he guessed at nothing), and, sitting there in that bare little bank, I listened in silence what time he marched from Zoroaster down to Charlemagne, and from Rome to Paris. He quoted from Buckle and Bacon and Macaulay till I marveled at the contrast between his great shaggy head and its common-place surroundings, for in the midst of a discussion of the bleak problems of Agnosticism, or while considering Gibbon's contribution to the world's stock of historical knowledge, certain weather-worn Bavarian farmers came and went, studying us with half-stupid, half-suspicious glances, having no more kinship with Don Carlos Taft than so many Comanches.

It is probable that the lonely old scholar rejoiced in me as a comprehending, or at least a sympathetic, listener, for he talked on and on, a steady, slow-moving stream. I was content to listen. That I allowed him to think of me as a fellow-student, I confess, but in my failure to undeceive him I was only adding to the comfort which he took in my company. It would have been a cruelty to have confessed my ignorance. It was after all only a negative deception, one which did neither of us any harm.

Furthermore, I was aware that he was in a sense "trying me out." He not only wanted to measure my understanding—he was especially eager to know what my "religion" was. He dreaded to find me a sectarian, and when he discovered that I, too, was a student of Darwin and a disciple of Herbert Spencer, he frankly expressed his pleasure. He rejoiced, also, in the fact that I was earning my own living, and to him I seemed to be in possession of a noble income. With all his love of scholarship he remained the thrifty son of New England.

Here again I fear I permitted him to assume too much, but when one's prospective father-in-law is asking how one expects to support a wife, one is tempted to give a slightly more favorable report than the conditions will warrant. I explained my contract with Macmillans, and named the prices I obtained for my stories, and with these he was properly impressed. It was absurd yet gratifying to have

A Judicial Wedding

a son-in-law who could sell "lies" for hard cash, and his respect for me increased.

As we walked homeward that night, I expressed my wish to have the marriage a judicial ceremony. "I make no objection to having the service read by a clergyman," I explained, "but I prefer to employ the highest legal authority in the county—a judge, if possible. However, I will leave it all to Zulime. As an individualist I consider her a full and equal partner in all phases of this enterprise. I do not expect her to even promise to obey me, but I hope she will always find my requests reasonable—if she does not, she has the right to ignore them. Her signature shall be as good as mine at the bank."

This statement startled the banker, for he held rather old-fashioned ideas concerning women and money; but Zulime was his favorite child, and he hastened to assure me that she would not waste my substance. "I think we can induce the district judge to come over and perform the ceremony," he concluded.

If my notion to employ a judge of the district shocked my bride, she artfully deceived me, for she cheerfully consented, and a day or two later, with her brother Florizel for a guide, I drove over to the county town and laid my request before Judge Sturgis of the District Court.

The judge knew Don Carlos and (as a reader of the magazines) had some knowledge of me; therefore he at once declared his willingness to assist. "It will be an honor," he added heartily; "I'll adjourn court if necessary. You may depend on me."

He also agreed to meet our wishes as to the character of the ceremony. "I'll make it as short as you like," he said. "I'll reduce it to its lowest legal terms," and with this understanding I procured my license and returned to Hanover.

In spite of all these practical details the whole adventure seemed curiously unreal, as though it concerned some other individual, some character in one of my novels. It was a play in which I acted as manager rather than as leading man. There was nothing in all this preparation which remotely suggested any of the weddings in which I had been concerned as witness, and I suspect that Zulime was almost equally unconvinced of its reality. Poor girl! It was all as far from the wedding of her girlish dreams as her bridegroom fell short of the silver-clad knight of romance, but I promised her that she would find something grandiose and colorful in our wedding journey. "Our wedding will be prosaic, but wait until you see the sunset light on the Crestones! Our week in the High Country shall be a poem."

This was a characteristic attitude with me. I was always saying, "Wait! These flowers *are* lovely, but those just ahead of us are more beautiful still." Zulime's attitude, as I soon discovered, was precisely opposite: "Let us make the most of the flowers at our hand," was her motto.

The Taft home had something of the same unesthetic quality which marked Neshonoc. It was simple, comfortable, and entirely New England. Throughout the stern vicissitudes of his life on the Middle Border, Don Carlos Taft had carried the memories and the accents of his New Hampshire town. His beginnings had been as laboriously difficult as those of my father. In many ways they were alike; that is to say, they were both Yankee in training and tradition.

At last the epoch-marking day came marching across the eastern plain. The inevitable bustle began with the dawn. I packed my trunk and dispatched it to the station in confident expectation of our mid-afternoon departure, and Zulime did the same, although it must have seemed more illusory to her than to me. The Judge arrived precisely at noon, and at half-past twelve the family solemnly gathered in the living-room, and there, in plain traveling garb, Zulime Taft stood up with me, while the Judge gravely initiated her into a perilous partnership, a coalition in which she took the heaviest chances of sorrow and regret.

The Judge was as good as his word. He made the ceremony a short but very serious interchange of intentions, and at last, in sonorous and solemn tones, pronounced us man and wife.

Altogether, it did not take five minutes, and then, at twelve-forty, while the man of law was writing out the certificate, the "breakfast" was announced and we all sat down to what was really a dinner, a meal to which the Judge did full justice, for he had been up since early morning, and had ridden twelve or fifteen miles.

If the old professor retained any anxieties concerning his daughter's future, he masked them with a smile and discoursed genially of the campaigns of Cyrus—or some such matter. At the close of the meal, the Judge, comfortable and friendly, rose to go. With him, he said, it had not only been a duty but a pleasure, and as he had given to our brief wedding just the right touch of dignity, we were grateful to him. It was the kind of service which cannot be obtained by any fee.

At four o'clock we took a dusty, hesitating local train for the small town in Nebraska where we expected to catch the express for Colorado Springs. In such drab and unromantic fashion did Zulime Taft and Hamlin Garland begin their long journey together. "But wait!" I repeated. "Wait till you see the Royal Gorge and Shavano!"

CHAPTER TEN

The New Daughter and Thanks-giving

AT about half-past seven of a clear November morning I called my bride to the car window and presented to her, with the air of a resident proprietor, a first view of Pike's Peak, a vast silver dome rising grandly above the Rampart Range. "Well, there it is," I remarked. "What do you think of it?"

Her cry of surprise and her words of delight were both entirely genuine. "Oh, how beautiful!" she exclaimed, as soon as she recovered breath.

It *was* beautiful. Snow covered, flaming like burnished marble, the range, with high summits sharply set against the cloudless sky, upreared in austere majesty, each bleak crag gilded with the first rays of the morning sun. Above the warm, brown plain the giants towered remotely alien, like ancient kings on purple thrones, and the contrast of their gleaming drifts of snow, with the dry, grassy foothills through which we were winding our way, was like that of deep winter set opposite to early September. However, I would not permit Zulime to exhaust her vocabulary of admiration. "Keep some of your adjectives till we reach Ouray," I said with significant gravity.

Before the train came to a stop at the platform of Colorado Springs, I caught sight of the red, good-humored face of Gustave, coachman for Louis Ehrich, one of my Colorado friends. Gustave was standing beside the road wagon in which I had so often ridden, and when he saw me alight he motioned to me. "You are to come with me," he explained as I approached. "I have orders to bring you at once to the house—breakfast is waiting for you."

I had written to the Ehrichs, saying that my wife would be with me in the Springs for a few days, and that I wanted them to meet her—but I did not expect to be met or to receive an invitation to breakfast.

Zulime hesitated till I assured her that the Ehrichs were old friends and not the kind of people who say one thing and mean another. "They will never permit us to go to the hotel—I know them." With that she consented, and fifteen minutes later Louis and Henriette met us at their threshold and took Zulime to their hearts, as though they had known her for years.

The house stood on the bank of a stream, and, from the windows of the room they gave us, the Lord of the Range loomed in distant majesty directly above the Garden of the Gods, and our first day of married life was filled with splendor. Each hour of that day had for us its own magical color, its own drama of flying cloud and resisting rock. From the commonplace Kansas village we had been transported as if by an enchanted carpet to a land of beauty and romance, of changeful charm, a region of which I was even then beginning to write with joyous inspiration. That my bride and I would forever recall this day and this house with gratitude and delight I was even then aware.

"This compensates for the humble scene of our wedding, doesn't it?" I demanded.

"It is more than I dreamed of having," she replied.

In truth no blood relations could have been more sympathetic, more generous, more considerate than the Ehrichs. They rejoiced in us. Skilled and happy hosts, they did their utmost to make our honeymoon an unforgettable ex-

perience. Each hour of our stay was arranged with kind-
ness. We drove, we ate, we listened to music, with a
grateful wonder at our good fortune.

They would have kept us indefinitely had I not carefully
explained my plan to show my bride the Crestones and
Marshall Pass. "We must make the Big Circle and get
back to Wisconsin in time for Thanksgiving," I said to
Louis, who, as a loyal Colorado man, immediately granted
the force of this excuse. He understood also the pathos of
the old mother in West Salem, watching, waiting, longing
to see her new daughter. "You are right," he said. "To
fail of that dinner would be cruel."

That night we took the Narrow Gauge train, bound for
Marshall Pass and the splendors of the Continental Divide.

At daylight the next morning we were looping our way
up the breast of Mount Shavano, leaving behind us in
splendid changing vista the College Range, from whose lofty
summits long streamers of snow wavered like prodigious
silver banners. Unearthly, radiant as the walls of the sun,
lonely and cold they stood. For three hours we moved
amid colossal drifts and silent forests, and then, toward
midday, our train plunged into the snow-sheds of the high
divide. When we emerged we were sliding swiftly down
into a sun-warmed valley sloping to the west, where hills
as lovely as jewels alternated with smooth opalescent mesas
over which white clouds gleamed. The whole wide basin
glowed with August colors, and yet from Montrose Junction,
where we lunched, the rugged slopes of Uncompagre, hooded
with snow and dark with storms, were plainly visible, so
violently dramatic was the land.

"From here we proceed directly toward those peaks,"
I explained to Zulime, who was in awe of the land I was
exhibiting.

As we approached the gateway to Ouray, the great white

flakes began to fall athwart the pines, and when we entered the prodigious amphitheater in which the town is built, we found ourselves again in mid-winter, surrounded by icy cliffs and rimy firs. Dazzling drifts covered the rocks and almost buried the cottages from whose small windows, lights twinkled like gleaming eyes of strange and roguish animals. Every detail was as harmonious as an ideally conceived Christmas card. It was the antithesis of Kansas.

Upon entering our room at the hotel, I exultantly drew Zulime's attention to the fact that the sky-line of the mountains to the South cut across the upper row of our window panes. "You are in the heart of the Rockies now," I declared as if somehow that fact exalted me in her regard.

When we stepped into the street next morning, the snow had ceased to fall, but the sky was magnificently, grandly savage. Great clouds in career across the valley momentarily caught and clung to the crags, but let fall no frost, and as the sun rose laggardly above the dazzlingly white wall, the snow-laden pines on the lower slopes appeared delicate as lace with distance. At intervals enormous masses of vapor, gray-white but richly shot with lavender, slid suddenly in, filling the amphitheater till all its walls were hid, then quite as suddenly shifted and streamed away. From time to time vistas opened toward the west, wondrous aisles of blinding splendor, highways leading downward to the glowing, half-hid, irridescent plain. In all my experience of the mountains I had never seen anything more gorgeous, more stupendous—what it must have meant to my bride, who had never seen a hill, I can only faintly divine.

At two o'clock, the sky having cleared, I hired a team and sleigh, and we drove up the high-climbing mining trail which leads toward Telluride, a drive which in itself was worth a thousand-mile journey, an experience to be remembered all our lives. Such majesty of silent, sunny cliffs!

Such exquisite tones, such balance of lights and shadows, such tracery of snow-laden boughs! It was impossible for my lowland bride to conceive of any mountain scene more gorgeous, more sumptuous, more imperial.

For two hours we climbed, and then, at a point close to timber-line, I reluctantly halted. "We must turn here," I said regretfully. "It will be dark by the time we reach the hotel."

Slowly we rode back down the valley, entranced, almost oppressed, by the incommunicable splendor of forested hills and sunset sky. It was with a sense of actual relief that we reëntered our apartment. Our eyes ached with the effort to seize and retain the radiance without, and our minds, gorged with magnificence, were grateful for the subdued light, the ugly furniture, the dingy walls of our commonplace little hotel.

To some of my readers, no doubt, this wedding trip will seem a lunatic, extravagant fantasy on my part; but Zulime declared herself grateful to me for having insisted upon it, and for three days we walked and drove by daylight or by moonlight amid these grandiose scenes, absorbing with eager senses the sounds, sights and colors which we might never again enjoy, returning now and then to a discussion of our future.

"We'll go East after our visit to the old folks," I declared. "This is only the first half of our wedding journey; the other part shall include Washington, Boston, and New York."

Zulime looked somewhat incredulous (she didn't know me yet), but her eyes glowed with pleasure at the thought of the capital, of which she knew nothing, and of New York, which she knew only as a seaport. "I thought you were poor," she said.

"So I am," I replied, "but I intend to educate you in American geography."

The New Daughter and Thanksgiving

The railway enters the Ouray amphitheater from the west and stops—for the very good reason that it can go no farther!—but from the railway station a stage road climbs the precipitous eastern wall and leads on to Red Mountain, as through an Alpine pass. Over this divide I now planned to drive to Silverton, and thence to Durango by way of Las Animas Cañon. Zulime, with an unquestioning faith in me—a faith which I now think of with wonder—agreed to this crazy plan. Her ignorance of the cold, the danger involved, made her girlishly eager to set forth. She was like a child in her reliance on my sagacity and skill.

We left Ouray, at eight of a bitter morning, in a rude sleigh with only a couple of cotton quilts to defend us from the cold, and when, after a long climb up a wall of stupendous cliffs with roaring streams shouting from their icy beds upon our right, we entered an aisle of frosty pines edging an enormous ledge, where frozen rills hung in motionless cascades, Zulime, enraptured by the radiant avenues which opened out at every turn of our icy upward trail, became blind to all danger. The flaming, golden light flinging violet shadows, vivid as stains of ink along the crusted slopes, dazzled her, caused her to forget the icy wind or, at any rate, to patiently endure it.

At Red Mountain, a mournful, half-buried, deserted mining town, we left our sleigh and stumbled into the dingy little railway station, so chilled, so cramped, that we could scarcely walk, and yet we did not regret our ride. However, we were glad of the warmth of the dirty little coach into which we climbed a few minutes later. It seemed delightfully safe to Zulime, and I was careful not to let her know that from this town the train descended of its own weight all the way to Silverton!

Fortunately, nothing happened, and at Silverton we changed to a real train, with a real engine, and as we dropped into Las Animas Cañon we left December behind.

145

At six o'clock we emerged from the cañon at Durango into genial September—or so it seemed after our day of mid-winter in the heights. Next day we returned to Colorado Springs.

Our stay in the mountains was at an end, but the memory of those burnished domes, those dark-hued forests, and the sound of those foaming streams, remain with us to this day.—All the way down the long slope to the Mississippi River, we reverted to this "circuit," recalling its most impressive moments, its noblest vistas. It had been for my bride a procession of wonders, a colossal pageant—to me it was a double satisfaction because of her delight. With a feeling that I had in some degree atoned for my parsimony in the matter of an engagement ring and for the drab prose of our marriage ceremony, I brought the first half of our wedding journey to a close in Chicago.

I now looked forward to the meeting between my mother and her new daughter. This was, after all, the important part of my venture. Would my humble home content my artist bride?

In preparation I began to sing small. "Don't expect too much of the Garland Homestead," I repeated. "It is only an angular, slate-colored farm-house without a particle of charm outside or in. It is very far from being the home I should like you to be mistress of, and my people you must bear in mind, are pioneers, survivals of the Border. They are remote from all things urban."

To this the New Daughter responded loyally, "I am sure I shall like your home and I *know* I shall love your mother."

As women of her race have done from the most immemorial times, she had left her own tribe and was about to enter the camp of her captor, but she pretended to happiness, resolute to make the best of whatever came.

Our friends in Chicago smiled when I told them where we had been. Lorado said, "A Honeymoon in the heart of the

Rockies is just like you"—but I cared nothing for his gibes so long as Zulime was content, and I had but to over-hear her account of her trip to be reassured. To her it had been a noble exploration into a marvelous country.

This was the day before Thanksgiving, and with a knowledge that the old folks were counting the hours which intervened, I wrested Zulime from her friends, and hurried her to the train. "Dear old mother! I know just how she is waiting and watching for you. We must not fail her."

It was just daylight as we stepped down from the Pullman at West Salem, but father was there! Seated in our "canopy-top surrey" and holding restless ramping Black Dolly to her place, he was too busy to glance at us, but I could tell, by the set of his head, that he was emotionally intense.

"There's your new father," I said, pointing him out to Zulime, "and that is your family coach."

Father couldn't even shake hands, for Dolly was still pawing and plunging but he smiled as we approached and called out in reference to Dolly, "She'll quiet down in a minute."

While the train was pulling out I explained to Zulime that Dolly's fury was all assumed. "She'll soon be stolid as a stump."

It wasn't in the least the tender meeting I had expected to enjoy, but when at last my father was able to reach his hand down to Zulime, he said, "I'm glad to meet you, my daughter," and the tenderness in his vibrant voice touched me. "We were afraid you weren't coming," he added, and a little later I saw him wipe the tears from his eyes. The fact that he used a bandanna for this purpose, did not destroy the moving quality of his emotion.

The village looked woefully drab and desolate under that misty November sky. The elm trees, stripped of every leaf, the gardens weedy, ragged and forlorn, together with the ugly little houses suggested the sordid reality of the life to which I had brought my bride. It was all a far cry from the towering cliffs and colorful cañons of Colorado.

The Homestead shared in the general ugliness of that rain-swept dawn. Its maples were gaunt skeletons, its garden a sodden field over which the chickens were wandering in sad and aimless fashion. To my city-bred wife this home-coming must have been a cruel shock, but it was the best I could do, and whatever the girl felt, she concealed with a smile, resolute to make the best of me and mine.

Mother was waiting for us on the porch, tremulous with excitement, too eager to remain in doors, and as I took her in my arms, and kissed her, I said, "Mother, I've brought your new daughter."

For just a moment she hesitated (the grace and dignity of the tall girl awed her, confused her), then Zulime went to her, and the two women, so diverse, yet so dear to me, met in an embrace of mutual love and confidence.

Isabel Garland entered into possession of the daughter she had so long hoped for, and Zulime Taft became a member of the household of which Richard Garland was the head.

Breakfast was waiting for us, a noble meal, a sumptuous wedding breakfast, for mother and her two helpers (daughters of a neighboring farmer), had been up since five o'clock and while it was a good deal like a farmer's Sunday dinner, Zulime thanked the girls when father presented them to her, but was a bit startled when one of them took her seat at the table with us. She was not accustomed to this democratic custom of the village.

My aunt, Susan Bailey, a gentle, frail little body also joined our circle, adding one more pair of eyes to those whose scrutiny must have been somewhat trying to the bride. To meet these blunt, forthright folk at such a table without betraying amusement or surprise, required tact, but the New Daughter succeeded in winning them all, even Mary, the cook, who was decidedly difficult.

Almost immediately after taking his seat my father began: "Well now, daughter, you are the captain. Right here I abdicate. Anything you want done shall be done. What you say about things in the kitchen shall be law. I will furnish the raw materials—you and the girls must do the rest. We like to be bossed, don't we, Belle?" He ended addressing mother.

In her concise, simple fashion, she replied: "Yes, the house is yours. I turn it all over to you."

It was evident that all this had been discussed many times for they seemed in haste to get its statement off their minds, and I could not check them or turn them aside.

Zulime made light of it. "I'd rather not *be* captain," she laughingly protested. "I'd rather be passenger for a while."

Father was firm. "No, we need a commanding officer, and you must take charge. Now I've got a turkey out there—and cranberries—" He was off! He told just what he had laid in for the dinner, and ended by saying, "If there's anything I've forgot, you just let me know, and I'll go right up town and get it."

As he talked, the tones of his resonant voice, the motions of his hands, the poise of his head, brought back to me a boyish feeling of subordination. I laughed, but I submitted to his domination, entirely willing that he should play the part of the commander for the last time. It was amusing, but it had its pathetic side for my mother's silence was significant of her weakness. She said nothing—not a word, but with Zulime sitting beside her, she was content, so happy she could not find words in which to express her satisfaction. Her waiting was at an end!

My father made a handsome picture. His abundant white hair, his shapely beard, and his keen profile pleased me. Though a little stooped, he was still alert and graceful, and his voice rang like a trumpet as he entered upon an account of his pioneer experiences.

"I've always lived on the Border," he explained, "and I don't know much about the ways of city folks, so you must excuse me when I do the wrong thing. My will is the best in the world, and I'll do anything I can to please you."

That breakfast was the exact opposite of a "Continental Breakfast." Steak, doughnuts, buckwheat cakes, cookies, apple sauce made me groan but Zulime smiled. She understood the care which had gone into its making.

When at last she and I were alone in my study I began, "Well, how do you like West Salem and the Garlands?"

"Your mother is a dear!" she replied, and her voice was convincing—"and I like your father. He's very good looking. And the breakfast was—well it was like one of your stories—Do you *always* have steak and doughnuts for breakfast?"

"No," I replied, "not always, but breakfast is a real meal with us."

The sky darkened and a sleety rain set in during the forenoon, but mother did not mind the gloom outside, for within she had her daughter. Upon our return to the sitting room, she led Zulime out into the kitchen to take account of all that was going on for dinner, and while the maids, with excited faces stood about waiting for orders from their new boss, Zulime laughingly protested that she had no wish to interfere. "Go on in your own way," she said.

To me, on her return to the sitting room, she exclaimed: "You should see the food in preparation out there! Enough to feed all the Eagle's Nest campers.—How many are coming to dinner?"

"No one but the McClintocks—and only a few of them,"

I soberly replied. "Uncle William and Aunt Maria, Frank and Lorette—and Deborah, all old people now. I don't know of any one else." In fact, we had less than this number, for Maria was not well enough to come out in the rain.

Our circle was small, but the spirit of Thanksgiving was over it, and when I saw my stately city wife sitting among my rough-hewn relations, listening to the quaint stories of Uncle Frank, or laughing at the humorous sallies of Aunt Lorette, I wondered what they thought of her. She made a lovely picture, and all—even caustic Deborah— capitulated to her kindliness and charm. If she had failed of complete comprehension and sympathy I could not have blamed her, but to have her perfectly at home among these men and women of the vanishing Border displayed her in a new and noble guise.

If anything was lacking—any least quality of adaptation, it was supplied when, that evening, my uncles and my father discovered that Zulime could not only read music, but that she could play all the old songs which they loved to have me sing. This accomplishment completed their conquest, for under her deft hands the piano revived the wistful melodies of *Minnie Minturn*, *Maggie,* and *Nellie Wildwood,* and when my mother's voice, sweet as ever, but weak and hesitant, joined with mine in singing for our guests, I was both glad and sad, glad of my young wife, sad with a realization of my mother's weakness and age.

She did not reproach me for not bringing the daughter sooner. She had but one regret. "I wish Frank was here," she said, her thought going out to her other son.

How far away, how remote, how tender that evening seems to me after more than twenty years work and travel! To Zulime it unrolled like a scene from one of my novels, to me it was the closing, fading picture of an era, the end of an epoch, the passing of a race, for the Garlands and Mc-

Clintocks, warriors of the western conquest, representatives of a heroic generation were even then basking in the light of a dying. camp-fire, recounting the deeds of brave days gone.

When we were again alone in my study, Zulime said, "I'm going to enjoy it here. I like your people, and I hope they liked me."

*   *   *   *   *   *

It was in this humble fashion that I brought to my mother the new daughter for whom she had longed, and it was in this homely way that the Garlands and McClintocks received my wife. Amid surroundings which were without grace of art or touch of poetry, the informal and very plain ceremony took place, but the words were sincere, and the forms and features of the speakers deeply significant of the past. No matter what my mother's storms and sorrows had been, she was now at peace. With a smiling face she confronted the future.

CHAPTER ELEVEN

My Father's Inheritance

A T half-past six on the morning following our arrival at the Homestead, my father opened the stairway door and shouted, just as he had been wont to do in the days when I was a boy on the farm—"Hamlin! Time to get up!" and with a wry grin I called to Zulime and explained, "In our family, breakfast is a full and regular meal at which every member of the household is expected promptly at seven."

It was not yet fully dawn and the thought of rising in a cold room at that time of night was appalling to a city woman, but with heroic resolution Zulime dressed, and followed me down the narrow stairway to the lamp-lit dining-room, where a steaming throng of dishes, containing oatmeal, potatoes, flap-jacks and sausage (supplemented by cookies, doughnuts and two kinds of jam), invited us to start the day with indigestion.

The dim yellow light of the kerosene lamp, the familiar smell of the buckwheat cakes and my father's clarion voice brought back to me very vividly and with a curious pang of mingled pleasure and regret, the corn-husking days when I habitually ate by candlelight in order to reach the field by daybreak. I recalled to my father's memory one sadly-remembered Thanksgiving Day when he forced us all to husk corn from dawn to sunset in order that we might finish the harvest before the snowstorm covered the fallen stalks. "But mother's turkey dinner saved the day," I remarked to

Zulime. "Nothing can ever taste so good as that meal. As we came into the house, cold, famished and weary, the smell of the kitchen was celestial."

My mother smiled but father explained in justification, "I could feel a storm in the air and I knew that we had just time to reach the last row if we all worked, and worked hard. As a matter of fact we were all done at four o'clock."

"O, we worked!" I interpolated. "Frank and I had no vote in those days."

During the week which followed, most of my relatives, and a good many of the neighbors, called on us, and as a result Zulime spent several highly educational afternoons listening to the candid comments of elderly widows and sharp-eyed old maids. Furthermore, being possessed of a most excellent digestion, she was able to accept the daily invitations to supper, at which rich cakes and home-made jams abounded. She was also called upon to examine "hand-made paintings in oil," which she did with tender care. No one could have detected in her smile anything less than kindly interest in the quaint interior decorations of the homes. Her comment to me was a different matter.

That she was an object of commiseration on the part of the women I soon learned, for Mrs. Dunlap was overheard to say, "She's altogether too good for him" (meaning me), and Mrs. McIlvane, with the candor of a life-long friendship, replied, "That's what I told Belle."

Uncle William, notwithstanding a liking for me, remarked with feeling, "She's a wonder! I don't see how you got her."

To which I replied, "Neither do I."

In setting down these derogatory comments I do not wish to imply that I was positively detested but that I was not a beloved county institution was soon evident to my wife. Delegations of school children did not call upon me, and very few of my fellow citizens pointed out my house to travelers—at that time. In truth little of New England's regard for authorship existed in the valley and my head possessed no literary aureole. The fact that I could—and did—send away bundles of manuscript and get in return perfectly good checks for them, was a miracle of doubtful virtue to my relatives as well as to my neighbors. My money came as if by magic, unasked and unwarranted, like the gold of sunset. "I don't see how you do it," my Uncle Frank said to me one day, and his tone implied that he considered my authorship a questionable kind of legerdemain, as if I were, somehow, getting money under false pretenses.

Rightly or wrongly, I had never pretended to a keen concern in the "social doings" of my village. Coming to the valley out of regard for my father and mother and not from personal choice, the only folk who engaged my attention were the men and women of the elder generation, rugged pioneer folk who brought down to me something of the humor, the poetry, and the stark heroism of the Border in the days when the Civil War was a looming cloud, and the "Pineries" a limitless wilderness on the north. Men like Sam McKinley, William Fletcher, and Wilbur Dudley retained my friendship and my respect, but the affairs of the younger generation did not greatly concern me. In short, I considered the relationship between them and myself fortuitous.

Absorbed in my writing I was seldom in the mood during my visits to entertain curious neighbors, in fact I had met few people outside my relatives. All this was very ungracious, no doubt, but such had been my attitude for seven years. I came there to work and I worked.

Even now, in the midst of my honeymoon, I wrote busily. Each morning immediately after breakfast I returned to my study, where the manuscript of a novel (*Her Mountain Lover*) was slowly growing into final shape, but in the afternoons Zulime and I occasionally went sleighing with Dolly and the cutter, or we worked about the house.

It was a peaceful time, with only one thought to stir the pool of my content. I began to realize that the longer we stayed, the harder it would be for my mother to let us go. She could hardly permit her New Daughter to leave the room. She wanted her to sit beside her or to be in the range of her vision all day long. So far from resenting her loss of household authority she welcomed it, luxuriating in the freedom from care which the young wife brought.

This growing reliance upon Zulime made me uneasy. "I cannot, even for mother's sake, ask my city-bred wife to spend the winter in this small snow-buried hamlet," I wrote to my brother, "and, besides, I have planned a wedding trip to Washington and New York."

In announcing to my mother the date of our departure, I said, "We won't be gone long. We'll be back early in the spring."

"See that you do," she replied, but her eyes were deep and dark with instant sadness. She had hoped with childish trust that we would stay all winter with her.

It was beautiful in Neshonoc at this time. Deep, dazzling snows blanketed the hills, and covered the fields, and frequently at sunset or later, after the old people were asleep, Zulime and I went for a swift walk far out into the silent country, rejoicing in the crisp clear air, and in the sparkle of moonbeams on the crusted drifts. At such times the satin sheen of sled-tracks in the road, the squeal of dry flakes under my heel (united with the sound of distant sleigh bells) brought back to me sadly-sweet memories of boyish games, spelling school, and the voices of girls whose laughter had long since died away into silence.

The blurred outlines of the hills, the barking of sentinel dogs at farm-yard gates, and the light from snow-laden

cottage windows filled my heart with a dull illogical ache,
an emotion which was at once a pleasure and a pain.

> O, witchery of the winter night,
> (With broad moon shouldering to the west),
> Before my feet the rustling deeps
> Of untracked snows, in shimmering heaps,
> Lie cold and desolate and white.
> I hear glad girlish voices ring
> Clear as some softly-stricken string—
> (The moon is sailing toward the west),
> The sleigh-bells clash in homeward flight,
> With frost each horse's breast is white—
> (The moon is falling toward the west)—
> "Good night, Lettie!"
> "Good night, Ben!"
> (The moon is sinking at the west)—
> "Good night, my sweetheart,"—Once again
> The parting kiss, while comrades wait
> Impatient at the roadside gate,
> And the red moon sinks *beyond* the west!

Such moments as these were meeting places of the old
and the new, the boy and the man. The wistful, haunting
dreams of the past, contended with the warm and glowing
fulfillment of the present. For the past a song, for the
present the woman at my side!

Whether Zulime had similar memories of her girlhood or
not I do not know. She was not given to emotional expression, but she several times declared herself entirely content
with our orderly easeful life and professed herself willing
to remain in the homestead until spring. "I like it here,"
she repeated, but I was certain that she liked the city and
her own kind, better, and that a longer stay would prove
a deprivation and a danger. After all, she was an alien in
the Valley,—a gracious and kindly alien, but an alien nevertheless. Her natural habitat was among the studios of

Chicago or New York, and my sense of justice would not permit me to take advantage of her loyalty and her womanly self-sacrifice.

"Pack your trunk," I said to her one December day, with an air of high authority. "We are going East in continuation of our wedding trip."

Two days after making this decision we were in Washington, at a grand hotel, surrounded by suave waiters who had abundant leisure to serve us, for the reason that Congress was not in session, and the city was empty of its lobbyists and its law-makers.

The weather was like October and for several days we walked about the streets without thinking of outside wraps. We went at once to the Capitol from whose beautiful terraces we could look across the city, back and upward along our trail, above the snows of Illinois soaring on and up into the far cañons of the San Juan Divide, retracing in memory the first half of our wedding journey with a sense of satisfaction, a joy which now took on double value by reason of its contrast to the marble terrace on which we stood. From the luxury of our city surroundings the flaming splendors of the Needle Range appeared almost mystical.

We ate our Christmas dinner in royal isolation, attended by negroes whose dusky countenances shone with holiday desire to make us happy. With no visitors and no duties we gave ourselves to the business of seeing the Capitol and enjoying the gorgeous sunlight. Zulime, who looked at everything in the spirit of a youthful tourist, was enchanted and I played guide with such enthusiasm as a man of forty could bring to bear. It was a new and pleasant schooling for me, a time which I look back upon with wistful satisfaction, after more than twenty years.

Philadelphia, our next stop, had an especial significance to me (something quite apart from its historical significance). Outwardly professing a keen interest in the Liberty Bell, Independence Hall, and other objects which enthralled my young wife, I was secretly planning to offer Lorimer of *The Post*, the serial rights of my novel *The Eagle's Heart*, and I had an engagement to talk with Edward Bok about a novelette.

Bok, a friend of several years' standing, received us most cordially, and Mrs. Bok, who came in next day to meet us, not only instantly and heartily approved of my wife, but quite openly said so, a fact which added another quality to the triumphal character of our progress. I was certain that all of my other Eastern friends would find her admirable.

We reached New York on New Year's Eve, and the streets were roaring with the customary riot of youth, but in our rooms at the Westminster we were as remote from the tumult as if we had been at the bottom of a Colorado mine. We would have heard nothing of the horns and hootings of the throngs had not Zulime expressed a wish to go forth and mix with them. With a feeling of disgust of the hoodlums who filled Broadway, I took her as far north as Forty-second Street, but she soon tired of the rude men and their senseless clamor, and gladly returned to our hotel willing to forget it all.

In my diary I find these words, "I am beginning the New Year with two thousand dollars in the bank, and a pending sale which will bring in as much more. I feel pretty confident of a living during the year 1900."

Evidently the disposal of my serial to Lorimer, the results of my deal with Brett, and the growing interest of other publishers in my work had engendered a confidence in the future which I had never before attained—and yet I must admit that most of my prosperity was expected rather than secured, a promise, rather than a fulfillment, and the fact that I permitted Zulime to settle upon a three-room suite in an obscure Hotel on Fifteenth Street, is proof of my secret doubts. Eighteen dollars per week seemed a good deal of money to pay for an apartment.

As I think back to this transaction I am bitten by a kind of remorseful shame. It was such a shabby little lodging for my artist bride, and yet, at the moment, it seemed all that we could safely afford, and she cheerfully made the best of it. Never by word or sign did she hint that its tiny hall and its dingy and unfashionable furnishings were unworthy of us both, on the contrary she went ahead with shining face.

One extravagance I did commit, one that I linger upon with satisfaction—I forced her to choose a handsome coat instead of a plain one. It was a long graceful garment of a rich brown color, an "Individual model" the saleslady called it. It was very becoming to my wife—at any rate I found it so—but the price was sixty-five dollars—"marked down from eighty-five" the saleslady said. Neither of us had ever worn a coat costing more than twenty-five dollars and to pay almost three times as much even for a beautiful "creation" like this was out of the question—and my considerate young wife decided against it with a sigh.

I was in reckless mood. "We will take it," I said to the saleswoman.

"Oh no! We can't afford it!" protested Zulime in high agitation. "It is impossible!" She looked scared and weak.

"You may do up the old coat," I went on in exalted tone. "My wife will wear the new one."

In a tremor of girlish joy and gratitude Zulime walked out upon the street wearing the new garment, and the expression of her face filled me with desire to go on amazing her. She had owned so few pretty things in her life that I took a keen pleasure in scaring her with sudden presents. I bought a crescent-shaped brooch set with small diamonds which cost one hundred dollars—Oh, I was coming on!

[She is wearing these jewels yet and she says she loves

them—but as I think back to that brown cloak I am not so sure that her approval was without misgiving. It may be that she secretly hated that coat for it was an unusual color, and while its lines were graceful in my eyes it may have been "all out of style."—What became of it, finally, I am unable to say. No matter, it expressed for me a noble sentiment and it shall have a place on this page with the Oriental brooch and the amethyst necklace.]

Humble as our quarters were we rejoiced in distinguished visitors. William Dean Howells called upon us almost immediately and so did Richard Watson Gilder, Edmund Clarence Stedman, John Burroughs, and many other of my valued, old-time friends. Furthermore, with a courage at which I now marvel at, Zulime announced that we would be "at home" every afternoon, and thereafter our tiny sitting-room was often crowded with her friends—for she had begun to find out many of her artist acquaintances. In fact, we were forever discovering people she had known in Paris. It seemed to me that she had met the entire American Colony during her four years in France.

My social and domestic interests quite cut me off from my club, and we joked about this. "I am now one of the newly-weds," I admitted, "and my absence from the club is expected. Members invariably desert the club during the first year or two of their married life, but they all come back!—Sooner or later, they drop in for lunch or while wifey is away, and at last are indistinguishable from the bachelors."

Mrs. James A. Herne, who had meant so much to me in my Boston days, was one of our very first callers, and no one among all my friends established herself more quickly in my wife's regard. Katharine's flame-like enthusiasm, her never-failing Irish humor, and her quick intelligence, made her a joyous inspiration, and whilst she and Zulime compared experiences like a couple of college girls, I sat and smiled with a kind of proprietary pride in both of them.

Fortunately my wife approved of my associates. "You have a delightful circle," she said one night as we were on our way home from a dinner with a group of distinguished literary folk.

Her remark comforted me. Having no money with which to hire cabs or purchase opera tickets, I could at least share with her the good friendships I had won, confidently, believing that she would gain approval,—which she did. Not all of my associates were as poor as I (some of them, indeed, lived in houses of their own), but they were mostly concerned with the arts in some form, and with such people Zulime was entirely at ease.

With a lecture to deliver in Boston I asked her to go with me. "I cannot forego the pleasure of showing you about 'the Hub,'" I urged. "I want Hurd and other of my faithful friends of former days to know you. We'll take rooms at the Parker House which used to fill me with silent awe. I want to play the part, for a day or two, of the successful author."

As she had never seen Boston, she joyfully consented, and the most important parts of my grandiose design were carried out. We took rooms at the hotel in which I first met Riley, and from there we sent out cards to several of my acquaintances. Hurd, who was still Literary Editor of the *Transcript*, came at once to call, and so did Flower of the *Arena*, but for the most part Zulime and I did the calling for she was eager to see the homes and the studios of my artist friends.

By great good fortune, James A. Herne was playing "Sag Harbor" at one of the theaters, and as I had told Zulime a great deal about "Shore Acres" and other of Herne's plays, I hastened to secure seats for a performance. Herne was growing old, and in failing health but he showed no decline of power that night. His walk, his voice, his gestures filled

My Father's Inheritance

me with poignant memories of our first meeting in Ashmont, and our many platform experiences, while the quaint Long Island play brought back to me recollections of his summer home on Peconic Bay. How much he had meant to me in those days of Ibsen drama and Anti-poverty propaganda!

To go about Boston with my young wife was like reliving one by one my student days. Many of my haunts were unchanged, and friends like Dr. Cross and Dr. Tompkins, with whom I had lived so long in Jamaica Plain, were only a little grayer, a little thinner. They looked at me with wondering eyes. To them I was an amazing success. Flower, still as boyish in face and figure as when I left the city in '92, professed to have predicted my expanding circle of readers, and I permitted him to imagine it wider than it was.

Some of my former neighbors had grown in grace, others had stagnated or receded, a fact which saddened me a little. A few had been caught in a swirl of backwater, and seemed to be going round and round without making the slightest advance. Their talk was all of small things, or the unimportant events of the past.

Alas! Boston no longer inspired me. It seemed small and alien and Cambridge surprised me by revealing itself as a sprawling and rather drab assemblage of wooden dwellings, shops and factories. Even the University campus was less admirable, architecturally, than I had supposed it to be, and the residences of its famous professors were hardly the stately homes of luxury I had remembered them. Upon looking up the house on Berkley Street in which Howells had lived while editing *The Atlantic Monthly*, I found it smaller and less beautiful than my own house in Wisconsin. Dr. Holmes' mansion on "the water side of Beacon Street" and the palaces of Copley Square left me calm, their glamor had utterly vanished with my youth (I fear Lee's Hotel in Auburndale would have been reduced in grandeur); and when we took the train for New York, I confessed to a feeling of sadness, of definite loss.

Naturally, inevitably the Boston of my early twenties had vanished. My youthful worship of the city, my faith in the literary supremacy of New England had died out. Manifestly increasing in power as a commercial center, roaring with new interests, new powers, new people, the Hub had lost its scholastic distinction, its historic charm. Each year would see it more easily negligible in American art. It hurt me to acknowledge this, it was like losing a noble ancestor, but there was no escape from the conclusion.

"Little that is new is coming out of Boston," I sadly remarked to Zulime. "Her illustrious poets of the Civil War period are not being replaced by others of National appeal. Her writers, her artists, like those of Chicago, Cleveland, and San Francisco. are coming to New York. New England is being drained of talent in order that Manhattan shall be supreme."

While we were away on this trip my friends Grace and Ernest Thompson-Seton had sent out cards for a party "in honor of Mr. and Mrs. Hamlin Garland," but when, a few nights later, a throng of writers, artists and musicians filled the Seton studio, I was confirmed in a growing suspicion that I was only the lesser half of a fortunate combination. A long list of invitations to dinner or to luncheon testified to the fact that while they tolerated me, they liked my wife, and in this judgment I concurred.

One day while calling on a charming friend and fellow-fictionist, Juliet Wilbur Tompkins, we met for the first time Frank Norris, another California novelist, who captivated us both, not merely because of his handsome face and figure, but by reason of his keen and joyous spirit.

He had been employed for some time in the office of Doubleday and Page, and though I had often passed him at his desk, I had never before spoken with him. We struck up an immediate friendship and thereafter often dined together. He told me of his plan to embody modern California in a series of novels, and at my request read some of his manuscript to me.

Zulime, although she greatly admired Norris, still maintained that Edward MacDowell was the handsomest man of her circle, and in this I supported her, for he was then in the noble prime of his glorious manhood, gay of spirit, swift of wit and delightfully humorous of speech. As a dinner companion he was unexcelled and my wife quite lost her heart to him. Between Frank Norris and Edward MacDowell I appeared but a rusty-coat. I sang small. Fortunately for me they were both not only loyal friends but devoted husbands.

I remembered saying to Zulime as we came away: "America need not despair of her art so long as she has two such personalities as Edward MacDowell and Frank Norris."

Edwin Booth's daughter, Mrs. Grossman, who was living at this time in a handsome apartment on Eighteenth Street, was one of those who liked my wife, and an invitation to take tea with her produced in me a singular and sudden reversal to boyish timidity, for to me she had almost the quality of royalty. I thought of her as she had looked to me, fifteen years before, when on the occasion of Edwin Booth's last performance of *Macbeth* in Boston, she sat in the stage-box with her handsome young husband, and applauded her illustrious father.

"An enormous audience was present," I explained to Zulime, "and most of us were deeply interested in the radiant figure of that happy girl. To me she was a princess, and I observed that as the curtain rose after each act and the great tragedian came forth to bow, his eyes sought his daughter's glowing face. Each time the curtain fell his final glance was upon her. Her small hands seemed the only ones whose sound had value in his ears."

How remote, how royal, how unattainable she had appeared to me that night! Now here she was a kindly, charming hostess, the mother of a family who regarded me as "a distinguished author." To make that radiant girl in the stage box and my lovely hostess coalesce was difficult, but as I studied her profile and noted the line of her expressive lips I was able to relate her to the princely player whose genius I had worshiped from the gallery.

It will be evident to the reader that life in New York pleased me better than life in West Salem or even in Chicago, and I would gladly have stayed on till spring, but Zulime decided to go back to Chicago, and this we did about the first of February.

The last of the many notable entertainments in which my wife shared was an open meeting of the National Institute of Arts and Letters (which I had helped to found), where she met many of the leading writers and artists of the city. Howells, who presided over the program, was especially fine, restrained, tactful yet quietly authoritative, and when I told him that our wedding journey was nearly over he expressed a regret which was highly flattering to us both. At one o'clock on the day following this historic meeting we entered a car headed for the west, acknowledging with a sigh, yet with a comfortable sense of having accomplished our purpose, that it would be profitable to go into retirement and ruminate for a month or two. The glories of New York had been almost too exciting for Zulime, "I am ready to go home," she said.

Home! There was my problem. The only city residence I possessed was my bachelor apartment on Elm Street, and at the moment I had no intention of asking my wife to share its narrow space except as a temporary lodging, and to take her back into that snow-covered little Wisconsin village, back to a shabby farm house filled with ailing elderly folk would amount to crime. From the high splendor of our stay in New York we now fell to earth with a thump. My duties as a son, my cares as the head of a household returned upon me, and my essential homelessness took away all that assurance of literary success which my Eastern friends had helped me attain. Of the elation in which I had moved while in New York I retained but a shred. Once more the hard-working fictionist and the responsible head of a family, I began to worry about the future. My honeymoon was over.

The basic realities of my poverty again cropped out in a letter from my mother who wrote that my aunt was very ill and that she needed me. To Zulime I said, "You stay here with your sister and your friends while I go up to the Homestead and see what I can do for our old people."

This she refused to do. "No," she loyally said, "I am going with you," and although I knew that she was choosing a dreary alternative I was too weak, too selfishly weak, to prevent her self-sacrifice. We left that night at the usual hour and arrived in time to eat another farmer's breakfast with father and mother next morning. Aunt Susan was unable to meet us.

Her sweet spirit was about to leave its frail body, that was evident to me as I looked down at her, but she knew me and whispered, "I'm glad to have you at home." She showed no fear of death, in fact she appeared unconscious of her grave condition. She was a beautiful character and to see her lying there beneath her old-fashioned quilt, so small and helpless, so patient, lonely and sad, made speech difficult for me. She had meant much in my life. The serene dignity with which she and her mother had carried the best New England traditions into the rough front rank of the Border, was still written in the lines of her face. I had never seen her angry or bitter, and I had never heard her utter an unkind word.

Zulime took charge of the work about the house with a cheerfulness which amazed me. My mother with pathetic confidence leaned upon her daughter's strong young shoulders and the music of my stern old father's voice as he said, "Well, daughter, I'm glad you're here," was a revelation to me. He already loved her as if she were his very own, and she responded to his affection in a way which put me still more deeply in her debt. It would have been disheartening, but not at all surprising, had she found the village and my home intolerable, but she did not—she appeared content, sustained we will say, by her sense of duty.

Her situation was difficult. Imprisoned in the snowy silences of the little valley, dependent on her neighbors for entertainment, and confronted with the care of two invalids and a fretful husband, she was put to a rigid test.

Beside our base-burning stove she sat night after night playing cinch or dominoes to amuse my father, while creaking footsteps went by on the frosty board-walks and in a distant room my aunt lay waiting for the soft step of the Grim Intruder. It must have seemed a gray outlook for my bride but she never by word or look displayed uneasiness.

Without putting our conviction into words, we all realized that my aunt's departure was but a matter of a few days. "There is nothing to do," the doctor said. "She will go like a person falling asleep. All you can do is wait—" And so the days passed.

We went to bed each night at ten and quite as regularly rose at half-past six. Dinner came exactly at noon, supper precisely at six. Although my upstairs study was a kind of retreat, we spent less time in it than we had planned to do, for mother was so appealingly wistful to have us near her that neither of us had the heart to deny her. She could not endure to have us both absent. Careful not to interrupt my writing, she considered Zúlime's case in different light. "You can read, or sew or knit down here just as well as up there," she said. "It is a comfort for me just to have you sit where I can look at you."

She loved to hear me read aloud, and this I often did in the evening while she sat beside Zulime and watched her fingers fly about her sewing. These were blissful hours for her, and in these after years I take a measure of comfort in remembering the part I had in making them possible.

Slowly but steadily Susan Garland's vital forces died out, and at last there came a morning when her breath faltered on her lips. She had gone away, as she had lived, with quiet dignity. Notwithstanding her almost constant suffering she had always been a calmly cheerful soul and her passing, while it left us serious did not sadden us. Her life came to its end without struggle and her face was peaceful.

She was the last of my father's immediate family, and to him was transmitted in due course of law, the estate with which her husband had left her, a dower, which though small had enabled her to live independently of her relatives and in simple comfort. It was a matter of but a few thousand dollars, but its possession now made the most fundamental change in my father's way of life. The effect of this certain income upon his character was almost magical. He took on a sense of security, a feeling of independence, a freedom from worry such as he had been trying for over sixty years, without success, to attain.

It released him from the tyranny of the skies. All his life he had been menaced by the "weather." Clouds, snows, winds, had been his unrelenting antagonists. Hardly an hour of his past had been free from a fear of disaster. The glare of the sun, the direction of the wind, the assembling of clouds at sunset,—all the minute signs of change, of storm, of destruction had been his incessant minute study. For over fifty years he had been enslaved to the seasons.

His sister's blessing liberated him. He agonized no more about the fall of frost, the slash of hail, the threat of tempest. Neither chinch bugs nor drought nor army worms could break his rest. He slept in comfort and rose in confidence. He retained a general interest in crops, of course, but he no longer ate his bread in fear, and just in proportion as he realized his release from these corroding, long-endured cares, did he take on mellowness and humor. He became another man altogether. He ceased to worry and hurry. His tone, his manner became those of a citizen of substance, of genial leisure. He began to speak of travel!

Definitely abandoning all intention of farming, he put his Dakota land on sale and bought several small cottages in West Salem. As a landlord in a modest way, he rejoiced in the fact that his income was almost entirely free from the results of harvest. It irked him (when he thought of it) to admit that all his pioneering had been a failure, that all his early rising, and his ceaseless labor had availed so little, but the respect in which he was now held as householder, and as President of the village, compensated him in such degree that he was able to ignore his ill success as a wheat raiser.

"This legacy proves once again the magic of money," I remarked to Zulime. "Father can now grow old with dignity and confidence. His living is assured."

It remains to say that this inheritance also lifted indirectly a part of my own burden. It took from me something of the financial responsibility concerning the household whose upkeep I had shared for ten years or more. Mother was still my care, but not in the same sense as before, for my father with vast pride volunteered to pay all the household expenses. He even insisted upon paying for an extra maid and gardener. Now that he no longer needed the cash returns from the garden, he began to express a pleasure in it. He was content with making it an esthetic or at most a household enterprise.

CHAPTER TWELVE

We Tour the Oklahoma Prairie

ONE of the disadvantages of being a fictionist lies in the fact that the history of one's imaginary people halts just in proportion as one's mind is burdened with the sorrowful realities of one's own life. A troubled bank clerk can (I believe) cast up a column of figures, an actor can declaim while his heart is breaking, but a novelist can't— or at any rate I can't—write stories while some friend or relative is in pain and calling for relief. Composition is dependent in my case upon a delicately adjusted mood, and a very small pebble is sufficient to turn the currents of my mind into a dry channel.

My aunt's death was a sad shock to my mother and until she regained something of her cheerful temper, I was unable to take up and continue the action of my novel. I kept up the habit of going to my study, but for a week or more I could not write anything but letters.

By the tenth of March we were all longing with deepest hunger for the coming of spring. According to the old almanac's saying we had a right to expect on the twenty-first a relenting of the rigors of the north, but it did not come. "March the twenty-first is spring and little birds begin to sing" was not true of the Valley this year. For two weeks longer, the icy winds continued to sweep with Arctic severity across the crests of the hills, and clouds of snow almost daily sifted down through the bare branches of the elms. At times the landscape, mockingly beautiful, was white and bleak as January. Drafts filled the lanes and sleigh-bells jingled mockingly.

At last came grateful change. The wind shifted to the

South. At mid-day the eaves began to drip, and the hens, lifting their voices in jocund song, scratched and burrowed, careening in the dusty earth which appeared on the sunward side of the barn. Green grass enlivened the banks of the garden, and on the southern slopes of the hills warmly colored patches appeared, and then came bird-song and budding branches!—so dramatic are the changes in our northern country.

No sooner was spring really at hand than Zulime and I, eager to share in the art life which was so congenial to us both, returned to my former lodging in Chicago; and a little later we went so far as to give a party—our first party since our marriage. Fuller, who came early and stayed late, appeared especially amused at our make-shifts. "This isn't Chicago," he exclaimed as he looked around our rooms. "This is a lodging in London!"

It was at this party that I heard the first word of the criticism under which I had expected to suffer. One of our guests, an old and privileged friend, remarked with a sigh, "Well, now that Zuhl has married a writer, I suppose her own artistic career is at an end."

"Not at all!" I retorted, somewhat nettled. "I am an individualist in this as in other things. I do not believe in the subordination of a wife to her husband. Zulime has all the rights I claim for myself—no more, no less. If she fails to go on with her painting or sculpture the fault will not be mine. Our partnership is an equal one."

I meant this. Although dimly aware that mutual concessions must be made, it was my fixed intention to allow my wife the fullest freedom of action. Proud of her skill as an artist, I went so far as to insist on her going back into her brother's studio to resume her modeling. "You are not my house-keeper—you are a member of a firm. I prefer to have you an artist."

Smiling, evasive, she replied, "I haven't at the present

moment the slightest 'call' to be an artist. Perhaps I shall
—after a while; but at present I'd rather keep house."

"But consider *me!*" I insisted. "Here am I, a public
advocate of the rights of women, already denounced as your
'tyrant husband,' 'a selfish egotistic brute!'—I'll be accused
—I am already accused—of cutting short your career as a
sculptor. Consider the injustice you are doing *me!*"

She refused to take my protest or her friends' comment
seriously; and so we drifted along in pleasant round of
parties till the suns of May, brooding over the land lured
us back to the Homestead, in which Zulime could house-keep
all day long if she wished to do so, and she did!

Full of plans for refurnishing and redecorating, she was
busy as a bumble-bee. As the mistress of a big garden and
a real kitchen she invited all her Chicago friends to come
and share her good fortune. She was filled with the spirit
of ownership and exulted over the four-acre patch as if it
were a noble estate in Surrey.

It chanced that Lorado on his way to St. Paul was able
to stop off, and Zulime not only cooked a special dinner for
him, but proudly showed him all about the garden, talking
gaily of the number of jars of berries and glasses of jelly
she was planning to put up.

"Well, Zuhl," he said resignedly, "I suppose it's all for
the best, but I don't quite see the connection between your
years of training in sculpture and the business of canning
fruit."

It was a perfect spring day, and the Homestead was at
its best. The entire demesne was without a weed, and the
blooming berry patches, the sprouting asparagus beds and
the budding grape vines all come in for the eminent sculptor's enforced inspection, until at last with a yawn of un-
concealed boredom he turned away. "You *seem* to *like*
your slavery," he remarked to Zulime, a note of comical
accusation in his voice.

On the station platform when about to say good-bye to me, he became quite serious. "This marriage appears to be working out," he admitted, musingly. "I confess I was a little in doubt about it at first, but Zuhl seems to be satisfied with her choice and so—well, I've decided to let matters drift. Whether she ever comes back to sculpture or not is unimportant, so long as she is happy."

Knowing that Zulime had always been his intellectual comrade, and realizing how deeply he felt the separation which her growing interest in my affairs had brought about, I gave him my hand in silent renewal of a friendship into which something new and deeply significant had come. "I hope she will never regret it," was all I could say.

Zulime was not deceived as to my income. My property, up to this time, consisted of a small, a very small library, a dozen Navajo rugs, several paintings, a share in four acres of land and my book rights (which were of negligible value so far as furnishing a living was concerned), and my wife perceived very clearly that our margin above necessity was narrow, but this did not disturb her faith in the future, or if it did, she gave no sign of it—her face was nearly always smiling. Nevertheless I had no intention of keeping her in West Salem all summer. I could not afford to wear out her interest in it.

One day, shortly after Lorado's visit, I received a letter from Major Stouch, the Indian Agent with whom I had campaigned at Lamedeer in '97. He wrote: "I have just been detailed to take charge of the Cheyenne Agency at Darlington, Oklahoma. Mrs. Stouch and I are about to start on a survey of my new reservation and I should like to have you and your wife come down and accompany us on our circuit. We shall hold a number of councils with the Indians, and there will be dances and pow-wows. It will all be material for your pen."

This invitation appealed to me with especial force for

We Tour the Oklahoma Prairie

I had long desired to study the Southern Cheyennes, and a tour with Stouch promised a rich harvest of fictional themes, for me. Furthermore it offered a most romantic experience for Zulime—just the kind of enlightenment I had promised her.

With no time to lose, we packed our trunks and took train for Kansas City enroute for Indian Territory, the scene of many of the most exciting romances of my youth, the stronghold of bank robbers, and the hiding place of military renegades.

On our way to Oklahoma, we visited Professor Taft in Hanover and I find this note recorded: "All day the wind blew, the persistent, mournful crying wind of the plain. The saddest, the most appealing sound in my world. It came with a familiar soft rush, a crowding presence, uttering a sighing roar—a vague sound out of which voices of lonely children and forgotten women broke. To the solitary farmer's wife such a wind brings tears or madness. I am tense with desire to escape. This bare little town on the ridge is appalling to me. Think of living here with the litany of this wind forever in one's ears."

By contrast West Salem, with its green, embracing hills, seemed a garden, a place of sweet content, a summer resort, and yet in this Kansas town Zulime had spent part of her girlhood. In this sun-smit cottage she had left her mother to find a place in the outside world just as I had left my mother in Dakota. From this town she had gone almost directly to Paris! It would be difficult to imagine a more amazing translation—and yet, now that she was back in the midst of it, she gave no sign of the disheartenment she must have felt. She met all her old friends and neighbors with unaffected interest and gayety.

Twenty-four hours later we were in the midst of a wide, sunny prairie, across which, in white-topped prairie schooners, settlers were moving just as they had passed our door in Iowa thirty years before. Plowmen were breaking the sod as my father had done in '71, and their women washing and cooking in the open air, offered familiar phases of the immemorial American drama,—only the stations on the railway broke the spell of the past with a modern word.

Swarms of bearded, slouchy, broad-hatted men filled the train and crowded the platforms of the villages. Cow-boys, Indians in white men's clothing, negroes (black and brown), and tall, blonde Tennessee mountaineers made up this amazing population—a population in which libraries were of small value, a tobacco-chewing, ceaselessly spitting unkempt horde, whose stage of culture was almost precisely that which Dickens and other travelers from the old world had found in the Central West in the forties.

How these scenes affected my young wife I will not undertake to say; but I remember that she kept pretty close to my elbow whenever we mingled with the crowd, and the deeper we got into this raw world the more uneasy she became. "Where shall we spend the night?" she asked.

Had I been alone I would not have worried about a hotel, but with a young wife who knew nothing of roughing it, I became worried. To the conductor I put an anxious question, "Is there a decent hotel in Reno?"

His answer was a bit contemptuous, "Sure," he exclaimed. "What do you think you're doing—exploring?"

This was precisely what I feared we *were* doing. I said no more about it, although I hadn't much confidence in his notions of a first class hotel. There was nothing for it but to rest upon his assurance and go hopefully forward to the end of the line.

It must have been about ten of a dark warm night as we came to a final halt beside a low station marked "Reno," and at the suggestion of the brakeman I called for "the Palace Hotel Bus," although none of the waiting carriages or drivers seemed even remotely related to a palace. My wife, filled with a high sense of our adventure, took her seat in the muddy and smelly carriage, with touching trust in me.

The Palace Hotel, with its doorway brightly lighted with electricity, proved a pleasant surprise. It looked clean and bright and new, and the proprietor, a cheerful and self-respecting citizen, was equally reassuring. We went to our rooms with restored confidence in Oklahoma.

The next morning, before we had finished our breakfast, a messenger from the Agency came in to say that a carryall was at the door, and soon we were on our way toward the Fort.

The roads were muddy, but the plain was vividly, brilliantly green, and the sky radiantly blue. The wind, filled with delicious spring odors, came out of the west; larks were whistling and wild ducks were in flight. To my wife it was as strange as it was beautiful. It was the prairie at its best—like the Jim River in 1881.

Fort Reno (a cluster of frame barracks), occupied a low hill which overlooked the valley of the Canadian, on whose green meadows piebald cattle were scattered like bits of topaz. Flowers starred the southern slopes, and beside the stream near the willows (in which mocking birds were singing), stood clusters of the conical tents of the Cheyennes, lodges of canvas made in the ancient form. Our way led to the Agency through one of these villages, and as we passed we saw women at their work, and children in their play, all happy and quite indifferent to the white man and his comment.

The Stouchs met us at the door of the big frame cottage which was the agent's house, and while Mrs. Stouch took charge of Zulime the Major led me at once to his office, in order that I might lose no time in getting acquainted with his wards. In ten minutes I found myself deep in another world, a world of captive, aboriginal warriors, sorrowfully concerned with the problem of "walking the white man's trail."

All that day and each day thereafter, files of white-topped wagons forded the river, keeping their westward march quite in the traditional American fashion, to disappear like weary beetles over the long, low ridge past the fort which stood like a guidon to the promised land. Here were all the elements of Western settlement, the Indians, the soldiers, the glorious sweeping wind and the flowering sod, and in addition to all these the resolute white men seeking their fortunes beneath the sunset sky, just as of old, remorselessly carrying their women and children into hardship and solitude. Without effort I was able to imagine myself back in the day of Sam Houston and Satanka.

Our trip around the reservation with the Agent began a few days later with an exultant drive across the prairie to the South Fork of the Canadian River. It was glorious summer here. Mocking birds were singing in each swale, and exquisite flowers starred the sod beneath our wheels. Through a land untouched by the white man's plow, we rode on a trail which carried me back to my childhood, to the Iowa Prairie over which I had ridden with my parents thirty years before. This land, this sky, this mournful, sighing wind laid hold of something very sweet, almost sacred in my brain. By great good fortune I had succeeded in overtaking the vanishing prairie.

The arrival of the Agent at each sub-agency was the signal for an assembly of all the red men round-about and Zulime had the pleasure of seeing several old fashioned Councils carried on quite in the traditional fashion, the chiefs in full native costume, their head dresses presenting suggestions of the war-like past. The attitudes of the men in the circle were at all times serious and dignified, and the gestures of the orators instinct with natural grace.

One of the Cheyenne camps in which we lingered was

especially charming. Set amid the nodding flowers and waving grasses of a small meadow in the elbow of a river, its lodges were filled with happy children, and under sun-shades constructed of green branches, chattering women were at work. Paths led from tent to tent, and in the deep shade of ancient walnut trees, on the banks of the stream, old men were smoking in reminiscent dream of other days.

As night fell and sunset clouds flamed overhead, primroses yearned upward from the sward, and the teepees, lighted from within, glowed like jewels, pearl-white cones with hearts of flame. Shouts of boys, laughter of girls, and the murmur of mothers' voices suggested the care-free life of the Algonquin in days before the invading conqueror enforced new conditions and created new desires.

For two weeks we drove amid scenes like these, scenes which were of inspirational value to me and of constant delight to Zulime. My notebook filled itself with hints for poems and outlines for stories. In all my tales of the Cheyennes, I kept in mind Major Powell's significant remark, "The scalp dance no more represents the red man's daily life than the bayonet-charge represents the white man's civilization." Having no patience with the writers who regarded the Indian as a wild beast, I based my interpretation on the experiences of men like Stouch and Seger who, by twenty years' experience, had proved the red man's fine qualities. As leading actors in the great tragedy of Western settlement I resolved to present the Ogallallah and the Ute as I saw them.

At one of these informal councils between the Agent and some of the Cheyenne headmen, I caught a phrase which gave me the title of a story and at the same time pointed the moral of a volume of short stories. White Shield, one of John Seger's friends, in telling of his experiences, sadly remarked, "I find it hard to make a home among the white men."

Instantly my mind grasped the reverse side of the problem. I took for the title of my story these words: *White Eagle, the Red Pioneer,* and presented the point of view of a nomad who turns his back on the wilderness which he loves, and sets himself the task of leading his band in settlement among the plowmen. In a collection of tales, some of which have not been published even in magazines, I have grouped studies of red individuals with intent to show that a village of Cheyennes has many kinds of people just like any other village. "Hippy, the Dare Devil," "White Weasel, the Dandy," "Rising Wolf, the Ghost Dancer," are some of the titles in this volume. Whether it will get itself printed in my lifetime or not is a problem, for publishers are loath to issue a book of short stories, any kind of short stories. "Stories about Indians are no longer in demand," they say. Nevertheless, some day I hope these stories may get into print as a volume complementary to *Main Traveled Roads,* and *They of the High Trails.*

Among the most unforgettable of all our Oklahoma experiences was a dinner which we had with the Jesuit Missionary priest at "Chickashay" on the last day of our stay. It had been raining in torrents for several hours, and as the Mission was four miles out I would have despaired of getting there at all had it not been for the Agency Clerk who was a man of resource and used to Oklahoma "showers." Commandeering for us the Agency "hack," a kind of canvas-covered delivery wagon, he succeeded in reaching the priest's house without shipwreck, although the road was a river.

The priest, a short, jolly Alsatian, met us with shining face quite unlike any other missionary I had ever seen. He was at once a delight and an astonishment to Zulime. His laugh was a bugle note and his hospitality a glow of good will. The dinner was abundant and well served, the wine excellent, and our host's talk of absorbing interest.

We were waited upon by a Sister of severe mien, who, between courses, stood against the wall with folded arms eyeing us with disapproving countenance. It was plain that she was serving under compulsion, but Father Ambrose paying no attention to her frowns, urged us to take a second helping, telling us meanwhile of his first exploration of Oklahoma, a story which filled us with laughter at his "greenness." Chuckling with delight of the fool he was, he could not conceal the heroic part he had played, for the hardships in those days were very real to a young man just out of a monastery. "I was so green the cows would have eaten me," he said.

The whole incident was like a chapter in a story of some other land than ours. The Sisters, the little brown children, the book-walled sitting room, the sturdy little priest recounting his struggles with a strange people and a strange climate,—all these presented a charming picture of the noble side of missionary life. Nothing broke the charm of that dinner except an occasional peal of thunder which made us wonder whether we would be able to navigate the hack back to the hotel or not.

What a waste the plain presented as we started on our return at ten o'clock! The lightning, almost incessant, showed from time to time what appeared to be a vast lake, shorelessly extending on every side of us, a shallow sea through which the horses slopped, waded and all but swam while Carroll, the Clerk, as pilot, did his best to reassure my wife. "I know the high spots," he said, whereat I fervently (though secretly) replied, "I hope you do," and when we swung to anchor in front of our little hotel, I shook his hand in congratulations over his skill—and good luck!

On our return to Chicago I found Lorado in his studio, modeling a more or less conventional female form, and my resentment took words. "If you will come with me, down among the Cheyennes, I will show you men who can be nude without being naked. In White Eagle's camp you can study warriors who have the dignity of Roman Senators and the grace of Athenian athletes."

To illustrate one of my points, I caught up a piece of gray canvas and showed him how the chiefs of various tribes managed their blankets. Something in these motions or in the long gray lines of the robe which I used fired his imagination. For the first time in our acquaintanceship, I succeeded in interesting him in the Indian. He was especially excited by the gesture of covering the mouth to express awe, and a few days later he showed me several small figures which he had sketched, suggestions which afterwards became the splendid monuments of Silmee and Blackhawk. He never lost the effect of the noble gestures which I had reproduced for him. The nude red man was a hackneyed subject, but Brown Bear with his robe, afforded precisely the stimulus of which he stood in need.

This trip to Indian Territory turned out to be a very important event in my life. First of all it enabled me to complete the writing of *The Captain of the Gray Horse Troop,* and started me on a long series of short stories depicting the life of the red man. It gave me an enormous amount of valuable material and confirmed me in my conviction that the Indian needed an interpreter, but beyond all these literary gains, I went back to Wisconsin filled with a fierce desire to own some of that beautiful prairie over which we had ridden.

This revived hunger for land generated in me a plan for establishing a wide ranch down there, an estate to which we could retire in February and March. "We can meet the spring half-way," I explained to my father. "I want a place where I can keep saddle horses and cattle. You must go with me and see it sometime. It is as lovely as Mitchell County was in 1870."

To this end I wrote to my brother in Mexico. "Leave the rubber business and come to Oklahoma. I am going to buy a ranch there and need you as superintendent."

CHAPTER THIRTEEN

Standing Rock and Lake McDonald

IT was full summer when we got back to Wisconsin, and The Old Homestead was at its best. The garden was red with ripening fruit, the trees thick with shining leaves, and the thrushes and catbirds were singing in quiet joy. In the fields the growing corn was showing its ordered spears, and the wheat was beginning to wave in the gentle wind. No land could be more hospitable, more abounding or more peaceful than our valley.

With her New Daughter again beside her life seemed very complete and satisfying to my mother, and I was quite at ease until one night, as she and I were sitting alone in the dusk, she confided to me, for the first time, her conviction that she had but a short time to live. Her tone, as well as her words, shocked me, for she had not hitherto been subject to dark moods. She gave no reason for her belief, but that she was suffering from some serious inner malady was evident,—I feared it might concern the action of her heart—and I was greatly disturbed by it.

Of course I made light of her premonition, but thereafter I watched her with minute care, and called on the doctor at the slightest sign of change. We sang to her, we read to her, and Zulime spent long hours reading to her or sitting beside her. She was entirely happy except when, at intervals, her mysterious malady,—something she could not describe,—filled her eyes with terror.

She loved to sit in the kitchen and watch her new daughter presiding over its activities, and submitted, with pathetic pride, to any change which Zulime proposed. "I am perfectly contented," she said to me, "except——"

"Except what, mother?"

"The grandchild. I want to see my grandchild."

One of our regular excursions for several years had been a drive (usually on Sunday) over the ridge to Lewis Valley, where Frank McClintock still lived. Among my earliest memories is a terror of this road, for it led up a long, wooded hill, which seemed to me, as a child, a dangerous mountain pass. Many, many times since then I had made the climb, sometimes in the spring, sometimes in midsummer, but now my plans included my wife. Mother was eager to go. "I can stand the ride if you will drive and be careful going down hill," she said to me—and so, although I was a little in doubt about the effect upon her heart, I hired a team, and early of a clear June morning we started for Mindoro.

It was like riding back into the hopeful, happy past, for both the old people. Father was full of wistful reminiscences of "the early days," but mother, who sat beside Zulime, made no comment, although her face shone with inward joy of the scene, the talk—until we came to the steep descent which scared her. Clinging to her seat with pitiful intensity she saw nothing but dangerous abysses until we reached the level road on the opposite side of the ridge.

It was glorious June, and in this I now rejoice, for it proved to be the last time that we made the crossing of the long hill together. I was glad to have her visit her brother's home once more. Change was coming to him as well as to her. His prodigious muscles and his boyish gayety were fading away together. Though still delightfully jolly and hospitable, his temper was distinctly less buoyant. He still played the fiddle; but like his brother, David, he found less and less joy in it, for his stiffened fingers refused to do his bidding. The strings which once sang clear and sweet, failed of their proper pitch, and these discords irritated and saddened him.

Aunt Lorette, his handsome, rosy-cheeked wife, was beginning to complain smilingly, of being lame and "no account," but she provided a beautiful chicken dinner, gayly "visiting" while she did it, with mother sitting by to watch her at the job as she had done so many times before.

Lorette, like all the rest of us, felt under the necessity of putting her best foot forward in order that "Zuleema" should not be disappointed in any way, and to Zulime she was like a character in a novel; indeed, they all tried to live up to her notion of them. For her, father told his best stories of bears and Indians, for her, Uncle Frank fiddled his liveliest tunes, and for her Aunt Lorette recounted some of the comedies which the valley had from time to time developed, and which (as she explained) "had gone into one of Hamlin's books. Of course he fixed 'em up a little," she added, "you couldn't expect him to be satisfied with a yarn just as I told it, but all the same he got the idea of at least two of his stories from me."

Valiant Aunt Lorette! Her face was always sunny, no matter how deep the shadow in her heart; and her capacity for work was prodigious. She was an almost perfect example of the happy, hard-working farmer's wife, for her superb physical endowment and her serene temperament had survived the strain of thirty years of unremitting toil. Her life had been, thus far, a cheerful pilgrimage. She did not mind the loneliness of the valley. The high hill which lay between her door and the village could not wall her spirit in. She rejoiced in the stream of pure water which flowed from the hillside spring to the tank at her kitchen door, and she took pride in the chickens and cows and pigs which provided her table with abundant food.

Standing Rock and Lake McDonald

"Oh, yes, I like to go to town—once in a while," she replied, in answer to Zulime's question. "But I'd hate to live there. I don't see how people get along on a tucked up fifty-foot lot where they have to buy every blessed thing they eat."

How good that dinner was! Hot biscuit, chicken, short-cake, coffee and the most delicious butter and cream. At the moment it did seem a most satisfactory way to live. We forgot that the dishes had to be washed three times each day, and that the mud and rain and wind and snow often shut the homestead in for weeks at a stretch. Seeing the valley at its loveliest, under the glamor of a summer afternoon, we found it perfect.

After dinner we men-folks (leaving the women, in the "good old way," to clear away the dinner dishes) went out on the grass under the trees, and as I talked of my moun-taineering Uncle Frank said, with a wistful note in his voice, "I've always wanted to go out into that country with you. Chasing a deer through a Wisconsin swamp don't satisfy me—I'd like to get into the grizzly bear country— but now I'm too old."

Thereupon father stated his desires. "There are just two trips I want to make—I'd like to go. by a steamboat from Duluth to Detroit, and I want to see Yellowstone Park."

"Well, why don't you do it?" demanded my Uncle. "You can afford it now."

Father's face became thoughtful. "I believe I will. Lottridge and Shane are planning that boat trip. I could go with them."

"Sail ahead," said I, "and if you get back in time I'll take you through Yellowstone Park. Zulime and I are going to Montana in July."

Neither of them had the slightest desire to see London or Paris or Rome, but they both longed for a fuller knowledge of the West. They were still pioneers, still explorers over whose imagination the trackless waste exercised a deathless dominion. To my uncle I said, "If I could afford it, I would take you with me on one of my trailing expeditions and show you some real wilderness."

"I wish you would," he answered quickly. "I'd tend horses, cook, or anything else in order to go along."

Of course this wistful longing was only a mood on his part, for he was naturally of a cheerful disposition, but music and the wilderness always stirred him to his deeps. Ten minutes later he was joking with Zulime, giving a fine exhibition of the contented husbandman.

As the time came to leave, my mother glanced about her with an emotion which she brokenly expressed when she said, "I don't suppose I shall ever get over here again. You must come and see me, after this."

"Oh, you'll be comin' over oftener than ever, now that you've got a daughter to lean on," retorted Lorette with easy grace.

On our way home, at the crest of the hill, I drew rein in order that we might all look away over the familiar valley, stretching mistily toward the sun, and I, too, had the feeling—which I was careful not to express even by a look or tone—that mother and I would never again ride this road or look out upon this lovely scene together, and something in her eyes and the melancholy sweetness of her lips told me that she was bidding the landscape a long farewell.

We rode the remaining portion of our way in somber mood, although we all agreed that it was a colorful finish of a perfect day—a day to be recalled in after years with a tender heart-ache.

[It is all changed now. Aunt Lorette has gone to her reward. Uncle Frank, old and lonely, is living on the village side of the ridge and strangers are in the old house!]

That night, Zulime and I talked over the agreement I

had made with father, and we planned a way to carry it
out. Almost as excited about the Yellowstone as he, she
was quite ready to camp through as I suggested. "We
will hire a team at Livingston, and with our own outfit, will
be independent of stages and hotels—but first I must show
you some Indians. We will visit Standing Rock and see
the Sioux in their 'Big Sunday.' Father can meet us at
Bismark after we come out."

With the confidence of a child she accepted my arrangement and on the first day of July we were in the stage
ambling across the hot, dry prairie which lay between Bismark and Fort Yates. Empty, arid and illimitable the
rolling treeless landscape oppressed us both, and yet there
was a stern majesty in its sweep, and the racing purple shadows of the dazzling clouds lent it color and movement. To
me it was all familiar, but when, after an all-day ride, we
came down into the valley of the Muddy Missouri, the
sheen of its oily red current was quite as grateful to me as
to my weary wife.

Our only means of reaching the Agency was a small
rowboat which seemed a frail ferry even to me. How it
appeared to Zulime, I dared not ask—but she unhesitatingly
stepped in and took her seat beside me. I think she accepted it as a part of the strange and hardy world in which
her husband was at home.

We were both silent on that crossing, for our slender
craft struggled anxiously with the boiling, silent, turbid
current, and when we landed, the tense look on Zulime's
face gave place to a smile.—Half an hour later we were
sitting at supper in a fly-specked boarding house, surrounded by squaw-men and half-breed Sioux, who were enjoying the luxury of a white man's table as a part of their
Fourth of July celebration. My artist wife was being educated swiftly!

The tribe was again encamped in a wide circle just

west of the Fort, precisely as when my brother and I had visited it three years before, while the store and the Agency swarmed with native men and women, many in mixed costume of cloth and skin. Zulime's artistic joy in them filled me with complacent satisfaction. I had the air of a showman rejoicing in his exhibition hall. With keen interest we watched the young warriors as they came whirling in on their swift ponies, each in his gayest garments, the tail of his horse decorated with rosettes and ribbons. Possessing the swiftness and the grace of Centaurs, coming and going like sudden whirlwinds, they were superb embodiments of a race which was passing. Some of the older men remembered me, and greeted me as one friendly to their cause—but for the most part the younger folk eyed us with indifference.

That night a singular and savage change in the weather took place. The wind shifted to the southeast and took on the heat of a furnace. By ten o'clock next morning dirt was blowing in clouds and to walk the street was an ordeal. All day Zulime remained in her room virtually a prisoner. Night fell with the blast still roaring, and the dust rising from the river banks like smoke, presented a strange and sinister picture of wrath. It was as though the water, itself, had taken fire from the lightning which plunged in branching streams across the sky. Thunder muttered incessantly all through that singular and solemn night, a night which somehow foreshadowed the doom which was about to overtake the Sioux.

The following day, however, was clear and cool, and we spent most of it in walking about the camp, visiting the teepees of which there were several hundreds set in a huge ellipse, all furnished in primitive fashion—some of them very neatly. Over four thousand Sioux were said to be in this circle, and their coming and going, their camp fires and feasting groups composed a scene well worth the long journey we had endured. Strange as this life seemed to my wife it was quite familiar to me. To me these people were not savages, they were folks—and in their festivity I perceived something of the spirit of a county fair in Wisconsin.

Our guide about the camp, the half-breed son of a St. Louis trader, was a big, fine-featured, intelligent man of about my own age, whose pleasant lips, and deep brown eyes attracted me. He knew everybody, both white and red, and as soon as he understood my wish to write fairly of his people, he gave himself unreservedly to our service. Taking us from lodge to lodge, he introduced us to the men whose characters were of the most value in my study and told them of my wish to report them with sympathy and truth.

One of the games that day was a rough, outdoor drama, in which mimic war parties sallied forth, scouts were captured and captives rescued in stirring pantomime.

As I stood watching the play I observed that one man (no longer young) was serving as "the enemy," alternately captured or slain. His rôle was not only arduous—it was dangerous—dangerous and thankless, and as I saw him cheerfully volunteering to be "killed" I handed Primeau a dollar and said: "Give this to that old fellow, and tell him he should have many dollars for his hard, rough work."

Primeau gave him the coin, but before he had time to know who gave it, he was called back into the field.

At the Agency store I met a French-Canadian named Carignan who was a most valuable witness, for he had been among the red men for many years, first as a school teacher and later as trader. From him I secured much intimate history of the Sioux. He had known the Sitting Bull well, and gave me a very kindly account of him. "I taught the school in Rock Creek near the Sitting Bull's camp, and he was often at my table," he explained. "I saw no harm in him. I liked him and respected him. He was an Indian but he was a thinker."

Vaguely holding in my brain a tale in which the Sitting Bull should be protagonist, I talked with many who had known him, and a few days later I accepted Primeau's invitation to visit the valley in which the chief had lived, and which was the scene of the Ghost Dance, and the place of the chief's death.

I suggested to Zulime that she would be more comfortable at the Agency but she replied, "I'd rather go with you. I don't like being left here alone."

"You'll find the ride tiresome and the lodging rough, I fear."

"I don't care," she retorted firmly, "I'm going with you."

Primeau was a very intelligent man and a good talker, and as we rode along he gave us in detail the history of the rise of the Ghost Dance, so far as the Sioux were concerned. "There was nothing war-like about it," he insisted. "It was a religious appeal. It was a prayer to the Great Spirit to take pity on the red man and bring back the world of the buffalo. They carried no weapons, in fact they carried nothing which the white man had brought to them. They even took the metal fringes off their shirts. They believed that if they gave up all signs of the whites the Great Spirit would turn his face upon them again."

"Did Sitting Bull take part in this?" I asked.

"He encouraged the meeting at his camp and gave his cattle to feed the people, but he was never able to dream like the rest. He never really believed in it. He wanted to but he couldn't. He was too deep a thinker. He often talked with me about it."

At a point about twenty miles from The Fort, Primeau left us to visit a ranchman with whom he had some business and left us to drive on with a guide to his cattle-ranch where we were to stay all night.

The ranch house turned out to be a rude low shack, and here Zulime had her first touch of genuine cowboy life. The foreman had not been expecting ladies for supper and the food he had prepared was of the usual camp sort. He explained that he and his men had finished their meal, and then, leading the way to the kitchen, showed us the food and said heartily, "Help yourself."

On the back of the stove was a pot half filled with a mixture of boiled rice and prunes. In the oven was some soggy bread, and on the hearth some cold bacon. A can half filled with pale brown coffee added the finishing touch to a layout perfectly familiar to me. I thanked the cook and proceeded to dish out some of the rice whose grayish color aroused Zulime's distrust. She refused to even taste it. "It looks as if it were filled with dirt—or ashes."

"That's its natural complexion," I explained. "This is the unpolished kind of rice. It is much more nutritious than the other kind."

She could not eat any of the bread, and when she tried the coffee she was utterly discouraged. Nevertheless her kindliness of heart led her to conceal her disgust. She emptied her rice into the stove and threw her cup of coffee from the window in order that the cook might think that she had eaten her share of the supper.

The foreman who came in a few minutes later to see that we were getting fed politely inquired, "Is there anything else I can get you, miss?"

She really needed something to eat and yet she was puzzled to know what to ask for. At last, in the belief that she was asking for the simplest possible thing, she smiled sweetly and said, "I should like a glass of milk."

The foreman permitted no expression of surprise or displeasure to cross his face, he merely turned to a tall young man in the doorway and quietly remarked, "Mell, the lady would like some milk."

A glint of amusement was in the eyes of Mell, but he made no reply, just quietly "sifted out," and a few moments later, while the foreman was in the midst of a story, a most appalling tumult broke upon our ears. Calves bawled, bulls bellowed, galloping hooves thundered, men shouted and laughed—in a most amazing uproar.

Rushing to the door in search of the cause of this clamor, I found it to be related to my wife's innocent request.

Tied near the cabin was a leaping, blatting, badly frightened calf while inside the corral, a cow evidently its dam, was charging up and down the fence, her eyes literally blazing with fury, pursued by Mell on a swift pony, a rope swinging in his hand. On the top rails of the enclosure a row of delighted loafers laughed and cheered and shouted good advice to the roper.

"What is he doing?" asked my amazed wife, as Mell brought the cow to earth in a cloud of dust.

"Milking the cow," replied the boss with calmly hospitable inflection. "If you'll be patient jest a few minutes——"

The insane animal, strong as a lioness, in some way freed herself from the rope and charged her enemy—Mell's pony fled. "O, don't let him hurt her," pleaded Zulime. "I don't want any milk. I didn't know you had to do that."

"It's the only way to milk a range cow," I explained.

"Don't worry, Miss," the foreman added reassuringly. "It's all in the day's work for Mell."

Again the cow went to earth and Zulime, horrified at the sight, begged them to restore the calf to its dam. At last this was done, and a grateful peace settled over the scene.

The cowboys were highly delighted and I was amused, but Zulime was too shocked to see any humor in Mell's defeat. "Do they really milk their cows in that way?" she asked me.

"Yes, when they milk them at all," I replied, inwardly filled with laughter. "As a matter of fact they get all their cream out of cans. Milking that cow was a new departure for Mell, I think he was a little disappointed at not being allowed to go through with it."

"I'm glad he didn't. I'll never mention milk again—in this country."

We slept in the bed of our wagon-box that night while the crew rode away to fight a prairie fire. We heard them come quietly in toward dawn, and when we awoke and looked out of our cover we saw them lying all about us on the ground each rolled up in his tarpaulin like a boulder. Altogether it was a stirring glimpse of ranch life for my city-bred wife.

Primeau's home ranch and store which we reached about eleven the next forenoon was an almost equally sorry place for a delicate woman, a sad spot in which to spend even a single night. Flies swarmed in the kitchen like bees, and the air of our bedroom was hot and stagnant, and mosquitoes made sleep impossible. Zulime became ill, and I bitterly regretted my action in bringing her into this God forsaken land. "We shall return at once to the fort," I promised her.

It was an iron soil. The valley was a furnace, the sky a brazen shield. No green thing was in sight, and the curling leaves of the dying corn brought back to me those desolate days in Dakota when my mother tried so hard to maintain a garden. Deeply pitying the captive red hunters, who were expected to become farmers under these desolate conditions, I was able to understand how they had turned to the Great Spirit in a last despairing plea for pity and relief. "Think of this place in winter," I said to Zulime.

One of the men whom Primeau especially wished me to meet was Slohan, the annalist of his tribe, one of the "Silent Eaters," a kind of bodyguard to Sitting Bull. "He lives only a few miles up the valley," Primeau explained, and so to find him we set off in a light wagon next morning drawn by a couple of fleet ponies.

As we rode, Primeau told me more of "The Silent Eaters." "They were a small band of young warriors organized for defense and council, and were closely associated with Sitting Bull all his life. Slohan, the man we are to see to-day, is one of those who stood nearest the chief. No man living knows more about him. He can tell you just what you want to know."

An hour later as we were riding along close to the bank of the creek, Primeau stopped his team. "There he is now!" he exclaimed.

Looking where he pointed I discovered on a mound above the stream an old man sitting motionless as a statue, with bowed head, and lax hands. There was something strange, almost tragic in his attitude, and this impression deepened as we approached him.

He was wrinkled with age and clad in ragged white man's clothing, but his profile was fine, fine as that of a Roman Senator, and the lines of his face were infinitely sad. In one fallen hand lay a coiled rope.

He did not look up as we drew near, did not appear to hear Primeau's respectful greeting. Dejected, motionless, he endured the hot sunshine like an Oriental Yoghi or a man deadened by some narcotic drug.

Gently, almost timidly, Primeau addressed him. "Slohan, this white man has come a long way to see you. He wishes to talk with you about the Sitting Bull and of the days of the buffalo."

At last the old man turned and lifted his bloodshot eyes and uttered in a husky whisper, a few words which changed Primeau's whole expression. He drew back. "Come away!" he said to me.

While we were walking toward our team he explained. "Slohan is mourning the death of his little grandson. Long time he has been there wailing. His voice is gone. He can cry no more. His heart is empty. He will not talk with us."

What a revelation of the soul of a red warrior! Hopeless, tragic, inconsolable, he was the type of all paternity throughout the world.

Primeau went on, "I told him of you and I think his mind is turned to other things. I asked him to come to see you this afternoon. Perhaps he will. Perhaps I have lifted his mind from his sorrow."

All the way down the valley I pondered on the picture that grandsire had made there in the midst of that desolate valley.

Primeau told me of his grandson. "He was a handsome little fellow. I can't blame the old man for weeping over his loss."

Slohan was a redoubtable warrior. He had been the leader of Sitting Bull's bodyguard, he was accounted a savage, and yet for forty-eight hours he had been sitting ceaselessly mourning for a child, crying till his voice was only a husky whisper. Nothing that I had ever seen typed the bitterness of barbaric grief more powerfully than this bent and voiceless old man.

Late in the afternoon the mourner came in view, riding on a pony, without a saddle, his face still very sad, but not entirely despairing. His mind, in working backward to the splendid world of the past, the world in which his chief had played such heroic and stirring parts, his heart had been comforted—or at any rate lightened.

Although clothed in the customary rags of the mourner, his hair was neatly brushed and braided, and he met my wife with gentle grace. There was something tragic in his dim glance, something admirable in his low words of greeting.

We gave him food and drink, and then while we all sat on the earth in the scant shade thrown by Primeau's building, he began to talk, slowly, hesitantly of the part his chief had taken in the wars against the white man. He had the dignity and the eloquence of a fine New England judge. A notable sweetness and a lofty poetry were blended in his expression; and as he used the sign language in emphasizing his words (gestures finely expressive and nobly rhythmical) he became, to my perception, the native bard reciting the story of his clan. I was able to follow the broad lines of his discourse and when at the close of the afternoon he rose to go, I said to him, "I shall tell of the Sitting Bull as you have spoken," and we parted in the glow of mutual esteem.

Zulime was feeling much better, and the air being cooler, I asked permission to stay another day, in order that I might meet Looking Stag, another of the warriors who had known the Sitting Bull.

Looking Stag's home was a few miles down the valley, and we found him in his commodious lodge, entertaining a couple of headmen from Cheyenne River. He was seated on a low bed opposite the door, and his guests were placed on either hand of him. He glanced up at us, spoke a curt word to Primeau and went on with his story. His cold greeting, and the evident preoccupation of his manner made me feel like an intruder, which I was, and this feeling was deepened when I perceived that my guide was distinctly ill at ease. After all, he was only a half-breed trader, while these men were red chieftains.

The Looking Stag was not contemptuous of me—he was merely indifferent. Busied with honored guests he regarded the coming of a strange white man to his lodge as something of a nuisance. He went on cutting tobacco, and afterward ground it between his palms whilst his visitors talked on quite oblivious to me.

Standing Rock and Lake McDonald

Our host looked familiar, but as he was painted and wore a bonnet of eagle feathers I could not remember where I had seen him.

At last, in a pause of the talk, Primeau said something to him which caused him to break into a smile and thrust his open hand toward me. "How! How! my friend," he called heartily.

Then I recognized him. He was the man who had so unweariedly taken the part of "The Enemy" in the games at Standing Rock. Primeau had told him that I was the man who had given him the money, and he now accepted me as a friend.

He then told his visitors the story of my gift and message. They also laughed and shook hands with me. Thereafter we were all on terms of high respect and mutual confidence. I put my questions freely and they replied with an air of candor.

As they approached the Custer fight, however, they paused, pondered, checked up one another's statements, and at last produced what I believed to be the truth regarding the share in that battle—and the truth is incredible. They recreated the whole scene for me as Two Moons had done. They corroborated all that I had obtained from the northern Cheyennes.

I forgot the plow and the reaper while sitting there in conference with those men for they were thinkers as well as warriors. Within the walls of that lodge they were not despised outcasts, they were leaders, councillors, men of weight. They had reëntered a world which caused their faces to shine just as my father's face shone when he told of Grant at Vicksburg or recounted the days of his youth on The Old Wisconse. For a little while I inhabited their world, and when I left them I carried with me a deepened sense of their essential manliness.

Alas! Zulime was less enthusiastic. The flies, the heat,

the dust, the bad food—so commonplace to me—were horrifying to her, and so for her sake I cut short my historical studies and hurried her back to the Fort, back to the wholesome fare of the officers' mess. With no consuming literary interest to sustain her she found even the Agency a weariness; and as the date for meeting my father was near, we took the stage back to Bismark, she with a sense of relief, I with a feeling of regret that I had not been able to push my investigations deeper. There was a big theme here, but I had small faith in my ability to handle it. It required an epic poet, rather than a realistic novelist.

Father, excited as a boy, came along on the train which reached Bismark the morning following our arrival and we at once took him into the Pullman car and forced him to share some of the comforts of travel. We ate breakfast in the dining car at what seemed to him a wildly extravagant price but I insisted on his being a guest. "Just sit here and look out of the window and think of the Erie Canal Boats in which you came west, or remember your ox-team in fifty-eight."

"All right," he said with a quizzical smile. "If you can stand the expense, I can." A little later he said, "What a change my life has witnessed. I helped to grade the first railway in the State of Maine, and now here I am whirling along through 'the Great American Desert' eating a steak and drinking my coffee in a flying hotel. I wish your mother could be here with us."

This was the only shadow at our feast and we put it aside, taking comfort in the thought that she was happy in a tree-embowered home, surrounded by the abundance of a prolific garden. "Her days of travel are over," I said, and turned to the task of making my father's outing a shining success.

For ten days we camped with him in Yellowstone Park, moving from place to place, in our own wagon and tent,

and when we came out and he started on his homeward
way, he expressed complete satisfaction. "It has been up
to the bills," he conceded, and I could see that he was
eager to get back to Johnson's drug store, where he could
discuss with Stevens and McEldowney the action of gey-
sers and the habits of grizzly bears, on terms of equal information.

If he was satisfied, I was not. Insisting on showing
Zulime the Cascade Range and the Pacific Ocean, I kept
on to the West. Together we viewed Tacoma and Seattle,
and from the boat on Puget Sound discovered the Olympic
Mountains springing superbly from the sea. For us Rainier
disclosed his dome above the clouds, and Lake McDonald
offered its most gorgeous sunset.

One of the points which I had found of most interest in
'97 was the Blackfoot Agency, and as we sat in our tent on
the Northern shore of Lake McDonald I gained Zulime's
consent to go in there for a few days. "The train lands
us there late at night," I said, "and there is no hotel at
the station or the Agency, but we can set up our tent in a
few moments and be comfortable till morning."

To this she agreed—or perhaps I should say to this she
submitted, and at eleven o'clock the following night we
found ourselves unloaded on the platform of a lonely little
station on the plain. It was a starlit night, fortunately,
and dragging our tent and bedding out on the crisp, dry sod,
we set to work. In ten minutes we had a house and bed
in which we slept comfortably till a freight train thundered by along about dawn. Truly my artist wife was being
schooled in the tactics of the trail!

At the Agency we hired a wagon and drove to the St.
Mary's Lake. With a Piegan (old Four Horns) for a
guide we camped on the lower Lake, and Zulime caught
two enormous pike. At Upper St. Mary's, we set our tent
just below the dike. A "Chalet" on this spot now wel-

comes the tourist, but in those days St. Mary's was a lone, and stormful mountain water with not even a forest ranger's cabin to offer shelter. We lived in our own tent and cooked our own food—a glorious experience to me, but to Zulime (as I learned afterward) the trip was not an unmixed delight.

We visited several other Indian reservations on our way home, and all along the way my mind was busy with the splendid literary problems here suggested. Deep down in my brain a plan was forming to picture these conditions. "First I must put together a volume of short stories to be called *The Red Pioneer;* then I shall complete a prose poem of the Sitting Bull to be called *The Silent Eaters;* and third, and most important of all, I must do a novel of reservation life, with an army officer as the agent."

In these volumes I planned to put the results of all my studies of the Northwest during my many explorations of the wild. In this way I would be doing my part in delineating the swiftly changing conditions of the red man and the mountaineer.

Everywhere I went I studied soldiers, agents, missionaries, traders and squaw-men with insatiable interest. My mind was like a sponge, absorbing not facts, but impressions, pictures which were necessary to make my stories seem like the truth. While in camp and on the train, I took notes busily and actually formulated several tales while riding my horse along the trail.

Perfectly happy in this work, I believed my wife to be equally content, for she bravely declared that to tumble off a pullman in the middle of a moonless night, and help me set up a tent on the prairie grass was fun. She pretended to *enjoy* cooking our food at a smoking camp fire in a drizzle of rain; but I now know that she was longing for the comforts, the conveniences, the repose of West Salem.

"Oh, but it is good to be home," she said as we reached the old house, and I too was ready for its freedom from care and its opportunity for work, happy in the belief that I had bestowed on my wife some part of the store of heroic and splendid experiences, which made up so large a section of my own life, experiences which were to serve as the basis for all my future work.

The flame of my ambition burned brightly at the close of these weeks of inspirational exploration. "With nothing to distract or weaken me I ought now, at least to justify the faith which Howells and other of my literary friends and advisers had been kind enough to declare." Seizing my pen with new resolution I bent to the task of putting into fiction certain phases of the great Northwest which (up to this year) had not been successfully portrayed.

CHAPTER FOURTEEN

The Empty Room

MY father was a loyal G. A. R. man. To him, naturally, the literature, the ceremonies and the comradeship of the Grand Army of the Republic were of heroic significance for, notwithstanding all other events of his stirring life, his two years as a soldier remained his most moving, most poetic experience. On all special occasions he wore the regulation blue coat with the bronze button of the Legion in its lapel, and faithfully attended all the local meetings of his "Post," but he had not been able to take part in the National Conventions for the double reason that they were always too far away from his Dakota home and invariably came at the time when his presence was most needed on the farm. With a feeling of mingled envy and sadness he had seen his comrades, year after year, jubilantly set out for Washington or Boston or San Francisco whilst he remained at work.

Now the case was different. He had the money, he had the leisure and the Grand Review was about to take place in. Chicago. "Hamlin," said he, on the morning after my return from Montana, "I want you to go with me to the G. A. R. meeting in Chicago."

Although I did not say so, I was sadly averse to making this trip. Aching to write, impatient to get my new conceptions down on paper, I could hardly restrain an expression of reluctance, but I did, for the old soldier, more afraid of towns than of mountains, needed me in the city.

The Empty Room

"All right, father," I said, and put my notes away.

He made a handsome figure in his new suit, and his broad-rimmed hat with its gold cord. He was as excited as a boy when we set out for the station and commented with a tone of satisfaction on the number of his comrades to be seen on the train. He was not in need of me during this part of his excursion for he hailed every old soldier as "Comrade" and made a dozen new friendships before we reached Madison. No one resented his fraternal interest. Occasionally he brought one of his acquaintances over to my seat, explaining with perfectly obvious pride that I had written a history of General Grant and that I lived in Chicago. "I'm taking him along to be my scout," he declared, at the close of each introduction.

At my lodgings on Elm Street he made himself so beloved that I feared for his digestion. The landlady and the cook were determined that he should eat hot biscuit and jam and pie in addition to roast chicken and gravy, and I was obliged to insist on his going to bed early in order to be up and in good condition for the parade next day.

"I've no desire to march in the ranks," he said. "I'm perfectly content to sit on the fence and see the columns pass."

"You needn't sit on the fence," I replied. "I've got two of the best seats in the Grand Stand. You can rest there in comfort all through the parade."

He didn't know how much I paid for our chairs, but a knowledge that he was in the seats of the extravagant pleased him while it troubled him. He was never quite at ease while enjoying luxury. It didn't seem natural, someway, for him to be wholly comfortable.

We were in our places hours before the start (he was like a boy on Circus Day—afraid of missing something), but that he was enjoying in high degree his comfortable outlook, made me almost equally content.

At last with blare of bugle and throb of drum, that grand and melancholy procession of time-scarred veterans came to view, and their tattered flags and faded guidons brought quick tears to my father's eyes. Few of them stepped out with a swing, many of them limped pitifully—all were white-haired—an army on its downward slope, marching toward its final, silent bivouac.

None of them were gay and yet each took a poignant pleasure in sharing the rhythm of the column, and my father voiced this emotion when he murmured, "I ought to be down there with my company."

To touch elbows just once more, to be a part of the file would have been at once profoundly sad and sadly sweet, and he wiped the tears from his cheeks in a silence which was more expressive than any words could have been.

To me each passing phalanx was composed of piteous old men—to my sire they were fragments of a colossal dream—an epic of song and steel. "In ten years he and they will all be at rest in 'fame's eternal camping ground,'" I thought with a benumbing realization of the swift, inexorable rush of time—a tragedy which no fluttering of bright flags, no flare of brave bugles could lighten or conceal. It was not an army in review, it was an epoch passing to its grave.

After the parade was over, as we were going home in the car, tired, silent and sad, I perceived my father as others saw him, a white-haired veteran whose days of marching, of exploration were over. His powerful figure, so resilient and so brave was stooping to its end. His restless feet were weary.

However, this was only a mood with him. A night's sleep brought back his courage, and his energy to a most amazing degree, and I was again called upon to show him the "sights" of the city—that is to say, we once more viewed the Stock Yards, the Masonic Temple and Lincoln

The Empty Room

Park. He also asked me to go with him for a sail across the Lake, but at this point I rebelled. "I am willing to climb tall buildings or visit the Zoo, but I draw the line at a trip to Muskegon."

With guilty conscience I watched him start off for the dock alone, but this sentiment on my part was wasted. A score of "comrades" on the boat more than made up for my absence, and at sunset he returned beaming, triumphant, perfectly satisfied with his day's sail. "Now, I'm ready to go home," he announced.

After putting him on the train next day I opened my desk in my quiet room on Elm Street, with a feeling of being half-in and half-out of the state of matrimony. In some ways I liked being alone. A greater power of concentration resulted. With no disturbing household influences, no distracting interests, I wrote all the morning, but at night, when my work was done, my mind went out toward my young wife. To have her moving about the room would have been pleasant. To walk with her to the studio would have been a joy. As a novelist, I bitterly resented all the minute domestic worries, but as a human being I rejoiced in my new relationship. "Can I combine the two activities? Will being a husband and a householder cramp and defeat me as a novelist?"

These questions every writer who is ambitious to excel, must answer for himself. So far as I was concerned, the decision had been made. Having elected myself into the ranks of those who were carrying forward the immemorial traditions of the race, there was no turning back for me. I ended the week by going out to Eagle's Nest Camp, where Zulime met me to renew the delight of our days of courtship.

Even here, I did not neglect my task. Wallace Heckman gave me a desk in the attic and there each morning I hammered away, eager to get my material "roughed out" while it was hot in my memory. I often wrote four thousand words between breakfast and luncheon. One story took shape as a brief prose epic of the Sioux, a special pleading from the standpoint of a young educated red man, to whom Sitting Bull was a kind of Themistocles. Though based on accurate information, I intended it to be not so much a history as an interpretation. It interested me at the time and so—I wasted a week!

Life at camp was very pleasant, but as my brother wrote me that he must return to New York I felt it my duty to go home and see that my mother "attended" the County Fair, which was a most important event to her. "Mother's life retains so few interests," I explained to Zulime, "that to miss the Fair would be to her a great deprivation. You can stay here but I must go home and take her down to the old settlers' picnic in Floral Hall."

Zulime understood. Loyally cutting short her pleasant companionship with her fellow artists she returned with me to West Salem a few days before the fair opened.

Fuller, who timed his visit to be with us during the exhibition, professed a keen interest in every department of it. His attitude was comically that of a serious-minded European tourist. He not only purchased a catalogue, he treated it precisely as if it were the hand-book of the Autumn Salon in Paris. Carrying it in his hand, he spent busy hours minutely studying "Spatter Work," and carefully inspecting decorated bedspreads. He tasted the prize bread, sampled the honey, and twirled the contesting apples. Nothing escaped his notice. He was as alert, and (apparently) as vitally concerned as any of the "judges," but I, knowing his highly-critical mind, could only smile at his reports.

He was a constant joy, not only to Zulime and to me, but to our friends, the Eastons. One day as we were digging potatoes he gave me a lecture on my duty as a Wisconsin novelist. "You should do for this country what

The Empty Room

Thomas Hardy has done for Wessex," he said. "You have made a good start in *Main Traveled Roads,* and *Rose of Dutcher's Coolly,* but you should do more with it. It is a noble background."

"Why not do something with it yourself?" I retorted.

"You are almost as much a part of Wisconsin as I am. I've done my part and moved on. My keenest interests now are in the Mountain West—a larger field. There's no use saying 'Make more of this material!' I can only do what I feel. Just now I am full of Montana. Why don't you celebrate Eagle's Nest? If you weren't so myopic you'd perceive in that little artist colony something quite as literary as the life which Hawthorne lived at Brook Farm."

"I'm no Hawthorne," he replied. "I'm not even Margaret Fuller. I don't want to write about Camp—in fact I don't want to write about anything. I'd rather drive nails or superintend a tinner."

In this way our discussion usually ended—with each of us going his own gait. In this instance his way led back to Chicago. "I must return to my plumbing," he protested. "I've got some renters who are complaining of their furnaces," and that was the end of his visit. We knew better than to argue for delay. He was as inflexible as New England granite.

His going left a gap. We both liked to have him about. Never in the way, never interfering with my work, he was always a stimulant. His judgment (second only to Howells' in my estimation) kept me to my highest level. He was the only man with whom I could discuss all my perplexities and be enlightened.

As October came on my mother's condition called for increasing care. She could not walk across the road and her outings were all taken in a wheeled chair, which I pushed about the village each afternoon. She was very happy when we were at home, but as she could neither sew nor read she was piteously dependent upon the members of her household for diversion. Life's walls were narrowing for her, that was sorrowfully evident to me; and yet I did not—I would not consider the possibility of her early passing. I thought of her as living on for many years longer. It was her growing inability to employ her time which troubled me and I gave the most of my afternoons to her amusement.

As my father wrote from Dakota early in October setting November 1st as the date for his return, I began to plan another trip to New York, feeling that it was better to go in the early autumn than to wait till winter. "Winters are very hard on old folks in our valley," I remarked to Zulime. To mother I said, "Our absence will not be long. We'll be back in time for Thanksgiving," I assured her.

She dreaded our going. Clinging to us both as though she feared we might never return she pleadingly said, "Wait till your father comes," and her distress of mind caused me to put off our departure until father could arrive.

These moods of depression, these periods of suffering which she could not explain, were usually transitory, and this one soon passed. In a day or two she was free from pain, and quite cheerful. "You may go," she said at last, but warningly added, "Don't stay away too long!"

In spite of her smiling face, I kissed her good-by with a sense of uneasiness, almost of guilt. "It seems a selfish act to leave her at this time," I confessed to Zulime, "and yet if we are to get away at all, it is safer to go now."

In order to save time for our eastern trip, we went through Chicago almost without stopping, and upon reaching New York, took the same suite of rooms on Fifteenth Street in which we had lived the previous year. In an hour we were settled.

My brother, who was playing an engagement in the city, came at once to inquire about the old folks and I gave a good report. "Mother has her ups and downs," I explained, "but she is very comfortable in her new rooms. Of course she misses her sons and her new daughter—I am not sure, but she misses the new daughter more than she misses you and me, but we shall soon return to her."

The Eagle's Heart, which had been running with favor as a serial, was just being published in book form, and we were in high hopes of it.

At the same time the Century Company was preparing to issue *Her Mountain Lover,* which had already been printed in the magazine. Altogether my presence in New York seemed opportune, if not actually necessary, a fact which I made much of in writing to the old folks in the West.

Gilder, who met me on the street soon after our arrival in New York, spoke to me in praise of *Her Mountain Lover.* "I predict a great success for it. It has beauty——" here he smiled. "I am always preaching 'beauty' to you, but you need it! You should remember that the writing which is beautiful is the writing which lasts."

He was looking thin and bent and gray, and I experienced a keen pang of fear. "Gilder is growing old," I thought, and this feeling of change was deepened a few days later by the death of Charles Dudley Warner.

"The older literary men, the writers who have been my guides and my exemplars, are dropping away! I am no longer 'a young and promising novelist.' It is time I delivered my message—if I have any," I reminded myself, with a realization that I was now in the mid-ranks, pushed on by younger and more vigorous authors. Frank Norris and Stewart Edward White were crowding close upon my lagging heels. With this in my thought I got out my manuscript and set to work.

I would have been entirely happy in the midst of many delightful meetings with my fellow craftsmen had it not been for a growing sense of anxiety concerning my mother's condition. Father's brief notes were not reassuring. "Your mother needs you," he said, in effect, and I began to plan our return. "We have a few engagements," I wrote, "but you may expect us for our usual Thanksgiving Dinner."

I will not say that I had a definite premonition of trouble, I was just uneasy. I felt inclined to drop all our social engagements and start for home but I did not carry out the impulse.

On Sunday, the twenty-fifth of November, after a delightful dinner with Augustus Thomas in his home at New Rochelle, Zulime and I returned to our apartment in happiest humor, to be met by a telegram which went to my heart like the thrust of a bayonet. It was from my father. *"Your mother is very low. Come at once."*

For a few moments I remained standing, like a man stunned by a savage blow. Then I awoke to the need of haste in getting away to the West. It was five o'clock in the afternoon, and the last train which would enable us to connect with the Milwaukee train from Chicago to West Salem, left at half-past six. "We must make that train," I said to Zulime with a desperate realization of the need of haste.

The rush of packing, the excitement of getting to the station kept me from the sinking of spirit, the agony of self-accusation which set in the moment we were safely in the sleeping car, and speeding on our homeward way. "If only we can reach her before it is too late," was my prayer. "I shall never forgive myself for leaving her. I knew she was not well," I confessed to Zulime, whose serene optimism comforted me, or at least dulled the edge of my self-reproach. Again I telegraphed that we were coming, giving the name and number of our train, hoping to have an encouraging reply from father or the doctor during the evening, but none came.

The Empty Room

The long agonizing hours wore on. A hundred times I accused myself, "I should not have left her."

At all points where I attacked myself, my wife defended me, excused me, and yet I could not clear myself—could not rest. In imagination I pictured that dear, sweet face turned toward the door, and heard that faint voice asking for me.

It is true I had done many considerate things for her, but I had not done enough. Money I had given her, and a home, but I had not given her as much of my time, my service, as I might have done,—as I should have done. My going away to the city at the very moment when my presence was most necessary seemed base desertion. While she had been suffering, longing and lonely, I had been feasting. All my honors, all my writing, seemed at this moment too slight, too trivial to counter-balance my mother's need, my mother's love.

Midnight came without a message, and I went to bed, slightly comforted, hoping that a turn for the better had taken place. I slept fitfully, waking again and again to the bleak possibilities of the day. A persistent vision of a gray-haired mother watching and waiting for her sons filled my brain. That she was also longing for Zulime I knew, for she loved her, and thought of her as a daughter.

In this agony of remorse and fear I wore out the night, and as no word came in the morning, I ate my breakfast in half-recovered tranquillity.

"It must be that she is better," Zulime said, but at nine o'clock a telegram from the doctor destroyed all hope. "Your mother is unconscious. Do not hope to find her alive," was his desolating message.

Every devoted son who reads this line will shiver as I shivered. That warning came like a wind from the dark spaces of a bleak, uncharted deep. It changed my world. For twenty years my mother had been my chief care. My

daily thought ran to her. Only when deeply absorbed in
my work had she been absent from my conscious mind.
For her I had planned, for her I had saved, for her I had
built, and now——!

That day was the longest, bitterest, I had ever known,
for the reason that, mixed with my grief, my sense of remorse, was a feeling of utter helplessness. In desperate desire for haste I could only lumpishly wait. Another day
of agony, another interminable night of pain must pass
before I could reach the shadowed Homestead. Nothing
could shorten the interval. Then, too, I realized that she
whom I would comfort had already gone beyond my aid,
beyond any comfort I could send.

Over and over I repeated, "If only we had started a few
days sooner!" The truth is I had failed of a son's duty
just when that duty was most needed, and this conviction
brought an almost intolerable ache into my throat. Nothing that Zulime could do or say removed that pain. I could
not eat, and I could not rest.

We reached Chicago in time to catch the night train at
ten o'clock, and in almost utter mental exhaustion I fell
asleep about midnight, and slept till nearly daylight.

Father met us at the train, as he had so often done before, but this time there was something in the pinched gray
look of his face, something in the filmed light of his eagle
eyes which denoted, movingly, the tragic experiences
through which he had just passed. Before he spoke I knew
that mother had passed beyond my reach.

As he gripped my hand I perceived that he was smitten
but unbowed. He was taking his orders like a soldier,
without complaint or question.—Only when Zulime kissed
him did he give way.

As we entered the gate I perceived with a pang of dread
the wheeled chair, standing empty on the porch, pathetic

214

witness of the one who had no further need of it. Within doors, the house showed the disorder, the desolate confusion, the terror which death had brought. The furniture was disarranged—the floor muddy, and in the midst of the chill little parlor rested a sinister, flower-strewn box. In this was all that remained of Isabel McClintock, my mother.

For a few minutes I stood looking about me, a scalding blur in my eyes, a choking in my throat. The south room, *her* room, was empty, intolerably, accusingly empty. The gentle, gray-haired figure was no longer in its place before the window. The smiling lips which had so often touched my cheek on my return were cold. The sweet, hesitant voice was forever silent.

Her dear face I did not see. I refused to look upon her in her coffin. I wanted to remember her as she appeared when I said good-by to her that bright October evening, her white hair gleaming in the light of the lamp, while soft curves about her lips suggested a beautiful serenity. How patient and loving she had been! Even though she feared that she might never see us again she had sent us away in cheerful self-sacrifice.

Father was composed but tense. He went about his duties with solemn resignation, and, an hour or two later, he said to me, "You and I must go down and select a burial lot, a place for your mother and me."

It was a desolate November morning, raw and gloomy, but the gray sky and the patient, bare-limbed elms were curiously medicinal to my sore heart. In some strange way they comforted me. Snow was in the air and father mechanically weather-wise, said, without thinking of the bitter irony of his words—"Regular Thanksgiving weather."

Thanksgiving weather! Yes, but what Thanksgiving could there be for him or for me, now?

* * * * * *

The day of the funeral was still more savagely cold and bleak, and I resented its pitiless gloom. The wind which blew over the open grave of my dead mother was sinister as hate, and the snow which fell, intolerably stern. I turned away. I could not see that box lowered into the merciless soil. My mother's spirit was not there—I knew that—and yet I could not bear to think of those tender lips, those loving hands going into the dark. It was a harsh bed for one so gentle and so dear.

Back to the Homestead we drove—back to an empty shell. The place in which Isabel Garland's wish had been law for so many years was now desolate and drear, and return would have been impossible for me had it not been for the presence of my wife, whose serene soul was my comfort and my stay. "You have done all that a son could do," she insisted, and it was a comfort to have her say this even though I knew that it was not true, her faith in me and her youth and beauty partly redeemed me from the awful emptiness of that home. Without her (and all that she represented) my father and I would have been victims of a black despair.

I had never possessed a definite belief in immortality and yet, as we gathered about our table that night, I could not rid myself of a feeling that my mother was in her room, and that she might at any moment cough, or stir, or call to me. Realizing with appalling force that so far as my philosophy went our separation was eternal, I nevertheless hoped that her spirit was with us at that moment, I did not know it—I desired it. In the sense which would have made belief a solace and relief, I was agnostic.

"How strange it all seems!" my father exclaimed, and on his face lay such lines of dismay as I had never seen written there before. "It seems as though I ought to go and wheel her in to dinner."

I marvel now, as I marveled then, at the buoyant helpfulness, the brave patience of my wife in the presence of her stricken and bewildered household. She sorrowed but she kept her calm judgment, and set about restoring the interrupted routine of our lives. Putting away all signs of the gray intruder whose hands had scattered the ashes of ruin across our floor, she called on me to aid in uniting our broken circle. Under her influence I soon regained a certain composure. With a realization that it was not fair that she should bear all the burden of the family reorganization, I turned from death and faced the future with her. On her depended the continuation of our family. She was its hope and its saving grace.

BOOK II

CHAPTER FIFTEEN

A Summer in the High Country

MY first morning in the old Homestead without my
mother was so poignant with its sense of loss, so
rich with memories both sweet and sorrowful, that I shut
myself in my study and began a little tribute to her, a
sketch which I called *The Wife of a Pioneer*. Into this I
poured the love I had felt but failed to express as fully as
I should have done while she was alive. To make this her
memorial was my definite purpose.

As I went on I found myself deep in her life on the farm
in Iowa, and the cheerful heroism of her daily treadmill
came back to me with such appeal that I could scarcely see
the words in which I was recording her history. Visioning
the long years of her drudgery, I recalled her early rising,
and suffered with her the never-ending round of dish-
washing, churning, sewing, and cooking, realizing more
fully than ever before that in all of this slavery she was but
one of a million martyrs. All our neighbors' wives walked
the same round. On such as they rests the heavier part
of the home and city building in the West. The wives of the
farm are the unnamed, unrewarded heroines of the border.

For nearly a week I lingered upon this writing, and having
completed it I was moved to print it, in order that it might
remind some other son of his duty to his ageing parents

sitting in the light of their lonely hearth, and in doing this I again vaguely forecast the composition of an autobiographic manuscript—one which should embody minutely and simply the homely daily toil of my father's family, although I could not, at the moment, define the precise form into which the story would fall.

The completion of the memorial to my mother eased my heart of its bitter self-accusation, and a little later I returned to my accustomed routine, realizing that in my wife now lay my present incentive and my future support. She became the center of my world. In her rested my hope of happiness. My mother was a memory.

To remain longer in the old home was painful, for to me everything suggested the one for whom it had been established. The piano I had bought for her, the chair in which she had loved to sit, her spectacles on the stand—all these mute witnesses of her absence benumbed me as I walked about her room. Only in my work-shop was I able to find even momentary relief from my sense of irreparable and eternal loss.

Father, as though bewildered by the sudden change in his life, turned to Zulime with a pathetic weakness which she met with a daughter's tender patience and a woman's intuitive understanding. He talked to her of his first meeting with "Belle" and his tone was that of a lover, one who had loved long and deeply, and this I believe was true. In spite of unavoidable occasional moments of friction, he and Isabel McClintock had lived in harmony. They had been spiritually married, and now, in looking back over the long road he and she had traveled together, he recalled only its pleasant places. His memories were all of the sunlit meadows and starry nights along the way. Prairie pinks and wild roses hid the thorns and the thistles of the wayside.

His joy in the songs she had sung came back, intensified

now by tender association with her face and voice. The knowledge that she who had voiced them so often, could voice them no more, gave to some of the words an almost overpowering pathos, and when he asked me to sing them, I could not immediately comply. To him they brought grateful tears and a consoling sadness, to me they came with tragic significance.

> "But that mother she is gone
> Calm she sleeps beneath the stone"

was not a song but a reality.

More and more he dwelt upon the time when she was young, and as the weeks went by his sorrow took on a wistful, vague longing for the past. Through the gate of memory he reëntered the world of his youth and walked once more with William and David and Luke. The mists which filled his eyes had nothing hot or withering in their touch—they comforted him. Whether he hoped to meet his love in some other world or not I do not know—but I think he did.

In the midst of these deep emotional personal experiences, I began to write (almost as if in self-defense), a novel which I called *The Gray Horse Troop*, a story which had been slowly forming in my mind ever since my visit to Lame Deer in 1897. This was my first actual start upon its composition and I was soon in full drive again, and just in proportion as I took on these fictional troubles did my own lose their power. To Zulime, with a feeling of confidence in myself, I now said, "You need not remain here any longer. Go down to Chicago and wait for me. I'll come as soon as father feels like letting me go. I am all right now. I am at work."

She smiled but replied with firm decision, "I shall stay

right here until you can go with me. Father needs me more than he needs you."

This was true. She would have been deserting two men instead of one—and so she stayed while I worked away at my story, finding comfort in the realization of her presence.

At last my father said, "You mustn't stay here on my account; I can take care of myself."

Here spoke the stark spirit of the man. Accustomed to provide for himself in camp and on the trail, he saw no reason why he should not contrive to live here in the sheltered village, surrounded by his friends; but Zulime insisted upon his retaining our housekeeper, and to this he consented, although he argued against it. "I've been keeping house alone for six years out there in Dakota; I guess I can do as well here."

"All right, father," I said, "we'll go, but if you need me let me know."

A return to the city did not interrupt my writing. My new novel now had entire possession of me. So far as my mornings were concerned I was forgetful of everything else—and yet, often, as I put aside my work for the day, I caught myself saying, *"Now I must write to mother,"*— and a painful clutch came into my throat as I realized, once again, that I no longer had a mother waiting for a letter. For twenty years no matter where I had been or what I had been doing I had written to her an almost daily message and now she was no longer in my reach!—Was she near me on some other plane?

The good friendship of the Eagles' Nest Campers was of the highest value to me at this time. Without them Chicago would have been a desert. Henry Fuller's gay spirit, Lorado's swift wit and the good fraternal companionship of Charles Francis Browne were of daily comfort;

but above all others I depended upon my wife whose serenely optimistic spirit carried me over many a deep slough of despond. How I leaned upon her! Her patience with me was angelic.

A writer, like an artist, is apt to be a selfish brute, tending to ignore everything which does not make for the progress of his beloved manuscript. He resents every interruption every hindering distraction, as a hellish contrivance, maliciously designed to worry or obstruct him—At least I am that way. That I was a burden, an intolerable burden to my wife, at times—many times—I must admit—but she understood and was charitable. She defended me as best she could from interruption and smoothed my daily course with deft hand. Slowly my novel began to take shape and as I drew farther away from the remorseful days which made my work seem selfish and vain, I recovered an illogical cheerfulness.

We saw very few Chicago people and in contrast with our previous "season" in New York our daily walk was uneventful, almost rural, in its quiet round. Christmas came to us without special meaning but 1900 went out with *The Eagle's Heart* on the market, and *Her Mountain Lover* going to press. Aside from my sense of bereavement, and a certain anxiety concerning my lonely old father, I was at peace and Zulime seemed happy and confident.

There was no escaping my filial responsibility, however, for in the midst of this serene season, a sudden call for help came from West Salem. "Your father is ill and needs you," wrote the doctor and I went at once to his aid.

It was a cheerless home-coming,—one that I could hardly endure the thought of, and yet I was glad that I had not followed my first impulse to delay it, for as I entered the door of the desolate lonely house I found the old soldier stretched out on a couch, piteously depressed in mind and flushed with fever. I had not arrived a minute too soon.

What a change had come over the Homestead! It was but a shell, a mansion from which the spirit for whom it had been built was fled. Its empty, dusty rooms, so cold and silent and dead—were dreadful to me, but I did my best to fill them with cheer for my father's sake.

As the day wore on I said to him, "It seems like Sunday to me. I have a feeling that mother and Zulime are away at church and that they may, at any moment, come in together."

"I wish Zuleema would come," my father said, and as if in answer to his wish, she surprised us by a telegram. "I am coming home," she wired, "meet me at the station to-morrow morning," and this message made my father so happy that it troubled me, for it revealed to me how deeply he had missed her, and made plain to me also how difficult it would be for me to take her away from him thereafter.

Her coming put such life in the house that I decided to invite a number of my father's friends and neighbors to spend the evening with us, and the thought of this party quite restored him to his natural optimism. His confidence in his new daughter's ability had become fixed. He accepted her judgments almost instantly. He bragged of her skill as a cook, as an artist and as a musician, quite shamelessly; but as this only amused her I saw no reason for interfering —I even permitted him to boast of my singing. He believed me to be one of the most remarkable ballad singers in the world, and to hear me sing "The Ninety and Nine" with all the dramatic modulations of a professional evangelist afforded him the highest satisfaction.

At his urging we made elaborate preparations for feeding our guests, and Zulime arranged a definite program of entertainment. When conversation slackened I was to sing while she played my accompaniment, and to fill out the program I volunteered to read one of my short stories.

The outcome of the evening was amusingly destructive of all our kindly plans. Before the women had fairly removed their wraps, Lottridge drew a box of dominoes from his pocket, saying, "I didn't know but you'd be a little short on 'bones,'" and Shane called out, "Well, now, Richard, what about tables?"—In five minutes they were all— every mother's son and daughter of them—bent above a row of dominoes!

No entertainment on the part of host or hostess was necessary till the time came to serve supper. All our literary and musical preparations went for naught!—At ten o'clock they rose as one man, thanked us for a pleasant evening and went home!

Zulime laughed merrily over the wreck of our self-sacrificing program when we were alone. "Well, we'll know exactly what to do next time. All we need to do is to furnish dominoes and tables, our guests will do the rest."

My young wife's presence in the Homestead almost redeemed it from its gloom, and yet I was not content. The complications in the situation defied adjustment. My father needed us, but the city was essential to me. As a writer, I should have been remorselessly selfish. I should have taken my wife back to Chicago at once, but my New England conscience would not let me forget how lonely that old man would be in this empty house, silent, yet filled with voices of the moaning, swaying branches of its bleak midwinter elms.

My problem was, in fact, only another characteristic cruel phase of American family history. In a new land like ours, the rising generation finds itself, necessarily, almost cruelly, negligent of its progenitors. Youth moves on, away and up from the farm and the village. Age remains below and behind. The tragedy of this situation lies in the fact that there is no happy solution of the problem. Youth can not be shackled, age can not be transplanted.

In my case, I foresaw that the situation would inevitably become more and more difficult year by year. My father could not live in any city, and for me to give up my life in Chicago and New York in order to establish a permanent home in West Salem, involved a sacrifice which I was not willing to make,—either on my òwn account or Zulime's. I had no right to demand such devotion from her. Like thousands of other men of my age I was snared in circumstances—forced to do that which appeared unfilial and neglectful.

In the midst of these perplexities I was confronted by a new and surprising problem—I had money to invest! For the serial use of *The Eagle's Heart* and *Her Mountain Lover* I had received thirty-five hundred dollars, and as each of these books had also brought in an additional five hundred dollars advance royalty, I was for the moment embarrassed with cash.

In this extremity I turned, naturally, toward Oklahoma. I recalled the beautiful prairies I had crossed on my way to the Washitay. "Another visit to Darlington will not only furnish new material for my book of Indian stories, but enable me to survey and purchase a half-section of land," I explained to my father. "Like Henry George we both understand the value of unearned increment."

In this plan he agreed and two days after making this decision I was at Colony, Oklahoma, where I spent nearly the entire month of May, and when I returned I was the owner of three hundred and twenty acres of land.

My return to the Homestead found Zulime deep in the rush of the berry season. As mistress of a garden her interest in its produce was almost comical. She thought less of art, she neither modeled nor painted. She cared less and less for the Camp at Eagle's Nest, exulting more and more in the spacious rooms of her home, and in the abundance of her soil. Her love of the Homestead delighted me, but I was a little disappointed by the coolness with which she received my gift of a deed to a quarter section of Oklahoma land. She smiled and handed it back to me as if it were a make-believe deed.

It chanced that July came in unusually dry and hot, and in the midst of a dreadful week, she fell ill, so ill that she was confined to her bed for nearly three weeks, and as I watched beside her during those cloudless days and sultry nights, my mind turned with keenest longing toward the snow-lined crests of the Colorado mountains, and especially to the glorious forests of the White River Plateau. The roar of snowy Uncompagre, the rush of the deep-flowing Gunnison, and the serrate line of The Needle Peaks, called us both, and when at last, she was strong enough to travel, we packed our trunks and fled the low country, hurrying in almost desperate desire to reach the high, cool valleys of Colorado.

O, that torturing journey! As we neared Omaha the thermometer rose to 105 in the Pullman car, and remained there nearly all day. For twelve hours we steamed, sitting rigidly erect in our chairs, dreading to move, sweltering in silence, waiting with passionate intensity for the cool wind which we knew was certain to meet us somewhere on our upward course.

The sun went down in murky flame and the very shadows were hot, but deep in the night I was roused by a delicious puff of mountain air, and calling to Zulime, suffering in her berth, I said, "Worry no longer about the heat. From this hour on, every moment will be joy. You can forget the weather in Colorado."

What exquisite relief came with that change of air! What sweetness of promise! What buoyancy of expectation!—We went to sleep with the wind blowing in upon us, and when we woke the mountains were in sight.

At the station in the Springs, our good friend Louis Ehrich again met us, and in half an hour we stood in the same room which we had occupied on our wedding trip, a room whose windows faced directly upon the Rampart range, already deep purple with the shadow of the clouds. By contrast with our torrid railway car this was Paradise itself—so clean, so cool, so sweet, so tonic was the air, and when at noon a storm hid the peaks, and lightning crashed above the foot hills, the arid burning plain over which we came was forgotten—or remembered only to make our enjoyment of the mountain air more complete.

The splendor of that mighty wall, the kiss of that wind, the memory of that majestic peak looming amid the stars, comes back to me as I write, filling me with an almost intolerable longing to recover the magic of that summer, a summer which has receded with the speed of an eagle.

Each day we breakfasted and lunched and dined on a vine-clad porch in full view of the mountains. Each afternoon we drove or rode horseback or loitered on the lawn. Never in all my life had I come so near to flawless content, and Zulime, equally joyous, swiftly returned to perfect health. Her restoration was magical.

Louis Ehrich, one of the gentlest men I have ever known, rejoiced in our presence. He lived but to fill our days with pleasure. He and I had been friends for ten years, and his family now took my wife into favor—I was about to say into equal favor, but that would not be true. They very properly put her above me in the scale of their affection, and to this subordination I submitted without complaint, or even question.

A Summer in the High Country

It chanced that on the second day of our stay the Ehrichs were due at a garden party in "Glen Eyrie," General Palmer's palatial home in the foot hills, and kindly obtained permission to bring us with them. That drive across the mesa was like a journey into some far country—passage to a land which was neither America nor England, neither East nor West. To reach the Castle we entered a gate at the mouth of a narrow, wooded cañon and drove for nearly a mile toward the west through a most beautiful garden in which all the native shrubs and wild flowers had been assembled and planted with exquisite art.

People were streaming in over the mountain roads, some on horseback, some on bicycles, some in glittering, gayly-painted wagons, and when we reached the lawn before the great stone mansion, we found a very curious and interesting throng of guests, and in the midst of them, the General, tall, soldierly, clothed in immaculate linen and wearing a broad white western hat, was receiving his friends, assisted by his three pretty young daughters.

The house was a veritable chateau—the garden a wonderland of Colorado plants and flowers, skilfully disposed among the native ledges and scattered along the bases of the cliffs whose rugged sides enclosed the mansion grounds. The towers (of gray stone) were English, but the plants and blooms were native to the Rampart foot hills. In a very real fashion "Glen Eyrie" bodied forth the singular and powerful character of its owner, who was at once an English squire, a Pennsylvania civil war veteran, and a western railway engineer.

Food and drink and ices of various kinds were being served under the trees with lavish hospitality, and groups of young people were wandering about the spacious grounds —grounds so beautiful by reason of nature's adjustment, as well as by way of the landscape gardener's art, that they made the senses ache with a knowledge of their exquisite impermanency. It was a kind of poem expressed in green and gold and scarlet.

Zulime greatly interested the Palmer girls, and the General, who remembered me pleasantly, was most amiable to us both. "You must come again," he said, and to me he added, "You must come over some day and ride my trails with me."

As I mingled with that throng of joyous folk, I lost myself. I became an actor in a prodigious and picturesque American social comedy. For stage we had the lawn, banks of flowers, and the massive towers of the castle. For background rose the rugged hills!—Nothing could have been farther from our home in Neshonoc. Glowing with esthetic delight in the remote and singular beauty of the place, Zulime took an artist's keen interest in alien loveliness. It threw our life into commonplace drab. And yet it was factitious. It had the transient quality of a dream in which we were but masqueraders.

Two days later, at the invitation of General Palmer, we joined his party in a trip over the short-line railway to Cripple Creek, traveling in his private car, and the luxury of this novel experience made my wife's eyes shine with girlish delight.—I professed alarm, "I don't know where all this glory is going to land us," I warned, "after this Aladdin's-lamp luxury and leisure, how can I get you back into washing dishes and canning fruit in West Salem?"

She laughed at this, as she did at most of my fears. Serene acceptance of what came was her dominant characteristic. Her faith in the future was so perfect that she was willing to make the fullest use of the present.

The day was gloriously clear, with great white clouds piled high above the peaks, and as the train crept steadily upward, feeling its way across the mountain's shoulder, we were able to look back and down and far out upon the plain which was a shoreless sea of liquid opal. At ten thousand feet the foot hills (flat as a rug) were so rich in color, so alluring in their spread that we could scarcely believe them to be composed of rocks and earth.

After a day of sight-seeing we returned, at sunset, to the Springs, with all of the pomp of railway magnates *en tour*, and as we were about to part at the railway station, the General in curt, off-hand way, asked, "Why not join my camping party at Sierra Blanca? We're going down there for a week or two, and I shall be very glad to have you with us. Come, and stay as long as you can. We shall probably move on to Wagon Wheel Gap later. Wagon Wheel ought to interest you."

He said this with a quizzical smile, for he had been reading my novel of Colorado, and recognized in my scene the splendors of the San Juan country. "Your friend Ehrich is coming," he added, "and I expect Sterling Morton for a day or two. Why not all come down together?"

"Would you like me to bring my bed and tent?" I asked.

"As you please, although I have plenty of room in my own outfit."

It happened that Colorado Springs was holding a Quarto-Centenary, a kind of Carnival and Wild-West Pageant, to which Vice-President Roosevelt was coming as the chief guest of honor, and as soon as he arrived I called upon him at his hotel. Almost at once he asked, "Where is your wife? I want to see her. Is she here?"

"Yes, she is staying with some friends," I replied.

"I am very glad to know it. I shall call upon her to-morrow afternoon as soon as my duties at the carnival are ended."

The thought of having the Vice-President of the United

States go out of his way to make a call upon my wife gave me a great deal of pleasure for I realized how much it would mean to Zulime, but I replied, "We shall be very glad to call upon *you*."

"No," he replied in his decisive fashion—"I shall call to-morrow at four o'clock—if that is convenient to you. Meanwhile I want you and Mr. Ehrich to breakfast with me here, at the hotel. I shall have some hunters and rough riders at my table whom you will be interested to meet."

Of course I accepted this invitation instantly, and hurried home to tell my wife that "royalty" was about to call upon her.

The Vice-President's breakfast party turned out to be a very curious collection of mutually repellent, but highly-developed individualities. There was John Goff, well known as guide and hunter in western Colorado, and Marshall Davidson, a rough-rider from New Mexico, Lieutenant Llewellyn of the Rough Riders, Sterling Morton (former Secretary of Agriculture), a big impassive Nebraska pioneer; Louis Ehrich (humanist and art lover), and myself— I cannot say that I in any way reduced the high average of singularity, but I was at least in the picture—Morton and Ehrich were not; they remained curious rather than sympathetic listeners. While no longer a hunter I was a trailer and was able to understand and keenly enjoy the spirit of these hardy men of the open.

True to his word, Roosevelt called at the Ehrich's that afternoon, and no one could have been more charming, more neighborly than he. He told of our first meeting, smilingly called me "a Henry George crank," and referred to other differences which existed between us. "Differences which do not in the least interfere with our friendship," he assured Zulime. "Your husband, for example, doesn't believe in hunting, and has always stood out against my shooting," here he became quite serious—"However, I've given up shooting deer and elk. I kill only 'varmints' now."

After half an hour of lively conversation, he rose to go and as I went with him to the gate, where his carriage was waiting, he said with earnest emphasis, "I congratulate you most heartily, my dear fellow. Your wife is fine! fine!"

As Morton and Ehrich had accepted General Palmer's invitation to camp with him, we all took train for Fort Garland, a mysterious little town in Southern Colorado, near which the General was encamped. This expedition particularly pleased me for it carried me into the shadow of Sierra Blanca, one of the noblest of Colorado's peaks, and also into the edge of the Mexican settlement. It all seemed very remote and splendid to me that day.

We were met at the station by one of the General's retainers and ten minutes later found ourselves in a mountain wagon and on our way toward Old Baldy, the mountain which stands just north of Sierra Blanca, which forms the majestic southern bastion of the Crestones.

Mexican huts lined the way, and dark-skinned farmers working in the fields and about the corrals, gave evidence of the fact that this "land grant" had been, at one time, a part of Old Mexico.

"It contains nearly seven hundred thousand acres," Ehrich explained, " and is the property of General Palmer."

This statement aroused a sense of wonder in my mind. "Think of being proprietor of one-half of Sierra Blanca?" I said to Morton. "Has any individual a right to such a privilege?"

In a lovely grove on the bank of a rushing glorious stream, we found the Lord of this Demesne and his three daughters encamped, attended by a platoon of cooks, valets, maids, and hostlers. A "camp" which highly amused

Sterling Morton, although he had moments of resenting its luxury. "Now this is the kind of 'roughing it' I believe in," he declared with a smile. "It is suited to elderly old parties like Ehrich and myself, but you, Garland, a youngster, a trailer—should have no part in it. It's too corrupting."

Our luncheon, which contained five courses, came on with the plenitude and precision of a meal at Glen Eyrie. The rusticity of the function was altogether confined to the benches on which we sat and the tables from which we ate—the butlering was for the most part urban.

"Why didn't Mrs. Garland come?" asked the General.

"She had an engagement or two that prevented her."

"Oh! She must come down," commanded the General. "Telegraph her at once and ask her when she can get away. I'll send my car for her."

This he did. The private Pullman, with a maid and a steward in charge, went back that night and on the second morning Zulime came down the line in lonely state.

I met her at the station, and for ten days we lived the most idyllic, yet luxurious life beside that singing stream. We rode the trails, we fished, we gathered wild flowers. Sometimes of an afternoon we visited the ranches or mining towns round about, feasting at night on turtle soup, and steak and mushrooms, drinking champagne out of tin cups with reckless disregard of camp traditions, utterly without care or responsibility—in truth we were all under military discipline!

The General was a soldier even in his recreations. Each day's program was laid out in "orders" issued in due form by the head of the expedition—and these arrangements held! No one thought of changing them. Our duty was to obey—and enjoy.

Never before in all my life had anything like this freedom from responsibility, from expense, come to me. So carefree, so beautiful was our life, that I woke each morning with a start of surprise to find its magic a reality. It was like the hospitality of oriental kings in the fairy stories of my childhood.

For four weeks we lived this incredible life of mingled luxury and mountaineering, attended by troops of servants and squadrons of horses, threading the high forests, exploring deep mines, crossing Alpine passes, and feasting on the borders of icy lakes—always with the faithful "Nomad," the General's private Pullman car, waiting in the offing ready in case of accident—and then, at last, after riding through Slumgullion Gulch back to Wagon Wheel, Zulime and I took leave of these good friends and started toward Arizona. I had not yet displayed to her the Grand Cañon of the Colorado!

Five years before, on a stage drawn by four wild-eyed bronchos I had ridden from Flagstaff to Hance's Cabin in the glorious, exultant old-time fashion, but now a train ran from Williams to the edge of the abyss, and while I mourned over the prosaic change, I think Zulime welcomed it, and when we had set up our little tent on a point of the rim which commanded a view (toward the Southwest) of miles and miles of purple pagodas, violet towers and golden peaks we were content. Nothing could change the illimitable majesty of this view.

Day by day we watched the colorful play of sun-light and shadow along those mighty walls, and one night we camped in the deeps, a dramatic experience, for a mountain lion yowling from the cliffs gave voice to the savage grandeur of the scene. Then at last, surfeited with splendor, weary with magnificence, we turned our faces homeward. With only a stop at Laguna to watch the Indian Corn Dance, we slid down to Kansas City and at last to West Salem and home.

A Daughter of the Middle Border

What a vacation it had been! Pike's Peak, Cripple Creek, Glen Eyrie, our camp beside the singing stream at Baldy, Sierra Blanca, Wagon Wheel Gap, Creede, Red Mountain, Lake City, Slumgullion, Tennessee Pass, noble dinners on the car, trail-side lunches of goose-liver and sandwiches and jam, iced watermelon and champagne in hot camps on the mesas—all these scenes and experiences came back accompanied by memories of the good talk, the cosmopolitan humor, of the Palmers and their guests.

From this royal ease, this incessant shift of scene and personality, we returned to our shabby old homestead brooding patiently beneath its maples, reflecting upon the glittering panorama which our magic lamp and flying carpet had wrought so potently to display. As I had started out to educate my wife in Western Life, it must be admitted that this summer had been singularly successful in bringing to her a knowledge of the splendors of Colorado and a perception of the varied character of its population.—Best of all she returned in perfect health and happy as a girl.

"This being married to a poor novelist isn't so bad after all," I remarked with an air of self-congratulation. "True, our rewards come without reason, but they sometimes rhyme with joy and pride."

Strange to say, I got nothing out of this summer, in a literary way, except the story which I called *The Steadfast Widow Delaney*, a conception which came to me on my solitary ascent of Sierra Blanca. All the beauty and drama, all the humor and contrast of the trip with the Palmers, had no direct fictional value to me. It is hard to explain why, but so it was. I did not so much as write a poem based on that gorgeous experience.

CHAPTER SIXTEEN

The White House Musicale

THE Homestead on the day of our return, was not only a violent contrast to the castle in Glen Eyrie, but its eaves were dripping with water and its rooms damp and musty. It was sodden with loneliness. Father was in Dakota and mother was away never to return, and the situation would have been quite disheartening to me had it not been for Zulime who did not share my melancholy, or if she did she concealed it under that smiling stoicism which she derived from her deeply philosophic father. She pretended to be glad of the peace of our plain reality.

Life with her was not lacking in variety. From the splendors of Colorado and the luxury of private cars and palatial chambers, she now dropped, with a suddenness which should have been disconcerting, to the level of scouring pots and cooking her own meals. It was several days before we succeeded in finding a cook. "This is what it means to be the wife of an unpopular novelist," I said to her.

"I'm not complaining. It's fun," she replied.

The house was soon in order and when my brother arrived later in the week, she greeted him with the composure of a leisured hostess. In such wise she met every demand upon her.

It was Franklin's first night at home since mother went away, and I labored to cheer him with the fiction that she was "on a visit" to some of her old friends and would soon return.

The Junior as I called him, was in a serious mood for another reason. After more than twelve years of life as an actor, he had decided to quit the stage, something the player is traditionally supposed to be incapable of doing, and he had come to me for aid and encouragement. "I have a good opportunity to go into the management of a rubber plantation," he explained, "and I'd like to have you buy out my share in the Homestead in order to give me a little money to work on."

To this I agreed, although I had grave doubts of the rubber business. To have him give up the stage I considered a gain, for while he was a capable player of middle-aged character parts, I saw no lasting success ahead of him —on the contrary I imagined him getting into a more and more precarious condition. Nothing is more hopeless than an elderly actor out of a job and subject to the curt dismissals of contemptuous managers. Frank had always been gayly unconcerned about the future and he was not greatly troubled now; he was merely desirous of a fixed home and a place to vote. With the promise of my cash for his share of the Homestead, and my support in his Mexican venture, he cheered up markedly and went away almost as carefree as a boy.

In the quiet of the days which followed I worked each morning, sometimes on *The Steadfast Widow Delaney,* and sometimes on a revision of the novel which I had variously and from time to time called *On Special Duty,* and *The Captain of the Gray Horse Troop.* Having been accepted by Lorimer, this story was about to be printed under this latter title as a serial in the *Post.*

Each afternoon I saddled my Klondike horse who was in need of exercise, and galloped about over the hills for an hour or two. We were familiar figures by this time, and the farmers when they saw me leaping a pasture fence or climbing a hill, would smile (I assume that they smiled), and say, there goes that literary cuss, or words to that general effect. I took a boyish delight in showing that Ladrone would walk a log or leap a ditch at the mere touch of my heel.

Occasionally I went to LaCrosse with Zulime to visit our good friends the Eastons, and it was on one of these visits that I had my first long ride in an automobile. Incredible as it may seem now, there were very few motor cars in the county in 1901, and Easton's machine would excite laughter to-day. It was dumpy of form and noisy and uncertain of temper, but it made the trip to Winona and *almost* home again. It broke down helplessly in the last mile, a treachery which caused its owner the deepest chagrin, although it gave me the final touch for a humorous story of our outing, a sketch which I sold to *Harper's Weekly*. The editor had a fine illustration made for it, one which gave further force to my description of the terrific speed with which we whirled through the landscape. As I recall it we rose to nearly seventeen miles an hour!

As *The Captain of the Gray Horse Troop*, actually began to appear in *The Post*, I became sharply concerned with the question of preparing it for book publication. I decided to go to New York and look the ground over very carefully before making selection of another publisher.

My life in the Homestead was comfortable, almost too comfortable. It lacked stimulus. Riding my horse, gathering hickory nuts, and playing tennis or "rummy," were all very well in their way, but they left me dissatisfied, and after the cold winds began to blow and my afternoons were confined to the house, I stagnated. Like Prudden, Grinnell and other of my trailer friends, I was disposed to pitch my winter camp somewhere on Manhattan Island. The

Rocky Mountains for four months in summer and the rest of the year in New York City appeared an ideal division of my life for a western novelist.

I had some reason to think this arrangement was also satisfactory to my wife. To her the Wilderness was a strange and wonderful place in which to try her powers of endurance, but the trail had none of the charms of association which it possessed for me. She was quite ready to accompany me to the city although she professed to be content with Neshonoc. She was entirely urban whereas I was an absurd mixture of pioneer and trailer, fictionist and farmer.

We left West Salem in late October and in less than three days were settled in the little hotel in Fifteenth Street where we had lived during two previous winters. My confidence in my new novel was not sufficient to warrant me in paying more than twenty dollars per week for our little apartment, and as for Zulime—she professed to wonder how I dared to pay as much as seventeen.

One by one and two by two our faithful friends called, Burroughs, Gilder, Howells, Marion and Edward Mac-Dowell, the Pages, Juliet Tompkins—no one appeared to think ill of us because we returned to our shabby little suite. We dined at Katherine Herne's, finding James A., "away," and with Frank Norris and his wife who were (like ourselves), just beginning to feel a little more secure of a living, while from Seton and Bacheller who were passing from glory to glory, we had kindly invitations to visit their new houses, for both of them were building, Bacheller at Sound Beach and Seton at Coscob.

Seton admitted to me that he had already acquired five times the amount he had once named as the summit of his hopes, and Bacheller awed me by the quiet ease of his way of life. In the opulent presence of these men, I sang a very

meek and slender song. I hated to admit my poverty, but
what was the use of making any concealment?

It remains to say that neither Bacheller nor Seton expressed in the slightest degree the sense of superiority which
their larger royalties might have warranted. I am quite sure
they never went so far as to feel sorry for me although
they very naturally rejoiced in their own triumphant progress. In some ways I envied them, but I begrudged
them nothing.

It chanced that the Setons were far enough along with
their building to announce a House Warming, and on New
Year's Day, Zulime and I were fortunate enough to be included in the list of their guests. On the Saturday train
we found Lloyd Osbourne, Richard Le Gallienne and several others whom we knew and on arrival at the new house
on its rocky ledge above the lake, we found that the party
also included Mary Fanton, Carl Lumholz, Emery Pottle
and Gertrude Lynch.

Seton and I spent part of the afternoon fixing up a teepee
which we constructed out of an old Sibley tent, while the
other guests skated on the pond. What a dinner we
enjoyed that night! What youthful spirits we brought
to it! Afterward we sang and danced—we all danced, even
Zulime danced for the first time in her life—so she said.

No one had gray hair, no one doubted the future, no
one acknowledged impending cloud. We toasted the longev-
ity of "Wyndygoul" and the continued success of its
builder. We pledged eternal allegiance to our hostess, and
so without a care of the future, watched the New Year
dawn.

At two in the morning when I crept away to my bed, the
tom-tom and the piano were both sounding out with almost
undiminished vigor. It was a night to remember and I
do remember it with the pleasure an old man has in the days

of his early manhood—not so very early either for I was on the hither side of forty!

Upon our return to the city I found a letter from Bok with a check for eight hundred dollars in it. This was in response to a note of mine respecting an offer of seven hundred and fifty. "Better make it eight hundred," I wrote, and so, in my triumph, I led Zulime to Vantine's and there purchased for her a carved gold ring set with three rose diamonds, the handsomest present I had ever dared to buy for her. "This is to make amends for the measly little engagement ring you were forced to accept," I remarked by way of explanation.

She protested at my reckless waste of money (as she had done with regard to the brown cloak), but to no avail, and thereafter if she occasionally brought the conversation round to Oriental jewelry, I am sure she is not to be blamed. She is still wearing that ring, though she no longer finds the same girlish pleasure in displaying it.

The actual making of my serial into book form began soon after New Years, for I find records of my contract with Harper and Bros., and the arrival of bundles of proof. By the end of February the book was substantially made and ready for distribution, and a handsome book it was—to me. Whatever it had started out to be, it had ended as a fictional study of the red man in his attempt to walk the white man's road, and as a concept of his tragic outlook I still think it worth while.

The three men in control of the reorganized firm of Harper and Bros., George Harvey, Frederick Duneka and Frank Leigh, all professed a firm belief in *The Captain of the Gray Horse Troop,* and promised me such a boost as I had never had. This promise they set about to fulfill.

As the day of publication came on they took generous squares of space in the daily papers, and whole pages in the magazines. They astonished and somewhat daunted me by putting an almost life-size portrait on the bill boards of all the elevated roads, and then to the consternation of my wife, *The Weekly* published a full page reproduction of her photograph, a portrait which they had obtained from me to use, as I supposed, in the ordinary way in the literary column of the Sunday papers. I had no idea of its being a full page illustration. I was troubled and uneasy about this for a day or two, but realizing that the firm was doing its best to make my book known to the public, I could not with justice complain. In truth the use of the portrait seemed not to make any difference one way or the other. It certainly did Zulime no harm.

At my request the firm made up a very handsome special copy of the novel which I sent to President Roosevelt, with a word of explanation concerning the purpose which underlaid the writing of the tale.

Early in March the book appeared with everything in its favor. True there was opportunity for controversy in its delineation of aggressive cattlemen, but those who had so bitterly criticized my pictures of the prairie life in *Main Traveled Roads*, were off their guard with respect of the mountains. My reviewers quite generally accepted the novel as a truthful presentation of life on an Indian reservation in the nineties. Furthermore my sympathetic interpretation of the Army's attitude toward the red men caused the story to be quite generally commended by the officers. This surprised and delighted me, but I was especially gratified by Roosevelt's hearty praise of it. "It is your best work so far," he wrote me, "and I am in full sympathy with your position."

Requests for stories, interviews, articles and biographical notes, flowed in upon me. It really looked like a late second arrival of Hamlin Garland. Not since the excitement of putting *Main Traveled Roads* on the market had I been so hopeful and in the midst of my other honors came a note from the President, inviting me to visit him, and with it a card to a musicale at the White House.

Life in the East as the reader can see, was very alluring to Zulime as well as to me, and though as April came on, we both felt the call of the West, I am not sure whether we would have wrought our courage to the point of deserting our little apartment on Fifteenth Street, had it not been for the President's invitation, which was in effect a command, an honor as well as a pleasure, which we did not think of disregarding.

As I had not voted the Republican ticket and had no political standing with the Administration, this invitation was personal. It came from Roosevelt as a friend and fellow-trailer—a fact which enhanced its value to me. We began at once to plan our return to Chicago in such wise that it would include a week in Washington, which we had not visited since our wedding journey.

It must have been about this time that the Annual Meeting of the Institute took place. I recall Howells presiding with timidity and very evident embarrassment when it came to the duty of putting certain resolutions to vote. He seemed sad and old that night—indeed as I looked around the table, I was startled to find how many of the men I had considered "among the younger writers" were gray and haggard. Mabie, Page, Hopkinson Smith, Gilder and Stedman—all were older than I had remembered them. Edward MacDowell, who was sitting beside me, remarked upon the change, and I replied, "Yes, you and I are young only by contrast. To Frank Norris and Stewart White, we are already veterans."

[That was twenty years ago, and I am three score years and more, and most of those who dined with me that night

244

are in their graves, only Page, of all the group, is left. Another generation altogether is on the stage whilst I and Stewart White are grouped together as "older men." I am seeing literary history made whether I am credited with making any of it, myself, or not. At times I have an appalling sense of the onward sweep of the years. Are they carrying us to higher grounds in fiction and in other arts, or are they descending to lower levels of motive and workmanship?

It was glorious spring when we reached Washington, and in the glow of my momentary sense of triumph we went to one of the best hotels and enjoyed for the moment the sense of being successful and luxurious folk.

In calling on the President the following day I was a little taken aback by his frankness in speaking of my changing point of view. "You have pictured the reverse side of the pioneer," he said with a gleam of mischief in his eyes, "In your study of the Indian's case you have discovered the fact that the borderer is often the aggressor and sometimes the thief." He repeated his praise of the book and then said. "I shall make use of your knowledge of the conditions on the Western reservations. You and George Bird Grinnell know what is going on out there and I intend to use you both—unofficially."

To this I agreed, and when he gave me a card to the Secretary of the Interior and told me to take up with the Commissioner certain reforms which I had suggested, I put the card in my pocket and set about the task. It was only a small card, a visiting card, and when, in my ignorance of official life, I walked in on the Secretary with that tiny slip of pasteboard in my hand, I had no idea of its explosive power. The Secretary who was lounging at his desk like a tired and discouraged old man, did not think me important enough to warrant a rise out of his chair, until he read the card which I handed to him. After that I owned the office! That card made me the personal representative of the President—for the moment.

On the following day Roosevelt allowed me to sit in at some of the meetings in the Executive Chamber, and it was at one of these that I met for the first time the most engaging Chief of the Forestry Bureau, Gifford Pinchot. At night Zulime and I dined with William Dudley Foulke and at nine o'clock we went to the White House Musicale.

That musicale at the White House is one of the starry nights in Zulime's life, as well as in my own, for not only did we meet the President and Mrs. Roosevelt and many of the best known figures in American art, letters, politics, and statesmanship, we also heard Paderewski play as we had never heard him play before.

We were seated close to the piano and when that potent, shock-haired Pole spread his great hands above the keys I fancied something of the tiger in the lithe grace of his body, and in his face a singular and sultry solemnity was expressed. Inspired no doubt by the realization that he was playing before a mighty ruler—a ruler by the divine right of brain power,—he played with magnetic intensity. Something mysterious, something grandly moving went out from his fingers. No other living musician could, at that moment have equaled him.

For a few hours Zulime and I enjoyed the white light which beat upon two of the great personalities of that day—one the world's greatest piano player, the other the most powerful and the most popular man in all America—and when we retired to the obscurity of our hotel we were silent with satisfaction. For the moment it seemed that fortune was about to empty her golden horn at my feet. I was happily married, my latest book was a hit, and I had the friendship and the favor of the President.

CHAPTER SEVENTEEN

Signs of Change

A S a matter of record, and for the benefit of young readers who may be contemplating authorship, I here set down the fact that notwithstanding my increasing royalties, my gross income for 1901 was precisely $3,100. Out of this we saved five hundred dollars. Neither my wife nor I had any great hopes of the future. Neither of us felt justified in any unusual expenditures, and as for speculation—nothing could induce me to buy a share of stock—or even a bond (gilt-edged or otherwise), for I owned a prejudice, my father's prejudice, against all forms of intangible wealth. Evidences of wealth did not appeal to me. I wanted the real thing, I wanted the earth. Nothing but land gave me the needed sense of security.

In my most exalted moments I began to dream of using my income from *The Captain of the Gray Horse Troop* in the purchase of more Oklahoma land. In imagination I saw myself in a wide-rimmed hat and white linen suit sitting at ease on the porch of a broad-roofed house (built in the Mexican style with a patio) looking out over my thousand acres—I had decided to have just a thousand acres, it made such a mouth-filling announcement to one's friends.

I did not go so far as to think of a life without labor (I expected to work in the North till February, then rest and ride horse-back for three months in the South), but I did hope to relieve Zulime of some of her drudgery. Now that I think back to it, I am not at all sure that my wife rejoiced over my plan to go to Weatherford to purchase another farm. It is probable that I overcame her objections by telling her that I wanted more material for my book of Indian tales; anyhow I left her in Chicago almost as soon as we arrived there, and went again to Darlington and Colony to see Major Stouch and John Seger, and to make certain observations for President Roosevelt.

Seger, unskilled as he was with the pen, could talk with humor and pictorial quality, and some of his stories had so stimulated my imagination that I was eager to have more time with him among his wards. Without precisely following his narratives I had found myself able to reproduce the spirit of them in my own diction. His ability as a sign-talker was of especial service to me for, as he signed to his visitors, he muttered aloud, for my benefit, what he was expressing in gesture, and also what the red man signed in reply. In this way I got at the psychology of the Cheyenne to a degree which I could not possibly compass through an interpreter.

While looking for farms during the day, I drew from Seger night by night, the amazing story of his career among the Southern Cheyennes. It was a rough and disjointed narrative, but it was stirring and valuable as authentic record of the Southwest. "The Red Pioneer," "Lone Wolf's Old Guard," and many more of my tales of red people were secured on this trip. Several dealing with the Blackfeet and Northern Cheyennes, like "the Faith of His Fathers" and "White Weasel" I gained from Stouch. None of them are true in the sense of being precisely the way they were told, for I took very few notes. They are rather free transcripts of the incidents which chanced to follow my liking— but they reflect the spirit of the original narratives and are bound together by one underlying motive which is to show the Indian as a human being, a neighbor. "We have had plenty of the 'wily redskin' kind of thing," I said to

Signs of Change

Stouch. "I am going to tell of the red man as you and Seger have known him, as a man of the polished stone age trying to adapt himself to steam and electricity."

It happened that plenteous rains had made Oklahoma very green and beautiful, and as I galloped about over the wide swells of the Caddo country, I was disposed to buy all the land that joined me. Imagining myself the lord of a thousand acres, I achieved a profound joy of living. It was good to glow in the sunlight, to face the sweet southern wind, and to feel once more beneath my knees the swelling muscles of a powerful horse. In a very vivid sense I relived the days when, as a lad of twelve, I rode with Burton and my sister Harriet along the prairie swells of the Cedar Valley some thirty years before. "Washitay," at such moments was not only the land of the past but the hope of the future.

My red neighbors interested me. The whole problem of their future was being worked out almost within sight of my door. Here the men of the Polished Stone Age and the men of gasoline engines and electrical telephones met and mingled in a daily adjustment which offered material of surpassing value to the novelist who could use it. Humor and pathos, tragic bitterness and religious exaltation were all within reach of my hand.

The spring nights which came to me there at Colony were of a quality quite new to me. The breeze, amiable and moist, was Southern, and the moonlight falling from the sky like a silent, all-enveloping cataract of silver, lay along the ground so mystically real that I could feel it with my hand. The air was at once tropic and Western, and this subtle blending of the North and the South, the strange and the familiar, appealed to me with such power that I wrote Zulime a statement of my belief that in becoming a part-owner in this land, I had assured for us both a happy and prosperous future. "I shall come here every spring," I declared, and in the glow of this enthusiasm, I purchased another farm of two hundred and forty acres and arranged with Seger for its management.

Alas, for my piece of mind! On my way homeward, at Reno, I encountered a simoon of most appalling power. An equatorial wind which pressed against the car and screamed at the window—a hot, unending pitiless blast withering the grain and tearing the heart out of young gardens—a storm which brought back to me the dreadful blizzard of dust which swept over our Iowa farm in the spring of '72. There was something grand as well as sorrowful in this unexpected display of desert ferocity.

My dream of a thousand-acre ranch shriveled with the plants. The prairie abandoning its youthful, buoyant air, took on a sinister and savage grandeur. To escape from the ashes of these ruined fields was now a passionate desire. The value of my land in Washitay fell almost to the vanishing point. Illinois became a green and pleasant pasture toward which I drove with gratitude and relief.

[I insert a line to say that this was only a mood. I went on with my purchase of lands till I had my thousand acres, but these acres were in scattered plots and the house with the patio and the porch was never built.]

At the Agency just before I left for the North I had hired some Cheyenne women to make for me a large council teepee which I had in mind to set up as my dwelling at Eagle's Nest Camp, where Zulime and I had agreed to spend the summer. Boyishly eager to reproduce as well as I could a Cheyenne house, I assembled all my blankets, parfleches, willow beds and other furnishings and raised my lodge on poles on the edge of the wood just inside the Camp's entrance.

It made a singularly appropriate addition to the reservation, to my thinking, at least, and I took inordinate pride in its ownership. Trim and white and graceful it stood against the forest wall, its crossed poles sprangling from its top with poetic suggestion of aboriginal life, and when, with elaborate ceremony, I laid the fuel for its first fire, calling upon our patron, Wallace Heckman, to touch a match to the tinder, I experienced a sense of satisfaction.

To my artist friends it was a "picturesque accessory"— to me it was a talisman of things passing. The smoke of the hickory faggots filling that conical roof-tree brought back to me a cloud of memories of the prairies of the Sioux, the lakes of the Chippewa, and the hills of the Cheyenne. Thin as were its walls, they shut out (for me) the commonplace present, helping me to reconstruct the world of Blackhawk and the Sitting Bull, and when I walked past it, especially at night, my mind took joy in its form, and a pleasant stir within my blood made manifest of its power.

Browne acknowledged its charm and painted a moonlight sketch of it, and Seton, who came by one day, helped me dedicate its firehole. In the light of its embers, he and I renewed our youth while smoking the beautiful Pipe of Meditation, which a young Cheyenne chief had given me in token of his friendship.

It happened that I was scheduled to give a series of lectures at the University of Chicago on *The Outdoor Literature of America,* and with a delightful feeling of propriety in the fact I set to work to write these addresses in my canvas lodge, surrounded by all its primitive furnishings. It made an admirable study, but at night as I lay on my willow couch, I found the moonlight so intense and the converging lines of the lodge poles so suggestive of other folk and other times that slumber was fitful. The wistful ghosts of Blackhawk and his kind seemed all about me. Not till the moon set or the shadows of the forest covered me, was I able to compose myself to sleep.

For several weeks I wrote at ease upon my theme and then, into the carefree atmosphere of my Lodge of Dreams came the melancholy news that William McClintock, my giant uncle, had been stricken by the same mysterious malady which had broken my mother's heart, and that he was lying motionless on his bed in the narrow space of his chamber. The "stroke" (so my aunt wrote) had come upon him (as upon my mother) without the slightest warning, and with no discoverable cause.

On my return to the Homestead I went at once to see him. He was sitting in my mother's wheeled chair, quite helpless, yet cheerful and confident of ultimate recovery. He had always been a man of dignity, and singularly abstemious of habit, and these qualities were strongly accentuated by his sudden helplessness. He was very gentle, very patient, and the sight of him lying there made speaking very difficult for me.

When the doctor would permit, he loved to lie in his chair on the porch of his little cottage where he could look out upon the hills, his eyes reflecting his beloved landscape like those of a dreaming cage-weary lion. Inarticulate, like my mother, he was nevertheless the poet, and never failed to respond—at least with a meaning glance—to any imaginative word in my discourse.

How much he had meant to me in all the days of my boyhood! As the master of the threshing machine forty years agone, he had filled my childish heart with worship. As the swift-footed deer trailer, the patient bee-hunter, the silent lover of the forest, he had held my regard and though he had never quite risen to the high place which my Uncle David occupied in my boyhood's worship, he had always been to me a picturesque and kindly figure. Year by year I had watched his giant form stoop, and his black beard wax thin and white, and now, here he sat almost at the end of his trail, unable to move, yet expressing a kind of elemental bravery, a philosophic patience which moved me as no words of lamentation could have done.

Strange malady! He who had never met his match in stark strength could not now by the exercise of all his will, lift that limp arm from his side and as I sat beside him I recalled my last sad meeting with Major Powell, the man who first guided a canoe through the Grand Cañon of the Colorado, and in my mind arose a conception of what these two men, each in his kind represented in the story of American pioneering. One the far-famed explorer, the other the unknown rifleman behind the plow. With William McClintock—with my father, with Major Powell, a whole world, a splendid and heroic world was passing never to return, and when I took my uncle's hand in parting I was almost certain that I should never see him again.

Once he was king of forest men.
To him a snow-capped mountain range
Was but a line, a place of mark,
A view-point on the trail. Then
He had no dread of dark,
No fear of change.
Now an uprolled rug upon the floor
Appalls his feet. His withered arm
Shakes at the menace of a door,
And every wind-waft does him harm.

God! 'Tis a piteous thing to see
This ranger of the hills confined
To the small compass of his room
Like a chained eagle on a tree,
Lax-winged and gray and blind.
Only in dreams he sees the bloom
On far hills where the red deer run,

A Daughter of the Middle Border

Only in memory guides the light canoe
Or stalks the bear with dog and polished gun.

In him behold the story of the West,
The chronicle of rifleman behind the plow,
Typing the life of those who knew
No barrier but the sunset in their quest.
On his bent head and grizzled hair
Is set the crown of those who shew
New cunning to the wolf, new courage to the bear.

Another evidence of melancholy change came to me in
the failing powers of Ladrone, my mountain horse, who
had come through the winter very badly. I found him
standing in the pasture, weak and inactive, taking no interest in the rich grasses under his feet. In the belief that
exercise would do him good, I saddled him and started to
ride about the square, but soon drew rein. He had not the
strength to carry me!

Sadly dismounting I led him back to the stable. It was
evident that he would never again career with me across
the hills. Bowed and dejected he resumed his place in
the paddock. Standing thus, with hanging head, he appeared to be dreaming of the days when as a part of the
round-up, in the far Northwest, he had carried his master
over the range and through the herd with joyous zeal. Each
time I looked at him I felt a twinge of pain.

Everything I could do for him was done, every remedial
measure was tried, but he grew steadily worse, and at last,
I called a neighbor to my aid and said, "Oliver, my horse
is very sick. I fear his days are numbered. Study him,
do what you can for him, and if you find he cannot be
cured, put him away. Don't tell me when it is done or
how it is done—I don't want to know. You understand?"

He understood, and one morning, a few days later, as I

looked in the pasture for the gray pony, he was nowhere
to be seen. In the dust of the driveway, I detected the
marks of his small feet. The toes of his shoes pointed toward
the gate, and there were no returning foot-prints. He had
gone away on the long trail which leads to the River of
Darkness and The Wide Lands Beyond It.

His bridle and saddle were hanging in the barn (they
are still there), silent memorials of the explorations in
which he and I had played a resolute part.

Something grips me by the throat as I remember his
eyes,

> "Brown, clear and calm, with color down deep,
> Where his brave, proud soul seemed to lie."

I recall the first days we spent together, beautiful days
in the Frazer Valley, when jubilant cranes bugled from the
skies, and humming birds moved in myriads along the river's
banks—memories of those desperate days in the Skeena
forests, amid dank and poisonous plants—of marches on
the tundra along the high Stickeen Divide—all these come
back. I see him crowding close to my fire, thin and weak.

I relive once more that bitter night on the wharf in
Glenora when (chilled by the cold wind), he first began to
cough. I am thinking of his journey on the boat with me
to Wrangell; of the day when I left him there (the only
horse on the coast); of my return; of our long trip to
Seattle; of his trust in me as he faced the strange monsters
of the city; of his long dark ride to St. Paul; of the joyous
day when I opened his prison door and finding him safe and
well, rode him forth to the admiration of my uncles at the
county fair. A vast section of my life faded with the
passing of that small gray horse. "Lost my Ladrone, gone
the wild living. I dream, but my dreaming is vain."

My sense of uneasiness was deepened by another warning,

255

a third sign of decay. One morning my father while apparently in his usual health, suddenly grew dizzy and fell and as I bent above him he gazed up at me with an expression which I had never before seen in his face, a humble, helpless, appealing look. It seemed that he was going as William had gone.

Happily I was mistaken. His indomitable soul reasserted itself. He refused to surrender. He rallied. "I'm all right," he said at last, a grim line coming back into his mouth. "It's passing off. I can move," and lifting his arm he opened and shut his hand in proof of it. "I'm better than a dozen dead men yet."

He was distinctly stronger next day, and when, looking from my window I saw him going about his work in the garden, bareheaded as was his habit, resolute and unsubdued, I was reassured, but never again did he move with the same vigor as before. For the first time he acknowledged his age.

During all these melancholy experiences so significant of the dying border, I had the comfort of my undaunted wife whose happy spirit refused to be clouded by what she recognized as merely the natural decay of the preceding generation. Her mind was set on the future, our future. She refused to yield her youthful right to happiness, and under the influence of her serene philosophy I went back to my writing, or at least to the serious consideration of another mountain theme, which was taking shape in my brain.

With a mere love-story I had never been content. For me a sociological background was necessary in order to make fiction worth while, and I was minded to base my next novel on a study of the "war" which had just taken place, at Cripple Creek, between the Free Miner, the Union Miner and the Operator or Capitalist.

The suggestion for this theme had come to me during

a call on some friends in New York City, where I had been amused and somewhat embarrassed, by the ecstatic and outspoken admiration of a boy of fourteen, who was (as his mother put it) "quite crazy over miners, Indians and cowboys. His dream is to go West and illustrate your books," she had said to me.

This lad's enthusiasm for the West and his ambition to be an illustrator of western stories had started me on a tale in which a fine but rather spoiled New York girl was to be carried to Colorado by the enthusiasm of her youthful brother, and there plunged (against her will) into the warfare of mountaineers and miners, a turbulence which her beloved brother would insist on sharing. Such a girl might conceivably find herself in the storm center of a contest such as that which had taken place on Bull Hill in the late nineties.

I called this study *Hesper, or the Cowboy Patrol* for the reason that in "the Cripple Creek War," cattlemen had acted as outposts for the union miners, and in this fact I perceived something picturesque and new and telling, something which would give me just the imaginative impulse I required.

Some of my friendly critics were still occasionally writing to me to ask, "Why don't you give us more *Main Traveled Roads* stories," and it was not easy to make plain to them that I had moved away from that mood, and that my life and farm life had both greatly altered in thirty years. To repeat the tone of that book would have been false not only to my art, but to the country as well.

Furthermore, I had done that work. I had put together in *Main Traveled Roads* and its companion volumes a group of thirty short stories (written between 1887 and 1891), in which I had expressed all I had to say on that especial phase of western life. To attempt to recover the spirit of

my youth would not only have been a failure but a bore
—even to those who were urging me to the task. It was
my business to keep moving—to accompany my characters
as they migrated into the happier, more hopeful West.
Like them I was "Campin' through, podner, just a campin'
through."

As in *The Captain of the Gray Horse Troop*, I had
dealt with the three-cornered fight of the cattlemen, the
Indian, and the soldier, so now, in 1902, I returned to
the mountain West, to picture another conflict, equally
stirring and possessing a still finer setting and back-ground.
In *Hesper* I was concerned with a war, in which most of
the action had taken place among the clouds, on the hill-
tops nearly two miles above sea-level. There was something
grandly pictorial in this drama; but, after writing a few
chapters of it, I felt the need of revisiting the scene.

Zulime again accompanied me and as our train slid
down the familiar road leading to Colorado Springs and we
could see the lightning flashing among the high summits on
which I had laid the scenes of my story, Zulime glowed
with joy and I took on a renewed sense of power. For an
hour I felt equal to my task, to be historian of the free
miner seemed to me a worthy office.

The Ehrichs were again our hosts and they (as well as
Russell Wray, the Editor of the *Gazette*) took the keenest
interest in my design. From Wray and his friends I began
at once to derive an understanding of the part which "Little
London" (as the miners called the Springs) had taken in
the war. I relied on a visit to Bull Hill and Victor to
furnish the Sky-town or "Red-neck" point of view.

Wray was especially valuable to me, for he had taken
part in the famous expedition of the "Yaller Legs" and his
experiences as a reporter and his sense of humor had
enabled him to report both sides of the controversy. He

had many friends in the camp, to whom he gave me letters.

The character which interested me most, in all the warring factions, was the free miner, the prospector, the man of the trail. Him I clearly understood. He had been companion in most of my trips into the wild. He was blood brother to my father, and cousin to my heroic uncles. He represented the finest phases of pioneering. "Matt Kelley," "Rob Raymond" and "Jack Munroe," I knew and loved, and their presence in this labor war redeemed it from the sordid, uninspired struggle which such contests usually turn out to be. In my design these three characters filled heroic place.

Zulime (with no literary problems to distract her) had another easeful, idyllic summer. The Ehrichs, the Wrays and the Palmers welcomed her as an old friend, and in their companionship she rode and camped and dined in easeful leisure, but I was on the move. I visited a ranch on the plains of Eastern Colorado, joined a round-up in the Sierra Blanca country, explored the gambling-houses and mines of Cripple Creek and Victor, and spent two weeks reëxploring the White River Plateau, this time with Walter Wykoff, of Princeton. For a week or two, Wykoff, Miss Ehrich and Zulime and I camped high on the shoulder of Pike's Peak. Vast and splendid scenes of storm and sun were printed on my mind, and, while the actual writing of my novel halted, I felt certain that I was doing just the right thing. I felt sure of finishing it in the proper spirit of enthusiasm.

The trip not only enabled me to finish *Hesper*—it suggested several of the stories which went into *They of the High Trails* and gave me the plan of *The Forester's Daughter*. I returned to West Salem, brown as an Indian and bursting with energy, and for several weeks toiled with desperate haste to put my impressions, imaginings in form.

Each morning of those peaceful days I took to mother's

room, on the sunward side of the old Homestead, and there wrought into final shape the materials I had gathered. I had only to shut my eyes to see again the clouds circling the walls of Shavano. In imagination I rode once more with Matt Kelley up Bull Hill, or, sitting opposite the chief of the Miners' Union, reënjoyed his graphic account of the coming of the Federal troops. The bawling roar of the round-up on the meadow came back to fill my eyes with pictures of the Sierra Blanca foothills. In truth I had no need of notes. I was embarrassed with material. I threw my note-books into a drawer and forgot them.

Letters from my publishers informed me that *The Captain of the Gray Horse Troop* was marching on, but that they hoped I was at work on something to follow it. To this I replied:

"Yes, I am in the midst of a story which I hope will be as good as *The Captain,* but don't hurry me!"

Whilst I, busied with my fiction, kept to my study, Zulime was ecstatically rearranging furniture. During our absence in Colorado, father had moved to another house, relinquishing all claim on the Homestead, and for the first time in our lives my wife and I were authentic householders in full possession of every room. We had a door-bell, and our clock was our own. Our meal-times conformed to our will, and not to another's. We went to bed when we pleased, and rose when we got ready.

Zulime's joy of ownership was almost comical. Leading me from room to room she repeated, "This is *our* house. Don't you like our house? Isn't it fun to have it all to ourselves?"

Her rapture instructed me. I perceived that the old Homestead had not yet served its purpose. So far as my father was concerned it was a story told, a drama almost ended, but as the undivided home of my young wife it developed new meaning. Another soul was coming into being; another tenant was about to take its place beneath our roof. Small feet would soon be dancing through those silent rooms, careless of the men and women whose gray heads and gaunt limbs had been carried out over their thresholds to a final resting-place beneath the sod.

A new interest, a new phase of life, was coming to Zulime, and to me.

CHAPTER EIGHTEEN

The Old Pioneer Takes the Back Trail

I N the midst of this period of hard work on *Hesper*, news of the death of Frank Norris came to me. Frank Norris the most valiant, the happiest, the handsomest of all my fellow craftsmen. Nothing more shocking, more insensate than the destruction of this glorious young fictionist had come to my literary circle, for he was aglow with a husband's happiness, gay with the pride of paternity, and in the full spring-tide of his powers. His going left us all poorer and took from American literature one of its strongest young writers.

The papers at once wired me for tributes, and these I gave, gladly, and later when one of the magazines paid me for an article, I used the money in the purchase of a tall clock to serve as a memorial. This time-piece stands in the hall of my city home and every time I pass it I am reminded of the fine free spirit of Frank Norris. In my small corner of the world he remains a vital memory.

All through October I wrote on my novel, but as the dark days of autumn came on, I began as usual to dwell upon my interests in the city and not even Zulime's companionship could keep me from a feeling of restlessness. I longed for literary comradeship. Theoretically my native village was an ideal place in which to write, actually it sapped me and after a few weeks depressed me. With no literary "atmosphere," damnable word, I looked away to New York for stimulus. I did not go so far as one of my friends who declined to have anything to do with his relatives simply because he did not like them, but I clearly recognized that my friends in the city meant more to me than any of my Wisconsin neighbors and it became more and more evident that to make and keep an arbitrary residence in a region which did not in itself stimulate or satisfy me, was a mistake. There was nothing to do in West Salem but write.

Above all other considerations, however, I had a feeling, perhaps it was a mistaken one,—that my powers grew in proportion as I went Eastward. In West Salem I was merely an amateur gardener, living a life which approached the vegetable,—so far as external action went. In Chicago I was a perversity, a man of mis-directed energy. In New York I was, at least respected as a writer.

In short New York allured me as London allures the writers of England, and as Paris attracts the artists of Europe. It was my literary capital. Theoretically I belonged to Wisconsin, as Hardy belonged to Wessex or Barrie to Scotland, actually my happiest home was adjacent to Madison Square. Only as I neared the publishing centers did I feel the slightest confidence in the future. This increased sense of importance may have been based upon an illusion but it was a very real emotion nevertheless.

Why should I not feel this? From my village home, from digging potatoes and doing carpenter work, I went (almost directly) to a luncheon at the White House, and the following night I attended a dinner given to Mark Twain on his sixty-seventh birthday with William Dean Howells, Thomas B. Reed, Wayne McVeagh, Brander Matthews, H. H. Rogers, George Harvey, Pierpont Morgan, Hamilton Wright Mabie and a dozen others who were leaders in their chosen work, as my table mates. Perhaps I was not deserving of these honors—I'm not urging that point—I am merely stating the facts which made my home in West Salem seem remote and lonely to me. Acknowledging myself a weak mortal I could not entirely forego the honors which the East seemed willing to bestow, and as father was in good health with a household of his own, I felt free to spend the entire winter in New York. For the first time in many years, I felt relieved of anxiety for those left behind.

New York was in the worst of its subway upheaval when we landed there, but having secured a small furnished apartment in a new but obscure hotel on Forty-seventh street, Zulime and I settled down for the winter. Our tiny three-room suite (a lovely nest for a woman) was not in the least like a home for an old trailer and corn-husker like myself. Its gas log and gimcrack mantel, its "Mission" furniture and its "new art" rugs were all of hopeless artificiality, but our sitting-room (on the quiet side of the building) received the sun, and there on the lid of a small desk I took up and carried forward the story of *Hesper* which my publishers had asked me to prepare for the spring trade.

Before we had time to unpack, a note came from President Roosevelt asking me to return to Washington to confer on a phase of the Indian service with which I was familiar, and I went at once—glad to be of any service—especially an unofficial service.

It was always a pleasure as well as an honor to meet Roosevelt. He was our first literary president. His esthetic interests were not only keen, but discriminating. He knew what each of us had published, and valued each of us for the particular contributions we were making to American literature. Each of us gave him something—in my case it was a knowledge of the West. Notwithstanding the multiple duties of his office, he put aside a part of each day for reading and when he read, he concentrated upon his page with such intensity that he remembered all that was important in the writing.

He knew the masters in the other arts also. If he had a

problem in architecture or medaling or painting to decide, he went to Mead or St. Gaudens, or Blashfield. Under his administration the White House had resumed its fine colonial character. At his direction Mead and McKim had restored it to the noble simplicity of Madison's time. They had cleared out the business offices and removed the absurd mixture of political machinery and household furniture which had accumulated under the rule of his predecessors, most of whom (coming from small inland towns) knew nothing of any art but government, and in some cases not too much of that. On this particular visit I recall the fact that repairs were going on, for the President invited me to take luncheon with his family, and we ate in a small room on the front of the house for the reason that the dining-room was in process of being restored and the howl of the floor polisher was resounding through the hall.

It may interest the reader to know that while my wife and I occasionally lunched or dined with "the choice ones of the earth," we prudently practiced "light housekeeping" between our splendid feasts. Like a brown-bearded Santa Claus I often ran the gauntlet of the elevator boy with pockets bulging bottles of milk, hunks of cheese, hot muffins, and pats of butter, and frequently, when the weather was bad, or when some one had neglected to invite us out, we supped in our room.

Once when I entered laden in this fashion I was sharply taken aback by the presence of several belated callers, very grand ladies, and only the most skilful manœuvering enabled me to slide into the closet and out of my overcoat without betraying my cargo. My predicament highly amused Zulime, while at the same time she inwardly trembled for fear of a smash. I mention this incident in order to reveal the reverse side of our splendid social progress. We were in no danger of becoming "spoiled" with feasting, so long as we kept to our Latin Quarter methods of lunching.

We had many notable dinners that winter, but our long anticipated visit to Mark Twain's house in Riverdale stands out above them all. We reached the house about seven o'clock, by way of an ancient hack which met us at the depot and carried us up the hill, into the yard of an old-fashioned mansion sheltered by great trees.

Mark came running lightly down the broad stairs to meet us in the hall, seemingly in excellent health, although his spirits were not at all as boyish as his step. "I'm glad to see you," he said cordially, "but you'll find the house a hospital. The girls have both been miserable and Mrs. Clemens, I'm sorry to say, is still too ill to see you. I bring her greetings to you and her apology."

Thereupon he related with invincible humor and vivid phraseology, the elaborate scheme of deception to which they had been forced during Jean's illness. "Mrs. Clemens was very weak, so low that the slightest excitement—so the doctor warned us—might prove fatal; hence we were obliged to pretend that Jean was well but busy doing this or doing that, in order that her mother might not suspect the truth of the situation.

"I was protected by the doctor's orders, which forbade me from spending more than two minutes in Mrs. Clemens' room, but Clara, who was allowed to nurse her mother, was forced to enter upon a season of unveracity which taxed her imagination to the uttermost. She had to pretend that Jean was away on a visit, or that she was in town shopping or away at a dinner. Together we invented all kinds of social engagements for her and that involved the description of new gowns and a list of the guests of each entertainment. Oh, it was dreadful. Fortunately Clara had a good reputation with her mother, and was able to carry conviction, whereas I had a very hard time. I kept getting into shoal water."

He was very funny—I can only report the substance of

266

his tale—and yet there was a tone in his voice which enabled me to understand the tragic situation. Mrs. Clemens' illness was hopeless.

All through the dinner he talked on in the same enthralling fashion, picturesque, humorous, tragic. He dealt with June bugs, alcohol, Christian Science, the Philippine outrage and a dozen other apparently unrelated subjects. He imitated a horse-fly. He swore. He quoted poetry. We laughed till our sides ached—and yet, all the while, beneath it all, he had in mind (as we had in mind)—that sweetly-patient invalid waiting upstairs for his good-night caress.

As a bitter agnostic as well as a tender humorist Mark Twain loomed larger in my horizon after that night. The warmly human side of him was revealed to me as never before, and thereafter I knew him and I felt that he knew me. That remote glance from beneath those shaggy eyebrows no longer deceived me. He was a tender and loyal husband. Later when I came to read the marvelous story of his life as related by Albert Bigelow Paine, I found a part of my intuitions recorded as facts. He was an elemental western American—with many of the faults and all of the excellencies of the border.

Meanwhile I was at work. In my diary of this date I find these words, "This is living! The sunlight floods our tiny sitting-room whose windows look out on a blue-and-white mountainous 'scape of city roofs. We have dined and the steam is singing in our gilded radiator. The noise and bustle of the city is far away.—I foresee that I shall be able to do a great deal of work on my novel."

In that last sentence I was reckoning without the effect of my wife's popularity. Invitations to luncheons, dinners, and theater parties began to pile up, and I could not ask Zulime to deny herself these pleasures, although I tried to keep my forenoons sacred to my pen. I returned to the manuscript of *Hesper* and succeeded in writing at least a thousand words each day; on fortunate mornings I was able to turn off a full chapter.

It was a gay and satisfying season. We met all our old friends and made many new ones, finding ourselves more and more at home in the city. We rode to grand receptions in the street cars—as usual—and while we ate our luncheons at inexpensive cafés, we often dined with our more prosperous fellow-craftsmen. In spite of many interruptions I managed to complete my novel. By the first of March *Hesper* was ready for the printer and I turned it over to Duneka.

On Zulime's birthday as I was putting the last chapter in final shape, I received a letter from father which said, "I am coming East. Meet me in Washington on the 21st." To this request there was but one answer: "I'll be there."

It was the first time that the old pioneer had taken "the back trail" since leaving Boston, nearly fifty years before, and I rejoiced in his decision. The thought of leading him into the halls of Congress and pointing out for him the orators whose doings had been so long his chief concern, was pleasureable to me. From my earliest childhood I had heard him comment on the weekly record of Congressional debates. He loved oratory. He was a hero-worshiper. With him the Capitol meant Lincoln and Grant and Blaine and Sherman. It was not a city, it was a shrine.

When he stepped from the train in Washington the following week, I was there to meet him, and for several days I led him from splendor to splendor. With me he saw Mount Vernon, the White House, Congress, the library, and his patriotism intensified as the glories of his country's capital unrolled before his eyes. He said little, only looked, and when he had harvested as much of Washington as he could carry I took him to Philadelphia, in order that he might breathe the air of Continental Hall and gaze upon its sacred Liberty Bell. His patriotism had few reservations. All these relics were of high solemnity to him.

At last as a climax we approached New York, whose glittering bays, innumerable ships and monstrous buildings awed him and saddened him. It was a picture at once incredible and familiar, resembling illustrations he had seen in the magazines, only mightier more magnificent than he had imagined any of it to be. It overwhelmed him, wearied him, disheartened him, and so it came about that the quiet dinners he took with me at my club were his most enduring pleasures, for there he rested, there he saw me at home. He acquired an understanding of my endurance of the vast and terrible town.

Up to this time the story of my doings in the East had been to him like those of characters in highly-colored romance. He had believed me (in a sense) when, in West Salem, I had spoken of meetings with Roosevelt and Howells and other famous men, and yet, till now, he had never been able to realize the fact that I *belonged* in New York, and that men of large affairs were actually my friends. He comprehended now (in some degree) my good fortune, and it gratified him while it daunted him. He understood why I could not live in West Salem.

If he was proud to acknowledge me as a son, I, on my part, was proud to acknowledge him as my father, for as he sat with me in the dining-room of the club or walked about the Library to examine the relics and portraits of Booth (for whom he had a passionate admiration) he was altogether admirable.

At the end of our third day, I suggested Boston. To this he replied, "No, I've had enough," and there was a tired droop in his voice. "I'm ready to go home. I'm all tired out with 'seeing things,' and besides it's time to be getting back to my garden."

To urge him to remain longer would have been a mistake. Boston would have disturbed and bewildered him.

Not only would he have failed to find the city of his youth, he would have been saddened by the changes. His loss of power to remember troubled me. He retained but few of his impressions of Washington, and with sorrow I acknowledged that it no longer mattered whether he saw Boston or not. He had waited too long for his great excursion. He was old and timid and longing for rest.

As he went to his train (surfeited with strange glories, crowds and exhibitions) he repeated that his dinners with me at the club remained his keenest pleasures. In tasting a few of my comforts he understood why I loved the great city. He saw me also in an established position, and this he considered a gain. His faith in my future was now complete.

*   *   *

For years he had talked of this expedition, planned for it, calculated upon its expense, and now it was accomplished. He went back to his garden with a sense of pride, of satisfaction which he would share with his cronies as they met in Johnson's Drug Store or Anderson's Meat Market. What he said of me I do not know, but I fear he reported me as living in unimaginable luxury and consorting on terms of equality with the great ones of New York.

CHAPTER NINETEEN

New Life in the Old House

MEANWHILE, Chicago rushing toward its two million mark, had not, alas! lived up to its literary promise of '94. In music, in painting, in sculpture and architecture it was no longer negligible, but each year its authors appeared more and more like a group of esthetic pioneers heroically maintaining themselves in the midst of an increasing tumult of material upbuilding.

One by one its hopeful young publishing houses had failed, and one by one its aspiring periodicals had withered in the keen wind of Eastern competition. *The Dial* alone held on, pathetically solitary, one might almost say alien and solitary.

Against all this misfortune even my besotted optimism could not prevail. My pioneering spirit, subdued by years of penury and rough usage, yielded more and more to the honor and the intellectual companionship which the East offered. To Fuller I privately remarked: "As soon as I can afford it I intend to establish a home in New York."

"I'd go further," he replied. "I would live in Italy if I could."

It was a very significant fact that Chicago contained in 1903 but a handful of writers, while St. Louis, Cleveland, Cincinnati, Detroit and Kansas City had fewer yet. "What is the reason for this literary sterility?" I asked of my companions. "Why should not these powerful cities produce authors? Boston, when she had less than three hundred thousands citizens had Lowell, Longfellow, Emerson and Holmes."

The answer was (and still is), "Because there are few supporters of workers in the fine arts. Western men do not think in terms of art. There are no literary periodicals in these cities to invite (and pay for) the work of the author and the illustrator, and there is moreover a tendency on the part of our builders to give the eastern sculptor, painter or architect the jobs which might be done by local men. Until Chicago has at least one magazine founded like a university, and publishing houses like Scribners and Macmillans our authors and artists must go to New York." Of course none of these answers succeeded in clearing up the mystery, but they were helpful.

Some of the writers in the Little Room were outspokenly envious of my ability to spend half my winters in the East, but Lorado Taft stoutly declared that the West inspired him, satisfied him. "Chicago suits me," he asserted, "and besides I can't afford to run away from my job. You should be the last man to admit defeat, *you* who have been preaching local color and local patriotism all your days."

In truth Taft was one of the few who could afford to remain in Chicago for its public supported him handsomely, but those of us who wrote had no organizations to help sustain our self-esteem. Nevertheless I permitted him to imagine my pessimism to be only a mood which, in some degree it was, for I had many noble friends in the city who invited me to dinner even if they did not read my books.

The claims of Chicago upon me had been strengthened by the presence of Professor Taft who had given up his home in Kansas and was now settled not far from his son and near the University. He had brought all his books and other treasures with intent to spend the remaining years of his life in the neighborhood of his illustrious son and his two daughters, a fact which I could not overlook in any plans for changing my own residence.

Don Carlos Taft was a singular and powerful figure, as I have already indicated, a stoic, of Oriental serenity, one who could smile in the midst of excruciating pain. With his eyes against a blank wall he was able to endlessly amuse himself by calling up the deep-laid concepts of his earlier years of study. Though affected with some obscure spinal disorder which made every movement a punishment, he concealed his suffering, no matter how intense it might be, and always answered, "Fine, fine!" when any of us asked "How are you to-day?"

He lived in Woodlawn as he had lived in Kansas, like a man in a diving bell. His capacious brain filled with "knowledges" of the days when Gladstone was king and Darwin an outlaw, had little room for the scientific theories of Bergson and his like. He remained the old-fashioned New England theologian converted to militant agnosticism.

Although at this time over seventy years of age his mind was notably clear, orderly and active, and his talk (usually a carefully constructed monologue) was stately, formal and precise. He used no slang, and retained scarcely a word of his boyhood's vernacular. The only emotional expression he permitted himself was a chuckle of glee over an intellectual misstatement or a historical bungle. Novels, theaters, music possessed no interest for him.

He had read, I believe, one or two of my books but never alluded to them, although he manifested a growing respect for my ability to earn money, and especially delighted in my faculty for living within my means. He watched the slow growth of my income with approving eyes. To him as to my father, earning money was a struggle, saving it a virtue, and wasting it a crime.

In almost every other characteristic he was my father's

direct antithesis—my father, whose faith approximated that of a Sioux warrior. "I take things as they come," was one of his sayings. He was not concerned with the theories of Evolution, the Pragmatic Philosophy or any other formal system of learning or ethics. With him the present was filled with duties, the remote past or the distant future was of indifferent concern. To deal justly and to leave the world a little better than he found it, was his creed.

The one point of contact between these widely divergent pioneers was their love of Zulime, for my father was almost as fond of her as Don Carlos himself, and distinctly more expressive of his love—for Father Taft held affection to be something not quite decorous when openly declared. He never offered a caress or spoke an affectionate word so far as I know.

There was something pathetic in his situation in these days. Full of learning and eager to share it with youth he could find no one willing to listen to him—not even his children. In the midst of a vast city he was sadly solitary. None of his children appeared interested in his allusions to Hammurabi or Charlemagne, on the contrary, monologues of any kind were taboo in the artistic circles where Lorado reigned. We was too busy, we were all too busy with our small plans and daily struggles, to take any interest in Locke or Gibbon or Hume, therefore the ageing philosopher sat forlornly among his faded, musty books, dreaming his days away on some abstruse ethical problem, or carving with his patient knife some quaintly ornate piece of furniture, while my own father (at the opposite pole of life) weeded his garden, read the daily paper or played cinch with the men at the village drugstore.

Nevertheless, with full knowledge of these fundamental divergencies in the lives of our sires, I urged Zulime to invite Professor Taft to spend a few weeks in West Salem. "He and father will disagree, but the one is a philosopher

274

accustomed to pioneer types and the other a man of reason and I am willing to risk their coming together if you are."

Don Carlos seemed pleased by this invitation and promised to come "one of these days."

Our return to Wisconsin in April was a return to winter. On looking from our car windows at dawn, we found the ground white with snow, and flakes of frost driving through the budding branches of the trees. Every bird was mute, as if with horror and the tender amber-and-green leaves of the maples shone through the rime with a singular and pathetic beauty.

Happily this was only a cold wave. Toward noon the sun came out, the icy cover sank into the earth and the robins began to sing again as if to reassure themselves as well as us.

We came back to the Homestead now with a full sense of our proprietorship. It was entirely ours and it was waiting for us. Father was at the gate, it is true, but he was there this time merely as care-taker, as supervisor of the garden—our garden.

His greeting of Zulime had a deeper note of tenderness than he had ever used hitherto, for he was aware of our hope, and shared our joyous expectancy. "I'm glad you've come," he said simply. "I hate to see the house standing here cold and empty. It don't seem natural or right."

His first act was to lead us out to the garden where orderly beds of springing vegetables testified to his care. "I didn't do anything about the flowers," he confessed rather shamefacedly. "I'm no good at that kind of work."

As the days went by I discovered that father's heart clung to the old place. He loved to spend his days upon it. He was comfortable in his own little cottage, but it seemed too small and too "slick" for him. He liked our trees and lawn and barn, and I was glad to have him continue his supervision of them. They gave him something to think about, something to do. The curse of the "tired farmers" of the village was their enforced idleness. There was almost nothing for them to exercise upon.

He spent most of each day tinkering around the barn, overseeing the garden or resting on the back porch where mother used to sit and look out on the valley. On Sunday he came in to supper, and afterward called for "The Sweet Story of Old" and "The Palace of the King." He listened in silence, a blur in his dreaming eyes, for the past returned on the wings of these songs.

Nobly considerate in his attitude toward Zulime he seemed to understand, perfectly, her almost childish joy in the possession of a nest of her own. He never came to a meal without invitation, though he was seldom without the invitation, for Zulime was fond of him and had only one point of contention with him: "I wish you wouldn't wear your working clothes about the street," she said—and artfully added, "You are so handsome when you are in your Sunday suit, I wish you would wear it all the time."

He smiled with pleasure, but replied: "I'd look fine hoeing potatoes in my Sunday suit, wouldn't I!" Nevertheless he was mindful of her request and always came to dinner in, at worst, his second best.

Each day the gardens about us took on charm. The plum and cherry trees flung out banners of bloom and later the apple trees flowered in pink-and-white radiance. Wonder-working sap seemed to spout into the air through every minute branch. Showers of rain alternated with vivid sunshine, and through the air, heavy with perfume, the mourning dove sang with sad insistence as if to remind us of the impermanency of May's ineffable loveliness. Butterflies suddenly appeared in the grass, and the bees toiled like harvesters, so eager, so busy that they tumbled over one another in their haste. Nature was at her sweetest and loveliest, and in the midst of it walked my young wife, in quiet anticipation of motherhood.

Commonplace to others our rude homestead grew in beauty and significance to us. Day by day we sat on our front porch, and watched the clouds of blossoms thicken. If we walked in our garden we felt the creative loam throbbing beneath our feet. Each bird seemed as proud of the place as we. Each insect was in a transport of activity.

Into the radiant white of the cherry blossoms, impetuous green shoots (new generations) appeared as if in feverish haste, unwilling to await the passing of the flowers. The hills to the south were soaring bubbles of exquisite green vapor dashed with amber and pink and red. Each morning the shade of the maple trees deepened, and on the lawn the dandelions opened, sowing with pieces of gold the velvet of the sward. The songs of the robin, the catbird and the thrush became more confident, more prolix until, at last, the drab and angular little village was transfigured into celestial beauty by the heavenly light and melody of completed spring.

In a certain sense here was the wealth I had been struggling to secure. Here were—seemingly—all the elements of man's content, a broad roof, a generous garden, spreading trees, blossoming shrubs, a familiar horizon line, a lovely wife—and the promise of a child!

Truly, I should have been happy, and in my sour, big-fisted way I was happy. I tried, honestly, to grasp and hold the ecstasy which these days offered. I who had lived for twelve years on railway trains, in camp, on horse-back or in wretched little city hotels, was now a portly householder, a pampered husband and a prospective parent. And yet—such is my perverse temperament—I could not overlook the fact that this tranquil village like thousands of others scattered over the West, was but a half-way house, a pleasant hospital into which many of the crippled, worn-out and white-haired farmers and their wives had come to rest for a little while on their way to the grave.

As I walked the shaded street, perceiving these veterans of the hoe and plow, digging feebly in the earth of their small gardens, or sitting a-dream on the narrow porches of their tiny cottages my joy was embittered. Age, age was everywhere. Here in the midst of the flowering trees the men of the Middle Border were withering into dust.

In the city one does not come into anything like this close relationship with a dying generation. The tragedy is obscured. Here Zulime and I, young and strong, were living in the midst of an almost universal senility and decay. There was no escape from these grim facts.

Looked at from a distance there was comfort in the thought of these pioneers, released from the grind of their farm routine, dozing at ease beneath the maple trees, but closely studied they became sorrowful. I knew too much about them. Several of them had been my father's companions in those glorious days in fifty-five. Yonder white-haired invalid, sitting in the sun silently watching his bees, had been a famous pilot on the river, and that bushy-haired giant, halting by on a stick, was the wreck of a mighty hunter. The wives of these men equally worn, equally rheumatic and even more querulous, had been the rosy, laughing, dancing companions of Isabel McClintock in the days when Richard Garland came a-courting. All, all were camping in lonely cottages while their sons and daughters, in distant cities or far-off mountain valleys, adventuring in their turn, were taking up the discipline and the duties of a new border, a new world.

As a novelist I could not fail to observe these melancholy features of a life which on its surface seemed idyllic. In New York, in Chicago I was concerned mainly with happy, busy people of my own age or younger,—here I was brought

New Life in the Old House

into close contact daily—almost hourly—with the passing of my father's generation and, also, I was made aware of the coming in of an alien, uninspiring race. The farms of the Dudleys, the McKinleys, the Coburns were being taken by the Smeckpeffers, the Heffelfingers, and the Bergmans! Already the pages of the village newspaper were peppered with such names, and a powerful Congregation was building a German church on the site of the old-time Methodist meeting house of my boyhood. My strain was dying out— a new and to my mind less admirable America was coming on.

As June deepened my father (who realized something of the changes going on) proposed a trip to the town in Iowa near which we had lived for twelve years, and to this I consented, feeling that this visit could not safely be postponed another year.

He had never been back to our prairie farm in Mitchell County since leaving it, over twenty years before, and now (with money and leisure) he was eager to go, and as my old Seminary associates had asked me to speak at their Commencement, we rode away one lovely June day up along the Mississippi to Winona, thence by way of a winding coulee, to the level lands, and so across to Mitchell County, our old home. The railroad, which was new to us, ran across Dry Run prairie within half a mile of our schoolhouse, but so flat and monotonous did the whole country now appear, we could not distinguish any familiar landmarks. The "hills" along the creek were barely noticeable from the car, and all the farm-steads were hidden by groves of trees. We passed our former home without recognizing it!

Osage, we soon discovered, was almost as much of an asylum for the aged as West Salem. It, too, was filled with worn-out farmers, men with whom my father had subdued the sod in the early days. Osmond Button, William Frazer,

Oliver Cole, David Babcock were all living "in town" on narrow village lots, "taking it easy" as they called it, but they were by no means as contented as they seemed to the casual onlooker. Freed from the hard daily demands of the farm, many of them acknowledged a sense of uselessness, a fear of decay.

As fast as they learned of our presence, scores of loyal friends swarmed about us expressing a sincere regard for my father, and a kind of wondering respect for me. Some of them clung to my father's hand as though in hope of recovering through him some gleam of the beauty, some part of the magic of the brave days gone—days when the land was new and they were young. "You must come home with me," each man insisted, "the women folks all want to see you."

Twenty years had wrought great changes in the men as well as in the county, and my father was bewildered and saddened by the tale. One by one he called the names of those who had been his one-time friends and neighbors. Some were dead, others had moved away—only one or two remained where he had left them, and it was in the hope of seeing these men and at the same time to visit the farm and school-house on Dry Run, and the church at Burr Oak, that I hired a carriage and drove my father out along the well-remembered lane to the north and east—I say "well-remembered" although the growth of the trees and the presence of new buildings made its appeal mixed and unsatisfactory to us both.

We found our house almost hid in the trees which we had planted on the bare prairie thirty years before. As we stood in the yard I spoke of the silver wedding which took place there. The yard was attractive but the house (infested by the family of a poor renter) was repulsive. The upstairs chamber in which I had slept for so many years presented a filthy clutter of chicken feathers, cast-off furniture and musty clothing. Our stay was short.

Strangers were in all of the other houses along the way—we found but two of our former neighbors at home, and the farther we drove the more melancholy we both became.

One of the places which I wished especially to revisit was the school-house at Burr Oak, the room which had been our social center in the early eighties. In it we had listened to church service in summer, and there in winter our Grange Suppers and Friday Lyceums had been held. It was there, too, that I had worshiped at the shrine of Hattie's girlish beauty, when as a shock-haired lad I forgot, for a day, the loneliness of my prairie home.

Alas! the tall oaks which in those days had given dignity and charm to the yard had all been cut down, and the building, once glorified by the waving shadows of the leaves, now stood bare as a bone beside the road. An alien lived where Betty once reigned, and the white cottage from which Agnes was wont to issue in her exquisite Sunday frock, was untenanted and falling into decay.

How lovely those girls had seemed to me as I watched them approach, walking so daintily the path beside the fence! What rich, alluring color flamed in Bettie's cheek, what fire flashed in Aggie's dark and roguish eyes!

To a stranger, Burr Oak—my Burr Oak—even in Seventy-two was only a pleasant meeting place of prairie lanes on the margin of a forest, but to me it had been a temple of magic. I had but to shut my eyes to desolating changes, turning my vision inward, in order to see myself (a stocky awkward boy in a Sunday suit with a torturing collar) standing on the porch waiting to see those white-clad maidens pass into the vestibule.

Too shy in those days to meet their eyes, too worshipful to ever hope for word or smile, I remained their silent adorer. Here and now I set down the tribute which I could not then express:

> O maids to whom I never spoke, to whom
> My dreaming ran in lonely field,
> Because of you I saw the bloom
> Of Maytime more abundantly revealed.
> From you each bud new magic caught.
> When you were near, my skies
> Were brighter, for your beauty brought
> A poet's rapture to my eyes.
>
> Men tell me you are bent and gray,
> And worn with toil and pain;
> And so I pray the Wheel of Chance
> May never set us face to face again.
> Better that I should think of you
> As you then were, strong and sweet,
> Walking your joyous sunlit way
> Between the wheat and roses of the lane—
> *Pass on, O weary women of today—*
> *Remain forever 'mid the roses and the wheat,*
> *O girls with laughing lips and dancing feet!*

That ride and the people I met closed a gate for me. I accomplished a painful relinquishment. That noon-day sun divided my past from my present as with the stroke of a flaming sword. Up to this moment I had retained, in formless fashion, a belief that I could some time and somehow reach out and regain, at least in part, the substance of the life I had once lived here in this scene. Now I confessed that not only was my youth gone but that the friends and the place of my youth had vanished. My heart, wrung with a measureless regret filled my throat with pain, and as I looked in my father's face I perceived that he, too, was feeling the force of Time's inexorable decree.

We started homeward in silence, speaking only now and then when some object made itself recognizable to us.

New Life in the Old House

"I shall never ride this lane again," I said as we were nearing the town. "It has been a sad experience. The world of my boyhood—the world we both knew—is utterly gone. It exists only in your memory and mine. I want to get away—back to Zulime and the present."

"I'm ready to go," replied my father. "I thought I'd enjoy visiting the old place and seeing old neighbors, but I haven't. It's all too melancholy. I'm ready to go back to the LaCrosse Valley and stay there what little time I've got left to me."

That night, at the Seminary, I met the Alumni and spoke to them on some subject connected with the early history of the school, and in doing so I obtained once again a perception of the barrier which had risen between my classmates and myself. They were not only serious, they were piteously solemn. No one laughed, no one took a light and airy view of life. Once or twice I tried to jest or ventured a humorous remark, but these attempts to lighten the gloom were met with chilling silence. No one whispered or smiled or turned aside. It was like a prayer meeting in the face of famine.

Part of this was due no doubt to their habit of listening to sermons, but some of it arose I am sure from a feeling of poignant regret similar to that which burdened my own heart. As usual in such reunions the absent ones were named and the faces of the dead recalled. In all our songs the rustling of withered leaves could be heard. All felt the pitiless march of time and I respected them for their perception of life's essential enigma.

After the "Services" were finished, several of the women came up to me and introduced themselves. One handsome gray-haired woman said: "I am Rosa Clinton," and it shocked me to be unable to find in her the girl I once knew. Another matron whom I recognized at once, retained something inescapably girlish in both face and voice. It hurt

283

me to detect in her withered lips the quaint twist which had once been so charming to me—but then she undoubtedly discovered in me equally distressing reminders of decay.

Not all my philosophy could prevent me from falling into profound melancholy. I went back to my hotel thinking of these men and women as they were when, as a youth of twenty, I trod with them the worn plank walks beneath the magical murmuring maple trees. The bitter facts of their lives gave rise to question. What was it all about? What was the value of their efforts or my own? Has the life of man any more significance than that of an insect?

Just before leaving for the train next day we called on Osmond Button, who clung to my father with piteous intensity. "Stay another day," he pleaded, but father would not listen to any postponement.

This old neighbor went to the train with us, knowing full well that he and my father would never meet again.

Thus it happened—curiously, yet most naturally—that the last man we saw as we left Osage was our first neighbor on Dry Run prairie in the autumn of Seventy-one.

From this melancholy review of the bent forms of ancient friends and neighbors, dreaming of the past, I returned to my wife, who was concerned entirely with the future. What had she to do with elderly folk? Life to her was sweet and promiseful. Intently toiling over the adornment of tiny caps, socks and gowns, joyful as a girl of seven making dresses for a doll, she insisted on displaying to me all of that lilliputian wardrobe. A dozen times each day she called on me to admire this or that garment, and I was greatly relieved to find that the growing wonder of the experience through which she was about to pass, prevented her from giving way to fear of it. Over me, at times, an icy shadow fell. Suppose—suppose——!

One night she dreamed that a babe had come to us, and

that the nurse had carelessly allowed it to chill and die, but I had no such disturbing premonitions. Contrary to the statements of sentimental novelists and poets I almost never dreamed of my wife. I more often dreamed of Howells or Roosevelt or some of my editorial friends, indeed I often had highly technical literary dreams wherein I prepared manuscripts for the press or composed speeches or poems, and sometimes my mother or Jessie came back to me—but Zulime had never up to this time entered my sleep.

One afternoon during this period of waiting and just after I had finished the writing of *Hesper* we joined our good friends the Eastons on an excursion up the Mississippi on their house-boat, a glorious outing which I mention because it was the farthest removed from my boyhood life on Dry Run prairie whose scenes had just been vividly brought to mind.

Here was the flawless poetry of recreation, the perfection of travel. To sit in a reclining chair on the screened-in forward deck of a beautiful boat, what time it was being propelled by some invisible silent machinery, up a shining river, reflecting wooded bluffs, was like taking flight on the magic carpet of my boyhood's story book. The purple head-lands projecting majestically into the still flood took on once more the poetry and the mystery of the prehistoric. One by one those royal pyramids ordered and adorned themselves for our inspection while the narrow valleys opening their gates, displayed all their tranquil pastoral charm.

Our meals, delicately cooked and perfectly served, appeared as if by conjury, on a table in the dining-room amidships, and as we ate we watched the glory deepen on the clouds, while the waters, soundless as oil, rolled past our open doors. It was all a passage to the Land of the Lotos to me. How had I, whose youth had been so full of penury and toil, earned a share in such leisure, such luxury?

Was it right for me to give myself up to the enjoyment of it? For Zulime's sake I rejoiced in it, knowing that her days were long with waiting and suspense:

Without knowing much of the bitter anguish of the ordeal, I held maternity to be (as the great poets had taught me to hold it) a noble heroism. "If mankind is worth continuing on this earth," I had written, "then the mother is entitled to the highest honor, the tenderest care. Science should do its best to lessen her pain, to make her birth-bed honorable."

In spite of my wife's brave smile I sensed in her a subconscious dread of what was coming, and this anxiety I shared so fully that I ceased to write and gave all my time to her. Together we walked the garden or drove about the country in the low-hung, easy-riding old surrey, tracing the wooded ways we loved the best, or climbing to where a wide view of the valley offered. I understood her laughing stoicism much better now, and it no longer deceived me. She made light of her own fears in order that I might not worry. The fact that she was past her first youth was my torment, for I had read that the danger increased with every year beyond twenty-five and the thought that we might never ride these lanes again came into my mind and would not be exorcised. At such moments as I could snatch I worked on a series of lectures which I was scheduled to deliver at the University of Chicago—lectures on Edwin Booth which brought back my Boston days.

At last the dreaded day came!—I shall not dwell upon the long hours of the mother's pain, or on the sleepless anxiety of my household, for I have no desire to relive them. I would rather make statement of my relief and gratitude when after many, many hours of suffering, Edward Evans of LaCrosse, a scientific, deft and powerful surgeon, came to the mother's rescue. He was a master—the man who knew!

At last the time came when I was permitted to take my wife—
lovely as a Madonna—out into the sunshine, and, as she sat
holding Mary Isabel in her arms, she gathered to herself an
ecstasy of relief, a joy of life which atoned, in part, for the
inescapable sufferings of maternity.

New Life in the Old House

He saved both mother and child, and when the nurse laid in my arms a little babe, who looked up at me with grave, accusing blue eyes,—the eyes of her mother,—I wondered whether society had a right to put any woman to this cruel test—whether the race was worth maintaining at such a price.

Our loyal friend, Mary Easton (mother of five children), who was present to help us through our stern trial, assured me that maternity had its joys as well as its agonies, and after she had peered into the face of my small daughter she remarked to me with a delightful note of admiration, "Why, she is already a *person!*"

So indeed she was. Her head, large and shapely and her eyes wide, dark and curiously reflective, were like her mother's. True, she hadn't much nose, but her hair was abundant and her fingers exquisite. She lay in my big paws with what seemed to me to be tranquil confidence, and though her legs were comically rudimentary, her glance manifested an unassailable dignity. My father insisted she resembled her grandmother.

* * * * * *

At last came the blessed day when the nurse permitted me to wheel the convalescent out upon the porch. The morning was lovely, with just a hint of autumn in its coolness, and to Zulime it was heavenly sweet, for it seemed that she had emerged from a long dark night of agony and doubt.

As she sat with the babe in her lap looking over the familiar hills, she was more beautiful than she had ever been before. She was a being glorified.

Later in the day, as the sun was going down in a welter of gold and crimson, she came out again and in its splendor I chose to read the promise of a noble future for Mary Isabel. It gave me joy to know that she had taken up her life beneath the same roof and almost in the same room in which Isabel Garland had laid her burden down.

Yes, the Homestead had a new claimant. In the midst of my father's decaying world a new and vigorous life had miraculously appeared. Beneath the moldering leaves of the leaning oaks a tender yet tenacious shoot was springing from the soil.

CHAPTER TWENTY

Mary Isabel's Chimney

NO one who reads the lives of writers attentively can fail of perceiving the periods of depression—almost of despair—into which we are all liable to fall—days when nothing that we have done seems worth while—moods of groping indecision during which we groan and most unworthily complain. I am no exception. For several months after the publication of *Hesper* I experienced a despairing emptiness, a sense of unworthiness, a feeling of weakness which I am certain made me a burden to my long-suffering wife.

"What shall I do now?" I asked myself.

From my standpoint as a novelist of The Great Northwest, there remained another subject of study, the red man —The Sioux and the Algonquin loomed large in the prairie landscape. They were, in fact, quite as significant in the history of the border as the pioneer himself, for they were his antagonists. Not content with using the Indian as an actor in stories like *The Captain of the Gray Horse Troop,* I had done something more direct and worthy through a manuscript which I called *The Silent Eaters,* a story in which I tried to put the Sitting Bull's case as one of his partisans might have depicted it. I had failed for lack of detailed knowledge, and the manuscript lay in my desk untouched.

It was in this period of doubt and disheartenment that I turned to my little daughter with gratitude and a deep sense

289

of the mystery of her coming. The never-ending surprise of her presence filled me with delight. Like billions of other Daddies I forgot my worries as I looked into her tranquil eyes. To protect and educate her seemed at the moment my chiefest care.

During the mother's period of convalescence I acted—in my hours of leisure—as nurse-maid quite indifferent to the smiles of spectators, who made question of my method. I became an expert in holding the babe so that her spine should not be over-taxed, and I think she liked to feel the grip of my big fingers. That she appreciated the lullabies I sang to her I am certain, for even my Aunt Deborah was forced to admit that my control of my daughter's slumber period was remarkably efficient.

The coming of this child changed the universe for me. She brought into my life a new element, a new consideration. The insoluble mystery of sex, the heroism of maternity, the measureless wrongs of womankind and the selfish cruelty of man rose into my thinking with such power that I began to write of them, although they had held but academic interest hitherto. With that tiny woman in my arms I looked into the faces of my fellow men with a sudden realization that the world as it stands to-day is essentially a male world —a world in which the female is but a subservient partner. "It is changing, but it will still be a man's world when you are grown," I said to Mary Isabel.

My devotion, my slavery to this ten-pound daughter greatly amused my friends and neighbors. To see "the grim Klondiker," in meek attendance on a midget sovereign was highly diverting—so I was told by Mary Easton, and I rather think she was right. However, I was undisturbed so long as Mary Isabel did not complain.

She was happy with me. She rode unnumbered joyous miles upon my left elbow and cantered away into dreamland by way of the ancient walnut rocker in which her grandmother had been wont to sit and dream. Deep in her baby brain-cells I planted vague memories of "Down the River," "Over the Hills in Legions," and "Nellie Wildwood," for I sang to her almost every evening of her infant life.

> "Rock-a-bye, baby, thy cradle is green.
> Papa's a nobleman—mother's a queen,"

was one of her most admired lullabys. It was a marvelous time for me—the happiest I had known since boyhood. Not even my days of courtship have greater charm to me now.

The old soldier was almost as completely subordinated as I. Several times each day he came into the house to say, "Well, how is my granddaughter getting on?" and upon seeing her, invariably remarked, "She's the very image of Belle,"—and indeed she did resemble my mother. He expressed the wish which was alive in my own heart, when he said, "If only Belle could have lived to see her granddaughter."

My new daughter was all important, but the new book could not be neglected. *Hesper* was scheduled for publication in October and copy must go to the printer in August, therefore I was forced to leave my wife and babe and go East to attend to the proof-reading and other matters incidental to the birth of another novel. Some lectures in Chicago and Chautauqua took up nearly two weeks of my time and when I arrived in New York, huge bundles of galley-proof were awaiting me.

My publishers were confident that the new book would equal *The Captain of the Gray Horse Troop* in popularity, but I was less sanguine. For several weeks I toiled on this job, and at last on the eleventh of September, a day of sweltering heat, I got away on the evening train for the West. In spite of my poverty and notwithstanding the tender age of my daughter, I had decided to fetch my family to New York.

On November tenth, we found ourselves settled in a small apartment overlooking Morningside Park, which seemed a very desirable playground for Mary Isabel.

Relying on my books (which were selling with gratifying persistency) we permitted ourselves a seven-room apartment with a full-sized kitchen and a maid—whom we had brought on from West Salem. We even went so far as to give dinner parties to such of our friends as could be trusted to overlook our lack of plate, and to remain kindly unobservant of the fact that Dora, the baby's nurse, doubled as waitress after cooking the steak.

In this unassuming fashion we fed the Hernes, the Severances, and other of our most valued friends who devoured the puddings which Zulime "tossed up," with a gusto highly flattering to her skill, while the sight of me as baby-tender proved singularly amusing—to some of our guests. It will be seen that we were not cutting entirely loose from the principles of economy in which we had been so carefully schooled—our hospitalities had very distinct (enforced) limits.

Our wedding anniversary came while we were getting settled and my present to Zulime that year was a set of silver which I had purchased with the check for an article called "A Pioneer Wife"—the paper which I had written as a memorial to my mother. In explanation of the fact that all these silver pieces bore the initials I. G., I said, "You are to think of them as a gift from my mother. Imagine that I gave them to her long ago, and that they now come to you, from her, as heirlooms. Let us call them 'The family silver' and hand them down to Mary Isabel in her turn."

Zulime, who always rose to a sentiment of this kind, gratefully accepted this vicarious inheritance and thereafter

Mary Isabel's Chimney

I was pleased to observe that whenever Mary Isabel wished to break a plate she invariably reached for one of her grandmother's solid silver spoons—they were so much more effective than the plated ones!

Christmas came to us this year with new and tender significance, for "Santy Claus" (who found us at home in New York, rejoicing in our first baby) brought to us our first tree, and the conjunction of these happy events produced in my wife almost perfect happiness. Furthermore, Mary Isabel achieved her first laugh. I am sure of this fact, for I put it down in my notebook, with these words, "She has a lovely smile and a chuckle like her grandmother's. She robs us of solitude, and system, and order, but our world would now be desolate without her." Only when I thought of what her grandfather was missing did I have a sense of regret.

At our feast our daughter sat in the high chair which Katherine Herne had given her, and looked upon the tiny, decorated tree with eyes of rapture, deep, dark-blue eyes in which a seraphic light shone. Her life was beginning far, very far, from the bleak prairie lands in which her Daddy's winter holidays had been spent, and while the silver spoon in her mouth was not of my giving, the one with which she bruised her chair-arm, was veritably one of my rewards.

In order to continue my practice as an Author, I managed to sandwich the writing of an occasional article between spells of minding the baby—and working on club committees. I recall going to Princeton to tell Henry Van Dyke's Club about "The Joys of the Trail," and it pleased me to be introduced as a "Representative of the West." West Point received me in this capacity, and I also read at one of Lounsbury's "Smokers" at Yale, but I was kept from any undue self-congratulation by recognition of the fact that my income was still considerably below the standard of a railway engineer—as perhaps it should be. My "arriving" was always in an accommodation train fifty minutes late.

Evidence of my literary success, if you look at it that way, may have lain in an invitation to dine at Andrew Carnegie's, but a suspicion that I was being patronized made me hesitate. It was only after I learned that Burroughs and Gilder were going that I decided to accept, although I could not see why the ironmaster should include me in his list. I had never met him and was not eager for his recognition.

The guests (nearly all known to me) were most distinguished and it was pleasant to meet with them, even in this palace. We marched into the dining-room keeping step to the music of a bagpipe. The speaking which followed the dinner was admirable. Hamilton Wright Mabie and John Finley were especially adroit and graceful, and Carnegie, who had been furnished with elaborate notes by his secretary, introduced his speakers with tact and humor, although it was evident that in some cases he would have been helpless without his literary furnishing—to which in my case he referred with especial care.

He was an amazement to me. I could not imagine him in the rôle of "Iron King," on the contrary he appeared more like a genial Scotch school-master, one genuinely interested in learning. Had it not been for his air of labored appreciation, and the glamour of his enormous wealth, the dinner would have been wholly enjoyable.

One charming human touch saved the situation. The tablecloth (a magnificent piece of linen) was worked here and there with silken reproductions of the signatures of former distinguished guests. "Mrs. Carnegie," our host explained, "works these signatures into the cloth with her own hands." Each of us was given a soft pencil and requested to add his name.

It happened that Gilder, Seton, Burroughs and myself went away together, and the doorman showed a mild sur-

Mary Isabel's Chimney

prise in the fact that no carriage awaited us. Gilder with comic intonation said, "Some of you fellows ought to have saved this situation by ordering a cab."

"As the only man with a stovepipe hat the job was yours," I retorted.

This struck the rest of the party as funny. In truth, each of us except Gilder wore some sort of soft hat, and all together we formed a sinister group. "I don't care what *Andrew* thinks of us," Gilder explained, "but I hate to have his butler get such a low conception of American authorship." On this point we all agreed—and took the Madison Avenue street car.

Meanwhile, I was secretly dreaming of getting rich myself.

Every American, with a dollar to spare, at some time in his life takes a shot at a gold mine. It comes early in some lives and late in others, but it comes! In my case it came after the publication of *Hesper* just as I was verging on forty-five, and was the result of my brother's connections in Mexico. Impatient of getting money by growing trees he had resigned his position on a rubber farm and was digging gold in Northern Mexico.

Our mine, situated about twenty miles from Camacho, was at the usual critical stage where more capital is needed, therefore in April I persuaded Irving Bacheller and Archer Brown to go down with me and take a look at the property. Of course I had a lump of ore to show them—and it was beautiful!

I recall that when this sample came to me by express, I had my first and only conviction that my financial worries were over. Even Zulime was impressed with my brother's smelter reports which gave the proportion of gold to the ton, precisely set down in bold black figures. All we had to do was to ship a sufficient number of car lots for the year and our income would rival that of Carnegie's.

A Daughter of the Middle Border

We decided to break up our little home, and while I went to Mexico, Zulime planned to visit Chicago and await my return. I was loth to dismantle our apartment, and when at the station I said good-by to my little daughter and her mother, I was almost persuaded that nothing was worth the pain of parting from that small shining face and those seeking, clinging hands. She had grown deep into my heart during those winter months.

I felt very poor and lonely as I went to my bed at the club that first night after our separation, and when next day Bacheller invited me out to his new home at Sound Beach, I gratefully accepted, although I was in the middle of getting a new book through the press—a job which my publishers had urged upon me against my better judgment. I felt that I was being hurried.

Bacheller, highly prosperous, was living at this time in a handsome waterside bungalow, with a big sitting-room in which a generous fire glowed. It happened that he was entertaining General Henderson of Iowa, and when in some way it developed that we were all famous singers, a spirited contest arose as to which of us could beat the others. Henderson sang Scotch lyrics very well, and Bacheller was full of tunes from his North Country, whilst I—well if I didn't keep my whiffletree off the wheel, it was not for lack of effort. I sang "Maggie" and "Lily Dale" and "Rosalie the Prairie Flower," all of which made a powerful impression on Henderson; but it was not till I sang "The Rolling Stone," that I fully countered. Irving asked me to repeat this song, but I refused. "You might catch the tune," I explained.

The general's face shone with pleasure but a wistful cadence was in his voice. "Your tunes carry me back to my boyhood," he said, "I heard my mother sing some of them."

He was near the end of his life, although none of us realized it that night, and we all went our ways in the glow of a tender friendship—a friendship deepened by this reminiscent song. Three days later Bacheller and I were entering Mexico on our way to my mine.

Although Bacheller declined to go into partnership with me we had a gorgeous trip, and that was the main object so far as the other fellows were concerned, and as I wrote an article on the caverns of Cacawamilpa which paid my expenses I was content.

In returning to the North by way of El Paso and the Rock Island road, I encountered a sandstorm, whose ferocity dimmed the memory of the one in which my father's wheat was uprooted. It was frightful. From this I passed almost at once to the bloom, the green serenity, and the abundance of my native valley. It was a kind of paradise by contrast to the South-west and to take my little daughter to my bosom, to look into her eyes, to feel her little palms patting my cheeks, was a pleasure such as I had never expected to own. Every father who reads this line will understand me when I declare that she had "developed wonderfully" in the month of my absence. To me every change in my first born was thrilling—and a little sad—for the fairy of to-day was continually displacing the fairy of yesterday.

Believing that this had ended my travels for the summer, I began to work on a novel which should depict the life of a girl, condemned against her will to be a spiritualistic medium,—forced by her parents to serve as a "connecting wire between the world of matter and the world of spirit."

This theme, which lay outside my plan to depict the West, had long demanded to be written, and I now set about it with vigor. As a matter of fact, I knew a great deal about mediums, for at one time I had been a member of the Council of the American Psychical Society, and as a special committee on slate writing and other psychical phenomena had conducted many experiments. I had in my mind (and in my notebooks) a mass of material which formed the background of my story, *The Tyranny of the Dark*. It made a creditable serial and a fairly successful book, but it will probably not count as largely in my record as "Martha's Fireplace," a short story which I wrote at about the same time. I do not regret having done this novel, because at the moment it seemed very much worth while, but I was fully aware, even then, that it had a much narrower appeal than either *Hesper* or *The Captain of the Gray Horse Troop*.

In the midst of my work on this book our good friends, Mary and Fred Easton, invited us to go with them, in their houseboat, on a trip to the World's Fair in St. Louis. Mrs. Easton offered to take Mary Isabel and her nurse into her own lovely home during our absence, and as Zulime needed the outing we joined the party.

It was a beautiful experience, a kind of dream journey, luxurious, effortless, silent and suggestive,—suggestive of the great river as it was in the time of Dubuque. Sometimes for an hour or more we lost sight of the railway, and the primitive loneliness of the stream awed and humbled us.

For ten days we sailed in such luxury as I had never known before; and when we reached home again it was the splendor of the stream and not the marvels of the Fair which had permanently enriched me. I have forgotten almost every feature of the exhibition, but the sunset light falling athwart the valleys and lighting the sand-bars into burning gold fills my memory to this day.

Here I must make another confession. Up to this time our big living-room had no fireplace. I had thrown out bay-windows, tacked on porches, and constructed bathrooms; but the most vital of all the requisites of a homestead was still lacking. We had no hearth and no outside chimney.

A fireplace was one of the possessions which I really envied my friends. I had never said, "I wish I had Bacheller's house," but I longed to duplicate his fireplace.

Mary Isabel's Chimney

Like most of my generation in the West I had been raised beside a stove, with only one early memory of a fireplace, that in my Uncle Davids's home, in the glow of which, nearly forty years before, I had lain one Thanksgiving night to hear him play the violin—a memory of sweetest quality to me even now. Zulime's childhood had been almost equally bare. She had hung her Christmas stockings before a radiator, as I had strung mine on the wall, behind the kitchen stove. Now suddenly with a small daughter to think of, we both began to long for a fireplace with a desire which led at last toward action—on my part, Zulime was hesitant.

"As our stay in the Old Homestead comes always during the summer, it seems a wilful extravagance to put our hard-earned dollars into an improvement which a renter would consider a nuisance," she argued.

"Nevertheless I'm going to build a fireplace," I replied.

"You mustn't think of it," she protested.

"Consider what a comfort it would be on a rainy day in June," I rejoined. "Think what it would do for the baby on dark mornings."

This had its effect, but even then she would not agree to have it built.

Another deterrent lay in the inexperience of our carpenters and masons, not one of whom had even built a chimney. Everybody had fireplaces in pioneer days, in the days of the Kentucky rifle, the broad-axe and the tallow-dip; but as the era of frame houses came on, the arches had been walled up, and iron stoves of varying ugliness had taken their places. In all the country-side (outside of La-Crosse) there was not a hearthstone of the old-fashioned kind, and though some of the workmen remembered them, not one of them could tell how they were constructed, and the idea of an outside chimney was comically absurd.

All these forces working against me had, thus far, prevented me from experimenting, and perhaps even now the towering base-burner would have remained our family shrine had not Mary Isabel put in a wordless plea. Less than four hundred days old, she was, nevertheless wise in fireplaces. She had begun to burble in the light of the Severances' hearth in Minnesota, and her eyes had reflected the flame and shadow of a noble open fire in Katherine Herne's homestead on Peconic Bay. Her cheeks had reddened like apples in the glory of that hickory flame, and when she came to our small apartment in New York City she had seemed surprised and sadly disappointed by the gas pipes and asbestos mat, which made up a hollow show under a gimcrack mantel. Now here, in her own home, was she to remain without the witchery of crackling flame?

As the cold winds of September began to blow my resolution was taken. "That fireplace must be built. My daughter shall not be cheated of beamed ceilings and the glory of the blazing log."

Zulime, in alarm, again cried out as mother used to do: "Consider the expense!"

"Hang the expense! Consider the comfort, the beauty of the embers. Think of Mary Isabel with her eyes reflecting their light. Imagine the old soldier sitting on the hearth holding his granddaughter——"

She smiled in timorous surrender. "I can see you are bound to do it," she said, "but where can it be built?"

Alas! there was only one available space, a narrow wall between the two west windows. "We'll cut the windows down, or move them," I said, with calm resolution.

"I hate a *little* fireplace," protested Zulime.

"It can't be huge," I admitted, "but it can be real. It can be as *deep* as we want it."

Having decided upon the enterprise I hurried forth to engage the hands to do the work. I could not endure a day's delay.

Mary Isabel's Chimney

The first carpenter with whom I spoke knew nothing about such things. The next one had helped to put in one small "hard-coal, wall pocket," and the third man had seen fireplaces in Norway, but remembered little about their construction. After studying Zulime's sketch of what we wanted, he gloomily remarked, "I don't believe I can make that thing *gee*."

Zulime was disheartened by all this, but Mary Isabel climbed to my knee as if to say, "Boppa, where is my fire place?"

My courage returned. "It shall be built if I have to import a mason from Chicago," I declared, and returned to the campaign.

"Can't you build a thing like this?" I asked a plasterer, showing him a magazine picture of a fireplace.

He studied it with care, turning it from side to side. "A rough pile o' brick like that?"

"Just like that."

"Common red brick?"

"Yes, just the kind you use for outside walls."

"If you'll get a carpenter to lay it out maybe I can do it," he answered, but would fix no date for beginning the work.

Three days later when I met him on the street he looked a little shame-faced. "I hoped you'd forgot about that fireplace," he said. "I don't know about that job. I don't just see my way to it. However, if you'll stand by and take all the responsibility, I'll try it."

"When can you come?"

"To-morrow," he said.

"I'll expect you."

I hastened home. I climbed to the top of the old chimney, hammer in hand, and began the work of demolition.

The whole household became involved in the campaign. While the gardener and my father chipped the mortar from the bricks which I threw down, Zulime drew another plan for the arch and the hearth, and Mary Isabel sat on the lawn, and shouted at her busy father, high in the sky.

A most distressing clutter developed. The carpenters attacked the house like savage animals, chipping and chiseling till they opened a huge gap from window to window, filling the room with mortar, dust and flies. Zulime was especially appalled by the flies.

"I didn't know you had to slash into the house like that," she said. "It's like murder."

Our neighbors hitherto vastly entertained by our urban eccentricities expressed an intense interest in our plan for an open fire. "Do you expect it to heat the house?" asked Mrs. Dutcher, and Aunt Maria said: "An open fire is nice to look at, but expensive to keep going."

Sam McKinley heartily applauded. "I'm glad to hear you're going back to the old-fashioned fireplace. They were good things to sit by. I'd like one myself, but I never'd get my wife to consent. She says they are too much trouble to keep in order."

At last the mason came, and together he and I laid out the ground plan of the structure. By means of bricks disposed on the lawn I indicated the size of the box, and then, while the carpenter crawled out through the crevasse in the side of the house, we laid a deep foundation of stone. We had just brought the base to the level of the sill when— the annual County Fair broke out!

All work ceased. The workmen went to the ball game and to the cattle show and to the races, leaving our living-room open to the elements, and our lawn desolate with plaster.

For three days we suffered this mutilation. At last the master mason returned, but without his tender. "No matter," I said to him. "I can mix mortar and sand," and I

Mary Isabel's Chimney

did. I also carried brick, splashing myself with lime and skinning my hands,—but the chimney grew!

Painfully, with some doubt and hesitancy, but with assuring skill, Otto laid the actual firebox, and when the dark-red, delightfully rude piers of the arch began to rise from the floor within the room, the entire family gathered to admire the structure and to cheer the workmen on their way.

The little inequalities which came into the brickwork delighted us. These "accidentals" as the painters say were quite as we wished them to be. Privately, our bricklayer considered us—"Crazy." The idea of putting common rough brick on the *inside* of a house!

The library floor was splotched with mortar, the dining-room was cold and buzzing with impertinent flies, but what of that—the tower of brick was climbing.

The mason called insatiably for more brick, more mortar, and the chimney (the only outside chimney in Hamilton township) rose grandly, alarmingly above the roof—whilst I gained a reputation for princely expenditure which it will take me a long time to live down.

Suddenly discovering that we had no fire-clay for the lining of the firebox, I ordered it by express (another ruinous extravagance), and the work went on. It was almost done when a cold rain began, driving the workmen indoors.

Zulime fairly ached with eagerness to have an end of the mess, and the mason catching the spirit of our unrest worked on in the rain. One by one the bricks slipped into place.

"Oh, how beautiful the fire would be on a day like this!" exclaimed Zulime. "Do you think it will ever be finished? I can't believe it. It's all a dream. It won't draw—or something. It's too good to be true."

"It will be done to-night—and it will draw," I stoutly replied.

At noon, the inside being done, Otto went outside to complete the top, toiling heroically in the drizzle.

At last, for the fourth time we cleaned the room of all but a few chips of the sill, which I intended to use for our first blaze. Then, at my command, Zulime took one end of the thick, rough mantel and together we swung it into place above the arch. Our fireplace was complete! Breathlessly we waited the signal to apply the match.

At five o'clock the mason from the chimney top cheerily called, *"Let 'er go!"*

Striking a match I handed it to Zulime. She touched it to the shavings. Our chimney took life. It drew! It roared!!

Pulling the curtains close, to shut out the waning daylight, we drew our chairs about our hearth whereon the golden firelight was playing. We forgot our troubles, and Mary Isabel pointing her pink, inch-long forefinger at it, laughed with glee. Never again would she sit above a black hole in the floor to warm her toes.

Out of the corners of the room the mystic ancestral shadows leapt, to play for her sake upon the walls. "She will now acquire the poet's fund of sweet subconscious memories," I declared. "The color of all New England home-life is in that fire. Centuries of history are involved in its flickering shadows. We have put ourselves in touch with our Anglo-Saxon ancestors at last."

"It already looks as ancient as the house," Zulime remarked, and so indeed it did, for its rude inner walls had blackened almost instantly, and its rough, broad, brick hearth fitted harmoniously into the brown floor. The thick plank mantle (stained a smoky-green) seemed already clouded with age. Its expression was perfect—to us, and when father "happened in" and drawing his armchair forward took Mary Isabel in his arms, the firelight playing over his gray hair and on the chubby cheeks of the child,

The old soldier and pioneer loved to take the children on his knees and bask in the light of the fire. At such times he made a picture which typed forth to me all the chimney corners and all the Anglo-Saxon grandsires for a thousand years. In him I saw the past. In them I forecast the future. In him an era was dying, in them Life renewed her swiftly passing web.

Mary Isabel's Chimney

he made a picture immemorial in its suggestion, typifying all the hearths and all the grandsires and fair-skinned babes of New England history.

The grim old house had a soul. It was now in the fullest sense a hearth and a home. Oh, Mother and David, were you with us at that moment? Did you look upon us from the dusky corners, adding your faint voices to the chorus of our songs? I hope so. I try to believe so.

That night when Mary Isabel was asleep and I sat alone beside the hearth, another and widely different magic came from those embers. Their tongues of flame, subtly inter-fused with smoke, called back to memory the many camp-fires I had builded beside the streams, beneath the pines of the mountain west.

Each of my tenting places drew near. At one moment, far in the Skeena Valley, I sat watching the brave fire beat back the darkness and the rain—hearing a glacial river roar-ing from the night. At another I was encamped in the shelter of a mighty cliff, listening in awe while along its lofty shelves the lions prowled and in the cedars, amid the ruins of prehistoric cities, the wind chanted a solemn rune filled with the voices of those whose bones had long since been mingled with the dust.

> Oh, the good days on the trail!
> I cannot lose you—I will not!
> Here in the amber of my song   6
> I hold you.
> Here where neither time nor change
> Can do you wrong.
> I sweep you together,
> The harvest of a continent. The gold
> Of a thousand days of quest.
> So, when I am old,
> Like a chained eagle I can sit

And dream and dream
Of splendid spaces,
The gleam of rivers,
And the smell of prairie flowers.
So, when I have quite forgot
The heritage of books, I still shall know
The splendor of the mountains, and the glow
Of sunset on the vanished plain.

CHAPTER TWENTY-ONE

The Fairy World of Childhood

ONE night just before leaving for the city, I invited a few of my father's old cronies to come in and criticize my new chimney. They all came,—Lottridge, Stevens, Shane, Johnson, McKinley, all the men who meant the most to my sire, and as they took seats about the glowing hearth, the most matter-of-fact of them warmed to its poetic associations, and the sternest of them softened in face and tone beneath its magic light.

Each began by saying, "An open fire is nice to sit by, but not much good as a means of heating the house," and having made this concession to the practical, they each and all passed to minute and loving descriptions of just the kind of fireplaces their people used to have back in Connecticut or Maine or Vermont. Stevens described the ancestral oven, Lottridge told of the family hob and crane, and throughout all this talk a note of wistful tenderness ran. They were stirred to their depths and yet concealed it. Not one had the courage to build such a chimney but every man of them covertly longed for it, dimly perceiving its value as an altar of memory, unconsciously acknowledging its poignant youthful associations. The beauty of vanished faces, the forms of the buried past drew near, and in the golden light of reminiscent dream, each grizzled head took on a softer, nobler outline. The prosaic was forgot. The poetry of their lives was restored.

Father was at his best, hospitable, reminiscent, jocund.

His pride in me was expressed in his faith in my ability to keep this fire going.

"Hamlin don't mind a little expense like this chimney," he said. "He put it in just to amuse the baby,—so he says and I believe him. He can afford it—so I'm not saying a word, in fact I like an open fire so well I'm thinking of putting one into my own house."

To this several replied by saying, "We'd have a riot in our house if we put in such an extravagance." Others declared, "It's all a question of dirt. Our wives would never stand the ashes."

We had provided apples and nuts, doughnuts, cider and other characteristic refreshments of the older day, but alas! most of our guests no longer took coffee at night, and only one or two had teeth for popcorn or stomach for doughnuts. As a feast our evening was a failure.

"I used to eat anything at any time," Lottridge explained, "probably that is the reason why I can't do it now. In those days we didn't know anything about 'calories' or 'balanced rations.' We et what was set before us and darn glad to get it."

Shane with quiet humor recalled the days when buckwheat cakes and sausages swimming in pork fat and covered with maple syrup, formed his notion of a good breakfast. "Just one such meal would finish me now," he added with a rueful smile.

These were the men who had been the tireless reapers, the skilled wood-choppers, the husky threshers of the olden time, and as they talked, each of them reverting to significant events in those heroic days, I sobered with a sense of irreparable loss. Pathos and humor mingled in their talk of those far days!

Shane said, "Remember the time I 'bushed' you over in Dunlap's meadow?" To this my father scornfully replied, "You bushed me! I can see you, now, sitting there under that oak tree mopping your red face. I had you 'petered' before ten o'clock."

It all came back as they talked,—that buoyant world of the reaper and the binder, when harvesting was a kind of Homeric game in which, with rake and scythe, these lusty young sons of the East contended for supremacy in the field. "None of us had an extra dollar," explained Stevens, "but each of us had what was better, good health and a faith in the future. Not one of us had any intention of growing old."

"Old! There *weren't* any old people in those days," asserted Lottridge.

Along about the middle of the evening they all turned in on a game of "Rummy," finding in cards a welcome relief from the unexpressed torment of the contrast between their decrepit, hopeless present and the glowing, glorious past.

My departure on a lecture trip at ten o'clock disturbed their game only for a moment, and as I rode away I contrasted the noble sanity and the high courage of those white-haired veterans of the Border, with the attitude of certain types of city men I knew. Facing death at something less than arm's length, my father and his fellows nevertheless remained wholesomely interested in life. None of them were pious, some of them were not even religious, but they all had a sturdy faith in the essential justice of the universe. They were still playing the game as best they knew.

Like Eugene Ware they could say—

> "Standing by life's river, deep and broad,
> I take my chances, ignorant but unawed."

As I sat among my fellow members at the Club, three days later, I again recalled my father and his group. Here, too, I was in the Zone of Age. A. M. Palmer, a feeble and melancholy old man, came in and wandered about with none to do him reverence, and St. Gaudens, who was in the city for medical treatment, shared his dry toast and his cereal coffee with me of a morning. George Warner, who kept a cheerful countenance, admitted that he did so by effort. "I don't like the thought of leaving this good old earth," he confessed one afternoon. "It gives me a pang every time I consider it." None of these men faced death with finer courage than my sire.

As I had a good deal of free time in the afternoon, and as I also had a room at the Club, I saw much of St. Gaudens. We really became acquainted. One morning as we met at breakfast he replied to my question with a groan and a mild cuss word: "Worse, thank you! I've just been to Washington, and on the train last night I ate ice-cream for dinner. I knew I'd regret it, but ice-cream is my weakness." He was at once humorous and savage for, as he explained, "the doctor will not let me work and there is nothing for me to do but sit around the Club library and read or write letters."

He wrote almost as many letters as I did, and so we often faced each other across a desk in the writing room. Sometimes he spoke of President Roosevelt who was employing him on the new designs for our coins, sometimes he alluded to the work awaiting him in his studio. Oh! how homesick we both were! Perhaps he felt the near approach of the hour when his cunning hand must drop its tool. I know the thought came to me, creating a tenderer feeling toward him. I saw him in a sorrowful light. He drew nearer to me, seeming more like a friend and neighbor.

I have said that I had a good deal of time on my hands, and so it seemed to me then and yet during this trip I visited many of my friends, prepared *The Tyranny of the Dark* for serial publication, attended a dinner to Henry James, was one of the Guests of Honor at the Camp Fire Club and acted as teller (with Hopkinson Smith) in the election which founded the American Academy of Arts and Letters—a fairly full program as I look back upon it, but I had a great many hours to spend in writing to Zulime and in dreaming about Mary Isabel. In spite of all my noble companions, my dinners, speeches and honors I was longing for my little daughter and her fireplace, and at last I put aside all invitations and took the westward trail, counting the hours which intervened between my laggard coach and home.

At times I realized the danger which lay in building so much of my content on the life of one small creature, but for the most part I rejoiced in the fact that she was in my world, even though I had a growing sense of its illusory and generally unsatisfactory character. I found comfort in the knowledge that billions of other men had preceded me and billions more would follow me, and that the only real things in my world were the human relationships. To make my wife and child happy, to leave the world a little better than I found it, these formed my creed.

It was cold, crisp, clear winter when I returned to West Salem and the village again suggested a Christmas card illustration as I walked up the street. The snow cried out under my shoe soles with shrill familiar squeal, carrying me back to the radiant mornings in Iowa when I trod the board-walks of Osage on my way to the Seminary Chapel, my books under my arm and the courage of youth in my heart. Now a wife and daughter awaited me.

A fire was crackling in the new chimney, and in the light of it, at her mother's feet, sat Mary Isabel. In a moment New York and Chicago were remote, almost mythic places. With my child in my arms, listening to Zulime's gossip of the town wherein the simple old-fashioned joys of life still persisted with wholesome effect, I asked myself, "Why struggle? Why travel, when your wife, your babe, and your hearthstone are here?

A Daughter of the Middle Border

"Once I threatened the world with fire,
And thrust my fist in the face of wrong,
Making my heart a sounding lyre—
Accusing the rulers of earth in song.
Now, counting the world of creeds well lost
And recking the greatest book no prize—
Withdrawn from the press and free from the cost
Of fame and war—in my baby's eyes—
In the touch of her tiny, slender palm,
I find the ease of a warrior's calm."

Calm! Did I say calm? It was the calm of abject
slavery. At command of that minute despot I began to toil
frenziedly. At her word I read over and over, and over once
again, the Rhymes of *Mother Goose* and the Tales of
Peter Wabbitt. The *Tin Tan Book* was her litany, and
Red Riding Hood her sweet terror. Her interest in books
was insatiate. She loved all verses, all melodies, even those
whose words were wholly beyond her understanding, and
her rapt eyes, deep and dark, as my mother's had been,
gave me such happiness that to write of it fills me with a
pang of regret—for that baby is now a woman.

It will not avail my reader to say, "You were but re-
enacting the experiences of innumerable other daddies," for
this was *my* child, these were *my* home and *my* fire. Without a shred of shame I rejoiced in my subjection then, as
I long to recover its contentment now. Life for me was ful-
filled. I was doing that which nature and the world required.

Here enters an incongruous fact,—something which I
must record with the particularity it deserves. My wife
who was accounted a genius, was in truth amazingly "clever"
with brush and pencil. Not only had she spent five years
in Paris, she had enjoyed several other years of study
with her sculptor brother. She could model, she could
paint and she could draw,—but—to whom did Mary Isabel
turn when she wanted a picture? To her artist mother?

Not at all! To me,—to her corn-husker daddy—of course. I was her artist as well as her reader.

To her my hand was a wonder-worker. She was always pleased with what I did. Hour after hour I drew (in amazing outlines) dogs and cows and pigs (pictographs as primitive as those which line the walls of cave dwellings in Arizona) on which she gazed in ecstasy, silent till she suddenly discovered that this effigy meant a cow, then she cried out, "tee dee moomo!" with a joy which afforded me more satisfaction than any acceptance of a story on the part of an editor had ever conveyed. Each scrawl was to her a fresh revelation of the omniscience, the magic of her father —therefore I drew and drew while her recreant mother sat on the other side of the fire and watched us, a wicked smile of amusement—and relief—on her lips.

My daughter was preternaturally interested in magazines, —that is to say she was (at a very early age) vitally concerned with the advertising columns, and forced me to spend a great deal of time turning the pages while she discovered and admired the images of shoes, chairs, tables and babies,—especially babies. It rejoiced her to discover in a book the portrait of a desk which was actually standing in the room, and in matching the fact with the artistic reproduction of the fact, she was, no doubt, laying the foundation of an esthetic appreciation of the universe, but I suffered. Only when she was hungry or sleepy did she permit me, her art instructor, to take a vacation.

In the peaceful intervals when she was in her bed, her mother and I discussed the question, "Where shall we make our winter home?"

My plan to take another apartment in New York seemed of a reckless extravagance to Zulime, who argued for Chicago, and in the end we compromised—on Chicago—where her father and brother and sister lived. November found us settled in a furnished apartment on Jackson Park Avenue, and our Christmas tree was set up there instead of in the Homestead, which was the natural place for it.

Another phase of being Daddy now set in. To me, as a father, the City by the Lake assumed a new and terrifying aspect. Its dirt, its chill winds, its smoke appeared a pitiless league of forces assaulting the tender form of my daughter. My interest in civic reforms augmented. The problems of street cleaning and sanitary milk delivery approached me from an entirely different angle. My sense of social justice was quickened.

In other ways I admitted a change. Something had gone out of my world, or rather something unexpected had come into it. I was no longer whole-hearted in my enjoyment of my Club. My study hours were no longer sacred. My cherub daughter allured. Sometimes as I was dozing in my sleeping car, I heard her chirping voice, "Bappa, come here. I need you." The memory of her small soft body, her trusting eyes, the arch of her brows, made me impatient of my lecture tours. She was my incentive, my chief reason for living and working, and from each of my predatory sorties, I returned to her with a thankfulness which was almost maudlin—in Fuller's eyes. To have her joyous face lifted to mine, to hear her clear voice repeating my mother's songs, restored my faith in the logic of human life. True she interrupted my work and divided my interest, but she also defended me from bitterness and kept me from a darkening outlook on the future. My right to have her could be questioned but my care of her, now that I had her, was a joyous task.

It would not be quite honest in me if I did not admit that this intensity of interest in my daughter took away something from my attitude as a husband, just as Zulime's mother love affected her relationship to me. A new law was at work in both our cases, and I do not question its necessity or its direction. Three is a larger number than

314

two,. and if the third number brings something unforeseen into the problem it must be accepted. Mary Isabel strengthened the bond between Zulime and myself, but it altered its character. Whatever it lost in one way it gained in another.

Dear little daughter, how she possessed me! Each day she presented some new trait, some new accomplishment. She had begun to understand that Daddy was a writer and that he must not be disturbed during the morning, but in spite of her best resolutions she often tip-toed to my door to inquire brightly, "Poppie, can I come in? Don't you want me?" Of course I wanted her, and so frequently my work gave place to a romp with her. In the afternoons I often took her for a walk or to coast on her new sled rejoicing in the picture she made in her red cloak and hood.

In her presence my somber conceptions of life were forgotten. Joyous and vital, knowing nothing of my worries, she comforted me. She was no longer the "baby" she was "Wenona," my first born, and in spirit we were comrades. More and more she absorbed my thought. "Poppie, I love you better than anything," she often said, and the music of her voice misted my eyes and put a lump into my throat.

When summer came and we went back to the Homestead, I taught her to drive Old Smoker, Uncle William's horse. Under my direction she studied the birds and animals. In city and country alike we came together at nightfall, to read or sing or "play circus." I sang to her all the songs my mother had taught me, I danced with her as she grew older, with Zulime playing the tunes for us, "Money Musk" and "The Campbells are Coming." As we walked the streets the trusting cling of her tiny fingers was inexpressibly sweet.

"Poppie, I'm so happy!" she often said to me after she was three, and the ecstasy which showed in her big blue eyes scared me with its intensity for I knew all too well that it could not last. This was her magical time. She was enraptured of the wind and sky and the grass. Every fact in nature was a revelation to her.

"Why, Poppie? What does it? What was that noise?" The dandelions, the dead bird, a snake—these were miracles to her—as they once were to me. She believed in fairies with devotional fervor and I did nothing to shake her faith, on the contrary I would gladly have shared her credence if I could.

Once as we were entering a deep, dark wood, she cautioned me to walk very softly and to speak in a whisper in order that we might catch the Forest Folk at play, and as we trod a specially beautiful forest aisle she cried out, "I *saw* one, Poppie! Didn't you see that little shining thing?"

I could only say, "Yes, it *must* have been a fairy." I would not destroy her illusion.

She inhabited a world of ineffable beauty, a universe in which minute exquisite winged creatures flashed like flakes of fire, through dusky places. She heard their small faint voices in the whisper of the leaves, and every broad toadstool was to her a resting place for weary elfin messengers hurrying on some mission for their queen. Her own imaginings, like her favorite books, were all of magic wands, golden garments and crystal palaces. Sceptered kings, and jeweled princesses trailing robes of satin were the chief actors in her dreams.

I am aware that many educators consider such reading foolish and harmful, but I care nothing for wire-drawn pedagogic theories. That I did nothing to mar the mystical beauty of the world in which my daughter then dwelt, is my present satisfaction, and I shamelessly acknowledge that I experienced keen pangs of regret as her tender illusions, one after another faded into the chill white light of later day. Without actually deceiving her, I permitted her to believe that I too, heard the wondrous voices of Titania and her elves in convention behind the rose bush, or the whispers of gnomes hiding among the cornrows.

Good republican that I was, I listened without reproof to her adoring fealty to Kings and Queens. Her love of Knights and tournaments was openly fostered at my hand. "If she should die out of this, her glorious imaginary world, she shall die happy," was my thought, "and if she lives to look back upon it with a woman's eyes, she shall remember it as a shining world in which her Daddy was a rough but kindly councillor, a mortal of whom no fairy need have fear."

The circus was my daughter's royal tournament, an assemblage of all the kings and queens, knights and fairies of her story books. She hated the clowns but the parade of the warriors and their sovereign exalted her. The helmeted spearmen, the lithe charioteers, the hooded drivers sitting astride the heads of vast elephants were characters of the Arabian Nights, passing veritably before her eyes. The winged dancers of the spectacle came straight from the castle of Queen Mab, the pale acrobats were brothers to Hector and Achilles.

As she watched them pass she gripped my hand as if to keep touch with reality, her little heart swollen with almost intolerable delight. "It makes me shiver," she whispered, and I understood.

As the last horseman of the procession was passing, she asked faintly—"Will it come again, Poppie?"

"Yes, it will come once more," I replied, recalling my own sense of loss when the Grand Entry was over.

As the queen, haughty of glance, superb in her robe of silver once more neared us, indolently swaying to the movement of the elephant, who bore his housings of purple and gold with stately solemnity, my daughter's tiny body quivered with ecstasy and her beautiful eyes dilated with an intensity of admiration, of worship which made me sad as well as happy, and then just as the resplendent princess was passing for the last time, Mary Isabel rose in her place and waving a kiss to her liege lady cried out in tones of poignant love and despair, "Good-by, dear Queen!" and I, holding her tender palpitant figure in my arms, heard in that slender silver-sweet cry the lament of childhood, childhood whose dreams were passing never to return.

Chicago did not offer much by way of magnificence but Mary Isabel made the most of what we took her to see. The gold room of the hotel was a part of her imaginary kingdom, conceivably the home of royalty. Standing timidly at the door, she surveyed the golden chairs, the gorgeous ceiling and the deep-toned pictures with a gaze which absorbed every detail. At last she whispered, "Is this the Queen's room?"

"Yes," I replied. "If the Queen should come to Chicago she would live here," and I comforted myself by saying, "You shall have your hour of wonder and romance, even at the expense of a prevarication."

With a sigh she turned away, or rather permitted me to lead her away. "I'm glad I saw it," she said. "Will the Queen ever come to Chicago again?"

"Yes, next spring she will come again," I answered, thus feeding her illusion without a moment's hesitation or a particle of remorse.

Her love of royal robes, gold chariots and Queens' houses did not prevent her from listening with deep delight while I read *Jock Johnstone, the Tinkler Lad,* or sang *O'er the Hills in Legions, Boys.* She loved most of the songs I was accustomed to sing but certain of the lines vaguely distressed her. She could not endure the pathos of Nellie Gray.

318

The Fairy World of Childhood

> "Oh, my poor Nellie Gray
> They have taken you away
> And I'll never see my darling any more"

put her into deepest anguish.

"*Why* did they take her away?" she sobbed. "Didn't they *ever* see her any more?"

Only after I explained that they met "down the river" and were very happy ever afterward, would she permit me to finish the ballad. She was similarly troubled by the words,

> "I can hear the children calling
> I can see their sad tears falling."

"*Why* are the children calling?" she demanded.

She had a curious horror of anything abnormal. Once I took her to see "Alice in Wonderland" thinking that this would be an enchanting experience for her. Not only was it intolerably repellent to her, it was terrifying, and when the bodies of the characters suddenly lengthened, she sought refuge under the seat. All deformities, grotesqueries were to her horrible, appalling. She refused to look at the actors and at last I took her away.

One afternoon as we were in the garden together she called to me. "Poppie, see the dead birdie!"

On looking I saw a little dead song sparrow. "It's been here all the night and all the day, Poppie. It fell out of the tree when Eddie shooted it. Put it up in the tree again, Poppie."

She seemed to think that if it were put back into its home it would go on living and singing. I don't know why this should have moved me as it did, but it blurred my eyes for a moment. My little daughter was face to face with the great mystery.

O those magical days! Knowing all too well that they could not last and that to lose any part of them was to be forever cheated, I gave my time to her. Over and over again as I met her deep serene glance, I asked (as other parents have done), "Whence came you? From what dusky night rose your starry eyes? Out of what unillumined void flowered your fairy face? Can it be, as some have said, that you are only an automaton, a physical reaction?"

She was the future, my father the past. Birth and death, equally inexplicable, were expressed to me in these two beings, so vital to me, so dependent upon me, and beside me, suffering, joying with me, walked the mother with unfaltering steps.

I was in the midst of a novel at this time, another story of Colorado, which I called *Money Magic*, and without doubt all this distraction and travel weakened it, although Howells spoke well of it. "It is one of your best books," he said, when we next met.

[Mary Isabel reads the book at intervals and places it next to *Hesper* and *The Captain of the Gray Horse Troop*.]

Marriage, paternity, householding, during these years unquestionably put the brakes on my work as a writer, but I had no desire to return to bachelorhood. Undoubtedly I had lost something, but I had gained more. As a human being I was enriched beyond my deserving by a wife and a child.

Perhaps I would have gone farther and mounted higher as a selfish solitary bachelor, but that did not trouble me then, and does not now. Concerned with the problem of providing a comfortable winter home for my family, and happy in maintaining the old house in West Salem as a monument to the memory of my mother, I wrote, committed carpentry and lectured.

My frequent absences from home soon made a deep impression on my daughter's mind, and whenever she was naughty I had but to say, "If you do that again Papa will go away to New York," and she would instantly say, "I'm doodie now papa, I'm doodie——" and yet my mention of going to New York could not have been altogether a punishment for I always brought to her some toy or book. Nothing afforded me keener joy than the moment when I showed her the presents I had brought.

The fact that she loved to have her heavy-handed old Daddy near her, was a kind of miracle, a concession for which I could not be too grateful.

"You shall have a happy childhood," I vowed, "no matter what comes later, you shall remember these days with unalloyed delight. They shall be your heaven, your fairyland."

Each month I set down in my diary some new phrase, some development, some significant event in her life, and when she found this out she loved to have me read what she had said, "When I was a little baby." She listened gravely, contrasting her ignorance at two with her wisdom at five. "Was I cute, Daddy? Did you like me then?" she would ask.

She early learned the meaning of Decoration Day, which she called "Flag Day," and took pride in the fact that her grand-sire was a soldier. Each year she called for her flag and asked to be taken to the cemetery to see the decorations and to hear the bugles blow above the graves, and I always complied; although to me, each year, a more poignant pathos quavered in the wailing cadence of "Lights out," and the passing of the veterans, thinning so rapidly— was like the march of men toward their open graves.

Happily my daughter did not realize any part of this tragic concept. For her it was natural that a soldier should be old and bent. Waving her little flag and shouting with silver-sweet voice she saluted with vague admiration those who were about to die—an age about to die—and in her eyes flamed the spirit of her grand-sire, the love of country which will carry the Republic through every storm no matter from which quarter the wind may spring.

So far as I could, I taught her to take up the traditions which were about to slip from the hands of Richard Garland and his sons, "She shall be our representative, the custodian of our faith."

For four years she remained our only child, and yet I can not say that she was either spoiled or exacting, on the contrary she was a constant, joyous pupil and a lovely appealing teacher. Through her I rediscovered the wonder of the sunrise and the stars. In the study of her face the lost beauty of the rainbow returned to me, in her presence I felt once more the mystic charm of dusk. I reaccepted the universe, putting aside the measureless horror of its recorded wars. I grew strangely selfish. My interests narrowed to my own country, my own home, to my fireside. Counting upon the world well lost, I built upon my daughter's love.

That my wife was equally happy in her parentage was obvious for at times she treated Mary Isabel as if she were a doll, spending many hours of many days designing dainty gowns and hoods for her delight. She could hardly be separated from the child, even for a night and it was in her battles with croup and other nocturnal enemies that her maternal love was tested to the full. I do not assume to know what she felt as a wife, but of her devotion as a mother I am able to write with certainty. On her fell the burden of those hours of sickness in the city, and when the time came for us to go back to the birds and trees of our beloved valley she rejoiced as openly as her daughter. "Now we shall be free of colds and fever," she said.

For the most part this was true. For several summers our daughter lived and throve at her birthplace, free of pain and in idyllic security—and then suddenly, one September day, like the chill shadow from an Autumn storm-

Entirely subject to my daughter, who regarded me as a wonder-
working giant, I paid tribute to her in song, in story, and in
frankincense and myrrh. Led by her trusting little hand I
re-discovered the haunts of fairies and explored once more
the land beneath the rainbow.

cloud, misfortune fell upon us. Our daughter became sick, how sick I did not realize until on the eighth day as I took her in my arms I discovered in her a horrifying weakness. Her little body, thinned with fever, hung so laxly, so lightly on my knee that my blood chilled with sudden terror.

With a conviction that I dared not even admit to myself, I put her back into her mother's keeping and hurried to the telephone. In ten minutes I had called to her aid the best medical men of the region. Especially did I appeal to Doctor Evans, who had helped to bring her into the world. "You must come," I said to him. "It is life or death."

He came, swiftly, but in a few moments after his arrival he gravely announced the dreadful truth. "Your child is in the last stages of diphtheria. I will do what I can for her but she should have had the antitoxin five days ago."

For forty-eight hours our baby's life was despaired of, yet fought for by a heroic nurse who refused to leave her for a single hour.

Oh, the suspense, the agony of those days and nights, when her mother and I, helpless to serve, were shut away from her, not even permitted to look at her. We could do nothing—nothing but wait through the interminable hours, tortured by the thought that she might be calling for us. During one entire dreadful night we writhed under one doctor's sentence, "The child can not live," and in these hours I discovered that it is the sweetest love that casts the blackest shadow. My joy in my daughter was an agony of fear and remorse—why had I not acted sooner?

As I imagined my world without that radiant face, that bird-like voice, I fell into black despair. My only hope was in the nurse, who refused to give her up. I could not talk or write or think of any other thing. The child's sufferings filled my mind with an intolerable ache of apprehension. I had possessed her only a few years and yet she was already woven into the innermost fibers of my heart.

That night, which I dare not dwell upon, put my youth definitely behind me. When the blessed word came that she would live, and I was permitted to look upon her small wasted face, I was a care-worn middle-aged man—willing to give up any part of my life to win that tiny sufferer back to health and happiness.

Pitiful little Mary Isabel, pale wraith of my sturdy comrade! When she lifted her beseeching eyes to me and faintly, fleetingly smiled—unable to even whisper my name, I, forbidden to speak, could only touch her cheek with my lips and leave her alone with her devoted nurse—for, so weak was she that a breath might have blown her away, back into the endless shadow and silence of the grave.

At that moment I asked myself, "What right have men and women to bring exquisite souls like this into a world of disease and death? Why maintain the race? What purpose is subserved by keeping the endless chain of human misery lengthening on?"

In times like these I was weaker than my wife. I grant her marvelous fortitude, sustained by something which I did not possess and could not acquire. She met every crisis. I leaned upon her serenity, her courage, her faith in the future which was in no sense a religious creed. It was only a womanly inheritance, something which came down the long line of her maternal Anglo-Saxon ancestors.

At last the day came when the nurse permitted me to take my daughter again in my arms and carry her out to the easy chair before the fire. The moment was perfect. The veil of snow falling without, the leaping firelight on the hearth, and the presence of my wife and father, united to fill me with happiness. I became the fond optimist again— the world was not so black—our year was worthy of Thanksgiving after all.

Nevertheless I was aware that a bitter ineradicable dusk had gathered in the corners and crannies of the old house.

Something depressing, repellent, was in the air. My sense of joy, my feeling of comfort in its seclusion were gone.

"Never again will this be a restful home for you or for me," I declared to my daughter. "Its shadow is now an enemy, its isolation a menace." To my wife I said, "Let us go back to the city where the highest type of medical science is at the end of the telephone wire."

She consented, and taking the child in my arms, I left the village with no intention of ever returning to it. The fire on my family altar seemed dead, never again to be rekindled.

CHAPTER TWENTY-TWO

The Old Soldier Gains a New Granddaughter

FOR nearly two years I did not even see the Homestead. My aversion to it remained almost a hatred. The memory of those desolate weeks of quarantine when my little daughter suffered all the agonies of death, still lingered over its walls, a poisonous shadow which time alone could remove. "I shall never live in it again," I repeated to my friends, and when some one wanted to rent it for the summer I consented—with a twinge of pain I must confess, for to open it to strangers even for a few weeks seemed an act of disloyalty to the memory of my mother.

Meanwhile I remained a moderately happy and very busy citizen of Chicago. Not content with esthetic conditions and in the belief that my home for years to come must be somewhere in the city's confines, I had resolved to establish a Club which should be (like the Players in New York) a meeting place for artists and writers, a rallying point for Midland Arts. Feeling very keenly the lack of such a rendezvous I said to Lorado, "I believe the time has come when a successful literary and artistic club can be established and maintained."

The more I pondered on the situation, the greater the discrepancy between the Chicago of my day and the Boston of my father's day became. "Why was it that the Boston of 1860, a city of three hundred thousand people, should have been so productive of great writers, while this vast

Old Soldier Gains a Granddaughter

inland metropolis of over two million of people remains almost negligible in the world of Art and Letters?"

Fuller, who refused, characteristically, to endorse my plan, was openly discouraging. To him the town was a pestilential slough in which he, at any rate, was inextricably mired, and though he was not quite so definite with me, he said to others, "Garland's idea is sure to fail."

Clarkson, Browne and Taft, however, heartily joined my committee, and the "Cliff Dwellers," a union of workers in the fine arts, resulted. As president of the organization, I set to work on plans for housing the club, and for months I was absorbed in this work.

On the eighteenth of June, 1908, in the midst of my work on the club affairs, another daughter was born to us, a vigorous and shapely babe, with delicate limbs, gray eyes, and a lively disposition, and while my wife, who came through this ordeal much better than before, was debating a choice of names for her, Mary Isabel gravely announced that she had decided to call her sister "Marjorie Christmas," for the reason, as she explained, that these were the nicest names she knew. Trusting first born!—she did not realize the difference which this new-found playmate was about to make in her life, and her joy in being permitted to hold the tiny stranger in her arms was pathetic.

My own attitude toward "Marjorie Christmas" was not indifferent but I did not receive her with the same intensity of interest with which I had welcomed my first child. Her place was not waiting for her as was the case of Mary Isabel. She was a lovely infant and perhaps I would have taken her to my arms with keen paternal pride had it not been for the realization that in doing so I was neglecting her sister whose comradeship with me had been so close (so full of exquisite moments) that it could not be transferred to another daughter, no matter how alluring. A second child is—a second child.

A Daughter of the Middle Border

To further complicate our problem, Constance (as we finally called her), passed under the care of a nursemaid, and for two years I had very little to do with her. I seldom sang this child to sleep as I had done countless times with Mary Isabel. She did not ride on the crook of my elbow, or climb on my back, or look at picture books with me, until she was nearly three years old. We regained her, but we could not regain the hours of companionship we had sacrificed. This experience enables me to understand the unhappiness which comes to so many homes, in which the children are only boarders, foundlings in the care of nurses and governesses. My poverty, my small dwelling have given me the most precious memories of my daughters in their childish innocence.

[Connie, who is now as tall as her mother and signs her drawings "Constance Hamlin Garland" is looking over my shoulder at this moment with a sly smile. It has long been known to her that she was, for several years, very much "in the discard" but she does not hold it against me. She knows that it would be hard for me to make a choice between my two jewels to-day—I allude to them as mine because I am writing this book. My wife has a different angle of vision concerning them.]

My father came down from West Salem to see this second granddaughter, and on the whole, approved of her, although his tenderest interest, like mine, remained with Mary Isabel, who was now old enough to walk and talk with him. To watch her trotting along the street with that white-haired warrior, her small hand linked with his, was to gain a deeply moving sense of the continuity of life. How slender the link between the generations appears in such a case!

Nothing, not even the birth of a new grandchild, could divert my father from his accustomed round of city sight-seeing. As in other times, so now he again demanded to be shown the Stockyards, the Wheat Pit, the Masonic Temple and Lincoln Park. I groaned but I consented.

It happened that Ira Morris, one of the owners of the Stockyards, was an acquaintance, and the courtesy and attentions which were shown us gave the old farmer immense satisfaction—and when he found that Frank Logan, of "Logan & Bryan," (a Commission firm to which he had been wont to send his wheat) was also my friend, he began to find in my Chicago life certain compensating particulars, especially as in his presence I assumed a prosperity I did not possess.

On paper I sounded fairly well. I was one of the vice-presidents of the National Institute of Arts and Letters. I had a "Town house" as well as a "country place," and under cover of the fact that very few of my friends had ever inspected both properties, I was able in some degree to camouflage my situation. In the city I alluded casually to "my Wisconsin Homestead," and when in West Salem I referred with quiet affluence to "my residence in Woodlawn." Explaining that it was a three story house I passed lightly over the fact that it was only eighteen feet wide! Similarly, in speaking of "our country home" I did not explain to all my friends that it was merely an ugly old farmhouse on the edge of a commonplace village. I stated the truth in each case but not the whole truth.

If my city friend, Charles Hutchinson, imagined me spending my summers in a noble mansion on the bank of a shining river it was not my duty to shock him by declaring that there was no water in sight and that my garden was only a truck patch. On the other hand, if my neighbors in West Salem thought of me as living in a handsome brick mansion in Chicago, and writing my stories in a spacious study walled with books, I was not obliged to undeceive them.

Fuller, alas! knew all the facts in both cases, and so did

Ernest Seton, who had visited us in the country as well as in our city home. Fuller not only knew the ins and outs of my houses; he was also aware that my royalties were dwindling and that my wife was forced to get along with one servant and that we used the street cars habitually.

Being president of the Cliff Dwellers was an honor, but the distinction carried with it something of the responsibility of a hotel-keeper as well as the duties of a lecture agent, for one of our methods in building up attendance at the Club, was to announce special luncheons in honor of distinguished visitors from abroad, and the task of arranging these meetings fell usually to me. In truth, the activities of the club took a large part of my time and carried a serious distraction from my work, but I welcomed the diversion, and was more content in my Chicago residence than I had been for several years.

Whenever I spoke to Zulime of my failure as a money-getter she loyally declared herself rich in what I had given her, although she still rode to grand dinners in the elevated trains, carrying her slippers in a bag. It was her patient industry, her cheerful acceptance of endless household drudgery which kept me clear of self-conceit. I began to suspect that I would never be able to furnish her with a better home than that which we already owned, and this suspicion sometimes robbed me of rest.

This may seem to some of my readers an unworthy admission on the part of a man of letters but it is a perfectly natural and in a sense, logical result of my close associations with several of the most successful writers and artists of my day. It was inevitable that while contrasting my home with theirs, I should occasionally fall into moods of self-disparagement, almost of despair.

To see my wife (whom everybody admired) wearing thread-bare cloaks and home-made gowns, to watch her making the best of our crowded little dining-room with its pitiful furniture and its sparse silver, were constant humiliations, an accusation which embittered me especially as I saw no prospect of ever providing anything more worthy of her care.

For a woman of taste, wearing made-over gowns is a very real hardship, but Zulime bore her deprivations with heroic cheerfulness, taking a never-failing delight in our narrow home. She made our table a notable meeting place, for, if we had few dollars we owned many friends who found their way to us, and often from our commonplace little portal we plodded away in the rain or snow to dine in the stately palaces of the rich,—kings of commerce and finance.

Apparently we were everywhere welcome, and that this was due almost entirely to the winning personality of my wife, I freely acknowledge. That she had scores of devoted admirers was only too evident, for the telephone bell rang almost continuously of a morning. Always ready to give her time, her skill and her abounding sympathy to those who made piteous demands upon her, she permitted these incessant telephone interruptions, although I charged her with being foolishly prodigal in this regard. If she felt resentful of the narrow walls in which I had confined her, she did not complain.

Whatever my wife's state of mind may have been these were restless years for me. As an officer of several organizations and as lecturer, I was traveling much of the time, mostly on the trail between New York City and Chicago. Even when at home I had only three morning hours for writing—but that was not the worst of it. My convictions concerning my literary mission were in process of disintegration.

My children, my manifold duties as theatrical up-lifter and club promoter, together with a swift letting down of my mental and physical powers, caused me to question the value of all my writing. I went so far as to say, "As a writer I have failed. Perhaps I can be of service as a citizen," with my Oklahoma farms bringing in a small annual income, the scrape of my pen became a weariness.

That I was passing from robust manhood to middle age was also evident to me and I didn't like that. I resented deepening wrinkles, whitening hairs and the sense of weariness which came over me at the end of my morning's work. My power of concentration was lessening. Noises irritated me and little things distracted me. I could no longer bend to my desk for five hours in complete absorption. How my wife endured me during those years I can not explain. The chirp of my babies' voices, the ring of the telephone, the rattle of the garbage cart, the whistle of the postman— each annoyance chopped into my composition, and as my afternoons and evenings had no value in a literary way, I was often completely defeated for the day. Altogether and inevitably my work as a fictionist sank into an unimportant place. I was on the down-grade, that was evident. Writing was a tiresome habit. I was in a rut and longing to get out—to be forced out.

The annual dinner of the Institute of Arts and Letters that year was not cheering. With the loss of four members, Stedman, Aldrich, MacDowell and St. Gaudens, I realized as never before the swift changes at work in American letters. It was my duty and my privilege to speak that night in memory of MacDowell who had so often been my seat-mate, and as I looked around that small circle of familiar faces, a scene of loss, a perception of decay came over me like a keen wind from out a desolate landscape. On every head the snows had thickened, on every face a shadow rested. All—all were hastening to be history.

* * * * * *

From that circle of my elders in the East, I returned to my children in the West with a sense of returning to the

future. The radiant joy of Mary Isabel's face as I displayed her presents, a ring and a story book, restored me
to something like a normal faith in the world. "Wead
to me, wead to me!" was now her insistent plea, and putting aside all other concerns I turned the pages of her new
book, realizing that to her the universe was still a great
and never-ending fairy tale, and her Daddy a wonder-
working magician, an amiable ogre. Her eager voice, her
raptured attention enabled me to recover, for a moment,
a wholesome faith and joy in my world—a world which was
growing gray and wan and cold with terrifying swiftness.

"Your childhood shall be as happy as my powers will
permit," I vowed once again as I looked into her uplifted
face. "You shall have only pleasant memories of me,"
and in this spirit I gave her the best of myself. I taught
her to read, I told her stories which linked her mind with
that of her pioneer grandmother, filling her brain with traditions of the middle border. Dear little daughter, her daddy
was veritably a nobleman, her mother a queen—in those
days!

My wife says that for ten years I was always either on
the point of going somewhere, or just returning, and as I
turn the pages of my diaries, I find this to be true, but also
I find frequent mention of meetings with John Burroughs,
Bacheller, Gilder, Alexander, Madame Modjeska, William
Vaughn Moody and many others of my friends distinguished
in the arts.

All my publishing interests and most of my literary
friends were in New York (my support came from there),
hence my frequent coming and going. Whether this constant change, these sudden and violent contrasts in my way
of life strengthened my fictional faculty or weakened it, I
can not say, but I do know that as the head of a family I
found concentrated effort increasingly difficult and at times
very nearly impossible. Constance was ailing for a year,

and was a source of care, of pain to me, as to her mother. At times, many times, her sufferings filled me with a passionate pity, a sense of rage, of helplessness. Indeed both children were subject to throat and lung disorders, especially when in the city.

Oh, those cruel coughing spells, those nights of burning fever, those alarming hours of stupor or of terrifying delirium! "Can science find no check upon these recurrent forms of disease?" I demanded of our doctor. "Must humanity forever suffer the agonies of diphtheria and pneumonia? If so why bring children into the world?"

We always knew when these disorders had set in, we knew all the signs but no medicine availed to stop their progress. Each attack ran its course in spite of nurse and drug whilst I raged helplessly and Zulime grew hollow-eyed with anxious midnight vigil. Death was a never-absent hovering shadow when those bitter winter winds were blowing, and realizing this I came to hate the great desolate city in which we lived, and to long with the most passionate ardor for the coming of April's sun.

One of the first signs of spring (so far as Mary Isabel was concerned) was the opening of the "White City," a pleasure park near us, and the second event quite as conclusive and much more exciting was the coming of the circus. These were the red letter days in her vernal calendar, and were inescapable outings, for her memory was tenacious. Each May she demanded to be taken to the "Fite City" and later "the Kings and Queens" and "the fairies" of the circus claimed her worship. Together we saw these glorious sights, which filled her little soul with rapture.

For two years my estrangement from the old Homestead was complete, but when one April day I found myself passing it on my way to St. Paul, I was constrained to stop off just to see how my father and the garden were coming on.

This was late April, and the day warm, windless and

musical with sounds of spring. The maples and the elms had adorned themselves with most bewitching greens, the dandelions beckoned from sunny banks, and through the radiant mist, the nesting birds were calling. In a flood, all the ancient witchery of the valley, all of the Homestead's loveliest associations came back to soften my mood, to regain my love. Wrought upon by the ever-returning youth of the world—a world to which my daughters were akin, I relented, "We will come back. Cruel as some of its memories are, this is home, I belong here, and so does Mary Isabel."

The sunlight streaming into my mother's chamber lay like a fairy carpet on the floor, waiting for the dancing feet of her grandchildren. Her spirit filled the room, calling to me, consoling me, convincing me.

All day I worked at trimming vines, and planting flowers while the robins chuckled from the lawn, and the maples expanded overhead. How spacious and wide and safe the yard appeared, a natural playground for the use of children.

And so it came about that on June seventeenth, just before Constance's second birthday, Mary Isabel and I took the night train for West Salem, leaving Zulime and the nurse to follow next morning. Greatly excited at the prospect of going to sleep on the cars my daughter went to her bed. "I kick for joy," she said, her eyes shining with elfin delight.

She loved the "little house" as she called her berth, and for an hour she lay peering out at the moon. "It follows us!" she cried out in pleased surprise.

"Yes, it is a kindly moon. It will keep right along overhead all the way to West Salem. But you must go to sleep now. I shall call you early in the morning to meet Grandfather."

She was a reasonable soul, entirely confident of my care, and so, putting her head on my arm, she went away to

dreamland. At such times my literary ambitions and failures were of no account. [To wish myself back there with
that tiny form beside me is folly—but I do—I do!]

In the cool lusciousness of the June morning we met
Grandpa, and as we entered the gate of the Homestead
(which Mary Isabel only dimly remembered), I said, "This
is your home, daughter, you belong here."

"Can I pick the flowers? Can I walk on the grass?" she
asked quickly.

"Yes, pick all you want. You can *roll* on the grass if
you wish."

Too excited to eat any breakfast, she ran from posy
bed to posy bed, and from tree to tree, indefatigable as a
bee or humming-bird. At five in the afternoon Zulime and
Constance came.

In the weeks which followed I renewed my childhood.
To Mary Isabel as to me at her age, the cornfield was a
vast mysterious forest, and the rainbow an overpowering
miracle.

"Don't they have rainbows in the city?" she asked one
evening as we were watching a glorious arch fade out of
the sky above the hills.

"Not such big beautiful double ones," I replied. "They
haven't room for them in the city."

She took the same delight in the flame and flare of the
Fourth of July which I once owned. She loved to walk in
the fields. Snakes, bugs, worms and spiders enthralled
her. Each hour brought its vivid message, its wonder and
its delight, and when now and again she was allowed to
explore the garden with me at night, the murk and the
stars, and the stealthily moving winds in the corn, scared,
awed her. At such moments the universe was a delicious
mystery. Keeping close hold upon my hand she whispered
with excitement, "What was that, Poppie? What was that
noise? Was it a gnome?"

Old Soldier Gains a Granddaughter

For her I built a "House" high in the big maple, and there she often climbed, spending many happy hours singing to her dollies or conning over her picture books. Her face shone down upon me radiant with life's ecstasy. Baby Constance was to her a toy, a doll, I was her companion, her playmate. The garden seemed fashioned for her uses, and whenever I saw her among the flowers or sitting on the lawn, I forgot my writing, realizing that these were golden days for me as well as for her,—days that would pass like waves of light across the wheat.

Together with Zulime I received the house back into my affection. Once more I thought of it as something permanent, a sure refuge in time of trouble. It gave us both a comforting sense of security to know that we could, at need, come back to it and live in comfort. With no hope of attaining a larger income, saving money was earning money for us both. In this spirit I put in another bathroom, and enlarged the dining-room—doing much of the work with my own hands.

Nothing could be more idyllic than our daily routine that summer. Our diversions, dependent on a love of odorous fields, colorful hills and fruitful vines, were of arcadian content. Our wealth expressed in nuts and apples and berries was ample. With Mary Isabel I assumed that wild grapes were enormously important articles of food. "Without them we might grow hungry this winter," I warned her. In this spirit we harvested, intent as chipmunks.

After the nurse left us the two children slept together on an upstairs screened-in porch, and every night, just before they went to sleep, it was my habit to visit them. Lying down between them with a small head on each arm, I told them stories or answered the questions which were suggested by the trees and the sky. "What are stars? What makes the moon spotted? What does iron come from? How do people make wall paper?" and many others equally

337

elemental. It was a tender hour for me and a delicious one for them.

Gradually as they grew older, they fell into the habit of saying, "Now tell us about when you were a little boy," and so I was led to freshen up on *A Son of the Middle Border,* which I had begun to rewrite. They could never get enough of these reminiscences and when, at nine o'clock, I said, "Daughties, you must go to sleep," they pleaded for "Just one more," and from this interest I derived a foolish hope that the book, if it should ever get published, would be successful.

It was sweet to hear those soft voices demanding an explanation of the universe whose wonders they were rediscovering in their turn. Every changing season, every expanding leaf was magical to them. A bat skittering about the chimney, the rustle of a breeze in the maples, were of sinister significance requiring explanation, and when at last I went away and they began to softly sing their wistful little evening prayer, one which Mary Isabel had composed, life seemed worthwhile even to me. I forgot the irrevocable past and confronted old age with composure.

Meanwhile my father's mind was becoming more and more reminiscent. His stories once so vivid and so full of detail had narrowed down to a few familiar phrases. "Just then Sherman and his staff came riding along," or "When I was camped on the upper waters of the Wisconsin." His memory was failing and so was his sense of hearing. He seldom quoted from a book, but he still cited Blaine's speeches or referred to Lincoln's anecdotes, and certain of Grant's phrases were often on his lips. In all his interests he remained objective, concerned with the world of action not with the library, and while he made no effort to talk down to Mary Isabel, he contrived to win her adoration, perhaps because she detected in his voice his adoring love for her. In the mist of his glance was the tender worship of youth on the part of age.

Always of a Sunday we sang for him and sometimes Uncle Frank, the last of the McClintocks, gray haired and lean and bent, came in with his fiddle and played while the children danced in the light of our fire, so lithe, so happy, so fairy-like in their loveliness that he and Lorette sat in silence, a silence which was at once tender and tragic. There was something alien as well as marvelous in the dramatic movements of those small forms.

Witnessing such scenes, moved by something elemental in their decay, I continued to brood over the manuscript which was to be a kind of autobiography, the blended story of the vicissitudes of the Garlands and the McClintocks. At times I worked upon it to the exclusion of all else, and when I read a part of the tale to Mary Isabel and found that she understood it and liked it, I was heartened.

Consider this! I now had a daughter to whom I could read my manuscript! Where did that personality come from? Was her soul merely the automatic reaction of a material organism against a material environment? Was her spirit dependent on the life of its little body or could it live on independent of the flesh? Acknowledging the benumbing, hopeless mystery of it all, I continued to live for my children, finding in them my comfort and my justification.

I have never known anything more perfect than some of those mid-August days when on some woodland slope, we gathered the luscious musky fruit of wild blackberry vines and at our camp fire broiled our steak and made our coffee for our evening, open-air meal.

There were no flies, no mosquitoes, no snakes, and the hillsides were abloom with luscious shining berries, berries so ripe they fell into our hands with the slightest touch, and so tender that they melted in our mouths. The wind filled with the odor of yellowing corn, and the smell of nuts and leaves, carried our songs to the mist-filled valley below us, and the children playing on the smooth sward found our world a paradise.

As the cool dusk began to cover the farms below us, we sang "Juanita" and "Kentucky Home" and told our last stories while the children lay at our feet, silent with rapture as I used to be, in similar circumstances, forty years before.

And then when the fire had died down and sleepy babies were ready to turn their faces bedward, we drove slowly down the winding lane to the dust-covered bridge, past the small cemetery where mother was sleeping, back to where the broad-roofed old house was waiting for us like some huge, faithful creature yearning to receive us once again beneath its wings. It was commonplace to our neighbors and without special significance to the world, but to my children it was noble and beautiful and poetic—it was home.

CHAPTER TWENTY-THREE

"Cavanagh" and the "Winds of Destiny"

NO doubt the reader has come to the conclusion, at this point, that my habits as an author were not in the least like those of Burroughs or Howells. There has never been anything cloistered about my life, on the contrary my study has always been a point of departure rather than a cell of meditation. From Elm Street, from the Homestead, I frequently darted away to the plains or the Rocky Mountains, keenly aware of the fact that the miner and cattleman, the trapper and the trailer were being pushed into ever remoter valleys by the men of the hoe and the spade, and that the customs and habits which the mountaineer had established were about to pass, precisely as the blossoming prairies had long since been broken and fenced and made commonplace by the plow.

That the destruction of the eagle and the mountain lion marked another stage of that remorseless march which is called civilization I fully recognized and—in a certain sense —approved, although the raising of billions of hens and pigs admittedly useful, was not to me an inspiring employment of human energy. The long-horn white-faced steer was more picturesque than a "Mooly" cow.

Doubtless a dairyman is a more valuable citizen in the long run than a prospector or miner, but he does not so easily appeal to the imagination. To wade irrigating ditches, hoe in hand, is not incompatible with the noblest manhood, but it is none the less true that men riding the trail or exploring ledges of quartz are more alluring characters to the novelist—at least that was the way I felt in 1909 when I began to shape another book concerning the great drama which was going on in the forests of the High Country.

For more than fifteen years, while trailing among the mountains of Colorado, Montana and Wyoming, I had seen the Forest Service, under Gifford Pinchot's leadership, gradually getting into effect. I had seen the silver miner disappear and the army of forest rangers grow from a handful of hardy cowboys and "lonesome men" into a disciplined force of over two thousand young foresters who represented in some degree the science and the patriotism of their chief.

As in *Hesper* and *The Captain of the Gray Horse Troop* I had attempted to depict certain types of the red men, miners and ranchers. I now began to study the mountain vedettes from the point of view of the Forest Ranger, a federal officer who represented our newly acquired ideals of Conservation, and whose duty it was to act as custodian of the National Forests. I decided to write a novel which should, in some degree, delineate the heroic side of this warden's solitary life as I had seen it and shared it in a half-dozen forests in Colorado, Wyoming and Montana.

In this writing I put myself at the opposite pole from the scenes of *The Shadow World*, a study of psychic phenomena with which I had been deeply involved for a year or more. From dark cabinets in murky seance chambers, from contact with morbid, death-fearing, light-avoiding residents of crowded apartments, I now found myself riding once again ten thousand feet above sea level with men who "took chances" almost every hour of their lives—not from any reckless defiance of death but merely by way of duty, men who lived alone and rode alone, men in whose ears the mountain streams as they fell from the white silences of the snows, uttered songs of exultation. In the presence of these hardy trailers the doings of darkened seance rooms seemed morbid, if not actually insane.

The stark heroism of these forest guards, their loyalty to a far-off chieftain (whom they knew only by name) appealed to me with increasing power. Their problem became my problem. More than this they kindled my admiration, for many of them possessed the cowboy's masterful skill with bronchoes, his deft handling of rope and gun and the grace which had made him the most admired figure in our literature,—but in addition to all this, they had something finer, something which the cowboy often lacked. At their best they manifested the loyalty of soldiers. Heedful of the Federal Government, they strove to dispense justice over the lands which had been allotted to their care, and their flags—the Stars and Stripes—as I came upon them fluttering from the peaks of their cabins were to me the guidons of a new and valiant skirmish line. They were of the Border in a new and noble sense. In short the Federal Ranger was a hero made to my hand.

Not all the soldiers in the service were of this large mold, I admit, but many of those I had met did possess precisely the qualities I have outlined. Ready, cheerful, undaunted in the face of danger, some of them had the capacity for lonely action which rendered them as admirable in their way as any of the long line of frontiersmen who had made the winning of the West an epic of singular hardihood. To fight cold and snow and loneliness during long months, with no one looking on, calls for stern resolution. Such work is directly antithetic to that of the city fireman who goes to his duties with a crowd looking on. The ranger has only his own conscience as spectator. For many weeks he does not even see his supervisor.

To the writing of *Cavanagh* I came, therefore, in the spirit of one who had discovered not only a new hero but the reverse side of the squatter's shield. Just as in my studies for *The Captain of the Gray Horse Troop,* I had come upon the seamy side of the cattleman's activity, so now I perceived that many of the men who had settled on the national forests were merely adventurers trying to get something for nothing. To filch Uncle Sam's gold, to pasture on his grass, to dig his coal and seize his water-power—these were the real designs of the claim-holders, while the ranger was in effect a federal policeman, the guardian of a domain whose wealth was the heritage of us all. He was the prophet of a new order, the evangel of a new faith.

The actual composition of *Cavanagh* began as I was riding the glorious trails around Cloud Peak in the Big Horn Mountains of northern Wyoming in the summer of 1908, one of the most beautiful of all my outings, for while the Big Horns are low and tame compared to the Wind River Range, yet the play of their lights and shadows, their clouds, and their mist was as romantic as anything I had ever encountered.

I recall riding alone down the eastern slope one afternoon, while prodigious rivers of cloud—white as wool and soundless as light—descended the cañon on my right and spread above the foothills, forming a level sea out of which the high dark peaks rose like rocky islands. This flood came so swiftly, flowed so marvelously and enveloped my world so silently that the granite ledges appeared to melt beneath my horse's feet.

At times the vapor closed densely round me, shutting out even the rocks of the trail and as I cautiously descended, I almost bumped astonished steers whose heads burst from the mist as if through a covered hoop. The high granite crags on the opposite side of the ravine took on the shapes of ruined castles seated on sloping shores by foaming seas, their smooth lawns reaching to the foam.

At one point, as I came out upon a ledge which overlooked the valley, I perceived my horse's shadow floating on the phantom ocean far below me, a dark equestrian statue encircled with a triple-ringed halo of fire. In all my mountain experiences I had never seen anything so marvelous.

At another time while riding up the trail, I perceived above my head a far-stretching roof of seamless cloud. As I rose, coming closer and closer to it, it seemed a ceiling just above my reach, then my head merged in it. A kind of dry mist surrounded me—and for ten or fifteen minutes I mounted through this luminous, strangely shrouding, all pervasive, mountain cloud. My horse, feeling his way with cautious care, steadily mounted and soon we burst out into the clear sunlight above. While still the mist curled about my horse's hoofs, I looked across a shoreless ocean with only Cloud Peak and its granite crags looming above its surface.

I describe these two spectacular effects out of many others merely to suggest the splendors which inspired me, and which, as I imagined, enriched the daily walk of the forest guard. "To get into my story some part of this glory, my hero must be something of a nature lover—as many rangers are," I argued, and this was true. Before a man will consent to ride the lonely road which leads to his cabin high in the forest, he must not only have a heart which thrills to the wonder of the lonely places, he must be self-sufficing and fearless. I rode with several such men and out of my experiences with them I composed the character of *Ross Cavanagh*.

The actual writing of this novel was begun on my forty-ninth birthday at my desk in the old Homestead, and I started off with enthusiasm notwithstanding the fact that Fuller, who was visiting me at the time, expressed only a tepid interest in my "theme." "Why concern yourself with forestry?" he asked. "No one wants to read about the ranger and his problems. Grapple with Chicago—or New York. That's the only way to do a 'best seller.'"

Henry always amused me but never so much as when tolerating rural joys. He was the exact opposite of my *Cavanagh*. Everything pastoral wearied him or irritated him. The "yelping" of the robins, the "drone" of the katydids, the "eternal twitter" of the sparrows infuriated him. The "accursed roosters" unseasonably wakened him in the morning, the "silly cackle" of the chickens prevented him from writing. Flowers bored him and the weather was always too cold or too hot, too damp or too dusty. Butterflies filled him with pessimistic forebodings of generations of cabbage worms. Moths suggested ruined coat collars— only at night, before our fire, with nature safely and firmly shut out, did he regain his customary and charming humor.

He belonged to the brick pavement, the electric-car line. He did not mind being awakened by the "twitter" of a milk cart. The "yelp" of the ice man, the snort of a six o'clock switch engine and the "cackle" of a laundry wagon formed for him a pleasant morning symphony. The clatter of an elevated train was with him the normal accompaniment of dawn, but the poetry of the pastoral—well, it didn't exist, that's all—except in "maudlin verses of lying sentimentalists." "I'm like George Ade's clerk: I never enjoy my vacation till I get back to the city."

To all such diatribes Zulime and I gave delighted ear. We rejoiced in his comment, for we did not believe a word of it, it was all a part of Henry's delightful perversity.

For six consecutive weeks I bent to the work of writing my novel undisturbed. A peaceful season which I shall long remember, for almost every afternoon, when the weather permitted, we joined the Dudleys and McKees and drove to some lovely spot on the river bank or sought out some half-hidden spring at the far end of a coulee and

346

there, while the children picked nuts or apples and the women read magazines or stitched, George Dudley and I lighted our fire and broiled our steak. Nothing could be simpler, homelier, more wholesome, than this life, and I was able to do nearly half my story before a return to Chicago became necessary.

Practically all of the spring months of 1910 were given to revising and proof-reading *Cavanagh, Forest Ranger,* which had genuinely interested me and which should have been as important in my scheme of delineating the West as *The Captain of the Gray Horse Troop,* but it wasn't. It was too controversial, and besides I did not give it time enough. I should have taken another year to it—but I didn't. I permitted myself to be hurried by Duneka, who was (like most publishers) enslaved to a program. By April it was off my hands.

After the last page of this proof was returned to the printer a sense of weakness, of age, a feeling altogether new to me, led me to say to Fuller, "I shall never do another book. I have finished what I started out to do, I have pictured certain broad phases of the West as I know it, and I'm done. I am out of commission."

Fuller, who had been of this mood for several years, was not content to have me assume a despairing attitude. "You're just tired, that's all," he insisted. "You'll come to a new theme soon."

Movement is swift on the Border. Nothing endures for more than a generation. No family really takes root. Every man is on his way. Cities come and builders go. Unfinished edifices are left behind in order that something new and grander may be started. Some other field is better than the one we are reaping. I do not condemn this, I believe in it. It is America's genius. We are all experimenters, pioneers, progressives.

347

A Daughter of the Middle Border

For years I had in mind to write a book to be called *The Winds of Destiny,* in which I should take up one by one the differing careers of my classmates and friends who had found our little prairie town too narrow and too poor to afford them fullest action. I never got to it, but from time to time I found some new material for it—material which, alas! I can not now find imagination enough to vitalize.

For example: One morning during a stay in New York, I found among my letters a note from an almost forgotten school-fellow, inviting me to dine with himself and wife at the Ritzdorf. The name on this note-head developed on the negative plate of my memory, the picture of two shock-headed, slender-legged schoolboys pacing solemnly, regularly, morning after morning, into the campus of the Seminary in Osage, Iowa. Their arms were always laden with books, their big brows bulging with thought. Invariably marching side by side like a faithful team of horses, turning aside neither to fight nor to play, they provoked laughter.

They were the sons of a farmer (a man of small means, who lived a mile or two from the village), and although they were familiar figures in the school they could hardly be said to be a part of it. Their poverty, their homespun trousers which were usually too short and too tight, and their poverty together with a natural shyness, kept them out of school affairs, although they were always at the top of their classes. To me they were worthy—though a bit grotesque.

My letter of invitation was from the younger of these boys, and having accepted his invitation, I was a bit in doubt as to what I should wear, for he had written, "with Mrs. Roberts and myself," and something in the tone of the letter had decided me to play safe. I put on evening dress, and it was well I did, for Ben met me in irreproachable dinner coat and presented his wife, a handsome and beautifully gowned woman, quite in the manner of a city-bred host. No one looking at us as we sat at our flower-decked table would have imagined that he or I had ever been plowboys of the Middle Border.

As the dinner went on I lost all my conviction that the preternaturally solemn, heavy-footed lad of 1880 was in any way connected with this rich middle-aged inventor, but then he was probably having the same difficulty relating me with the beardless senior of 1881.

On the surface our dinner was a pleasant and rather conventional meeting, and yet the more it is dwelt upon the more significant it becomes. Starting from almost the same point, with somewhat similar handicaps, we two had "arrived," though at widely separated goals. Each of our courses was characteristically American, and each was in demonstration—for the millionth time—of the magic power of the open lands.

In the free air of the Middle Border, this man's genius for inventing had full power of expansion, and in result he was in possession of a fortune, whilst I, in my literary way, had won what my kindest critics called success—by another kind of service. My position though less secure and far less remunerative, was none the less honorable—that I shall insist on saying even though I must admit that in the eyes of my Seminary classmates the inventor made the handsomer showing. As the owner of a patent bringing in many thousands of dollars per year in royalty he had certain very definite claims to respect which I lacked. My home in contrast with his would have seemed very humble. Measured by material things, his imagination had proved enormously more potent than mine.

This meeting not only led me to re-value my own achievement, it brought up to me with peculiar pathos the career of another classmate, my comrade Burton Babcock, whom I (in 1898) had left standing on the bank of the Stickeen River in Alaska. He, too, was characteristically American.

349

He had carried out his plan. After leading his pack train across the divide to the upper waters of the Yukon, he had built a raft and floated down the Hotalinqua. He had been frozen in, and had spent the winter in a windowless hut in the deep snow of an arctic landscape—and when, after incredible hardships, he had reached the Klondike, he had found himself almost as far from a gold claim as ever. All the mines were monopolized.

For the next four years he had alternately worked for wages and prospected for himself. One year he had "mushed" in the Copper River Country and later in the Tanana. In these explorations he went alone, and once he sledged far within the Arctic circle with only two dogs to keep him company. He became one of the most daring and persistent prospectors and yet he had always been just a little too late. He had never shared in any of the big strikes.

At last, after five years of this disheartening life, he had succeeded in breaking away from the fatal lure of the North. Returning to Anacortes on Puget Sound, he had taken up the threads of his life at the point where he had dropped them, to meet me, at Ashcroft, in '98, and on my little daughter's wrist was a bracelet, a string of nuggets, which represented all that he had been able to win from the desolate North.

He left his youth in Alaska. He was an old and broken man when he landed in Seattle, a silent, gray and introspective philosopher. Seeking out the cabin he had built on the Skagit River, he resumed his residence there, solitary and somber. In winter he cooked for a nearby lumber camp, in summer he served as watchman for an electric power company, patient, faithful, brooding over his books, austere, taciturn, mystical.

He read much on occult subjects, and corresponded ceaselessly with a certain school of esoteric philosophy, reaching at last a lofty serenity which approached content. He wrote me that the men of the lumber camp spoke of him as a "queer old cuss," but that disturbed him not at all. To me, however, he uttered his mind freely, and as I followed him thus, in imagination, remembering him as he once was, my graceful companion on the bright Iowa prairie, my sense of something futile in his whole life was deepened into pain.

His letters contained no complaint. He dwelt mainly upon his trips into the forest (occasional vacations from repulsive labor), but I was able to infer from a word here and there, his detestation of the coarse jests and senseless arguments of his "Siwash" companions. His philosophy prevented repining; but he could not entirely conceal his moods of loneliness, of defeat.

My heart ached as I thought of him, wearing his life away in the solitude of the forest, or in waiting on a crowd of unthinking lumber jacks, but I could do little to aid him. I had sent him books and loaned him money whenever he would accept it (which was seldom), and I had offered each year to bring him back to the Middle West and put him on a farm; but to all these suggestions he continued to repeat, "I can't bring myself to it. I can't return, a defeated explorer."

Like my uncle David, he preferred to walk the path he had chosen, no matter to what depth it might descend.

Not long after this meeting with Ben and while I was still absorbed in youthful memories, dreaming of my prairie comrades, a letter came to me from Blanche Babcock, telling me that her brother Burton, my boyhood chum, my companion on The Long Trail to the Yukon, had crossed the Wide Dark River, and with this news, a sense of heavy loss darkened my day. It was as if a part, and no small part, of my life had slipped away from me, irrecoverably, into a soundless abyss.

For more than forty years this singular soul had been a

subject of my care (at times he had been closer to me than my own brother), and now he had vanished from the tangible realities of his mountain home into the unmapped region whose blind trails we had so often manfully discussed.

By all the laws which his family recognized, his life was a failure. To Ben Roberts he was a derelict—and yet to me a kind of elemental dignity lay in the attitude he had maintained when surrounded by coarse and ignorant workmen. He remained unmoved, uncontaminated. His mind inhabited a calm inner region beyond the reach of any coarse word or mocking phrase. Growing ever more mystical as he grew older he had gone his lonely way bent and gray and silent, a student of the forest and the stream. So far as I know he never uttered a bitter or despairing word, and when the final great boundary river confronted him he entered it with the same courage with which he ferried the Yukon or crossed the ice fields of Iskoot.

It happened that on the day this news came to me one of my Chicago friends sent their beautiful motor car to fetch Zulime and me to the opera, and as the children saw us in our evening dress, they cried out, "Oh papa, mama is a queen and you look like a king!" Thus it happened that I rode away in a luxury which I had not earned at the very moment when my faithful trail-mate, after toiling all his life, was passing to his grave wifeless, childless and unknown.

"I wish I could have shared just a little of my good fortune with him," I said to Zulime, who really was as stately as a queen. But the best of all my possessions I would not, could not, share with any one—I mean the adoration of my little daughters to whom I possessed the majesty of an emperor.

> "Here his trail ends. Here by the landing I wait the
> same oar—the slow, silent one.
> We each go alone—no man with another,

"Cavanagh" and "Winds of Destiny"

Each into the gloom of the swift, black flood.
Burt, it is hard, but here we must sever.
The gray boatman waits, and you—you go first.
All is dark over there where the dim boat is rocking,
But that is no matter—no trailer need fear,
For clearly we're told, the powers which lead us,
Will govern the game till the end of the day.
Good-by!—Here the trail ends!"

* * *

Christmas came this year with special significance. Two pairs of eager eyes now peered at all bundles which came into the house. The faith and love and eager hope of my daughters made amends for the world's lack of interest in my writings. They and their mother were my wealth, their love compensated me for the slender dribble of my royalties.

"Our Christmas shall be as happy as that of any millionaire," was the thought which actuated me in the purchase and decoration of our tree. Wealth was highly desirable, but absurd as it may seem I had no desire to change places with any merchant or banker. The foolish notion that something historical in my work made it worth while, supported me in my toil. It was a hazy kind of comfort, I will concede, but I wrapped myself in it, and stole away out into the street to buy and sneak a Christmas tree up the back stairs. It was a noble tree, warranted to reach the ceiling of our library.

Father came down from Wisconsin and Franklin came up from Oklahoma to help me decorate it, and when, on Christmas morning, they both rose with me, and went down to light the candles, they were almost as gleeful as I. Mary Isabel was awake and piping from the top of the stairs, "Is it time, papa? Can we come now, papa?" and at last when the tower of glory was alight I called back, "Yes, now you may all come."

353

Slowly she descended step by step, clinging to her mother, who was carrying Constance. Very slowly the procession approached, for the little voluptuary in front was loath as well as eager—avid to enjoy yet hesitating to devour. Suddenly she saw, and into her face flamed an expression of wonder, of awe, of adoration, a look such as a cherub angel might wear while confronting The Great White Throne, a kind of rapture, humble yet exultant.

Silently she crept toward the center of the room, turning her eyes from this and to that unearthly splendor, yet always bringing them back to rest upon the faces of the dollies, sitting so still and so radiant beneath the glittering boughs. At last with a little gasping cry of joy she seized the largest and most splendid of these wondrous beings and clasped it to her breast, while Constance sat silent with her awe.

Their Christmas was complete. Another shining mark had been set in the upward slope of their happy march! Nothing, not even Death himself, can rob me of that precious memory.

CHAPTER TWENTY-FOUR

The Old Homestead Suffers Disaster

THE summer of 1912, so stormy in a political sense was singularly serene and happy for us. The old house had been received back into favor. It was beloved by us all but especially was it dear to my children. To Mary Isabel it possessed a value which it could not have to any of us, for it was her birth-place and she knew every stick and stone of it. To her it had all the glamor of a childhood home in summer time.

On Sunday, October 6, we began to plan our return to the city, and as we sat about our fire that night the big room never looked so warm, so homelike, so permanent. The deep fireplace was ablaze with light, and the walls packed with books and hung with pictures spoke of a realized ideal. On the tall settee (which I had built myself), lay a richly-colored balletta Navajo blanket, one that I had bought of a Flathead Indian in St. Ignatius. Others from Zuni and Ganado covered the floor. Over the piano "Apple Blossom Time," a wedding present from John Ennecking glowed like a jewel in the light of the quaint electric candles which had been set in the sockets of hammered brass sconces. In short, the place had the mellow charm of a completed home, and I said to Zulime "There isn't much more to do to it. It is rude and queer, a mixture of Paris, Boston, and the Wild West; but it belongs to us." It was in truth a union of what we both represented, including our poverty, for it was all cheap and humble.

My father, white-haired, eighty-two years of age was living with us again, basking in the light of our fire and smiling at his grandchildren, who with lithe limbs and sweet young voices were singing and circling before him. I was glad to have him back in mother's room, and to him and to those who were to be his care-takers for the winter I gravely repeated, "I want everything kept just as it is. I want to feel that we can come back to it at any time and find every object in place, including the fire."

To which father replied, "I don't want to change it. It suits me."

The children, darting out of the music-room (which was the "dressing-room" of their stage), swung their Japanese lanterns, enacting once again their pretty little play, and then our guests rose two by two and went away. Zulime led the march to bed, the lights were turned out and the clear, crisp, odorous October night closed over our scene.

As I was about to leave the low-ceiled library, I took another look at it saying to myself, "It seems absurd to abandon this roomy, human habitation for a cramped little dwelling on a city lot." But with a sense of what the city offered by way of compensation, I climbed the old-fashioned, crooked, narrow stairway to my bed in the chamber over the music-room, content to say good-by for the winter. . . .

It was dusky dawn when I awoke, with a sense of alarm, unable to tell what had awakened me. For several seconds I lay in confusion and vague suspense. Then a cry, a strange cry—a woman's scream—arose, followed by a rush of feet. Other cries, and the shrieks of children succeeded close, one upon the other.

My first thought was, "Constance has fallen." I sprang from my bed and was standing in the middle of the room when I heard Zulime cross the floor beneath me, and a moment later she called up the stairway, "Hamlin, *Fan has set the house on fire!*"

My heart was gripped as if by an icy hand for I knew how inflammable the whole building was, and without stopping to put on coat or slippers, I ran swiftly down the stairs. As I entered the sitting-room so silent, so peaceful, so undisturbed, it seemed that my alarm was only a part of a dream till the sobbing of my daughters and my wife's voice at the telephone calling for help, convinced me of the frightful reality. I heard, too, the ominous crackling of flames in the kitchen.

Pushing open the swinging door I confronted a wall of smoke. One-half of the floor was already consumed, and along the linoleum a sharply-defined line of fire told that it rose from burning oil—and yet I could not quite believe it, even then. It was like a scene in a motion picture play.

My first thought was to check, to hold back the flames, till help came. The garden hose was lying out under a tree (I had put it there the day before) and with desperate haste I hurried to attach it to the water pipes. I saw father in the yard, but he uttered no word. We were each thinking the same thought—"*The old homestead is doomed. Our life here is ended.*"

The hose was heavy and sanely perverse, and it seemed an age before I had the water turned on. Catching up the nozzle I approached the kitchen door. The thin stream had no effect, and the heat was so intense I could not face it. Throwing down the hose I reëntered the house.

The children, hysterical with fright, were just leaving by the east door and Zulime was upstairs. Opening the front door I stepped out upon the porch to call for help. The beauty of the morning, its stillness, its serenity, its odorous opulence, struck upon my senses with a kind of ironic benignancy, as if to say, "Why agonize over so small a thing?"

I shouted "Fire!" and my voice went ringing far up the street. I cried out again, a third time, a fourth, but no one answered, no one appeared, and behind me the crackling roar of the flames increased. In despair I turned back into the sitting-room.

It had been arranged between Zulime and myself that in case of fire (once the children were safe), she was to secure the silverware and her jewelry whilst I flew to collect my manuscripts.

With this thought in my mind, and believing that I had but a few minutes in which to work, I ran up the stairs to my study and began gathering such of my manuscripts as had no duplicates. As I thought of the hundreds of letters from my literary friends, of the many family records, of the innumerable notes, pictures, keepsakes, souvenirs and mementoes which had been assembling there for a quarter of a century, I became confused, indecisive. It was so hard to choose. At last I caught up a sheaf of unpublished stories which filled one drawer, and beating off the screen of the north window threw the manuscripts out upon the grass.

A neighbor's wife, quick to understand the meaning of my anxiety about these sheets, ran to her home across the way and bringing a valise, began to stuff them into it. Having cleared my desk of its most valuable papers I hurried to my dressing-room to secure shoes and trousers; but by this time the hall was full of the most nauseating smoke. The fire having swept entirely through the library, was burning the front porch. My escape by way of the stairway was cut off. Blinded and gasping I gave up the search for clothes and turned back into my study.

I was not in the least scared; on the contrary, I was filled with a kind of fatalistic rage. In imagination I saw the old house, with all that it meant to me, in ruins. I saw the great elms and maples scorched, dead, the tall black locust burned to a ship's mast. As I peered from the window, a neighbor called earnestly, "You'd better get off there; the whole house is going."

From the window I could see the villagers rapidly assembling, and not knowing how far advanced the flames might be I yielded to the advice of my friend, and swinging myself from the window dropped to the ground.

My next care was for the children. I could hear them crying frantically for "papa!" and I hurried to where they stood cowering in the door of the barn. "O, papa, put it out. I don't want it to burn. *Put it out!*" moaned Mary Isabel with passionate intensity.

Her faith in her father had an infinite pathos at the moment. She loved the house. It was a part of her very brain and blood. To have it burn was a kind of outrage. Little Connie, five years old, with chattering teeth, joined her pleading cry, *"Can't you put it out, papa?"* she asked piteously.

"No," I answered sadly. "Papa can not put it out. Nobody can. You must say good-by to our dear old home."

Wrapping a quilt about her I started across the road toward my neighbor's porch. The yard was full of my fellow-citizens, and young men were heroically dragging out smoking furniture from the lower floor, while over in the Sander's yard piles of books, bedding and furniture were accumulating. It was all curiously familiar and typical.

In the full belief that the homestead would soon be a heap of charcoal, we took the children back into our friend's dining-room. "Pull down the curtain," entreated Zulime, "we don't want to see the old place go."

Helpless for lack of street clothing, with my children on

my knees, I sat in silence, noting the flickering glare of the light on the walls, and hearing the shouts of the firemen and the sound of their axes.

Huldah, our neighbor's daughter, entered. "They're checking it!" she exclaimed. "It is under control."

This seemed incredible, but it was confirmed by George Dudley, who came in bringing my shoes and a suit of my clothing.

When at last I was fully clothed and could go out into the street I was amazed to find a part of the house standing. Most of the east wing seemed quite untouched, except of smoke and water. The west wing and front porch were in black disarray, but the roof held its place and the trees seemed scarcely scorched. A few firemen, among them the village plumber, the young banker, and a dentist, were on guard, watchfully intent that the flames should not break out again. The sun was rising gloriously over the hills. The fire, my fire, was over.

No doubt this event appeared most trivial to the travelers in a passing train. From the car windows it was only a column of smoke in the edge of a small village. Our disaster offered, indeed, only a mild sensation to the occupants of an early automobile party, but to my father, to Zulime and to the children, it was a desolate and appalling ruin. They had grown to love this old house foolishly, illogically, for it was neither beautiful nor historic, nor spacious. It was only a commonplace frame cottage, inwrought with memories and associations, but it was home—all we had.

The yard was piled with furniture, half-burned, soaked and malodorous, but none of my manuscripts were in sight. I had expected to find them scattered like feathers across the garden or trampled into the muddy sward. In reply to my question my friend Dudley replied, "They're all safe. I had the boys carry them down in blankets. You'll find them in the barn."

As I moved about silently, studying the ruins, the kindliest of my neighbors said, "You'll have to entirely rebuild." And to this a carpenter, a skilled and honest workman, agreed. "The cheapest thing to do is to tear it all down and start from the foundation."

Slowly, minutely, I studied the ruin. Surely here was gruesome change! Black, ill-smelling, smoking debris lay where our pretty dining-room had been. The library with all my best books (many of them autographed) was equally desolate, heaped with steaming, charred masses of tables, chairs, rugs and fallen plaster. I thought of it as it had been the night before, with the soft lights of the candles falling upon my children dancing with swinging lanterns. I recalled Ennecking's radiant spring painting, and Steele's "Bloom of the Grape," which glowed above the mantle, and my heart almost failed me—"Is this the end of my life in Wisconsin?"

For twenty years this little village had been the place of my family altar, not because it was remarkable in any way, but because since 1850 it had been the habitat of my mother's people and because it was filled with my father's pioneer friends. "Is it worth while to rebuild?" I asked myself. For the time I lost direction. I had no plan.

The sight of my white-haired father wandering about the yard, dazed, bewildered, his eyes filled with a look of despair at last decided me. Realizing that this was his true home; that no other roof could have the same appeal, and he could not be transplanted, I resolved to cover his head; to make it possible for him to live out his few remaining years under this roof with his granddaughters. "For his sake and the children's sake," I announced to Zulime, "I shall begin at once to clear away and restore. Before the winter comes you shall all be back in the old House. Perhaps we can eat our Thanksgiving dinner in the restored dining-room."

Whether she fully shared my desire to rebuild or whether she believed in my ability to carry out my plan so quickly I can not say. In such matters she was not decisive—she rested on my stubborn will.

The day came on—glorious, odorous, golden—but we saw little of its beauty. Engaged in digging the family silver out of the embers, and collecting my scattered books and papers I had no time to look at the sky. Occasionally, as I looked up from my work I saw my little daughters playing with childish intentness among the fallen leaves in my neighbor's yard, and in mistaken confidence I remarked what a blessing it is that childhood can so easily forget disaster.

I did not realize then, nor till many months after, how profound the shock had been to them. For years after the event they started at every unusual sound and woke at night screaming of fire.

All that day and all the days of the week which followed they played with the same singular insect-like absorption and at last I began to get some notion of their horror. They refused to enter the yard. "I don't want to see it," Mary Isabel wailed. Then she asked, "Will it ever be home for us again?"

"Yes," I answered with final determination. "I'll put it back just as it was before the fire came. It shall be nicer than ever when I am done."

Before night I had engaged a crew of men to clear away. Thereafter I lived like a man in a tunnel. I saw almost nothing of the opulent, golden sunshine, nothing of the exquisite foliage, nothing of the far hills, purple with Indian summer haze. Busily sorting my burned books or spreading out my treasured rugs, I toiled as long as light lasted. There were a few pleasant surprises. From one charred frame the face of Frank Norris, miraculously fresh and handsome and smiling, looked out through smoked and broken glass. In one corner of the sideboard (decorated by Thompson-Seton), a part of the silver bearing my mother's initials lay quite unharmed, though all of the pieces on the top were melted into a flat mass of bullion. Autographed books from Howells, Riley, Gilbert Parker, Conan Doyle, Arnold Bennett, fell to pieces in my hand, or showed so deep a stain of smoke as to make their rebinding impossible. My best Navajo rug, a fine example of the ancient weaving, was a frail cinder on the back of the charred settee, and a Hopi ceremonial dress which hung upon the wall was a blackened shred.

All these things had small money value, and to many men, would have represented no interest whatsoever, but to me they were precious. They were a part of my life. To burn them was to char a section of my brain. Pitiful possessions! Worthless rags! And yet they were the best I could show after thirty years of labor with the pen!

My father's condition troubled me most. To have him rendered homeless at eighty-two with winter coming on seemed to me an intolerable cruelty, and so with a driving haste I set to work with my own hands to clear away and restore. Wielding the wrecking bar and the spade each day, I toiled like a hired man—even after the carpenters were gone at night I scraped paint and shoveled rubbish.

Let no one pity me! A curious pleasure came with all this, for it seemed to advance the reconstruction with double swiftness.

At the end of the week I sent my wife and the children back to their city home, and thereafter I had but one interest, one diversion—to plan and execute my rebuilding.

To close the walls, to make the rooms secure against wind and rain was imperative.

The insurance inspector came pleasantly to the rescue, and with a small balance in the bank I hired roofers, plumbers, carpenters, masons, till the street resounded with their clamor. In a week I had the rooms cleared, the doors and windows closed, and my father living in one corner of the house, whilst I camped down in my study. Water-soaked, ill-smelling, but inhabitable, the old house again possessed a light and a hearth.

"The children and their grandsire shall eat Thanksgiving dinner in the rebuilt dining-room," was my secret sentimental resolution. "To do that will turn a wail into a song—a disaster into a poem."

All very foolish, you say. No doubt, but it interested me and I was of an age when very few things interested me vitally. With clothing black as soot, with hands brown with stain and skinned and swollen and feverish, I kept to my job without regard to Sundays or the ordinary hours of labor. I was not seeking sympathy,—I was renewing my youth. I was both artist and workman. My muscles hardened, my palms broadened, my appetite became prodigious. I lost all fear of indigestion and ate anything which my friend Dudley was good enough to provide. I even drank coffee at every opportunity, and went so far as to eat doughnuts and pancakes at breakfast! To be deliciously hungry as of old was heartening.

The weather continued merciful. Each day the sun rose red and genial, and at noon the warm haze of Indian summer trailed along the hills—though I had little time in which to enjoy it. Each sunset marked a new stanza in my poem, a completed phrase, a recovered figure. "Our small affairs have shut out the light of the sun," I said to father, "the political situation has lost all interest for me."

364

The Old Homestead Suffers Disaster

Bare, clean and sweet, the library and music-room at last were ready for furniture. All these must be replaced. A hurried trip to the city, three days of determined shopping with Zulime, and a stream of new goods (necessary to refurnish), began to set toward the threshold. The draymen plied busily between the station and the gate.

By November first my father and I were camping in the library and cooking our own food in the dining-room. We rose each day before dawn and ate our bacon and coffee while yet the stars twinkled in the west, and both of us were reminded of the frosty mornings on our Iowa farm, when we used to eat by candle-light in order to husk corn by starlight. My hands felt as they used to feel when, worn by the rasping husks, they burned with fever. Heavy as hams, they refused to hold a pen, and my mind refused to compose even letters—but the pen was not needed. "My poem is composed of wood and steel," I remarked to Dudley.

At last the yard was cleared of its charred rubbish, the porch restored to its old foundation, and the new metal roof, broad-spreading and hospitable, gleamed like snow in dusk and dawn, and from the uncurtained windows our relighted lamps called to the world that the Garland household was about to reassemble and the author permitted himself to straighten up. Changing to my city garments I took the train for Chicago, promising to bring the children with me when our Thanksgiving turkey was fatted for the fire.

My daughters listened eagerly to my tale of the new house, but expressed a fear of sleeping in it. This fear I determined to expel.

On the Saturday before Thanksgiving I rejoined my workmen, finding the house in a worse state of disarray than when I had last seen it. The floors were littered with dust and shavings, and in the dining-room my father, deeply discouraged, was gloomily cooking his breakfast on

365

an oil stove set in the middle of the floor. "It'll take another month to finish the job," he said.

"Oh, no it won't," I replied. "It won't take a week.

Fortunately the stain on the floor was dry and with the aid of two good men I finished the woodwork and beat the rugs. In a couple of days the lower house was livable.

On Wednesday at five o'clock I went to the train, leaving the electric lights all ablaze and the fire snapping in the chimney. It looked amazingly comfortable, restored, settled, and I was confident the children would respond to its cheer.

"Is it all made new?" they asked wistfully.

"Wait and see!" I confidently replied.

The night was cold and dark but as they neared the old house its windows winked a cheery welcome. "Why, it looks just as it used to!" exclaimed Mary Isabel.

"There are lights in our room!" exclaimed Constance.

"Run ahead, and knock," I urged.

She hung back. "I'm afraid," she said.

"So am I," echoed Connie.

The new metal roof gleaming like frost interested them as they entered the gate.

"Why, the porch is all here!" shouted Constance.

"But the screens are off," commented Mary Isabel.

"Knock!" I commanded.

Reaching up to the shining old brass knocker she banged it sharply.

The house awoke! White-haired old father came to the door and, first of all, the children sprang to his arms.

Then as they looked around they shouted with joy. "Why, it's just as it was—only nicer," was their verdict.

While Zulime looked keenly and smilingly around, Connie ran from settee to bookcase. "Everything is here—our books, the fireplace."

The Old Homestead Suffers Disaster

"Isn't it wonderful!" Mary Isabel exclaimed.

After greeting father Zulime surveyed the result of my six weeks' toil with critical but approving eyes. "I like it. It's much better than I expected. It *is* wonderful. But we must have new curtains for the windows," she added, with the housewife's attention to details.

The children danced through the brilliantly lighted rooms, but declined to go into the dining-room or to open the door to the kitchen which they remembered only as a mass of black embers and steaming ashes. I did not urge them to do so. On the contrary, I gathered them round me on the restored hearth and talked of the Thanksgiving dinner of the morrow.

As the hour for bedtime came Connie's eyes grew big and dark, and every small unusual sound startled her. Daddy's presence at last reassured them both and they went to sleep and, with only one or two restless intervals, slumbered till daylight.

Two of our neighbors—two capable women, came in next morning to help, and in a few hours the windows were curtained, the linen laid out and the turkey in the oven. Under Zulime's hands the rooms bloomed into homeliness. The kitchen things fell into orderly array. Pictures took their places on the walls, little knick-knacks which had been brought from the city were set on the mantels and bookcases, and when our guests arrived they each and all exclaimed, "No one would ever know you'd *had* a fire!"

At one o'clock the cooks, the children and Zulime all agreed that the fowl was ready for the carver and so we all assembled in the new and larger dining-room. No formal Thanksgiving was spoken, but vaguely forming in my mind was a poem which should express our joy and gratitude. My brother's seat was empty and so were those of other loved ones, but we did not dwell upon these sad things. I was living, working and planning now for the vivid souls of my daughters whose glowing cheeks and laughing eyes repaid me for all my toil. For them I had rebuilt this house—for them and their grandsire—whose trail was almost at its end. How happy he was in their presence! They, too, were happy because they were young, the sun was shining and their home was magically restored.

The happiest time of all was at night, when the evening shadows closed round the friendly walls, and the trees sighed in the chill wind—for beside the fire we gathered, the Garlands and McClintocks, in the good old fashion, while our neighbors came in to congratulate and rejoice. All the black terror of the dismantled house, all the toil and worry of the months which lay between, were forgotten as the children, without a care, sang and danced in the light of our new and broadened hearth.

That night as my daughters, "dressed up" as princesses, danced like fairies in the light of our restored and broadened hearth, I forgot all the toil, all the disheartenment which the burning of the house had brought upon me. To them the re-built homestead was only another evidence of their Daddy's magic power. His lamp was not less potent than Aladdin's.

CHAPTER TWENTY-FIVE

Darkness Just Before the Dawn

IN going back over the records of the years 1912 and 1913, I can see that my life was lacking in "drive." It is true I wrote two fairly successful novels which were well spoken of by my reviewers and in addition I continued to conduct the Cliff Dwellers' Club and to act as one of the Vice Presidents of the National Institute of Arts and Letters, but I was very far from a feeling of satisfaction with my position. My life seemed dwindling into futility. I was in physical pain much of the time and tortured by a fear of the future.

Naturally and inevitably the burden of my increasing discontent, worse health, fell with sad reiteration upon my wife, who was not only called upon to endure poverty, but to bear with a sick and disheartened husband. The bravery of her smile served to increase my sense of unworthiness. Her very sweetness, her cheerful acceptance of never-ending household drudgery, was an accusation.

She no longer touched brush or clay, although I strongly urged her to sketch or model the children. She had no time, even if she had retained the will, to continue her work as an artist. With a faculty for entertaining handsomely and largely, with hosts of friends who would have clustered about her with loyal admiration, she remained the mistress of a narrow home and one more or less incompetent housemaid. All these considerations added to my sense of weakness and made the particular manuscript upon which I was spending most of my time, a piece of selfish folly.

For ten years I had been working, from time to time, on an autobiographical manuscript which I had called by various names, but which had finally solidified into *A Son of the Middle Border*. Even in my days of deepest discouragement I turned most of my energy to its revision. In the belief that it was my final story and with small hope of its finding favor in any form, I toiled away, year after year, finding in the aroused memories of my youthful world a respite from the dull grind of my present.

My duties as head of the Cliff Dwellers and as Secretary of The Theater Society tended to keep me in Chicago. My lecture engagements became fewer and I dropped out of Eastern Club life, retaining only long distance connection with the world of Arts and Letters. In losing touch with my fellows something vital had gone out of me.

In spite of all my former protestations, the city began to take on the color of Henry Fuller's pessimism. My youthful faith in Chicago's future as a great literary center had faded into middle-aged doubt. One by one its writers were slipping away to Manhattan. The Midland seemed farther away from publishers than ever, "The current is all against us," declared Fuller.

As a man of fifty-two I found myself more and more discordant with my surroundings. With sadness I conceded that not in my time would any marked change for the better take place. "Such as Chicago now is, so it will remain during my life," I admitted to Fuller.

"Yes, if it doesn't get worse," was his sad reply.

I would have put my Woodlawn house on sale in 1912 had it not been for my father's instant protest. "Don't take Zulime and the children so far away," he pleaded. "If you move to New York I shall never see any of you again.

Stay where you are. Wait till I am 'mustered out'—it won't be long now."

There was no resisting this appeal. With a profound sense of what Zulime and the children meant to him, I gave up all thought of going East and settled back into my groove. "We will remain where we are so long as father lives," I declared to my friends.

My wife, who had perceived with alarm my growing discontent with Chicago, was greatly relieved by this decision. To her the thought of migration even to the North Side was disturbing, for it would break her close connection with the circle whose center was in her brother's studio. I am not seeking to excuse my recreancy to The Middle West; I am merely stating it as a phase of literary history, for my case is undoubtedly typical of many other writers who turned their faces eastward.

The plain truth is I had reached an age where I no longer cared to pioneer even in a literary sense. Desirous of the acceptances proper to a writer with gray hair and a string of creditable books, I wished to go where honor waited. I craved a place as a man of letters. That my powers were deteriorating in the well-worn rut of my life in Woodlawn I knew too well, and my need of contact with my fellow craftsmen in the East sharpened. The support and inspiration which come naturally to authors in contact with their kind were being denied me. Age was bringing me no "harvest home." In short, at the very time when I should have been most honored, most recompensed, in my work, I found myself living meanly in a mean street and going about like a man of mean concerns, having little influence on my art or among my fellows.

That Chicago was still on the border in a literary sense was sharply emphasized when the National Institute of Arts and Letters decided (after much debate), to hold its Annual Meeting for 1913 in the midland metropolis. "It is a long way out to Chicago," its Secretary wrote, "and I don't know how many members we can assemble, but I think we shall be able to bring twenty-five at least. You have been appointed chairman of the Committee of Arrangements, with full powers to go ahead."

The honor and responsibility of this appointment spurred me to action. I decided to accept and make the meeting a literary milestone in western history. My first thought was to make the Cliff Dwellers' Club the host of the occasion, but on further consideration, I reckoned that the City's welcome would have greater weight if all its literary and artistic forces could be in some way combined. To bring this about I directed letters to the heads of seventeen clubs and educational organizations, asking them to meet with me and form a joint Reception Committee.

This they did, and in a most harmonious session elected Hobart Chatfield-Taylor chairman. To this Committee I then said, "If we are to have any considerable number of our distinguished eastern authors and artists at this dinner we must make it very easy for them to travel. We should have a special train for them or at least special sleeping cars so that they can come as if in a moving club."

In this plan I had instant support. The sturdy group of men who had been so ready to aid me in building up the Cliff Dwellers (men like Hutchinson, Logan, Glessner, Ryerson, Aldis, and Heckmen), all took vital interest in the arrangements for the reception and dinner. The necessary funds were immediately subscribed, and my report to the Institute Council created a fine feeling of enthusiasm in the ranks of both organizations. The success of the meeting was assured. Some of the oldest members wrote, "It is a long way out there but we are coming."

The press of the city responded generously and some of its editors perceived and stated the historical significance of this pilgrimage of poets, artists, and historians to "the sparsely settled Border of Esthetic Culture." A trainload of men who painted, sculptured and composed, men who were entirely concerned with the critical or esthetic side of life, an academy of arts and letters rolling westward, was a new and wondrous phase of national exploration. The invasion was also capable of comic interpretation and a few graceless wags did allude to it as "a missionary expedition to Darkest Illinois."

To Fuller, to Chatfield-Taylor and to me, this joke was not altogether pleasant. We knew all too well the feeling of some of the writers who were coming. Several of them were seeing "the West" for the first time in their lives, others had not been in Chicago since the World's Fair in '93. All were conscious of the effort involved in reaching the arid and unknown frontier.

The entire Middle West had only ten resident members of the Institute although a large proportion of its membership was drawn from the Southern and Central Western States. "All trails lead to New York and there are no returning footsteps," commented Fuller. "Once a writer or painter or illustrator pulls his stakes and sets out for Manhattan, Chicago sees him no more."

All this was disheartening to those of us who, twenty years before, had visioned Chicago as a shining center of American art, but we went forward with our preparations, hoping that a fairly representative delegation could be induced to come.

Some thirty-five arrived safely, and the Dinner of Welcome in Sculpture Hall not only set a milestone in the progress of the city, but was in itself a beautiful and distinctive event.

The whole panorama of western settlement and its city building unrolled before me, as Charles L. Hutchinson,

President of the Art Institute, rose in his place, and in the name of the most aspiring of Chicago's men and women, welcomed the members of the American Academy and the National Institute as representatives of American Art and American Literature. Once again and for the moment our city became a capital in something like the character of Boston a generation before. This conception was illusory, of course, but we permitted ourselves the illusion and accepted the praise which our visitors showered upon us with a belief that we had gained, at last, a recognized place in the Nation's esthetic history.

During the weeks of preparation for this event I had been happy and content, but a few days later, after the clubs had fallen back to their normal humdrum level I acknowledged with a sense of hopeless weariness that our huge city had a long way to go before it could equal the small Boston of Emerson, Lowell, Holmes, and Howells. My desire to rejoin my fellows in New York was intensified. "As there is only one London for England so there is only one New York for America."

All through the autumn of 1913 I ground away at my story of the Middle Border, conscious of the fact that— in a commercial sense—I was wasting my time, for several of my editorial friends had assured me of that fact—but each morning as I climbed to my study I forgot my drab surroundings. Closing the door of the bitter present and turning my back on the stormy future I relived my audacious youth and dreamed of the brave days of old.

Thanksgiving Day in West Salem was misty, dark and still, but the children—bless their shining faces—regarded it as just the right kind of weather for our festival. They were up early and running of errands for their mother who was chief cook. Our only guests were three lonely old women, and it gave me a pang of pity for the children who were forced thus to tolerate a group of gray-heads to whom life was a closing, mournful dirge. Happily, my daughters had the flame of invincible youth in their blood and danced and sang as if the world were new and wholly beautiful, which it was, to them.

Dear little daughters! They didn't know that Daddy was worried about his future and theirs, and no sooner were we back in our Chicago home than they began to look away toward Christmas. "Poppie!"—Mary Isabel would repeat—"only three weeks till—you know what! Remember!"

I remembered. Once again their stockings were stuffed to the hem, and their tree, a marvel of light, touched the ceiling with its pliant tip on which sparkled a golden star. To them I was still a wonder-worker. For a week I put aside my dark musings and rejoiced with them in their fairy world.

Now it chanced that the University Club of Pittsburg had booked me for a lecture early in January and in taking account of this, I planned to invade Manhattan once again, in a desperate attempt to dispose of my rewritten *Son of the Middle Border,* and to offer, also, one or two short stories which I had lately put into clean copy. Humbly, sadly, unwillingly I left my home that cold, bleak, dirty day, staggering under the weight of my valises, for I was not in good health and my mood was irresolute.

Change was in my world and change of an ominous kind was in my brain. Subjects which once interested me had lost their savor, and several tales in which I had put my best effort had failed to meet my own approval and had been thrown aside. No mechanic, no clerk, would have envied me as I boarded a filthy street car on my way to the Englewood station. That I had reached a fork in my trail was all too evident. The things for which I had labored all my days were as ashes in my hand. I walked with a stoop and the bag containing my manuscript dragged at my shoulder like a fifty-pound weight as I painfully climbed the steps leading to the waiting-room of the grimy, noisy, train station. I was a million miles from being a "distinguished man of letters" at that moment, and with a sense of my poverty and declining health, took a seat in the crowded day coach and rode all day in gloomy silence. At noon I dined on a sandwich. Dollars looked as large as dinner plates that day. "Your only way to earn money is to save it," I accused myself.

At the University Club in Pittsburg I recovered slightly. The lecture having been announced to take place in the dining-room could not be staged till nine o'clock—a fact which worried me for I had arranged to take the night train for the East—and this alarm, this fear of losing my train led me to begin by address while my audience was assembling, and my hurried utterance led to weariness on the part of my hearers. My performance was a failure, and to complete my disheartenment I reached the station about five minutes after the last eastern train had pulled out.

Dismayed by this mishap, I took a seat in a corner and darkly ruminated. "What shall I do now? Shall I go back to Chicago? Or shall I go on?"

Decision was in reality taken out of my hands by the baggageman who said in response to inquiry, "I put your trunk on the 8:40 train. It is well on its way to New York."

Accepting this as a mandate to go on, I returned to my room in the University Club and went to bed, but not to sleep. For hours I tossed and turned in self-questioning, self-accusing fury.

"What a fool you have been to waste years of labor on

a book which nobody wants and which has put you—temporarily at least—out of conceit with fiction. Why go on? Why spend more time and money on a vain attempt to dispose of this manuscript.

Falling asleep at last, I regained a part of my courage, and at breakfast a faint glow of hope crept into my thinking. At nine o'clock I took the day train and in silence rode for nearly twelve hours, retracing the thirty years which lay between my first view of Manhattan and this my hundredth reëntrance. With no thrill of excitement I crossed the ferry and having registered at a small hotel on Thirty-fourth Street, went to bed at nine o'clock completely worn out with my journey.

A long night's sleep and a pot of delicious coffee for breakfast put so much sunshine into my world that I set out for Franklin Square with a gambler's countenance, resolute to conceal my dismay from my friends and especially from my publisher. There was something in the very air of Broadway which generated confidence.

Harpers' editors were genial, respectful, but by no means enthusiastic concerning my autobiographic manuscript, although I assured Duneka that I had vastly improved it since he had read it a year before.

"That may be," he granted, "but it is not fiction and nothing serializes but fiction. We'll be glad to schedule it as a book, but I don't see any place for it in our magazine." And then—more to get rid of me than for any other reason, he added, "You might see *Collier's*. Mark Sullivan is the editor up there now; it might be that he could use something of yours."

Duneka's indifference even more than his shunting my precious manuscript into the street brought back my cloud of doubt, for it indicated a loss of faith in me. To him I was a squeezed lemon. Nevertheless I took his hint.

Sullivan, I knew and liked, and while I had small hope of interesting him in *The Middle Border*, I did think he might buy one or two of my short stories.

The *Collier's* plant humming with speed, prosperous and commercial, was not reassuring to me, but I kept on through the maze until I reached Sullivan's handsome room, where I was given an easy chair and told to wait, "the editor will see you in a few minutes."

Alert, kindly, cordial, Mark greeted me and taking a seat, fixed his keen blue, kindly eyes upon me. "I'm glad to see you," he said, and I believed he meant it. He went on, "This is the psychological moment for us both. I am looking for American material and I want something of yours. What have you to show me?",

Thus encouraged I told him of *A Son of the Middle Border*.

He was interested. "Where is the manuscript? Is it complete?"

"It is. I have it with me at the hotel."

"Send it down to me," he said quickly, "I'll read it and give you a verdict at once."

In an illogical glow of hope I hastened to fetch the manuscript, and in less than two hours it was in his hands.

I speak of my hope as "illogical" for if the literary monthly of my own publishers could not find a place for it, how could I reasonably expect a hustling, bustling popular weekly like *Collier's* to use it?

Nevertheless something in Sullivan's voice and manner restored my confidence, and when I called on the editor of the *Century* I was able to assume the tone of successful authorship. The closer I got to my market the more assured I became. I counted for something in New York. My thirty years of effort were remembered in my favor.

On Tuesday Sullivan, who had been called to the West,

wired me from Chicago that *A Son of the Middle Border*
would make an admirable serial and that his assistants
would take the matter up with me. "I predict a great success for it."

That night I sent a message to my wife in which I exultantly said, "Rejoice! I've sold *The Middle Border* to
Collier's Weekly. Our troubles are over for a year at least."

Two days later *Collier's* took a short story at four hundred dollars and the *Century* gave me three hundred for an
article on James A. Herne, and when I boarded the train
for Chicago the following week I was not only four thousand
dollars better off than when I came—I had regained my
faith in the future. My task was clearly outlined. For the
seventh time I set to work revising *A Son of the Middle
Border,* preparing it for serial publication.

My father, who knew that I had been writing upon this
story for years, stared at me in silent amazement when I
told him of its sale. That the editor of a great periodical
should be interested in a record of the migrations and failures
of the McClintocks and Garlands was incredible. Nevertheless he was eager to see it in print—and when in March
the first instalment appeared, he read it with absorbed attention and mixed emotions. "Aren't you a little hard on
me?" he asked with a light in his eyes which was half-
humorous, half-resentful.

"I don't think so, Father," I replied. "You must admit
you were a stern disciplinarian in those days."

"Well maybe I was—but I didn't realize it."

My first understanding of the depths this serial sounded
came to me in the letters which were written to the editor
by those who could not find words in which to express their
longing for the bright world gone—the world when they
were young and glad. "You have written my life," each

one said—and by this they meant that the facts of my family history, and my own emotional experiences were so nearly theirs that my lines awoke an almost intolerable regret in their hearts—an ache which is in my own heart to-day—the world-old hunger of the gray-haired man dwelling upon the hope and illusions of youth.

These responses which indicated a wider and more lasting effect than I had hoped to produce, led me to plan for the publication of the book close on the heels of the concluding instalment of the serial but in this I was disappointed. The Mexican war suddenly thrust new and tremendously exciting news articles into the magazine, separating and delaying the printing of my story. Had it not been for the loyalty of Mark Sullivan it would have been completely side-tracked, but he would not have it so; on the contrary he began to talk with me about printing six more instalments, and this necessarily put off the question of finding a publisher for the book.

Nevertheless I returned to my desk in the expectation that the Mexican excitement was only a flurry and that the magazine would be able to complete the publication of the manuscript within the year. My harvest was not destroyed; it was only delayed.

CHAPTER TWENTY-SIX

A Spray of Wild Roses

ALTHOUGH for several years my wife and children had spent four months of each year in West Salem, and notwithstanding the fact that my father was free to come down to visit us at any time, I suffered a feeling of uneasiness (almost of guilt), whenever I thought of him camping alone for the larger part of the year in that big, silent house. His love for the children and for Zulime made every day of his lonely life a reproach to me, and yet there seemed no way in which I could justly grant him more of our time. The welfare of my wife and the education of the children must be considered.

He was nearing his eighty-fourth birthday, and a realization that every week in which he did not see his granddaughters was an irreparable loss, gave me uneasiness. It was a comfort to think of him sitting in an easy chair in the blaze of a fireplace which he loved and found a solace and yet he was a lonely old man—that could not be denied. He made no complaint in his short infrequent letters although as spring came on he once or twice asked, "Why don't you come up? The best place for the children is on the lawn under the maples."

In one note to me he said, "My old legs are giving out. I don't enjoy walking any more. I don't stand the work of the garden as well as I did last year. You'd better come up and help me put in the seed."

A Daughter of the Middle Border

This confession produced in me a keen pang. He who had marched so tirelessly under the lead of Grant and Thomas; he who had fearlessly cruised the pine forests of Wisconsin, and joyously explored the prairies of Iowa and Minnesota, was now uncertain of his footing. Alarmed more than I cared to confess, I hurried up to help him, and to tell him of the success of *The Middle Border*, which was in truth as much his story as mine.

The air was thick with bird songs as I walked up the street, for it was late April, and I came upon him at work in the garden, bareheaded as usual, his white hair gleaming in the sunlight like a silver crown.

Outwardly serene, without a trace of bitterness in his voice, he spoke of his growing weakness. "Oh, the old machine is wearing out, that's all." Aware of his decline he accepted it as something in the natural course of human life and was content.

Several of his comrades had dropped away during the winter and he was aware that all of his generation were nearing their end. "There's only one more migration left for us," he said composedly, yet with a note of regret. Not on the strength of any particular religious creed but by reason of a manly faith in the universe he faced death. He was a kind of primitive warrior, who, having lived honorably, was prepared to meet what was to come. "I've no complaint to make," he said, "I've had a long life and on the whole a happy life. I'm ready for the bugle."

This was the faith of a pathfinder, a philosophy born of the open spaces, courage generated by the sun and the wind. "I find it hard to keep warm on dark days," he explained. "I guess my old heart is getting tired," and as he spoke I thought of the strain which that brave heart had undergone in its eighty years of action, on the battlefield, along the river, in the logging camps, and throughout all the stern, unceasing years of labor on the farm. His tireless energy and his indomitable spirit came back, filling my mind with pictures of his swift and graceful use of axe and scythe, and when I spoke of the early days, he found it difficult to reply—they were so beautiful in retrospect.

The next day was Sunday, and Sunday afternoon was for him a period of musing, an hour of dream, and as night began to fall he turned to me and with familiar accent called out, "Come, Hamlin, sing some of the songs your mother used to love," and I complied, although I could play but a crude accompaniment to my voice. First of all I sang "Rise and Shine" and "The Sweet Story of Old" in acknowledgment of the Sabbath, then passed to "The Old Musician and His Harp," ending with "When You and I Were Young, Maggie," in which I discerned a darker significance—a deeper pathos than ever before. It had now a personal, poignant application.

Tears misted his eyes as I uttered the line, "But now we are aged and gray, Maggie, the trials of life are nearly done," and at the close he was silent with emotion. He, too, was aged and gray, his trials of life nearly done, and the one who had been his solace and his stay had passed beyond recall.

To me, came the insistent thought, "Soon he must go to join Mother in the little plot under the pines beyond Neshonoc." In spite of my philosophy, I imagined their reunion somehow, somewhere.

Tender and sweet were the scenes which the words of my songs evoked—pictures which had nothing to do with the music except by association, forms and faces of far-off days, of Dry Run Prairie and its neighbors, and of the still farther and dimmer and more magical experiences of Green's Coulee, before the call to war.

I sang the song my uncle Bailey loved. A song which took him back to his boyhood's home in Maine.

> "The river's running just the same,
> The willows on its side
> Are larger than they were, dear Tom,
> The stream appears less wide,
> And stooping down to take a drink,
> Dear Heart, I started so,
> To see how sadly I was changed
> Since forty years ago!"

His songs, his friends, his thoughts were all of the past except when they dwelt on his grandchildren—and they, after six months' absence, were shadowy, fairy-like forms in his memory. He found it difficult to recall them precisely. He longed for them but his longing was for something vaguely bright and cheerful and tender. David and William and Susan and Belle were much more vividly real to him than Constance or Mary Isabel.

*   *   *   *   *   *

On Monday morning he was up early. "Now let's get to work," he said. "I can't hoe as I used to do, and the weeds are getting the start of me." To him the garden was a battlefield, a contest with purslane and he hated to be worsted.

"Don't worry about the garden," I said. "It is not very important. What does it matter if the 'pussley' does cover the ground?"

He would not have this. "It matters a good deal," he replied with hot resentment, "and it won't happen so long as I can stand up and shove a hoe."

To relieve his anxiety and to be sure that he did not overwork, I hired Uncle Frank McClintock to come down for two or three days a week to help kill the weeds. "The

384

A Spray of Wild Roses

crop is not important to me," I said to him privately, "but it *is* important that you should keep a close watch on Father while I am away. He is getting feeble and forgetful. See him every day, and wire me if he is in need of anything. I must go back to the city for a few weeks. If you need me send word and I'll come at once."

He understood, and I went away feeling more at ease. I relied on Uncle Frank's interest in him.

Now, it chanced that just before the date of our return to the Homestead, Lily Morris, wife of the newly-appointed ambassador to Sweden, invited my wife and children to accompany her on a trip to the Big Horn Mountains and we were all torn between opposing duties and desires.

Eager to see "Papa's Mountains," yet loath to lose anything of dear old West Salem, Mary Isabel was pathetically perplexed. Connie was all for West Salem but Zulime who knew the charm of the West decided to go, and again I visited Father to tell him the news and to explain that we would all be with him in August. The fear of disappointing him was the only cloud on the happy prospect.

With a feeling of guilt I met him with the news of our change of plan, softening the blow as best I could. He bore it composedly, though sadly, while I explained that I could not possibly have shown the children the mountains of my own accord. "I have some lectures in Colorado," I explained, "but I shall not be gone long."

"I had counted on seeing Zulime and the children next week," was all he said.

Just before my return to the city, he sent for a team, and together we drove down to the little Neshonoc burying ground. "I want to inspect your mother's grave," he explained.

On the way, as we were passing a clump of wild roses, he asked me to stop and cut some of them. "Your mother

385

was fond of wild roses," he said, "I'd like to put a handful on her grave."

The penetrating odor of those exquisite blooms brought to my mind vistas of the glorious sunlit, odorous prairies of Iowa, and to gather and put into his hand a spray of them, was like taking part in a poem—a poignant threnody of age, for he received them in silence, and held them with tender care, his mind far away in the past.

Silently we entered the gate of the burial ground, and slowly approached the mound under which my mother's body rested, and as I studied the thin form and bending head of my intrepid sire, I realized that he was in very truth treading the edge of his own grave. My eyes grew dim with tears and my throat ached with a sense of impending loss, and a pity for him which I could conceal only by looking away at the hills.

Nevertheless, he was calmer than I. "Here is where I want to lie," he said quietly and stooping, softly spread his sprays of roses above the mound. "She loved all the prairie flowers," he said, "but she specially liked wild roses. I always used to bring them to her from the fields. We had oceans of them in Dakota in those days."

It was a commonplace little burial ground with a few trees and here and there a bed of lilies or phlox, yet it had charm. It was a sunny and friendly place, a silent acre whose name and history went back to the beginning of the first white settlement in the valley. On its monuments were chiseled the familiar names of pioneers, and it was characteristic of the time and deeply characteristic of the McClintocks, to be told, by my father, that in some way the exact location of my grandmother's grave had been lost and that no stone marked the spot where my grandfather was buried.

We wandered around among the graves for half an hour

A Spray of Wild Roses

while Father spoke of the men and women whose names were on the low and leaning stones. "They were American," he said. "These German neighbors of ours are all right in their way, but it isn't our way. They are good citizens as far as they know how to be, but they don't think in our words. Soon there won't be any of the old families left. My world is just about gone, and so I don't mind going myself, only I want to go quick. I don't want to be bedridden for months as Vance McKinley was. If I could have my wish, I'd go out like a candle in a puff of wind,—and I believe that's the way I shall go."

It was a radiant June afternoon and as we drove back along the familiar lane toward the hills softened by the mist, we looked away over a valley throbbing with life and rich with the shining abundance of growing grain—a rich and peaceful and lovely valley to me—but how much more it all meant to my father! Every hill had its memories, every turn in the road opened a vista into the past. The mill, the covered bridge, the lonely pine by the river's bank,—all, all spoke to him of those he had loved and lost.

With guilty reluctance I confessed that the return of the children had again been postponed. "Mrs. Morris cannot tell just when she will return—I fear not before the first of September. It is a wonderful opportunity for the children to see the mountains. I could not afford to take them on such a trip—much as I should like to do so—and there is no telling when such another opportunity will offer. Mary Isabel is just at the right age to remember all she sees and a summer in the mountains will mean much to her in after life. Even Constance will be profoundly changed by it. Zulime is sorry to disappoint you but she feels that it would be wrong to refuse such an opportunity."

He made no complaint, offered no further opposition, he only said gently and sadly, "Don't let them stay away too long. I want them here part of the summer. I miss them terribly—and you must remember my time on earth is nearly ended."

"We shall all be here in August," I assured him, "and I may return late in July."

This was the twelfth of June and as I left the house for the train the picture of that lonely, white-haired man, sitting at the window, took away all the anticipation of pleasure with which our expedition had filled my mind. I was minded to decline the wondrous opportunity and send the children to the old Homestead and their grandsire.

CHAPTER TWENTY-SEVEN

A Soldier of the Union Mustered Out

ON my return to Chicago, I made good report of Father's condition and said nothing of his forebodings, for I wanted Zulime to start on her vacation in entire freedom from care. Had it not been for my lecture engagements I might not have gone with them, but as certain dates were fixed, I bought tickets for myself on the same train which Mrs. Morris had taken, and announced my intention to travel with the party at least as far as Sheridan. "I want to watch the children's faces and hear their words of delight when they see the mountains," I explained to Mrs. Morris. "My lectures at the Colorado Normal School do not begin till the second week in July—so that I can be with you part of the time."

My decision gave the final touch to the children's happiness. They liked their shaggy father—I don't know why, but they did—and during the days of preparation their voices were filled with bird-like music. They were palpitant with joy.

On the day appointed the Morris automobile called for us and took us to the train, and when the children found that they were to travel in a private pullman and that the stateroom was to be their own little house they were transported with pride. Thereafter they knew nothing of heat or dust or weariness. Their meals came regularly, and they went to bed in their berths with warbles of satisfaction.

The plains of the second day's travel absorbed them. The prairie dogs, the herds of cattle, the cactus blooms all came in for joyous recognition. They had read about them: now here they were in actuality. "Are those the mountains?" asked Mary Isabel as we came in sight of the buttes of Eastern Wyoming. "No, only hills," I replied.

Then, at last, came the Big Horns deep blue and lined with snow. Mary Isabel's eyes expanded with awe. "Oh, they are so much finer than I expected them to be," she said, and from that moment, she gave them her adoration. They were papa's mountains and hence not to be feared. "Are we really going up there?" she asked. "Yes," I replied pointing out Cloud Peak, "we shall go up almost directly toward that highest mountain of all."

At a camp just above Big Horn City we spent a month of just the sort of riding, trailing and camping which I was eager to have my children know, and in a few days under my instruction, they both learned to sit a horse in fearless confidence. Mary Isabel, who was eleven, accompanied me on a ride to Cloud Peak Lake, a matter of twenty miles over a rough trail, and came into camp almost unwearied. She was a chip of the old block in this regard, and as I listened to her cheery voice and looked down into her shining face I was a picture of shameless parental pride. For several weeks I was able to remain with them and then at last set forth for Colorado on my lecture tour.

Meanwhile, unsuspected by Americans, colossal armies were secretly mobilizing in Europe, and on August first, whilst we were on our way home, the sound of cannon proclaimed to the world the end of one era and the beginning of another. Germany announced to the rulers of the Eastern Hemisphere that she intended to dominate not merely the land but the seas, and in my quiet hotel in a Colorado college town this proclamation found amazed readers. I, for one, could not believe it—even after my return to Chicago in August, while the papers were shouting "War! War!" I remained unconvinced. Germany's program seemed monstrous, impossible.

The children and their mother arrived two days later and to Zulime I said "Father is patiently waiting for us and in the present state of things West Salem seems a haven of rest. We must go to him at once." She was willing and on August six, two days after England declared war, the old soldier met us, looking thin and white but so happy in our coming that his health seemed miraculously restored.

With joyous outcry the children sprang to his embrace and Zulime kissed him with such sincerity of regard that he gave her a convulsive hug. "Oh, but I'm glad to see you!" he exclaimed while tears of joy glistened on his cheeks.

"Well, Father, what do you think about the European situation?" I asked.

"I don't know what to think," he gravely answered. "It starts in like a big war, the biggest the world has ever seen. If you can believe what the papers say, the Germans have decided to eat up France."

Although physically weaker, he was mentally alert and read his *Tribune* with a kind of religious zeal. The vastness of the German armies, the enormous weight and power of their cannons, and especially the tremendous problem of their commissariat staggered his imagination. "I don't see how they are going to maintain all those troops," he repeated. "How can they shelter and clothe and feed three million men?"

To him, one of Sherman's soldiers, who had lived for days on parched corn stolen from the feedboxes of the mules, the description of wheeled ovens, and hot soup wagons appeared mere fiction. Although appalled by the rush of the Prussian line, he was confident that the Allies would check the invasion. Sharply resenting the half-veiled pro-Germanism of some of his neighbors, he declared hotly: "They claim to be loyal to America, but they are hoping the Kaiser will win. I will not trade with such men."

How far away it all seemed on those lovely nights when with my daughters beside me I lay on their broad bed out on the upper porch and heard the crickets sleepily chirping and the wind playing with the leaves in the maples. To Connie's sensitive ears the rustle suggested stealthy feet and passing wings—but to me came visions of endless rivers of helmeted soldiers flowing steadily remorselessly through Belgium, and Mary Isabel said, "Papa, don't you think of going to war. I won't let you."

"They wouldn't take me anyway," I replied, "I'm too old. You needn't worry."

I could not conceal from myself the fact that my father's work was almost done. That he was failing was sorrowfully evident. He weeded the garden no more. Content to sit in a chair on the back porch or to lie in a hammock under the maples, he spent long hours with me or with Zulime, recalling the battles of the Civil War, or relating incidents of the early history of the valley.

He still went to his club each night after supper, but the walk was getting to be more and more of a task, and he rejoiced when we found time to organize a game of cinch at home. This we very often did, and sometimes, even in the middle of the afternoon I called him in to play with me; for with a great deal of time on his hands he was restless. "I can't read all the time," he said, "and most of the fellows are busy during the middle of the day."

Each morning regular as the clock he went to the post-office to get his paper, and at lunch he was ready to discuss the news of the battles which had taken place. After his meal he went for a little work in the garden, for his hatred of weeds was bitter. He could not endure to have them overrun his crops. They were his Huns, his menacing invaders.

In this fashion he approached his eighty-fourth birthday. His manner was tranquil, but I knew that he was a little troubled by some outstanding notes which he had signed in order to purchase a house for my brother in Oklahoma, and to cure this I bought up these papers, canceled them and put them under his breakfast plate. "I want him to start his eighty-fifth year absolutely clear of debt," I said to Zulime.

He was much affected by the discovery of these papers. It pleased him to think that I had the money to spare. It was another evidence of my prosperity.

Nearly half of *A Son of the Middle Border* had now been printed and while he had read it he was shy about discussing it. Something almost sacred colored the pictures which my story called up. Its songs and sayings vibrated deep, searching the foundation chords of his life. They told of a bright world vanished, a landscape so beautiful that it hurt to have some parts of it revealed to aliens— and yet he was glad of it and talked of it to his comrades.

Zulime made a birthday cake for him and the children decorated it, and when Mary Isabel brought it in with all its candles lighted, and we lifted our triumphant song, he was overwhelmed with happiness and pride.

"I never had a birthday cake or a birthday celebration before in all my life," he said, and we hardly knew whether to laugh or to cry at that confession.

We ended the day by singing for him—that was the best of it all; for both the children could now join with me in voicing the tunes which he loved. They knew his enthusiasms and were already faithful heirs of his traditions. Singers of the future, they loved to hear him recount the past.

All through the month of September as we walked our peaceful way in Wisconsin the Germans were pounding at the gates of Paris. It comforts me at this moment to recall how peaceful my father was. He heard of the war only as of a far-off storm. He had us all, all but Franklin, and there was no bitterness in his voice as he spoke of his increasing uselessness. "I'm only a passenger now," he said. "I've finished my work."

As the Interstate Fair came on, he quietly engaged a neighbor to take us all down to La Crosse in an automobile. "This is my treat," he said, and knowing how much it meant to him I gladly accepted. With a fine sense of being up-to-date he reverted to the early days as we went whirling down the turnpike, and told tales of hauling hay and grain over these long hills. He pointed out the trail and spoke of its mud and sand. "It took us six hours then. Now, see, it's just like a city street."

He was greatly pleased to find an aëroplane flying above the grounds as we drew near. "They say the Germans are making use of these machines for scouting—and they are building others to fight with. I can't understand how they make a ton of iron fly."

Once inside the gates we let him play the host. He bought candy for the children, paid for our dinners at the restaurant and took us to the side-shows. It wearied him, however, and about three o'clock he said "Let's go home by way of Onalaska. I want to visit the cemetery and see if Father's lot is properly cared for." It seemed a rather melancholy finish to our day, but I agreed and as we were crossing the sandy stretch of road over which I limped as a child, I remarked "How short the distance seems." He smiled like a conqueror, "This is next thing to flying," he said.

A Soldier of the Union Mustered Out

This lonely little burial ground, hardly more impressive than the one at Neshonoc, contained the graves of all the Garlands who had lived in that region. "There is a place here for me," he said, "but I want you to put me in Neshonoc beside your mother."

On the way home he recovered his cheerfulness with an almost boyish resiliency. The flight of the car up the long hill which used to be such a terror to his sweating team, gave a satisfaction which broke out in speech. "It beats all how a motor can spin right along up a grade like this— and the flies can't sting it either," he added in remembering the tortured cattle of the past. When I told him of an invitation to attend a "Home Coming of Iowa Authors" which I was considering, he expressed his pleasure and urged me to accept. Des Moines was a real city to him. It possessed the glamour of a capital and to have me claimed by the State of Iowa pleased him more than any recognition in New York.

The following day he watched while the carpenter and I worked at putting my study into shape. Ever since the fire two years before its ceiling had needed repair, and even now I was but half-hearted in its restoration. As I looked around the square, bare, ugly room and thought of the spacious libraries of Longfellow, Lowell and Holmes, I realized my almost hopeless situation. I was only a literary camper after all. My life was not here—it couldn't be here so far from all that makes a writer's life worth while. "Soon for the sake of the children I must take them from this pleasant rut," I said to Zulime. "It is true an author can make himself felt from any place, but why do it at a disadvantage? If it were not for Father, I would establish our winter home in New York, which has the effect of increasing my power as well as my happiness."

On the twentieth of October Father called me to his

room. "I'm getting near the end of my trail," he said, "and I want to talk to you about my will. I want you two boys to share equally in all I've got and I'd like to have you keep this property just as it is, then you'll be safe, you'll always have a home. I'm ready to go—any time, only I don't like to leave the children—" His voice failed him for a moment, then he added, "I know I can't last long."

Though refusing to take a serious view of his premonition I realized that his hold on life was loosening and I answered, "Your wishes shall be carried out."

He did not feel like going up to the club that night, and so we played cards with him. Wilson Irvine, a landscape painter, who was visiting us chose Constance as a partner against Mary Isabel and her grandsire. Luck was all in Constance's favor, she and Irvine won, much to the veteran's chagrin. "You little witch," he said, "what do you mean by beating your granddad?" He was very proud of her skill, for she was only six years old.

To end the evening to his liking, we all united in singing some old war songs and he went away to his bed in better spirits than he had shown for a week or more.

He was at the breakfast table with me next morning, but seemed not quite awake. He replied when I spoke to him, but not alertly, not as he should, and a few minutes later rose with effort. This disturbed me a little, but a few minutes later he left the house as if to do some work at the barn, and I went to my writing with a feeling that he was quite all right.

It was a glorious October morning and from my desk as I looked into the yard I could see him standing in the gate, waiting for the man and team. He appeared perfectly well and exhibited his customary impatience with dilatory workmen. He was standing alertly erect with the sunshine

396

falling over him and the poise of his head expressed his characteristic energy. He made a handsome figure. My eyes fell again to my manuscript and I was deep in my imaginary world when I heard the voice of my uncle Frank calling to me up the stairs:

"Hamlin! Come quick. Something has happened. Come, quick, quick!"

There was a note in his voice which sent a chill through my blood, and my first glance into his eyes told me that he had looked upon the elemental. "Your father is lying out on the floor of the barn. I'm afraid he's gone!"

He was right. There on the rough planking of the carriage way lay the old pioneer, motionless, just as he had fallen not five minutes before. The hat upon his head and his right hand in his pocket told that he had fallen while standing in the door waiting for the drayman. His eyes were closed as if in sleep, and no sign of injury could be seen.

Kneeling by his side I laid my hand on his breast. It was still! His heart invincible through so many years had ceased to beat. His breath was gone and his empty left hand, gracefully lax, lay at his side. The veteran pioneer had passed to that farther West from whose vague savanahs no adventurer has ever returned.

"He must have died on his feet," said my uncle gravely, tenderly.

"Yes, he went the way he wished to go," I replied with a painful stress in my throat.

Together we took him up and bore him to the house, and placed him on the couch whereon he had been wont to rest during the day.

I moved like a man in a dream. It was all incredible, benumbing. Tenderly I disposed his head on its pillow and drew his hands across his breast. "Here is the end of a good man," I said. "Another soldier of the Union mustered out."

His hands, strong, yet singularly refined, appealed to me with poignant suggestion. What stern tasks they had accomplished. What brave deeds they had dared. In spite of the hazards of battle, notwithstanding the perils of the forests, the raft, the river, after all the hardships of the farm, they remained unscarred and shapely. The evidence of good blood was in their slender whiteness. Honorable, skilfull, indefatigable hands,—now forever at rest.

My uncle slipped away to notify the coroner, leaving me there, alone, with the still and silent form, which had been a dominant figure in my world. For more than half a century those gray eyes and stern lips had influenced my daily life. In spite of my growing authority, in spite of his age he had been a force to reckon with up to the very moment of his death. He was not a person to be ignored. All his mistakes, his weaknesses, faded from my mind, I remembered only his heroic side. His dignity, his manly grace were never more apparent than now as he lay quietly, as though taking his midday rest.

A breath of pathos rose from the open book upon his table. His hat, his shoes, his gloves all spoke of his unconquerable energy. I thought of the many impatient words I had spoken to him, and they would have filled me with a wave of remorse had I not known that our last day together had been one of perfect understanding. His final night with us had been entirely happy, and he had gone away as he had wished to go, in the manner of a warrior killed in action. His unbending soul had kept his body upright to the end.

All that day I went about the house with my children like one whose world had suddenly begun to crumble. The head of my house was gone. Over and over again I stole softly into his room unable to think of him as utterly cold and still.

For seventy years he had faced the open lands. Starting from the hills of Maine when a lad, he had kept moving, each time farther west, farther from his native valley. His life, measured by the inventions he had witnessed, the progress he had shared, covered an enormous span.

"He died like a soldier," I said to the awed children, "and he shall have the funeral of a soldier. We will not mourn, and we will not whisper or walk tip-toe in the presence of his body."

In this spirit we called his friends together. In place of flowers we covered his coffin with the folds of a flag, and when his few remaining comrades came to take a last look at him, my wife and I greeted them cordially in ordinary voice as if they had come to spend an evening with him and with us.

My final look at him in the casket filled my mind with love and admiration. His snowy hair and beard, his fair skin and shapely features, as well as a certain firm sweetness in the line of his lips raised him to a grave dignity which made me proud of him. Representing an era in American settlement as he did I rejoiced that nothing but the noblest lines of his epic career were written on his face.

This is my consolation. His last days were spent in calm content with his granddaughters to delight and comfort him. In their young lives his spirit is going forward. They remember and love him as the serene, white-haired veteran of many battles who taught them to revere the banner he so passionately adored.

The art career which Zulime Taft abandoned (against my wish)
after our marriage, is now being taken up by her daughter Constance who, at fourteen, signs herself C. Hamlin Garland, Artist.

AFTERWORD

To Mary Isabel, who, as a girl of eighteen, still loves to impersonate
the majesty of princesses, I entrust the future literary history of
Neshonoe.

Afterword

A T this point I make an end of this chronicle, the story
of two families whose wanderings and vicissitudes (as
I conceive them) are typical of thousands of other families
who took part in the upbuilding of the Middle Western
States during that period which lies between the close of
the Civil War and the Great War of Nineteen Fourteen.
With the ending of the two principal life-lines which bind
these pages together my book naturally closes.

In these two volumes over which I have brooded for
more than ten years, I have shadowed forth, imperfectly,
yet with high intent, the experiences of Isabel McClintock
and Richard Garland, and the lives of other settlers closely
connected with them. For a full understanding of the
drama—for it is a drama, a colossal and colorful drama—
I must depend upon the memory or the imagination of my
readers. No writer can record it all or even suggest the
major part of it. At the end of four years of writing I
go to press with reluctance, but realizing that my public,
like myself, is growing gray, I have consented to publish
my manuscript with its many imperfections and omissions.

My Neshonoc is gone. The community which seemed so
stable to me thirty years ago, has vanished like a wisp of
sunrise fog. The McClintocks, the Dudleys, the Baileys,
pioneers of my father's generation, have entered upon their
final migration to another darkly mysterious frontier. My
sunset World—all of it—is in process of change, of disintegration, of dissolution. My beloved trails are grass-
grown. I have put away my saddle and my tent-cloth,

realizing that at sixty-one my explorations of the wilderness are at an end. Like a captive wolf I walk a narrow round in a city square.

With my father's death I ceased to regard the La Crosse Valley even as my summer home. I decided to make my permanent residence in the East, and my wife and daughters whose affections were so deeply inwound with the Midland, loyally consented to follow, although it was a sad surrender for them. As my mother, Isabel McClintock, had given up her home and friends in the Valley to follow Richard Garland into the new lands of the West, so now Zulime Taft, A Daughter of the Middle Border, surrendered all she had gained in Illinois and Wisconsin to follow me into the crowded and dangerous East. It was a tearing wrench, but she did it. She sold our house in Woodlawn, packed up our belongings and joined me in a small apartment seven stories above the pavement in the heart of Manhattan.

The children came East with a high sense of adventure, with no realization that they were leaving their childhood's home never to return to it. They still talk of going back to West Salem, and they have named our summer cabin in the Catskills "Neshonoc" in memory of the little pioneer village whose graveyard holds all that is material of their paternal grandparents. The colors of the old Homestead are growing dim, and yet they will not permit me to deed it to others. We still own it and shall continue to do so. It has too many memories both sweet and sacred,—it seems that by clinging to its material forms we may still retain its soul.

We think of it often, and when around our rude fireplace in Camp Neshonoc in a room almost as rough as a frontier cabin, we sit and sing the songs which are at once a tribute to our forebears and a bond of union with the past, the shadows of the heroic past emerge. David and Luke,

Richard and Walter, and with them Susan and Lorette—all
—all the ones I loved and honored——

My daughters are true granddaughters of the Middle
Border. Constance at fourteen, Mary Isabel at eighteen,
are carrying forward, each in her distinctive way, the traditions of the Border, with the sturdy spirit of their forebears
in the West. To them I am about to entrust the work
which I have only partially completed.

Too young at first to understand the reasons for my
decision, they are now in agreement with me that we can
never again live in the Homestead. They love every tree,
every shrub on the old place. The towering elms, the
crow's nest in the maples, the wall of growing woodbine,
the gaunt, wide-spreading butternut branches,—all these
are very dear to them, for they are involved with their
earliest memories, touched with the glamour which the
imagination of youth flings over the humblest scenes of
human life. To them the Fern Road, The Bubbling Spring,
and the Apple Tree Glen, scenes of many camping places,
are all a part of childhood's fairy kingdom. The thought of
never again walking beneath those familiar trees or sitting
in those familiar rooms, is painful to them, and yet I am
certain that their Neshonoc, like my own, is a realm remembered, a region to which they can return only on the wings
of memory or of dream.

Happily the allurement of art, the stimulus of ambition
and the promise of love and honor already partly compen-
sate them for their losses. Their faces are set to the future.
On them I rest my hopes. By means of them and their
like, Life weaves her endless web.

A CATALOG OF SELECTED DOVER
BOOKS IN ALL FIELDS OF INTEREST

CONCERNING THE SPIRITUAL IN ART, Wassily Kandinsky. Pioneering work by father of abstract art. Thoughts on color theory, nature of art. Analysis of earlier masters. 12 illustrations. 80pp. of text. 5⅜ x 8½.   23411-8 Pa. $3.95

ANIMALS: 1,419 Copyright-Free Illustrations of Mammals, Birds, Fish, Insects, etc., Jim Harter (ed.). Clear wood engravings present, in extremely lifelike poses, over 1,000 species of animals. One of the most extensive pictorial sourcebooks of its kind. Captions. Index. 284pp. 9 x 12.   23766-4 Pa. $12.95

CELTIC ART: The Methods of Construction, George Bain. Simple geometric techniques for making Celtic interlacements, spirals, Kells-type initials, animals, humans, etc. Over 500 illustrations. 160pp. 9 x 12. (USO)   22923-8 Pa. $9.95

AN ATLAS OF ANATOMY FOR ARTISTS, Fritz Schider. Most thorough reference work on art anatomy in the world. Hundreds of illustrations, including selections from works by Vesalius, Leonardo, Goya, Ingres, Michelangelo, others. 593 illustrations. 192pp. 7⅛ x 10¼.   20241-0 Pa. $9.95

CELTIC HAND STROKE-BY-STROKE (Irish Half-Uncial from "The Book of Kells"): An Arthur Baker Calligraphy Manual, Arthur Baker. Complete guide to creating each letter of the alphabet in distinctive Celtic manner. Covers hand position, strokes, pens, inks, paper, more. Illustrated. 48pp. 8¼ x 11.   24336-2 Pa. $3.95

EASY ORIGAMI, John Montroll. Charming collection of 32 projects (hat, cup, pelican, piano, swan, many more) specially designed for the novice origami hobbyist. Clearly illustrated easy-to-follow instructions insure that even beginning papercrafters will achieve successful results. 48pp. 8¼ x 11.   27298-2 Pa. $3.50

THE COMPLETE BOOK OF BIRDHOUSE CONSTRUCTION FOR WOOD-WORKERS, Scott D. Campbell. Detailed instructions, illustrations, tables. Also data on bird habitat and instinct patterns. Bibliography. 3 tables. 63 illustrations in 15 figures. 48pp. 5¼ x 8½.   24407-5 Pa. $2.50

BLOOMINGDALE'S ILLUSTRATED 1886 CATALOG: Fashions, Dry Goods and Housewares, Bloomingdale Brothers. Famed merchants' extremely rare catalog depicting about 1,700 products: clothing, housewares, firearms, dry goods, jewelry, more. Invaluable for dating, identifying vintage items. Also, copyright-free graphics for artists, designers. Co-published with Henry Ford Museum & Greenfield Village. 160pp. 8¼ x 11.   25780-0 Pa. $10.95

HISTORIC COSTUME IN PICTURES, Braun & Schneider. Over 1,450 costumed figures in clearly detailed engravings–from dawn of civilization to end of 19th century. Captions. Many folk costumes. 256pp. 8⅜ x 11¾.   23150-X Pa. $12.95

STICKLEY CRAFTSMAN FURNITURE CATALOGS, Gustav Stickley and L. & J. G. Stickley. Beautiful, functional furniture in two authentic catalogs from 1910. 594 illustrations, including 277 photos, show settles, rockers, armchairs, reclining chairs, bookcases, desks, tables. 183pp. 6½ x 9¼.   23838-5 Pa. $9.95

AMERICAN LOCOMOTIVES IN HISTORIC PHOTOGRAPHS: 1858 to 1949, Ron Ziel (ed.). A rare collection of 126 meticulously detailed official photographs, called "builder portraits," of American locomotives that majestically chronicle the rise of steam locomotive power in America. Introduction. Detailed captions. xi + 129pp. 9 x 12.   27393-8 Pa. $12.95

AMERICA'S LIGHTHOUSES: An Illustrated History, Francis Ross Holland, Jr. Delightfully written, profusely illustrated fact-filled survey of over 200 American light-houses since 1716. History, anecdotes, technological advances, more. 240pp. 8 x 10¾.
25576-X Pa. $12.95

TOWARDS A NEW ARCHITECTURE, Le Corbusier. Pioneering manifesto by founder of "International School." Technical and aesthetic theories, views of indus-try, economics, relation of form to function, "mass-production split" and much more. Profusely illustrated. 320pp. 6⅛ x 9¼. (USO)   25023-7 Pa. $9.95

HOW THE OTHER HALF LIVES, Jacob Riis. Famous journalistic record, expos-ing poverty and degradation of New York slums around 1900, by major social reformer. 100 striking and influential photographs. 233pp. 10 x 7⅞.
22012-5 Pa. $10.95

FRUIT KEY AND TWIG KEY TO TREES AND SHRUBS, William M. Harlow. One of the handiest and most widely used identification aids. Fruit key covers 120 deciduous and evergreen species; twig key 160 deciduous species. Easily used. Over 300 photographs. 126pp. 5⅜ x 8½.   20511-8 Pa. $3.95

COMMON BIRD SONGS, Dr. Donald J. Borror. Songs of 60 most common U.S. birds: robins, sparrows, cardinals, bluejays, finches, more–arranged in order of increasing complexity. Up to 9 variations of songs of each species.
Cassette and manual 99911-4 $8.95

ORCHIDS AS HOUSE PLANTS, Rebecca Tyson Northen. Grow cattleyas and many other kinds of orchids–in a window, in a case, or under artificial light. 63 illus-trations. 148pp. 5⅜ x 8½.   23261-1 Pa. $4.95

MONSTER MAZES, Dave Phillips. Masterful mazes at four levels of difficulty. Avoid deadly perils and evil creatures to find magical treasures. Solutions for all 32 exciting illustrated puzzles. 48pp. 8¼ x 11.   26005-4 Pa. $2.95

MOZART'S DON GIOVANNI (DOVER OPERA LIBRETTO SERIES), Wolfgang Amadeus Mozart. Introduced and translated by Ellen H. Bleiler. Standard Italian libretto, with complete English translation. Convenient and thoroughly portable–an ideal companion for reading along with a recording or the performance itself. Introduction. List of characters. Plot summary. 121pp. 5¼ x 8½.
24944-1 Pa. $2.95

TECHNICAL MANUAL AND DICTIONARY OF CLASSICAL BALLET, Gail Grant. Defines, explains, comments on steps, movements, poses and concepts. 15-page pictorial section. Basic book for student, viewer. 127pp. 5⅜ x 8½.
21843-0 Pa. $4.95

BRASS INSTRUMENTS: Their History and Development, Anthony Baines. Authoritative, updated survey of the evolution of trumpets, trombones, bugles, cornets, French horns, tubas and other brass wind instruments. Over 140 illustrations and 48 music examples. Corrected and updated by author. New preface. Bibliography. 320pp. 5⅜ x 8½. 27574-4 Pa. $9.95

HOLLYWOOD GLAMOR PORTRAITS, John Kobal (ed.). 145 photos from 1926-49. Harlow, Gable, Bogart, Bacall; 94 stars in all. Full background on photographers, technical aspects. 160pp. 8⅜ x 11¼. 23352-9 Pa. $12.95

MAX AND MORITZ, Wilhelm Busch. Great humor classic in both German and English. Also 10 other works: "Cat and Mouse," "Plisch and Plumm," etc. 216pp. 5⅜ x 8½. 20181-3 Pa. $6.95

THE RAVEN AND OTHER FAVORITE POEMS, Edgar Allan Poe. Over 40 of the author's most memorable poems: "The Bells," "Ulalume," "Israfel," "To Helen," "The Conqueror Worm," "Eldorado," "Annabel Lee," many more. Alphabetic lists of titles and first lines. 64pp. 5$\frac{3}{16}$ x 8¼. 26685-0 Pa. $1.00

PERSONAL MEMOIRS OF U. S. GRANT, Ulysses Simpson Grant. Intelligent, deeply moving firsthand account of Civil War campaigns, considered by many the finest military memoirs ever written. Includes letters, historic photographs, maps and more. 528pp. 6⅛ x 9¼. 28587-1 Pa. $11.95

AMULETS AND SUPERSTITIONS, E. A. Wallis Budge. Comprehensive discourse on origin, powers of amulets in many ancient cultures: Arab, Persian Babylonian, Assyrian, Egyptian, Gnostic, Hebrew, Phoenician, Syriac, etc. Covers cross, swastika, crucifix, seals, rings, stones, etc. 584pp. 5⅜ x 8½. 23573-4 Pa. $12.95

RUSSIAN STORIES/PYCCKNE PACCKA3bl: A Dual-Language Book, edited by Gleb Struve. Twelve tales by such masters as Chekhov, Tolstoy, Dostoevsky, Pushkin, others. Excellent word-for-word English translations on facing pages, plus teaching and study aids, Russian/English vocabulary, biographical/critical introductions, more. 416pp. 5⅜ x 8½. 26244-8 Pa. $8.95

PHILADELPHIA THEN AND NOW: 60 Sites Photographed in the Past and Present, Kenneth Finkel and Susan Oyama. Rare photographs of City Hall, Logan Square, Independence Hall, Betsy Ross House, other landmarks juxtaposed with contemporary views. Captures changing face of historic city. Introduction. Captions. 128pp. 8¼ x 11. 25790-8 Pa. $9.95

AIA ARCHITECTURAL GUIDE TO NASSAU AND SUFFOLK COUNTIES, LONG ISLAND, The American Institute of Architects, Long Island Chapter, and the Society for the Preservation of Long Island Antiquities. Comprehensive, well-researched and generously illustrated volume brings to life over three centuries of Long Island's great architectural heritage. More than 240 photographs with authoritative, extensively detailed captions. 176pp. 8¼ x 11. 26946-9 Pa. $14.95

NORTH AMERICAN INDIAN LIFE: Customs and Traditions of 23 Tribes, Elsie Clews Parsons (ed.). 27 fictionalized essays by noted anthropologists examine religion, customs, government, additional facets of life among the Winnebago, Crow, Zuni, Eskimo, other tribes. 480pp. 6⅛ x 9¼. 27377-6 Pa. $10.95

FRANK LLOYD WRIGHT'S HOLLYHOCK HOUSE, Donald Hoffmann. Lavishly illustrated, carefully documented study of one of Wright's most controversial residential designs. Over 120 photographs, floor plans, elevations, etc. Detailed perceptive text by noted Wright scholar. Index. 128pp. 9¼ x 10¾. 27133-1 Pa. $11.95

THE MALE AND FEMALE FIGURE IN MOTION: 60 Classic Photographic Sequences, Eadweard Muybridge. 60 true-action photographs of men and women walking, running, climbing, bending, turning, etc., reproduced from rare 19th-century masterpiece. vi + 121pp. 9 x 12. 24745-7 Pa. $10.95

1001 QUESTIONS ANSWERED ABOUT THE SEASHORE, N. J. Berrill and Jacquelyn Berrill. Queries answered about dolphins, sea snails, sponges, starfish, fishes, shore birds, many others. Covers appearance, breeding, growth, feeding, much more. 305pp. 5¼ x 8¼. 23366-9 Pa. $8.95

GUIDE TO OWL WATCHING IN NORTH AMERICA, Donald S. Heintzelman. Superb guide offers complete data and descriptions of 19 species: barn owl, screech owl, snowy owl, many more. Expert coverage of owl-watching equipment, conservation, migrations and invasions, etc. Guide to observing sites. 84 illustrations. xiii + 193pp. 5⅜ x 8½. 27344-X Pa. $8.95

MEDICINAL AND OTHER USES OF NORTH AMERICAN PLANTS: A Historical Survey with Special Reference to the Eastern Indian Tribes, Charlotte Erichsen-Brown. Chronological historical citations document 500 years of usage of plants, trees, shrubs native to eastern Canada, northeastern U.S. Also complete identifying information. 343 illustrations. 544pp. 6½ x 9¼. 25951-X Pa. $12.95

STORYBOOK MAZES, Dave Phillips. 23 stories and mazes on two-page spreads: Wizard of Oz, Treasure Island, Robin Hood, etc. Solutions. 64pp. 8¼ x 11. 23628-5 Pa. $2.95

NEGRO FOLK MUSIC, U.S.A., Harold Courlander. Noted folklorist's scholarly yet readable analysis of rich and varied musical tradition. Includes authentic versions of over 40 folk songs. Valuable bibliography and discography. xi + 324pp. 5⅜ x 8½. 27350-4 Pa. $9.95

MOVIE-STAR PORTRAITS OF THE FORTIES, John Kobal (ed.). 163 glamor, studio photos of 106 stars of the 1940s: Rita Hayworth, Ava Gardner, Marlon Brando, Clark Gable, many more. 176pp. 8⅜ x 11¼. 23546-7 Pa. $12.95

BENCHLEY LOST AND FOUND, Robert Benchley. Finest humor from early 30s, about pet peeves, child psychologists, post office and others. Mostly unavailable elsewhere. 73 illustrations by Peter Arno and others. 183pp. 5⅜ x 8½. 22410-4 Pa. $6.95

YEKL and THE IMPORTED BRIDEGROOM AND OTHER STORIES OF YIDDISH NEW YORK, Abraham Cahan. Film Hester Street based on Yekl (1896). Novel, other stories among first about Jewish immigrants on N.Y.'s East Side. 240pp. 5⅜ x 8½. 22427-9 Pa. $6.95

SELECTED POEMS, Walt Whitman. Generous sampling from *Leaves of Grass*. Twenty-four poems include "I Hear America Singing," "Song of the Open Road," "I Sing the Body Electric," "When Lilacs Last in the Dooryard Bloom'd," "O Captain! My Captain!"—all reprinted from an authoritative edition. Lists of titles and first lines. 128pp. 5³⁄₁₆ x 8¼. 26878-0 Pa. $1.00

THE BEST TALES OF HOFFMANN, E. T. A. Hoffmann. 10 of Hoffmann's most important stories: "Nutcracker and the King of Mice," "The Golden Flowerpot," etc. 458pp. 5⅜ x 8½. 21793-0 Pa. $9.95

FROM FETISH TO GOD IN ANCIENT EGYPT, E. A. Wallis Budge. Rich detailed survey of Egyptian conception of "God" and gods, magic, cult of animals, Osiris, more. Also, superb English translations of hymns and legends. 240 illustrations. 545pp. 5⅜ x 8½. 25803-3 Pa. $13.95

FRENCH STORIES/CONTES FRANÇAIS: A Dual-Language Book, Wallace Fowlie. Ten stories by French masters, Voltaire to Camus: "Micromegas" by Voltaire; "The Atheist's Mass" by Balzac; "Minuet" by de Maupassant; "The Guest" by Camus, six more. Excellent English translations on facing pages. Also French-English vocabulary list, exercises, more. 352pp. 5⅜ x 8½. 26443-2 Pa. $8.95

CHICAGO AT THE TURN OF THE CENTURY IN PHOTOGRAPHS: 122 Historic Views from the Collections of the Chicago Historical Society, Larry A. Viskochil. Rare large-format prints offer detailed views of City Hall, State Street, the Loop, Hull House, Union Station, many other landmarks, circa 1904-1913. Introduction. Captions. Maps. 144pp. 9⅜ x 12¼. 24656-6 Pa. $12.95

OLD BROOKLYN IN EARLY PHOTOGRAPHS, 1865-1929, William Lee Younger. Luna Park, Gravesend race track, construction of Grand Army Plaza, moving of Hotel Brighton, etc. 157 previously unpublished photographs. 165pp. 8⅞ x 11¾. 23587-4 Pa. $13.95

THE MYTHS OF THE NORTH AMERICAN INDIANS, Lewis Spence. Rich anthology of the myths and legends of the Algonquins, Iroquois, Pawnees and Sioux, prefaced by an extensive historical and ethnological commentary. 36 illustrations. 480pp. 5⅜ x 8½. 25967-6 Pa. $8.95

AN ENCYCLOPEDIA OF BATTLES: Accounts of Over 1,560 Battles from 1479 B.C. to the Present, David Eggenberger. Essential details of every major battle in recorded history from the first battle of Megiddo in 1479 B.C. to Grenada in 1984. List of Battle Maps. New Appendix covering the years 1967-1984. Index. 99 illustrations. 544pp. 6½ x 9¼. 24913-1 Pa. $14.95

SAILING ALONE AROUND THE WORLD, Captain Joshua Slocum. First man to sail around the world, alone, in small boat. One of great feats of seamanship told in delightful manner. 67 illustrations. 294pp. 5⅜ x 8½. 20326-3 Pa. $5.95

ANARCHISM AND OTHER ESSAYS, Emma Goldman. Powerful, penetrating, prophetic essays on direct action, role of minorities, prison reform, puritan hypocrisy, violence, etc. 271pp. 5⅜ x 8½. 22484-8 Pa. $6.95

MYTHS OF THE HINDUS AND BUDDHISTS, Ananda K. Coomaraswamy and Sister Nivedita. Great stories of the epics; deeds of Krishna, Shiva, taken from puranas, Vedas, folk tales; etc. 32 illustrations. 400pp. 5⅜ x 8½. 21759-0 Pa. $10.95

BEYOND PSYCHOLOGY, Otto Rank. Fear of death, desire of immortality, nature of sexuality, social organization, creativity, according to Rankian system. 291pp. 5⅜ x 8½. 20485-5 Pa. $8.95

A THEOLOGICO-POLITICAL TREATISE, Benedict Spinoza. Also contains unfinished Political Treatise. Great classic on religious liberty, theory of government on common consent. R. Elwes translation. Total of 421pp. 5⅜ x 8½. 20249-6 Pa. $9.95

MY BONDAGE AND MY FREEDOM, Frederick Douglass. Born a slave, Douglass became outspoken force in antislavery movement. The best of Douglass' autobiographies. Graphic description of slave life. 464pp. 5⅜ x 8½. 22457-0 Pa. $8.95

FOLLOWING THE EQUATOR: A Journey Around the World, Mark Twain. Fascinating humorous account of 1897 voyage to Hawaii, Australia, India, New Zealand, etc. Ironic, bemused reports on peoples, customs, climate, flora and fauna, politics, much more. 197 illustrations. 720pp. 5⅜ x 8½. 26113-1 Pa. $15.95

THE PEOPLE CALLED SHAKERS, Edward D. Andrews. Definitive study of Shakers: origins, beliefs, practices, dances, social organization, furniture and crafts, etc. 33 illustrations. 351pp. 5⅜ x 8½. 21081-2 Pa. $8.95

THE MYTHS OF GREECE AND ROME, H. A. Guerber. A classic of mythology, generously illustrated, long prized for its simple, graphic, accurate retelling of the principal myths of Greece and Rome, and for its commentary on their origins and significance. With 64 illustrations by Michelangelo, Raphael, Titian, Rubens, Canova, Bernini and others. 480pp. 5⅜ x 8½. 27584-1 Pa. $9.95

PSYCHOLOGY OF MUSIC, Carl E. Seashore. Classic work discusses music as a medium from psychological viewpoint. Clear treatment of physical acoustics, auditory apparatus, sound perception, development of musical skills, nature of musical feeling, host of other topics. 88 figures. 408pp. 5⅜ x 8½. 21851-1 Pa. $10.95

THE PHILOSOPHY OF HISTORY, Georg W. Hegel. Great classic of Western thought develops concept that history is not chance but rational process, the evolution of freedom. 457pp. 5⅜ x 8½. 20112-0 Pa. $9.95

THE BOOK OF TEA, Kakuzo Okakura. Minor classic of the Orient: entertaining, charming explanation, interpretation of traditional Japanese culture in terms of tea ceremony. 94pp. 5⅜ x 8½. 20070-1 Pa. $3.95

LIFE IN ANCIENT EGYPT, Adolf Erman. Fullest, most thorough, detailed older account with much not in more recent books, domestic life, religion, magic, medicine, commerce, much more. Many illustrations reproduce tomb paintings, carvings, hieroglyphs, etc. 597pp. 5⅜ x 8½. 22632-8 Pa. $11.95

SUNDIALS, Their Theory and Construction, Albert Waugh. Far and away the best, most thorough coverage of ideas, mathematics concerned, types, construction, adjusting anywhere. Simple, nontechnical treatment allows even children to build several of these dials. Over 100 illustrations. 230pp. 5⅜ x 8½. 22947-5 Pa. $7.95

DYNAMICS OF FLUIDS IN POROUS MEDIA, Jacob Bear. For advanced students of ground water hydrology, soil mechanics and physics, drainage and irrigation engineering, and more. 335 illustrations. Exercises, with answers. 784pp. 6⅛ x 9¼. 65675-6 Pa. $19.95

SONGS OF EXPERIENCE: Facsimile Reproduction with 26 Plates in Full Color, William Blake. 26 full-color plates from a rare 1826 edition. Includes "The Tyger," "London," "Holy Thursday," and other poems. Printed text of poems. 48pp. 5¼ x 7. 24636-1 Pa. $4.95

OLD-TIME VIGNETTES IN FULL COLOR, Carol Belanger Grafton (ed.). Over 390 charming, often sentimental illustrations, selected from archives of Victorian graphics—pretty women posing, children playing, food, flowers, kittens and puppies, smiling cherubs, birds and butterflies, much more. All copyright-free. 48pp. 9¼ x 12¼. 27269-9 Pa. $7.95

PERSPECTIVE FOR ARTISTS, Rex Vicat Cole. Depth, perspective of sky and sea, shadows, much more, not usually covered. 391 diagrams, 81 reproductions of drawings and paintings. 279pp. 5⅜ x 8½. 22487-2 Pa. $7.95

DRAWING THE LIVING FIGURE, Joseph Sheppard. Innovative approach to artistic anatomy focuses on specifics of surface anatomy, rather than muscles and bones. Over 170 drawings of live models in front, back and side views, and in widely varying poses. Accompanying diagrams. 177 illustrations. Introduction. Index. 144pp. 8⅜ x11¼. 26723-7 Pa. $8.95

GOTHIC AND OLD ENGLISH ALPHABETS: 100 Complete Fonts, Dan X. Solo. Add power, elegance to posters, signs, other graphics with 100 stunning copyright-free alphabets: Blackstone, Dolbey, Germania, 97 more–including many lower-case, numerals, punctuation marks. 104pp. 8⅛ x 11. 24695-7 Pa. $8.95

HOW TO DO BEADWORK, Mary White. Fundamental book on craft from simple projects to five-bead chains and woven works. 106 illustrations. 142pp. 5⅜ x 8. 20697-1 Pa. $4.95

THE BOOK OF WOOD CARVING, Charles Marshall Sayers. Finest book for beginners discusses fundamentals and offers 34 designs. "Absolutely first rate . . . well thought out and well executed."–E. J. Tangerman. 118pp. 7¾ x 10⅝. 23654-4 Pa. $6.95

ILLUSTRATED CATALOG OF CIVIL WAR MILITARY GOODS: Union Army Weapons, Insignia, Uniform Accessories, and Other Equipment, Schuyler, Hartley, and Graham. Rare, profusely illustrated 1846 catalog includes Union Army uniform and dress regulations, arms and ammunition, coats, insignia, flags, swords, rifles, etc. 226 illustrations. 160pp. 9 x 12. 24939-5 Pa. $10.95

WOMEN'S FASHIONS OF THE EARLY 1900s: An Unabridged Republication of "New York Fashions, 1909," National Cloak & Suit Co. Rare catalog of mail-order fashions documents women's and children's clothing styles shortly after the turn of the century. Captions offer full descriptions, prices. Invaluable resource for fashion, costume historians. Approximately 725 illustrations. 128pp. 8⅜ x 11¼. 27276-1 Pa. $11.95

THE 1912 AND 1915 GUSTAV STICKLEY FURNITURE CATALOGS, Gustav Stickley. With over 200 detailed illustrations and descriptions, these two catalogs are essential reading and reference materials and identification guides for Stickley furniture. Captions cite materials, dimensions and prices. 112pp. 6½ x 9¼. 26676-1 Pa. $9.95

EARLY AMERICAN LOCOMOTIVES, John H. White, Jr. Finest locomotive engravings from early 19th century: historical (1804–74), main-line (after 1870), special, foreign, etc. 147 plates. 142pp. 11⅜ x 8¼. 22772-3 Pa. $10.95

THE TALL SHIPS OF TODAY IN PHOTOGRAPHS, Frank O. Braynard. Lavishly illustrated tribute to nearly 100 majestic contemporary sailing vessels: Amerigo Vespucci, Clearwater, Constitution, Eagle, Mayflower, Sea Cloud, Victory, many more. Authoritative captions provide statistics, background on each ship. 190 black-and-white photographs and illustrations. Introduction. 128pp. 8⅞ x 11¾. 27163-3 Pa. $13.95

EARLY NINETEENTH-CENTURY CRAFTS AND TRADES, Peter Stockham (ed.). Extremely rare 1807 volume describes to youngsters the crafts and trades of the day: brickmaker, weaver, dressmaker, bookbinder, ropemaker, saddler, many more. Quaint prose, charming illustrations for each craft. 20 black-and-white line illustrations. 192pp. 4⅝ x 6.
27293-1 Pa. $4.95

VICTORIAN FASHIONS AND COSTUMES FROM HARPER'S BAZAR, 1867–1898, Stella Blum (ed.). Day costumes, evening wear, sports clothes, shoes, hats, other accessories in over 1,000 detailed engravings. 320pp. 9⅜ x 12¼.
22990-4 Pa. $14.95

GUSTAV STICKLEY, THE CRAFTSMAN, Mary Ann Smith. Superb study surveys broad scope of Stickley's achievement, especially in architecture. Design philosophy, rise and fall of the Craftsman empire, descriptions and floor plans for many Craftsman houses, more. 86 black-and-white halftones. 31 line illustrations. Introduction 208pp. 6½ x 9¼.
27210-9 Pa. $9.95

THE LONG ISLAND RAIL ROAD IN EARLY PHOTOGRAPHS, Ron Ziel. Over 220 rare photos, informative text document origin (1844) and development of rail service on Long Island. Vintage views of early trains, locomotives, stations, passengers, crews, much more. Captions. 8⅞ x 11¾.
26301-0 Pa. $13.95

THE BOOK OF OLD SHIPS: From Egyptian Galleys to Clipper Ships, Henry B. Culver. Superb, authoritative history of sailing vessels, with 80 magnificent line illustrations. Galley, bark, caravel, longship, whaler, many more. Detailed, informative text on each vessel by noted naval historian. Introduction. 256pp. 5⅜ x 8½.
27332-6 Pa. $7.95

TEN BOOKS ON ARCHITECTURE, Vitruvius. The most important book ever written on architecture. Early Roman aesthetics, technology, classical orders, site selection, all other aspects. Morgan translation. 331pp. 5⅜ x 8½. 20645-9 Pa. $8.95

THE HUMAN FIGURE IN MOTION, Eadweard Muybridge. More than 4,500 stopped-action photos, in action series, showing undraped men, women, children jumping, lying down, throwing, sitting, wrestling, carrying, etc. 390pp. 7⅞ x 10⅝.
20204-6 Clothbd. $25.95

TREES OF THE EASTERN AND CENTRAL UNITED STATES AND CANADA, William M. Harlow. Best one-volume guide to 140 trees. Full descriptions, woodlore, range, etc. Over 600 illustrations. Handy size. 288pp. 4½ x 6⅜.
20395-6 Pa. $6.95

SONGS OF WESTERN BIRDS, Dr. Donald J. Borror. Complete song and call repertoire of 60 western species, including flycatchers, juncoes, cactus wrens, many more–includes fully illustrated booklet. Cassette and manual 99913-0 $8.95

GROWING AND USING HERBS AND SPICES, Milo Miloradovich. Versatile handbook provides all the information needed for cultivation and use of all the herbs and spices available in North America. 4 illustrations. Index. Glossary. 236pp. 5⅜ x 8½.
25058-X Pa. $6.95

BIG BOOK OF MAZES AND LABYRINTHS, Walter Shepherd. 50 mazes and labyrinths in all–classical, solid, ripple, and more–in one great volume. Perfect inexpensive puzzler for clever youngsters. Full solutions. 112pp. 8⅛ x 11.
22951-3 Pa. $4.95

PIANO TUNING, J. Cree Fischer. Clearest, best book for beginner, amateur. Simple repairs, raising dropped notes, tuning by easy method of flattened fifths. No previous skills needed. 4 illustrations. 201pp. 5⅜ x 8½. 23267-0 Pa. $6.95

A SOURCE BOOK IN THEATRICAL HISTORY, A. M. Nagler. Contemporary observers on acting, directing, make-up, costuming, stage props, machinery, scene design, from Ancient Greece to Chekhov. 611pp. 5⅜ x 8½. 20515-0 Pa. $12.95

THE COMPLETE NONSENSE OF EDWARD LEAR, Edward Lear. All nonsense limericks, zany alphabets, Owl and Pussycat, songs, nonsense botany, etc., illustrated by Lear. Total of 320pp. 5⅜ x 8½. (USO) 20167-8 Pa. $6.95

VICTORIAN PARLOUR POETRY: An Annotated Anthology, Michael R. Turner. 117 gems by Longfellow, Tennyson, Browning, many lesser-known poets. "The Village Blacksmith," "Curfew Must Not Ring Tonight," "Only a Baby Small," dozens more, often difficult to find elsewhere. Index of poets, titles, first lines. xxiii + 325pp. 5⅝ x 8¼. 27044-0 Pa. $8.95

DUBLINERS, James Joyce. Fifteen stories offer vivid, tightly focused observations of the lives of Dublin's poorer classes. At least one, "The Dead," is considered a masterpiece. Reprinted complete and unabridged from standard edition. 160pp. 5³⁄₁₆ x 8¼. 26870-5 Pa. $1.00

THE HAUNTED MONASTERY and THE CHINESE MAZE MURDERS, Robert van Gulik. Two full novels by van Gulik, set in 7th-century China, continue adventures of Judge Dee and his companions. An evil Taoist monastery, seemingly supernatural events; overgrown topiary maze hides strange crimes. 27 illustrations. 328pp. 5⅜ x 8½. 23502-5 Pa. $8.95

THE BOOK OF THE SACRED MAGIC OF ABRAMELIN THE MAGE, translated by S. MacGregor Mathers. Medieval manuscript of ceremonial magic. Basic document in Aleister Crowley, Golden Dawn groups. 268pp. 5⅜ x 8½. 23211-5 Pa. $8.95

NEW RUSSIAN-ENGLISH AND ENGLISH-RUSSIAN DICTIONARY, M. A. O'Brien. This is a remarkably handy Russian dictionary, containing a surprising amount of information, including over 70,000 entries. 366pp. 4½ x 6⅛. 20208-9 Pa. $9.95

HISTORIC HOMES OF THE AMERICAN PRESIDENTS, Second, Revised Edition, Irvin Haas. A traveler's guide to American Presidential homes, most open to the public, depicting and describing homes occupied by every American President from George Washington to George Bush. With visiting hours, admission charges, travel routes. 175 photographs. Index. 160pp. 8¼ x 11. 26751-2 Pa. $11.95

NEW YORK IN THE FORTIES, Andreas Feininger. 162 brilliant photographs by the well-known photographer, formerly with *Life* magazine. Commuters, shoppers, Times Square at night, much else from city at its peak. Captions by John von Hartz. 181pp. 9¼ x 10¾. 23585-8 Pa. $12.95

INDIAN SIGN LANGUAGE, William Tomkins. Over 525 signs developed by Sioux and other tribes. Written instructions and diagrams. Also 290 pictographs. 111pp. 6⅛ x 9¼. 22029-X Pa. $3.95

ANATOMY: A Complete Guide for Artists, Joseph Sheppard. A master of figure drawing shows artists how to render human anatomy convincingly. Over 460 illustrations. 224pp. 8⅜ x 11¼.
27279-6 Pa. $10.95

MEDIEVAL CALLIGRAPHY: Its History and Technique, Marc Drogin. Spirited history, comprehensive instruction manual covers 13 styles (ca. 4th century thru 15th). Excellent photographs; directions for duplicating medieval techniques with modern tools. 224pp. 8⅜ x 11¼.
26142-5 Pa. $12.95

DRIED FLOWERS: How to Prepare Them, Sarah Whitlock and Martha Rankin. Complete instructions on how to use silica gel, meal and borax, perlite aggregate, sand and borax, glycerine and water to create attractive permanent flower arrangements. 12 illustrations. 32pp. 5⅜ x 8½.
21802-3 Pa. $1.00

EASY-TO-MAKE BIRD FEEDERS FOR WOODWORKERS, Scott D. Campbell. Detailed, simple-to-use guide for designing, constructing, caring for and using feeders. Text, illustrations for 12 classic and contemporary designs. 96pp. 5⅜ x 8½.
25847-5 Pa. $2.95

SCOTTISH WONDER TALES FROM MYTH AND LEGEND, Donald A. Mackenzie. 16 lively tales tell of giants rumbling down mountainsides, of a magic wand that turns stone pillars into warriors, of gods and goddesses, evil hags, powerful forces and more. 240pp. 5⅜ x 8½.
29677-6 Pa. $6.95

THE HISTORY OF UNDERCLOTHES, C. Willett Cunnington and Phyllis Cunnington. Fascinating, well-documented survey covering six centuries of English undergarments, enhanced with over 100 illustrations: 12th-century laced-up bodice, footed long drawers (1795), 19th-century bustles, 19th-century corsets for men, Victorian "bust improvers," much more. 272pp. 5⅜ x 8¼.
27124-2 Pa. $9.95

ARTS AND CRAFTS FURNITURE: The Complete Brooks Catalog of 1912, Brooks Manufacturing Co. Photos and detailed descriptions of more than 150 now very collectible furniture designs from the Arts and Crafts movement depict davenports, settees, buffets, desks, tables, chairs, bedsteads, dressers and more, all built of solid, quarter-sawed oak. Invaluable for students and enthusiasts of antiques, Americana and the decorative arts. 80pp. 6½ x 9¼.
27471-3 Pa. $8.95

HOW WE INVENTED THE AIRPLANE: An Illustrated History, Orville Wright. Fascinating firsthand account covers early experiments, construction of planes and motors, first flights, much more. Introduction and commentary by Fred C. Kelly. 76 photographs. 96pp. 8¼ x 11.
25662-6 Pa. $8.95

THE ARTS OF THE SAILOR: Knotting, Splicing and Ropework, Hervey Garrett Smith. Indispensable shipboard reference covers tools, basic knots and useful hitches; handsewing and canvas work, more. Over 100 illustrations. Delightful reading for sea lovers. 256pp. 5⅜ x 8½.
26440-8 Pa. $7.95

FRANK LLOYD WRIGHT'S FALLINGWATER: The House and Its History, Second, Revised Edition, Donald Hoffmann. A total revision–both in text and illustrations–of the standard document on Fallingwater, the boldest, most personal architectural statement of Wright's mature years, updated with valuable new material from the recently opened Frank Lloyd Wright Archives. "Fascinating"–*The New York Times*. 116 illustrations. 128pp. 9¼ x 10¾.
27430-6 Pa. $11.95

PHOTOGRAPHIC SKETCHBOOK OF THE CIVIL WAR, Alexander Gardner. 100 photos taken on field during the Civil War. Famous shots of Manassas Harper's Ferry, Lincoln, Richmond, slave pens, etc. 244pp. 10⅝ x 8¼. 22731-6 Pa. $9.95

FIVE ACRES AND INDEPENDENCE, Maurice G. Kains. Great back-to-the-land classic explains basics of self-sufficient farming. The one book to get. 95 illustrations. 397pp. 5⅜ x 8½. 20974-1 Pa. $7.95

SONGS OF EASTERN BIRDS, Dr. Donald J. Borror. Songs and calls of 60 species most common to eastern U.S.: warblers, woodpeckers, flycatchers, thrushes, larks, many more in high-quality recording. Cassette and manual 99912-2 $9.95

A MODERN HERBAL, Margaret Grieve. Much the fullest, most exact, most useful compilation of herbal material. Gigantic alphabetical encyclopedia, from aconite to zedoary, gives botanical information, medical properties, folklore, economic uses, much else. Indispensable to serious reader. 161 illustrations. 888pp. 6½ x 9¼. 2-vol. set. (USO)
Vol. I: 22798-7 Pa. $9.95
Vol. II: 22799-5 Pa. $9.95

HIDDEN TREASURE MAZE BOOK, Dave Phillips. Solve 34 challenging mazes accompanied by heroic tales of adventure. Evil dragons, people-eating plants, blood-thirsty giants, many more dangerous adversaries lurk at every twist and turn. 34 mazes, stories, solutions. 48pp. 8¼ x 11. 24566-7 Pa. $2.95

LETTERS OF W. A. MOZART, Wolfgang A. Mozart. Remarkable letters show bawdy wit, humor, imagination, musical insights, contemporary musical world; includes some letters from Leopold Mozart. 276pp. 5⅜ x 8½. 22859-2 Pa. $7.95

BASIC PRINCIPLES OF CLASSICAL BALLET, Agrippina Vaganova. Great Russian theoretician, teacher explains methods for teaching classical ballet. 118 illustrations. 175pp. 5⅜ x 8½. 22036-2 Pa. $5.95

THE JUMPING FROG, Mark Twain. Revenge edition. The original story of The Celebrated Jumping Frog of Calaveras County, a hapless French translation, and Twain's hilarious "retranslation" from the French. 12 illustrations. 66pp. 5⅜ x 8½. 22686-7 Pa. $3.95

BEST REMEMBERED POEMS, Martin Gardner (ed.). The 126 poems in this superb collection of 19th- and 20th-century British and American verse range from Shelley's "To a Skylark" to the impassioned "Renascence" of Edna St. Vincent Millay and to Edward Lear's whimsical "The Owl and the Pussycat." 224pp. 5⅜ x 8½. 27165-X Pa. $4.95

COMPLETE SONNETS, William Shakespeare. Over 150 exquisite poems deal with love, friendship, the tyranny of time, beauty's evanescence, death and other themes in language of remarkable power, precision and beauty. Glossary of archaic terms. 80pp. 5$\frac{3}{16}$ x 8¼. 26686-9 Pa. $1.00

BODIES IN A BOOKSHOP, R. T. Campbell. Challenging mystery of blackmail and murder with ingenious plot and superbly drawn characters. In the best tradition of British suspense fiction. 192pp. 5⅜ x 8½. 24720-1 Pa. $6.95

THE WIT AND HUMOR OF OSCAR WILDE, Alvin Redman (ed.). More than 1,000 ripostes, paradoxes, wisecracks: Work is the curse of the drinking classes; I can resist everything except temptation; etc. 258pp. 5⅜ x 8½.　20602-5 Pa. $5.95

SHAKESPEARE LEXICON AND QUOTATION DICTIONARY, Alexander Schmidt. Full definitions, locations, shades of meaning in every word in plays and poems. More than 50,000 exact quotations. 1,485pp. 6½ x 9¼. 2-vol. set.
Vol. 1: 22726-X Pa. $16.95
Vol. 2: 22727-8 Pa. $16.95

SELECTED POEMS, Emily Dickinson. Over 100 best-known, best-loved poems by one of America's foremost poets, reprinted from authoritative early editions. No comparable edition at this price. Index of first lines. 64pp. 5³⁄₁₆ x 8¼.
26466-1 Pa. $1.00

CELEBRATED CASES OF JUDGE DEE (DEE GOONG AN), translated by Robert van Gulik. Authentic 18th-century Chinese detective novel; Dee and associates solve three interlocked cases. Led to van Gulik's own stories with same characters. Extensive introduction. 9 illustrations. 237pp. 5⅜ x 8½.　23337-5 Pa. $6.95

THE MALLEUS MALEFICARUM OF KRAMER AND SPRENGER, translated by Montague Summers. Full text of most important witchhunter's "bible," used by both Catholics and Protestants. 278pp. 6⅝ x 10.　22802-9 Pa. $12.95

SPANISH STORIES/CUENTOS ESPAÑOLES: A Dual-Language Book, Angel Flores (ed.). Unique format offers 13 great stories in Spanish by Cervantes, Borges, others. Faithful English translations on facing pages. 352pp. 5⅜ x 8½.
25399-6 Pa. $8.95

THE CHICAGO WORLD'S FAIR OF 1893: A Photographic Record, Stanley Appelbaum (ed.). 128 rare photos show 200 buildings, Beaux-Arts architecture, Midway, original Ferris Wheel, Edison's kinetoscope, more. Architectural emphasis; full text. 116pp. 8¼ x 11.　23990-X Pa. $9.95

OLD QUEENS, N.Y., IN EARLY PHOTOGRAPHS, Vincent F. Seyfried and William Asadorian. Over 160 rare photographs of Maspeth, Jamaica, Jackson Heights, and other areas. Vintage views of DeWitt Clinton mansion, 1939 World's Fair and more. Captions. 192pp. 8⅞ x 11.　26358-4 Pa. $12.95

CAPTURED BY THE INDIANS: 15 Firsthand Accounts, 1750-1870, Frederick Drimmer. Astounding true historical accounts of grisly torture, bloody conflicts, relentless pursuits, miraculous escapes and more, by people who lived to tell the tale. 384pp. 5⅜ x 8½.　24901-8 Pa. $8.95

THE WORLD'S GREAT SPEECHES, Lewis Copeland and Lawrence W. Lamm (eds.). Vast collection of 278 speeches of Greeks to 1970. Powerful and effective models; unique look at history. 842pp. 5⅜ x 8½.　20468-5 Pa. $14.95

THE BOOK OF THE SWORD, Sir Richard F. Burton. Great Victorian scholar/adventurer's eloquent, erudite history of the "queen of weapons"—from prehistory to early Roman Empire. Evolution and development of early swords, variations (sabre, broadsword, cutlass, scimitar, etc.), much more. 336pp. 6⅛ x 9¼.
25434-8 Pa. $9.95

AUTOBIOGRAPHY: The Story of My Experiments with Truth, Mohandas K. Gandhi. Boyhood, legal studies, purification, the growth of the Satyagraha (nonviolent protest) movement. Critical, inspiring work of the man responsible for the freedom of India. 480pp. 5⅜ x 8½. (USO) 24593-4 Pa. $8.95

CELTIC MYTHS AND LEGENDS, T. W. Rolleston. Masterful retelling of Irish and Welsh stories and tales. Cuchulain, King Arthur, Deirdre, the Grail, many more. First paperback edition. 58 full-page illustrations. 512pp. 5⅜ x 8½. 26507-2 Pa. $9.95

THE PRINCIPLES OF PSYCHOLOGY, William James. Famous long course complete, unabridged. Stream of thought, time perception, memory, experimental methods; great work decades ahead of its time. 94 figures. 1,391pp. 5⅜ x 8½. 2-vol. set.
Vol. I: 20381-6 Pa. $12.95
Vol. II: 20382-4 Pa. $12.95

THE WORLD AS WILL AND REPRESENTATION, Arthur Schopenhauer. Definitive English translation of Schopenhauer's life work, correcting more than 1,000 errors, omissions in earlier translations. Translated by E. F. J. Payne. Total of 1,269pp. 5⅜ x 8½. 2-vol. set.
Vol. 1: 21761-2 Pa. $11.95
Vol. 2: 21762-0 Pa. $12.95

MAGIC AND MYSTERY IN TIBET, Madame Alexandra David-Neel. Experiences among lamas, magicians, sages, sorcerers, Bonpa wizards. A true psychic discovery. 32 illustrations. 321pp. 5⅜ x 8½. (USO) 22682-4 Pa. $8.95

THE EGYPTIAN BOOK OF THE DEAD, E. A. Wallis Budge. Complete reproduction of Ani's papyrus, finest ever found. Full hieroglyphic text, interlinear transliteration, word-for-word translation, smooth translation. 533pp. 6½ x 9¼.
21866-X Pa. $10.95

MATHEMATICS FOR THE NONMATHEMATICIAN, Morris Kline. Detailed, college-level treatment of mathematics in cultural and historical context, with numerous exercises. Recommended Reading Lists. Tables. Numerous figures. 641pp. 5⅜ x 8½.
24823-2 Pa. $11.95

THEORY OF WING SECTIONS: Including a Summary of Airfoil Data, Ira H. Abbott and A. E. von Doenhoff. Concise compilation of subsonic aerodynamic characteristics of NACA wing sections, plus description of theory. 350pp. of tables. 693pp. 5⅜ x 8½.
60586-8 Pa. $14.95

THE RIME OF THE ANCIENT MARINER, Gustave Doré, S. T. Coleridge. Doré's finest work; 34 plates capture moods, subtleties of poem. Flawless full-size reproductions printed on facing pages with authoritative text of poem. "Beautiful. Simply beautiful."–*Publisher's Weekly*. 77pp. 9¼ x 12. 22305-1 Pa. $6.95

NORTH AMERICAN INDIAN DESIGNS FOR ARTISTS AND CRAFTSPEOPLE, Eva Wilson. Over 360 authentic copyright-free designs adapted from Navajo blankets, Hopi pottery, Sioux buffalo hides, more. Geometrics, symbolic figures, plant and animal motifs, etc. 128pp. 8⅜ x 11. (EUK) 25341-4 Pa. $8.95

SCULPTURE: Principles and Practice, Louis Slobodkin. Step-by-step approach to clay, plaster, metals, stone; classical and modern. 253 drawings, photos. 255pp. 8⅛ x 11.
22960-2 Pa. $11.95

THE INFLUENCE OF SEA POWER UPON HISTORY, 1660–1783, A. T. Mahan. Influential classic of naval history and tactics still used as text in war colleges. First paperback edition. 4 maps. 24 battle plans. 640pp. 5⅜ x 8½. 25509-3 Pa. $12.95

THE STORY OF THE TITANIC AS TOLD BY ITS SURVIVORS, Jack Winocour (ed.). What it was really like. Panic, despair, shocking inefficiency, and a little heroism. More thrilling than any fictional account. 26 illustrations. 320pp. 5⅜ x 8½. 20610-6 Pa. $8.95

FAIRY AND FOLK TALES OF THE IRISH PEASANTRY, William Butler Yeats (ed.). Treasury of 64 tales from the twilight world of Celtic myth and legend: "The Soul Cages," "The Kildare Pooka," "King O'Toole and his Goose," many more. Introduction and Notes by W. B. Yeats. 352pp. 5⅜ x 8½. 26941-8 Pa. $8.95

BUDDHIST MAHAYANA TEXTS, E. B. Cowell and Others (eds.). Superb, accurate translations of basic documents in Mahayana Buddhism, highly important in history of religions. The Buddha-karita of Asvaghosha, Larger Sukhavativyuha, more. 448pp. 5⅜ x 8½. 25552-2 Pa. $12.95

ONE TWO THREE . . . INFINITY: Facts and Speculations of Science, George Gamow. Great physicist's fascinating, readable overview of contemporary science: number theory, relativity, fourth dimension, entropy, genes, atomic structure, much more. 128 illustrations. Index. 352pp. 5⅜ x 8½. 25664-2 Pa. $8.95

ENGINEERING IN HISTORY, Richard Shelton Kirby, et al. Broad, nontechnical survey of history's major technological advances: birth of Greek science, industrial revolution, electricity and applied science, 20th-century automation, much more. 181 illustrations. ". . . excellent . . ."–*Isis.* Bibliography. vii + 530pp. 5⅜ x 8¼. 26412-2 Pa. $14.95

DALÍ ON MODERN ART: The Cuckolds of Antiquated Modern Art, Salvador Dalí. Influential painter skewers modern art and its practitioners. Outrageous evaluations of Picasso, Cézanne, Turner, more. 15 renderings of paintings discussed. 44 calligraphic decorations by Dalí. 96pp. 5⅜ x 8½. (USO) 29220-7 Pa. $4.95

ANTIQUE PLAYING CARDS: A Pictorial History, Henry René D'Allemagne. Over 900 elaborate, decorative images from rare playing cards (14th–20th centuries): Bacchus, death, dancing dogs, hunting scenes, royal coats of arms, players cheating, much more. 96pp. 9¼ x 12¼. 29265-7 Pa. $11.95

MAKING FURNITURE MASTERPIECES: 30 Projects with Measured Drawings, Franklin H. Gottshall. Step-by-step instructions, illustrations for constructing handsome, useful pieces, among them a Sheraton desk, Chippendale chair, Spanish desk, Queen Anne table and a William and Mary dressing mirror. 224pp. 8⅛ x 11¼. 29338-6 Pa. $13.95

THE FOSSIL BOOK: A Record of Prehistoric Life, Patricia V. Rich et al. Profusely illustrated definitive guide covers everything from single-celled organisms and dinosaurs to birds and mammals and the interplay between climate and man. Over 1,500 illustrations. 760pp. 7½ x 10⅛. 29371-8 Pa. $29.95

Prices subject to change without notice.

Available at your book dealer or write for free catalog to Dept. GI, Dover Publications, Inc., 31 East 2nd St., Mineola, N.Y. 11501. Dover publishes more than 500 books each year on science, elementary and advanced mathematics, biology, music, art, literary history, social sciences and other areas.